York Manuscript and Early Print Studies
Volume 4

Re-using Manuscripts in Late Medieval England

YORK MEDIEVAL PRESS

York Medieval Press is published by the University of York's Centre for Medieval Studies in association with Boydell & Brewer Limited. Our objective is the promotion of innovative scholarship and fresh criticism on medieval culture. We have a special commitment to interdisciplinary study, in line with the Centre's belief that the future of Medieval Studies lies in those areas in which its major constituent disciplines at once inform and challenge each other.

Editorial Board (2022)

Professor Peter Biller, Emeritus (Dept of History): General Editor
Professor Tim Ayers (Dept of History of Art): Co-Director, Centre for Medieval Studies
Dr Henry Bainton: Private scholar
Dr J. W. Binns: Honorary Fellow, Centre for Medieval Studies
Dr K. P. Clarke (Dept of English and Related Literature)
Dr K. F. Giles (Dept of Archaeology)
Dr Shazia Jagot (Dept of English and Related Literature)
Dr Holly James-Maddocks (Dept of English and Related Literature)
Dr Harry Munt (Dept of History)
† Professor W. Mark Ormrod, Emeritus (Dept of History)
Dr L. J. Sackville (Dept of History)
Professor Elizabeth M. Tyler (Dept of English and Related Literature): Co-Director, Centre for Medieval Studies
Dr Hanna Vorholt (Dept of History of Art)
Dr Sethina Watson (Dept of History)
Professor J. G. Wogan-Browne (English Faculty, Fordham University)
Dr Stephanie Wynne-Jones (Dept of Archaeology)

All enquiries of an editorial kind, including suggestions for monographs and essay collections, should be addressed to: The Academic Editor, York Medieval Press, Department of History, University of York, Heslington, York, YO10 5DD (E-mail: pete.biller@york.ac.uk)

York Manuscript and Early Print Studies

Series Editors
Orietta Da Rold (Cambridge)
Holly James-Maddocks (York)

A description of the series and a list of published titles may be found at the end of this volume.

Re-using Manuscripts in Late Medieval England

Repairing, Recycling, Sharing

Hannah Ryley

THE UNIVERSITY *of York*

YORK MEDIEVAL PRESS

© Hannah Ryley 2022

All rights reserved. Except as permitted under current legislation no part of this work may be photocopied, stored in a retrieval system, published, performed in public, adapted, broadcast, transmitted, recorded or reproduced in any form or by any means, without the prior permission of the copyright owner

The right of Hannah Ryley to be identified as the author of this work has been asserted in accordance with sections 77 and 78 of the Copyright, Designs and Patents Act 1988

First published 2022
Paperback edition 2024

A York Medieval Press publication
in association with The Boydell Press
an imprint of Boydell & Brewer Ltd
PO Box 9, Woodbridge, Suffolk IP12 3DF, UK
and of Boydell & Brewer Inc.
668 Mt Hope Avenue, Rochester, NY 14620-2731, USA
website: www.boydellandbrewer.com
and with the
Centre for Medieval Studies, University of York

ISBN 978-1-91404-906-4 (Hardback)
ISBN 978-1-91404-922-4 (Paperback)

A CIP catalogue record for this book is available
from the British Library

The publisher has no responsibility for the continued existence or accuracy of URLs for external or third-party internet websites referred to in this book, and does not guarantee that any content on such websites is, or will remain, accurate or appropriate

Contents

	List of Illustrations	vii
	Acknowledgements	ix
	List of Abbreviations	xi
	Transcription Conventions	xv
	Introduction	1
1	Making Parchment For Books	19
2	Re-using Parchment In Books	61
3	Making Marks On Books	105
4	Second-Hand Books	141
	Conclusions	183
	Bibliography	189
	Index	217

Illustrations

Figures

1	TCC, MS R.14.45, fol. 57r (or p. 101), recipes for parchment and vellum.	38
2	Diagram to show mammalian skin layers, modelled on Ronald Reed, *Ancient Skins, Parchments and Leathers* (London, 1972), p. 14, fig. 1.	43
3	Diagram to show the prime cuts and off-cuts of skin, modelled on Jiří Vnouček, 'The Manufacture of Parchment for Writing Purposes and the Observation of the Signs of Manufacture Surviving in Old Manuscripts', *Care and Conservation* 8 (2005), 74–92 (p. 77) fig. 28a.	45
4	BodL, MS Douce 25, fol. 72r, off-cut.	70
5	Oxford, Hertford MS 4, fols. 49v–50r, palimpsested quire guards.	78
6	BodL, MS Ashmole 33 outer covers.	87
7	Diagram to show the inner and outer covers of BodL, MS Ashmole 33, modelled on Stephen H. Shepherd, 'Four Middle English Charlemagne Romances: A Revaluation of the Non-Cyclic Verse Texts and the Holograph Sir Ferumbras' (unpublished doctoral thesis, University of Oxford, 1988), p. 18.	89
8	Diagram to show the construction of the limp cover on SJC MS S.54.	94
9	BodL, MS Rawl. C.35, fols. 112v–113r, palimpsest and glimpse of undertext.	100
10	BodL, MS Douce 302, fol. 35v, markings on a back flyleaf.	106
11	BodL, MS Douce 109, fol. iv verso, markings on a front flyleaf.	119
12	BodL, MS Douce 103, fol. 15r, alphabet.	127
13	BodL, MS Douce 84, fols. ii verso–iii recto, recipes written across front flyleaves.	133
14	BodL, MS Laud misc.609, fol. 170va, verse added to the last leaf.	138
15	Lambeth Palace Library, MS 472, fol. 260r, common-profit inscription.	147
16	Lambeth Palace Library, MS 472, fol. 265r, memorandum.	148
17	BodL, MS Auct. D.5.14, fol. 578v, cautio inscription and stationer's mark.	167

18	BodL, MS Bodley 251, fol. iii verso, front flyleaf with two inscriptions.	169
19	BodL, MS Bodley 315, fol. iii verso, front flyleaf with donation inscription.	174

Table

1	The values of *precium* inscriptions in books (from the survey of *Summary Catalogue* II.i).	159

Full credit details are provided in the captions to the images in the text. The author and publisher are grateful to all the institutions and individuals for permission to reproduce the materials in which they hold copyright. Every effort has been made to trace the copyright holders; apologies are offered for any omission, and the publisher will be pleased to add any necessary acknowledgement in subsequent editions.

Acknowledgements

I would like to thank several people for making this book possible. Thank you to Prof Daniel Wakelin for helping me to shape this project and bring it to completion. I am also grateful to Prof Julia Boffey and Dr Jane Griffiths, and to my editors Dr Orietta Da Rold, Dr Holly James-Maddocks, Prof Pete Biller, and Caroline Palmer for their unstinting support.

Thank you to my fellow Oxford medievalists for the ongoing intellectual and literal nourishment. Further specific thanks to colleagues in Oxford and further afield: Prof Laura Ashe, Dr Tamara Atkin, Prof Mishtooni Bose, Prof Neil Cartlidge, Cavaliera Cristina Dondi, Dr Geri Della Rocca de Candal, Prof Mary C. Flannery, Prof Vincent Gillespie, Daryl Green, Dr Carrie Griffin, Prof Simon Horobin, Prof Heather O'Donoghue, Dr Nick Perkins, Prof Adam Smyth, Dr Annie Sutherland, Dr Laura Varnam and Dr Mary Wellesley.

At Worcester College in Oxford, the Wilkinson Assistant Dean & Junior Research Fellowship and the Martin Senior Scholarship enabled me to embark on this research. I am also deeply grateful for the disability support I have received.

This research would not have been possible without access to collections of medieval manuscripts, something that is keenly missed at the time of writing. To the Bodleian Library staff, special thanks for hefting so many heavy manuscripts! Thank you to Colin Harris, Dr Matthew Holford and Dr Martin Kauffmann. I would like to express my gratitude to the following research collections for welcoming me: in Cambridge, the University Library, Gonville & Caius College Library, St John's College Library, and the Wren Library at Trinity College; in London, the British Library, Lambeth Palace Library, and Gray's Inn Library; in California, the Henry E. Huntington Library; in addition, Eton College Library; Exeter Cathedral Library; and Worcester Cathedral Library. Also, particular thanks to the Henry E. Huntington Library for awarding me the Gilbert & Ursula Farfel Fellowship in 2015.

Images of manuscripts are published in this book by kind permission of: the Bodleian Library, the Principal, Fellows and Scholars of Hertford College in the University of Oxford, the Master and Fellows of Trinity College Cambridge, and Lambeth Palace Library. In addition, I would like to record my thanks to Darren Lingard for his excellent technical drawings, and to the Oxford Bibliographical Society and the Marc Fitch Fund for financially supporting the inclusion of manuscript images.

For verifying my translations, *merci beaucoup*: Dr Claire Harrill, Dr Kylie Murray, Dr Lizzie Sandis, and Costy Scarpa. For checking my forays into late medieval currencies, *Danke* Dr Katie Ball. For all your clear-sighted suggestions, thank you to my Research Assistants Eleanor Baker and Audrey Southgate. Any remaining errors are my own. For introducing me to real-life sheep rearing, thanks to Dr Yvonne Bohm and Dr Martin Nicholas. The following generously shared unpublished or forthcoming research with me and kindly permitted me to mention it in this book: Dr Jenny Adams, Prof A. S. G. Edwards, Prof Bruce Holsinger, Dr Stephanie Lahey, Dr Anna Reynolds, Dr Daniel Sawyer, Dr Jamieson Weetman, and Dr Tom White. In the final months of work on this book, several references were unavailable to me due to the COVID-19 pandemic.

Enormous thanks to all my friends for putting up with me (and, in many cases, for putting me up) during the course of this research: Seb and Dr Claire Allen-Johnstone, Beth Bathurst, Dr Edwina Christie, Dr Colleen Curran, Dr Emily Dolmans, Dr Gareth Lloyd Evans and Ruari Craig-Wood, Katie and Dan Franzen, Dr Kim Fuellenbach, Dr Rosie Hall, Jess and the Henderson family, Dr Louisa Hotson, Dr Alice Kelly, Dr Emily MacGregor, Tom Maitland, Dr J. R. Mattison, Dr James Misson, Dr Ally Paddock and Dan Jeffries, Dr Angéline Rais, Shokoofeh Rajabzadeh, Dr J. D. Sargan, Costy and the Scarpa family, Dr Sian Witherden, Drs Sarah and Tom Wright, and Dr Danielle Yardy. To the AWG Squad, the Secret English Nerd Society and the Medieval Baes: you know who you are and I salute you!

Finally, thanks go to my godparents and to my family. I owe my greatest debt of gratitude to my parents Simon and Di, my sister Imo, and my partner James. I could not have written this book without your support.

Oxford, 2021

MARC FITCH FUND

Abbreviations

Common abbreviations (for example, repr. for reprint and s. for shillings) are not listed here and are abbreviated silently throughout this book. Where locations of manuscripts are already indicated in the full shelfmark by the name of a library or collection (for example, Eton College or Worcester Cathedral) collection locations are not repeated. Full information about each item can be found in the Bibliography.

Bindings Thesaurus	*The Language of Bindings Thesaurus*, Ligatus project, online <http://www.ligatus.org.uk/lob/>.
BodL	Bodleian Library, Oxford.
BPPB	*Book Production and Publishing in Britain 1375–1475*, ed. J. Griffiths and D. Pearsall (Cambridge, 1989).
British Library Catalogue	*British Library Catalogue,* online <http://explore.bl.uk/primo_library/libweb/action/search.do?mode=Basic&vid=BLVU1&tab=local_tab&>.
British Library Illuminated Catalogue	*British Library Catalogue of Illuminated Manuscripts*, online <http://www.bl.uk/catalogues/illuminatedmanuscripts/welcome.htm>.
BRUC	*A Biographical Register of the University of Cambridge to 1500*, ed. A. B. Emden (Cambridge, 1963).
BRUO	*A Biographical Register of the University of Oxford to A. D. 1500*, ed. A. B. Emden, 3 vols. (Oxford, 1957, 1958, 1959).
BT	*Bosworth-Toller Anglo-Saxon Dictionary*, online <http://www.bosworthtoller.com>.
CCCC	Corpus Christi College, Cambridge.
CHBB II or III	*The Cambridge History of the Book in Britain.*
CHLBI I	*The Cambridge History of Libraries in Britain and Ireland.*
Christianson, *Directory*	*A Directory of London Stationers and Book Artisans, 1300–1500*, ed. C. P. Christianson (New York, 1990), online <http://hdl.handle.net/2027/heb.08874.0001.001>.
Clarke, *Crafte*	*The Crafte of Lymmyng and the Maner of Steynyng: Middle English Recipes for Painters, Stainers, Scribes and Illuminators*, ed. M. Clarke, EETS OS 347 (Oxford, 2016).
CUL	Cambridge University Library, Cambridge.

DIMEV	*The Digital Index of Medieval English Verse*, ed. L. Mooney, D. W. Mosser, E. Solopova, D. Thorpe, D. Hill Radcliffe, based on the *Index of Middle English Verse* (1943) and its *Supplement* (1965), online <http://www.dimev.net>.
DMLBS	*Dictionary of Medieval Latin from British Sources*, ed. R. E. Latham and others, online <http://www.dmlbs.ox.ac.uk/publications/online>.
Dutschke, *HEHL Catalogue*	*Guide to Medieval and Renaissance Manuscripts in the Huntington Library*, ed. C. W. Dutschke (San Marino, 1989).
EETS OS, OS, SS	Early English Text Society publications: OS (Original Series), ES (Extra Series), and SS (Supplementary Series).
Farming Glossary	*A Medieval Farming Glossary of Latin and English Words*, ed. J. L. Fisher revised by A. and R. Powell (Essex, 1997).
GCC	Cambridge, Gonville and Caius College Library.
Hardwick and Luard, *CUL Catalogue*	*A Catalogue of Manuscripts Preserved in the Library of the University of Cambridge*, ed. C. Hardwick and H. R. Luard, 6 vols. (Cambridge, 1856–67).
HEHL	Henry E. Huntington Library, San Marino, CA.
IMEP	*Index of Middle English Prose*, IV, VIII, X, XI, XIII, XVI, XVII, XIX.
James, *GCC Catalogue*	*A Descriptive Catalogue of the Manuscripts in the Library of Gonville and Caius College*, ed. M. R. James, 2 vols. (Cambridge, 1907–08).
James, *SJC Catalogue*	*A Descriptive Catalogue of the Manuscripts in the Library of St John's College, Cambridge*, ed. M. R. James (Cambridge, 1913).
James, *TCC Catalogue*	*The Western Manuscripts in the Library of Trinity College, Cambridge: A Descriptive Catalogue*, ed. M. R. James, 4 vols. (Cambridge, 1900–04).
LMES	*Late Medieval English Scribes*, ed. L. Mooney, S. Horobin, and E. Stubbs, online <http://www.medievalscribes.com>.
MED	*Middle English Dictionary*, gen. ed. R. E. Lewis, online <http://quod.lib.umich.edu/m/med/>.
MMBL	*Medieval Manuscripts in British Libraries*, ed. N. R. Ker and A. J. Piper, 5 vols. (Oxford, 1969–2002).
Muzerelle, *Vocabulaire codicologique*	D. Muzerelle, *Vocabulaire codicologique*, online <http://codicologia.irht.cnrs.fr>.

OED	*Oxford English Dictionary*, online <http://www.oed.com>.
PBE	*The Production of Books in England 1350–1550*, ed. A. Gillespie and D. Wakelin (Cambridge, 2011).
Quarto Catalogue	Bodleian Library *Quarto Catalogue*, II, III, V, IX, X.
Seymour, *Chaucer Catalogue*	*A Catalogue of Chaucer Manuscripts*, ed. M. C. Seymour, 2 vols. (Aldershot, 1995).
SJC	St John's College Library, Cambridge.
Summary Catalogue	Bodleian Library *Summary Catalogue*, II.i, II.ii, IV, V.
TCC	Trinity College Library, Cambridge.
Thomson, *Worcester Catalogue*	*A Descriptive Catalogue of the Medieval Manuscripts in Worcester Cathedral Library*, ed. R. M. Thomson and M. Gullick (Cambridge, 2001).

Transcription Conventions

All transcriptions are semi-diplomatic and follow each manuscript's use of **I** and **j, u** and **v**, and their word-division and capitalisation. Expanded abbreviations are marked with italics. Bold type is used when graphs are discussed as visual phenomena.

Symbol	Represents
[ct]	Square brackets surround cancelled letters (either by washing, scraping, or other damage), and any legible letters are placed within the square brackets.
[…]	Square brackets around an ellipsis indicate my selective omission of part of the transcription (also used where I omit part of a quotation from a secondary source).
/	Indicates a line break, or follows manuscript punctuation.
^ ^	Carets indicate an interlineated word, or words, which may function as corrections. These are placed as close as possible to the relevant word or phrase.
< >	Angled brackets indicate graphs or words that are difficult to read.
~~	Tildes represent space fillers.
⌐ ¬	Hooked dashes show words added in another hand.

Introduction

Fifteenth-century manuscript culture was generally disposed to make books well, and to make them to last. As Michael Sargent puts it, 'the production of medieval manuscript books was based on the expectation of longevity, rather than obsolescence'.[1] That longevity made possible repair, recycling and re-use. Parchment's longevity in the UK continues to be a topic of discussion even in the twenty-first century: debates in February 2016 noted the advantages of maintaining the practice of recording parliamentary statutes on parchment, and remarked on its potential for durability.[2] Medieval manuscripts' material features, such as repaired parchment leaves, overwritten palimpsests and fragments from other books bound in as flyleaves, constitute physical witnesses to the past, many of which signal that they were made and sustained well. These physical residues are not just leftover scraps; they prompt questions about the wider context of medieval manuscript culture and its evident and varied capacity for re-using book materiality. The durable qualities of books – and, therefore, multiple opportunities to repair, recycle and re-use them or their component materials – were achieved through practices and processes of craftsmanship and care. Indeed, the long-term survival of so many medieval manuscripts suggests that methods of medieval book production, handling and circulation enabled the extraordinary durability of these objects. What this study argues, then, is that the material remains of fifteenth-century manuscript culture offer a history of these re-use practices.

In manuscript culture, books can be traced through a sequence of stages: production, handling and circulation. Books may seem to be a coherent whole, especially today, accustomed as we are to the mechanised production of abundant print copies and digital interfaces. However, then (as now) all books were made from component parts, in a range of materials. The assembly of fifteenth-century books was often fluid in nature, and 'production was just one stage in the dynamic life cycle of a manuscript'.[3] That production could be ad hoc, occurring

---

[1] M. G. Sargent, 'What do the numbers mean? A Textual Critic's Observations on some Patterns of Middle English Manuscript Transmission', in *Design and Distribution of Late Medieval Manuscripts in England*, ed. M. Connolly and L. R. Mooney (York, 2008), pp. 205–44 (p. 220). Throughout, I use the terms 'book' and 'manuscript' interchangeably.

[2] D. Rundle, 'Parliament and the Vellum Debate, Part I', online, 6 March 2016 <https://bonaelitterae.wordpress.com/2016/03/06/parliament-and-the-vellum-debate-part-i/>. For details of the proposal, see House of Commons, 'Vellum: Printing Record Copies of Public Acts', online, 11 May 2016 <http://researchbriefings.parliament.uk/ ResearchBriefing/Summary/CBP-7451>; see also R. Mason, 'Tradition of Recording UK Laws on Vellum May Be Saved', the *Guardian*, 15 February 2016 <http://www.theguardian.com/politics/2016/feb/15/lords-overruled-recording-laws-vellum-goat-calf-skin>.

[3] M. Johnston and M. Van Dussen, 'Introduction: Manuscripts and Cultural History', in *The Medieval Manuscript Book: Cultural Approaches*, ed. M. Johnston and M. Van Dussen (Cambridge, 2015), pp. 1–16 (p. 3).

in fits and starts over time,[4] it could be commissioned from a stationer, it could be bought ready-made, or second-hand or it could be the result of do-it-yourself modes of production.[5] Studying the 'stratigraphy' of such manuscripts – essentially, manuscript archaeology – by looking back from a seemingly fully formed book to the origins of the various materials that come together to form it, can help answer a plethora of questions.[6] How were these materials made, and how did they come to be so durable, so potently available for re-use? In what ways did people recycle book materials? After the production of books, in the handling phase, did people re-use their books in other ways, for purposes other than reading? What about second-hand books, and their possession and circulation? These four questions are the basis of the four chapters in this study and form the underpinnings of an argument for the prevalence of re-use in late medieval manuscript culture. This story of manuscript materiality moves from animals in the field, through the processing of raw skins into parchment, on through myriad makers, handlers, users and re-users, to manuscripts' circulation in society. Thus, this study considers fifteenth-century manuscripts at various stages in their life cycle, assessing practices of re-use from a number of perspectives.

The long fifteenth century

The period selected for this study of manuscript re-use is, loosely, a date range known to literary scholarship as the 'long fifteenth century': the late fourteenth century through to the early sixteenth century.[7] For example, a typical long fifteenth-century period might stretch from Chaucer's death (1400) to the Reformation (1534 Act of Supremacy).[8] Scholars with more of an interest in late medieval book history have sometimes broadened or narrowed this date-range to 1350–1550, or 1375–1475, or have associated it more closely with the decades around the advent of printing in England, in 1476.[9] Throughout this study, the range of the long fifteenth century is relaxed, and always inclusive.

---

[4] A. Bahr refers to R. Hanna's work on the ad hoc practices that produced many vernacular manuscripts, 'Miscellaneity and Variance in the Medieval Book', in *The Medieval Manuscript Book*, ed. Johnston and Van Dussen, pp. 181–98 (p. 181).

[5] J. Boffey, 'Manuscript and Print: Books, Readers and Writers', in *A Companion to Medieval Poetry*, ed. C. Saunders (Oxford, 2010), pp. 538–54 (p. 542).

[6] J. P. Gumbert, 'Codicological Units: Towards a Terminology for the Stratigraphy of the Non-Homogeneous Codex', *Segno e testo: International Journal of Manuscripts and Their Transmission* 2 (2004), 17–42 (18); R. Clemens and T. Graham, *Introduction to Manuscript Studies* (Ithaca and London, 2007), p. 48, discuss the 'strata' in books.

[7] M. Woodcock, 'England in the Long Fifteenth Century', in *A Companion to Medieval Poetry*, ed. C. Saunders (Oxford, 2010), pp. 501–19 (p. 501).

[8] D. Gray, 'Introduction', in *The Oxford Book of Late Medieval Verse and Prose* (Oxford, 1989), pp. 3–44 (pp. 3–5); this focus is also reflected in *The Long Fifteenth Century: Essays for Douglas Gray*, ed. H. Cooper and S. Mapstone (Oxford, 1997).

[9] *Manuscripts and Printed Books in Europe 1350–1550: Packaging, Presentation and Consumption*, ed. E. Cayley and S. Powell (Liverpool, 2015); *BPPB* covers the years 1375–1475; A. Gillespie

Within this inclusive date range lie hundreds of surviving manuscripts.[10] Though estimates vary, copies suggest 'something like a tenfold increase in vernacular book production between 1350 and 1475', and others have suggested a 'spectacular transformation' in the production rate of vernacular books in Britain from 1375 to 1475.[11] But aside from the relatively high rate of production, why consider the fifteenth century when admittedly, one could well focus on books from the fourteenth or thirteenth centuries, or, for that matter, the sixteenth century? The long fifteenth century, I argue, represents a pivotal moment in book production: it was a period that saw the development of English vernacular literature, the increasing spread of literacy, and dynamic change in the activities of book production, and, as Alexandra Gillespie and Daniel Wakelin note, at this time people 'made, used and apparently wanted, or at least were able to obtain and preserve, more books than their forebears'.[12] Though they mention it in the introduction to their landmark collection of essays on late medieval English book production, Gillespie and Wakelin's book then largely elides the particular issue of 'preservation'. Their collection of essays does suggest the vital, burgeoning, and changing nature of fifteenth-century manuscript production, but what else does existing scholarship say about the re-use of manuscripts produced at this time?

Scholarship on the re-use or recycling of books is more commonly concerned with their damage, discarding, dispersal or destruction as fragments, waste or scrap. Whatever specific terms are used for the life cycles of books and their materials, there are often only fleeting references to recycling or re-use. For example, Ralph Hanna, Linne Mooney and Estelle Stubbs have each considered the appearance of a fragment of Chaucer's *Troilus and Criseyde* as a binding strip, but do not focus on its implications for manuscript re-use.[13] Erik Kwakkel mentions the economy of recycled materials in a chapter on ownership and miscellanies, and again in his work on discarded parchment, though the emphasis on 'discarding' parchment is notably distinct from my focus here on a more inclusive narrative

---

and D. Wakelin, 'Introduction', in *PBE*, pp. 1–11 (p. 4).

[10] Sargent states that he knows of 'no reliable method' of estimating the number of manuscripts, 'What Do the Numbers Mean?', p. 209. For various strategies and estimates, see E. Buringh, *Medieval Manuscript Production in the Latin West: Explorations with a Global Database* (Leiden, 2011). Manuscripts may be 'dated' or 'datable' to the fifteenth century, Clemens and Graham, *Introduction to Manuscript Studies*, p. 121.

[11] J. Raven, *The Business of Books: Booksellers and the English Book Trade, 1450–1850* (London, 2007) p. 13; see also A. S. G. Edwards and D. Pearsall, 'The Manuscripts of the Major English Poetic Texts', in *BPPB*, pp. 257–78 (p. 257), Sargent, 'What Do the Numbers Mean?', p. 243.

[12] Gillespie and Wakelin, 'Introduction', pp. 3, 8–9.

[13] R. Hanna discusses the fragment of *Troilus and Criseyde*, ll. 764–98, preserved in Hatfield House (Herts.), Cecil Papers, Box S/1, verso, in *Introduction to English Medieval Book History: Manuscripts, their Producers and their Readers* (Liverpool, 2013), p. 142; also, L. R. Mooney and E. Stubbs, *Scribes and the City: London Guildhall Clerks and the Dissemination of Middle English Literature, 1375–1425* (York, 2013 repr. 2014), pp. 68, 79, 106.

of manuscript re-use.¹⁴ Catalogues too make brief reference to recycling, such as Richard Gameson's remarks on fragments re-used in fifteenth-century bindings in a catalogue of the early Canterbury Cathedral collection.¹⁵ Numerous studies take a later, post-medieval emphasis, and frequently dwell on the aftermath of the Dissolution; many of these refer to the popular accounts of John Leland and John Bale.¹⁶ N. R. Ker's seminal study of pastedowns concentrates on the period *c.* 1520 to *c.* 1570, firmly focussing on the growing dominance of printed copies, and the effects of the Reformation and the dissolution of the monasteries (1536–41) on book production and trade.¹⁷ I am not taking such research to task for its passing reference to how durable or re-usable books were in the fifteenth century – sound arguments underlie these scholars' focuses and agendas. Nevertheless, the nexus of issues addressed in this book has not yet been explored to the extent that it warrants. As Gillespie notes, 'old books supplied handy material to binders long before the Reformation'.¹⁸ This study takes this reminder to heart: it extends attention to the pre-Reformation period, and looks beyond handy binding material to a fuller life cycle of the manuscript book.

Writing on books, writing on things

So, what are medieval manuscripts? What does *manuscript* mean? *Manuscript* comes from the Latin *manu* (by hand) and *scriptus* (written), and one of the most straightforward definitions of this word is simply something that has been handwritten.¹⁹ However, *manuscript* does not just refer to writing, or indeed to literary texts: it also refers to books as physical objects. Moreover, as material things as well as recording materials, manuscript books are multivalent. Adam Smyth and Gill Partington point out that books have a complicated 'two-faced' nature, being at once 'totems: carriers of culture, values, beliefs' and, at the

---

[14] E. Kwakkel, 'Late Medieval Text Collections: A Single Author Typology Based on Single-Author MSS', in *Author, Reader, Book: Medieval Authorship in Theory and Practice*, ed. E. Kwakkel and S. Partridge (Toronto, 2012), pp. 56–79 (pp. 72–73); E. Kwakkel, 'Discarded Parchment as Writing Support in English Manuscript Culture', in *Manuscripts Before 1400, English Manuscript Studies 1100–1700* 17 (2013), 238–61.

[15] R. Gameson, *The Earliest Books of Canterbury Cathedral: Manuscripts and Fragments to c. 1200* (London, 2008), pp. 34–37.

[16] For example, C. de Hamel, *Cutting Up Manuscripts for Pleasure and Profit* (Charlottesville, 1996), p. 6; C. Y. Ferdinand, 'Library Administration (*c.* 1475–1640)', *CHLBI* I, 565–91 (p. 581).

[17] N. R. Ker, *Pastedowns in Oxford Bindings* (Oxford, 2000); see also D. Rundle's online edition of this catalogue (POxBo) as part of the 'Lost Manuscripts' project, <https://www.lostmss.org.uk/pastedowns-oxford-bindings-online-poxbo>. For definitions of 'pastedown', see Beal, *Dictionary*, p. 288, and M. P. Brown, *Understanding Illuminated Manuscripts: A Guide to Technical Terms*, revised by E. C. Teviotdale and N. K. Turner (Los Angeles, 2018), p. 81.

[18] A. Gillespie, 'Bookbinding', in *PBE*, pp. 150–72 (p. 161).

[19] *OED*, manuscript, adj., etymology: borrowed from Latin; also, see 'manuscript' in P. Beal, *A Dictionary of English Manuscript Terminology 1450–2000* (Oxford, 2008), p. 244.

same time, 'quotidian objects: material and ephemeral things'.[20] This study emphasises the simultaneous functions of manuscripts as recorders of texts and as material objects in their own right. The following chapters pick up on this: books can carry economic, spiritual, and educational values (particularly relevant in Chapter 4), as well as existing as materials, such as parchment (especially Chapter 1), and as books, which were read but also written on (Chapter 3), and were reconstituted, sometimes as whole books, or in piecemeal parts (Chapter 2). Manuscripts are not just handwritten things, then, nor are they just literary works, nor indeed just material incarnations, but complex and sometimes conflicted carriers of all these values and more.

Medieval manuscripts occur in a range of physical incarnations, including fragmentary, re-used or recycled forms. Thanks to the representation of the medieval period in modern culture, in exhibitions, at historical attractions or on television programmes, today manuscripts tend to be conceived in the popular imagination as lavishly illuminated treasures.[21] Mainstream representations largely do not capture a sense of their lively diversity of form, their humdrum ephemerality or their re-usable, sustainable potential. Manuscripts could be valuable treasures, of course, but they could also be made from rough-and-ready parchment (Chapter 1), or to meet 'make-do-and-mend' specifications (Chapter 1 for repaired parchment, and Chapter 2 for book materials re-used in other books). And whatever the grade of production, fifteenth-century books could go on to carry esoteric notes and doodles (Chapter 3) and a range of attributed values, including many different kinds of second-handedness (Chapter 4). Many of these material forms suggest that there were options and opportunities for sustainable practices in book production.

How were these many physical incarnations known to their makers and users? Fifteenth-century references to what we would now call manuscripts would name these material objects *codex* or *liber*, both from Latin words for tree bark, or *bok*, from the Old English *boc*. The word *bok* or *boc* ultimately derives from the same Germanic base for the word *beech*, so a similarly woody origin.[22] Wood had long provided a durable surface for inscription and it was a common material for bookbinding. Leah Price notes the double

---

[20] A. Smyth and G. Partington, 'Introduction', in *Book Destruction in the West, from the Medieval to the Contemporary*, ed. A. Smyth and G. Partington (Basingstoke, 2014), pp. 1–14 (p. 8).

[21] M. Camille describes the manuscript, in its 'recent history', as undergoing a transformation from a 'family heirloom to something of a mass commodity fetish representing "Merry Olde England"' in *Mirror in Parchment: The Luttrell Psalter and The Making of Medieval England* (London, 2013), p. 12. A. Gillespie discussed the widespread understanding of manuscripts as 'treasures', in her keynote lecture, 4th Biennial BABEL Working Group Meeting: 'Off the Books', Toronto, Canada (9 October 2015). See, for example, the 'Book of Kells' exhibition at Trinity College, Dublin. Countless historical attractions feature the integration of 'snippets' or images plucked from luxury manuscripts, particularly illuminated miniatures. An example of a television series is J. Ramirez's *Illuminations: The Private Lives of Medieval Kings*, Oxford Film and Television collaboration with the British Library for the BBC, 2013.

[22] *MED*, *bok*, *n*., Sense 1a and etymology; *DMLBS*, *liber*, *n*., Sense 2.1 and 2.2; *codex* or *caudex*, *n*., Sense 1.1.c, *BT* connects *boc* with both beech-trees and books.

etymology of *liber*, which medieval commentators traced to either *liberare*, the act that texts were supposed to perform, as well as to the word for bark, a surface on which words could be inscribed.[23] This double etymology conveys the duality – and complexity – of books, as both cultural and physical objects.

Although these definitions of *liber* and *bok* pertain to the entities we would call manuscripts, people would have used *bok* to refer to other handwritten documents too, as well as conceptual divisions in a written work, and *liber* originally denoted a roll (as did the word *volumen* which developed into the modern English word *volume*).[24] This capaciousness of reference reached yet further: medieval books were understood to take their place in a wider contemporary culture of writing on things (discussed with reference to writing onto books in particular in Chapter 3). People also wrote on scrolls and scraps of parchment,[25] and on wax tablets, the medium on which many first learned to write.[26] In addition to these writerly surfaces, those living in the fifteenth century would have seen writing in public spaces.[27] Brasses and engraved inscriptions on stone tombs survive in medieval churches across Britain;[28] there would have been many wall paintings,[29] and surveys of churches have uncovered graffiti such as English and Latin names, lettering and phrases scratched into the walls.[30] However, writing was not just engraved, painted or scratched into surfaces; texts on parchment were pasted up on to walls of Westminster Abbey in the late fourteenth century,[31]

---

[23] L. Price, *How to Do Things with Books in Victorian Britain* (Princeton, 2013), p. 5.

[24] G. S. Ivy, 'The Bibliography of the Manuscript Book', in *The English Library Before 1700*, ed. F. Wormald and C. E. Wright (London, 1958), pp. 32–65 (p. 32).

[25] E. Kwakkel, 'Commercial Organization and Economic Innovation', in *PBE*, pp. 173–91 (p. 187); and throughout 'Discarded Parchment'.

[26] *Les tablettes à écrire de l'Antiquité à l'Epoque Moderne*, ed. É. Lalou *Bibliologia* 12 (Turnhout, 1992); R. H. Rouse and M. A. Rouse, 'The Vocabulary of Wax Tablets', *Vocabulaire du livre et de l'écriture au Moyen Age: Actes de la table ronde Paris 24–26 septembre 1987*, ed. O. Weijers (Turnhout, 1989), pp. 220–30.

[27] For a complementary study of sixteenth-century graffiti, see J. Fleming, *Graffiti and the Writing Arts of Early Modern England* (London, 2001).

[28] For surveys, see N. Saul, *English Church Monuments in the Middle Ages: History and Representation* (Oxford, 2009), pp. 335–65; and S. Badham, *Medieval Church and Churchyard Monuments* (Oxford, 2011), pp. 45–46.

[29] For example, R. Rosewell, *Medieval Wall Paintings* (Oxford, 2014) pp. 53–57.

[30] For a specific study of medieval wall graffiti, see K. Owen, 'Traces of Presence and Pleading: Approaches to the Study of Graffiti at Tewkesbury Abbey', in *Wild Signs: Graffiti in Archaeology and History*, ed. J. Oliver and T. Neal (Oxford, 2010), pp. 35–46. *DIMEV* notes examples of graffiti found on walls: Barrington in Oxfordshire, Duxford in Cambridgeshire, Great Bardfield in Essex, Landwade in Cambridgeshire, and Ridgewell in Essex. Norfolk Medieval Graffiti Survey, online <http://www.medieval-graffiti.co.uk>; Suffolk Medieval Graffiti Survey, online <http://www.medieval-graffiti-suffolk.co.uk>. M. Champion, *Medieval Graffiti: The Lost Voices of England's Churches* (London, 2015), gives an image of a prayer inscription at p. 8, images of Lydgate's inscription at St Mary's Church, Lidgate, Suffolk, and other inscriptions at pp. 130iii–v.

[31] Rosewell, *Wall Paintings*, p. 53.

and throughout the Middle Ages tapestries commonly featured embroidered writing.[32] In addition to these relatively public or large-scale instances of writing, lettering was also found on objects at a more intimate scale, including domestic items such as pottery[33] and personal accessories such as belts, rings and brooches.[34] So, the wider culture of materials inscribed with writing was varied in materials, scale and accessibility.

Inscribed surfaces also vary in terms of how well they might be re-used: some materials that bore writing could be extremely durable; others were highly ephemeral. Surfaces, such as stone or metal, were expected to be long-lasting. Writing on wax tablets was made with the possibility of erasure, as Roger Chartier comments, therefore it was 'necessarily ephemeral', but also, interestingly, re-usable.[35] In the physical space of the medieval church, Matthew Champion has contrasted the transient 'wisps' of burned *ex-voto* candles with graffiti, which possess a 'sense of permanence' and which constitute 'prayers made solid in stone'.[36] But just because stone or parchment *can* be long-lasting does not mean that all medieval stone monuments or parchment manuscripts have survived. While particularly well made and well-kept parchment possesses material properties that enable an array of re-usable outcomes – explored in this study – it is still subject to the same vagaries that apply to other materials too. Like most medieval wax, plenty of fifteenth-century parchment is lost forever. What matters for the ensuing discussion is that, like other medieval things, parchment manuscripts took their place on a spectrum of ephemerality to durability, and that cultivating that durability could make them re-useable in a range of ways.

This book is a focussed exploration of re-uses in fifteenth-century manuscripts. That said, I consider the physical properties of manuscripts in a wider context of 'manuscript culture', which Martha Dana Rust has defined as 'the network of beliefs and practices – pedagogical, technological, economic, devotional, agricultural, among others – that constituted the milieu of medieval book production and use'.[37] This inclusive understanding of a book-related medieval milieu opens up manuscripts to cross-disciplinary study, and positions them at the intersection of various beliefs and practices. Thus, the following chapters take into account medieval practices of animal husbandry, craftsmanship, penmanship, salesmanship and piety, among other aspects of medieval socio-economic and

---

[32] A. S. Cavallo, *Medieval Tapestries in the Metropolitan Museum of Art* (New York, 1993), p. 34.

[33] B. Jervis, *Pottery and Social Life in Medieval England: Towards a Relational Approach* (Oxford, 2014), p. 51.

[34] For belts or girdles decorated with letters, and appendices of inscriptions on objects, see R. Gilchrist, *Medieval Life: Archaeology and the Life Course* (Woodbridge, 2012), p. 175, appendices at pp. 527–29.

[35] R. Chartier, *Inscription and Erasure: Written Culture from the Eleventh to the Eighteenth Century*, trans. A. Goldhammer (Philadelphia, 2007), p. 4.

[36] Champion, *Medieval Graffiti*, pp. 172, 214.

[37] M. D. Rust, *Imaginary Worlds in Medieval Books: Exploring the Manuscript Matrix* (Basingstoke, 2007), p. 9.

cultural life. As a result, it is not just fifteenth-century books that populate this study, but also many of the people and places that produced books, were involved in their handling and enabled their circulation.

Although this study considers the contexts for making books, the sources for this research are mostly vernacular medieval manuscripts themselves. The manuscripts discussed in this book were for the most part made in England and are dated or datable to the long fifteenth century, or were made earlier but are considered for the signs of their circulation in the fifteenth century. Though the primary sources selected for study share this period of production, handling and circulation, in other ways they are remarkably wide-ranging. Occasionally groupings of manuscripts emerge, such as a survey of manuscripts containing codicological recipes (in Chapter 1), a series of Chaucer manuscripts (in Chapter 2), and a scattered group of books marked with sale prices (in Chapter 4). However, these groupings should not necessarily be taken to be more widely representative.[38] The manuscripts chosen for this book feature many different texts by different authors. They hail from a variety of genres, and demonstrate an array of production values and provenances. This diversity is deliberate, and it shows that re-use was a feature not just of any one milieu or tradition. My samples should not, though, be considered necessarily representative of the larger body of extant medieval manuscripts, or of manuscripts from the long fifteenth century, or indeed representative of medieval manuscripts in their own time. Sometimes they may well be, but because of losses we cannot ever know, with certainty, the true picture of medieval manuscripts in their own time.[39] In any case, such a picture would have been equally inaccessible to contemporaries.

Rather, this book sees manuscripts as sources for tentative *possible* histories. Although much evidence is lost irrevocably, or is not yet legible to us, manuscripts can carry traces of their participation in medieval culture in their material fabric, in signs such as the form of parchment, evidence of repair and re-use of book materials, and in many kinds of written markings. The lines of investigation into practices of re-use explored here are found in written notes and tangible traces. I draw on a range of approaches and fields of study, but above all else, this study is a work of book history. The main methods used in each chapter (outlined at more length in due course) will be familiar to book historians as commonplace techniques, such as undertaking surveys of catalogues, or case studies of particular books, or offering palaeographical and codicological interpretations of manuscripts. Nonetheless, these and other supplementary methods are influenced by a flexible, interdisciplinary, and cross-disciplinary outlook. This book also draws on approaches and ideas from ecocriticism, sustainability studies, archaeology, material culture studies,

---

[38] Seymour, *Chaucer Catalogue*; C. P. Christianson, 'Evidence for the Study of London's Late Medieval Manuscript-Book Trade', in *BPPB*, pp. 87–108.

[39] A. Bale summarises the scholarship, and suggests that 'the survival rate of medieval English books is estimated to be around 2 to 5 per cent, although a book, if destroyed efficiently, leaves no traces and so this is guesswork', 'Belligerent Literacy, Bookplates and Graffiti: Dorothy Helbarton's Book', in *Book Destruction*, pp. 89–111 (p. 89).

anthropology, sociology, zooarchaeology and animal studies, among others. However, concepts and key ideas drawn from these fields are used selectively in this book and are always grounded in book history.

* * *

Manuscripts are made of animal skins, as well as other organic products. They are also vehicles for education, status display and piety, among other socio-economic roles. They can be described as nonhuman objects, matter, stuff, artefacts, things, commodities, and they were made by skilled craftsmen – at this time, by hand. This makes books part of a much bigger theoretical conversation about the relationship between humans and nonhumans. This subject has been addressed by a number of different fields of enquiry, particularly by proponents of the 'material turn' and by ecocritics. 'Thing theory', developed by Bill Brown, has been influential and widely adopted in literary studies.[40] While I acknowledge and draw upon advocates of those theories, this book favours exploring the material culture of books without denying human agency.[41] This book engages with books and the relations between books and people, as part of material culture.

Of course, late medieval books are closely involved with craftsmanship. The human agency involved in bringing a manuscript into being is illuminated by the sociologist Richard Sennett's study of craftsmanship as a mode of relation between humans and nonhuman things. Moreover, craftsmanship is, to Sennett, 'an enduring, basic human impulse, the desire to do a job well for its own sake'.[42] That idea is most pertinent to Chapters 1 and 2's discussions of the production, repair, re-use and recycling of parchment. Emphasis on craft is filtering into manuscript scholarship, with Jonathan Wilcox describing a collection of essays as 'materially committed, craft conscious scholarship about medieval manuscripts'.[43] This book endeavours to be 'craft conscious', and follows

---

[40] B. Brown, 'Thing Theory', *Critical Inquiry* 28 (2001), 1–22; B. Brown, 'Objects, Others, and Us (The Refabrication of Things)', *Critical Inquiry* 36 (2010), 183–217. See also N. K. Turner, 'The Materiality of Medieval Parchment: A Response to "The Animal Turn"', *Revista Hispánica Moderna* 71 (2018), 39–67.

[41] J. Frow argues persuasively that a materialist approach should *not* neglect the human, in 'Matter and Materialism: A Brief Pre-History of the Present', in *Material Powers: Cultural Studies, History and the Medieval Turn*, ed. T. Bennett and P. Joyce (London, 2010), pp. 25–37 (p. 32).

[42] R. Sennett, *The Craftsman* (London, 2008), p. 9.

[43] J. Wilcox, 'Introduction: The Philology of Smell', in *Scraped, Stroked, and Bound: Materially Engaged Readings of Medieval Manuscripts*, ed. J. Wilcox (Turnhout, 2013), pp. 1–14 (p. 8); for more on craft in scribal work, see D. Wakelin, *Scribal Correction and Literary Craft: English Manuscripts 1375–1510* (Cambridge, 2014), pp. 101–83; and see also J. D. Sargan, 'The Scarlet Letter: Experimentation, Design and Copying Practice in the Coloured Capitals of MS Digby 86', in *Interpreting MS Digby 86: A Trilingual Book from Thirteenth-Century Worcestershire*, ed. S. Fein (York, 2019), pp. 219–54.

the conviction, reinforced by Sennett's ideas, that medieval parchmeners, book producers and book users, made and repaired books well, with the expectation of longevity. Investigating the making and repair of books from the fifteenth century deepens insight into the re-use activities of craftsmen.

The crafting of medieval manuscripts was influenced by other factors, such as social and economic considerations. Books were made for many purposes in fifteenth-century society, with its intersecting social and economic systems, and were attributed use-values.[44] Manuscripts were, after all, luxury goods, and even scrappier books made more cheaply were still luxuries inaccessible to most.[45] As manuscript production began to develop during the fifteenth century, the cheaper options it enabled were still relatively expensive compared with living costs.[46] Although this context is worlds away from early twentieth-century America, about which Thorstein Veblen wrote, many medieval manuscripts embody what he called 'conspicuous consumption'.[47] Whether or not late medieval England is regarded as proto-capitalist, then, as now, many people liked to display their wealth through luxury goods.[48] Taking this into account, this book pays attention to economic considerations, such as the different values attributed to parchment, particularly where it is understood to develop added value (Chapters 1 and 2), used or re-used in a 'waste not, want not' fashion (again, Chapters 1 and 2), the use of marginal spaces for jottings and doodles (Chapter 3), and second-hand books and their various attributed values (Chapter 4).

As well as being subject to social and economic pressures, manuscripts experience other pressures over time. Sometimes manuscripts are destroyed suddenly, by fire or flood, or altered dramatically, for example by someone clipping out miniatures for a scrapbook.[49] However, not all change was sudden. Rather than a residual stasis, there is a 'constant flux',[50] and a 'fluidity' to long-lasting manuscripts, 'which so often saw accretion and development over time'.[51] As well as experiencing dramatic transformations, manuscripts also

---

[44] W. H. Sherman discusses use-values, in *Used Books: Marking Readers in Renaissance England* (Philadelphia, 2008), pp. 177–78.

[45] H. E. Bell, 'The Price of Books in Medieval England', *The Library* 17 (1937), 312–32 (p. 330); see also W. L. Schramm, 'The Cost of Books in Chaucer's Time', *Modern Language Notes* 47 (1933) 139–45; O. Da Rold nuances Bell and Schramm's assertions, offering new perspectives on the cost of materials for writing, and plenty of hard data, in 'The Economics of Paper', in *Paper in Medieval England: From Pulp to Fictions* (Cambridge, 2020), pp. 58–93.

[46] See Chapter 4 for discussion of the cost and price of books.

[47] T. Veblen, *Theory of the Leisure Class* (New York, 1967), p. 64.

[48] For a discussion of capitalism and the fifteenth century, see C. Dyer, *Everyday Life in Medieval England* (London, 2000), pp. 305–27; the display of books as status-enhancing items is mentioned by L. Amtower, *Engaging Words: The Culture of Reading in the Later Middle Ages* (New York, 2000), pp. 11, 32.

[49] See de Hamel, *Cutting Up Manuscripts*.

[50] Johnston and Van Dussen, 'Manuscripts and Cultural History', p. 5.

[51] Wilcox, *Scraped, Stroked, and Bound*, p. 8.

change with a 'glacial slowness'.[52] The steady buckling of parchment in slightly-too-humid conditions, the gradual pull of thread sewn through parchment in repeated use and the fade of ink testify to this ongoing, slow change. The incremental mutability of manuscripts resonates with the thinking of some philosophers of materiality, who engage critically with this slowness of being, and the staying power and durability of things.[53] For example, Jane Bennett has outlined three important 'thing powers', and names one of these as 'slowness'.[54] Ironically, acknowledging the gradual change underway in manuscripts also emphasizes their remarkable durability, a quality which enables their continued existence and their sustainable use and re-use.

Sustainable re-use

While many of the theoretical underpinnings discussed here were not accessible to fifteenth-century people, there are fruitful points of contact between modern and medieval thinking. Two key concepts are explored in this book. The first is durability: the capacity to endure, to be long-lasting.[55] This engages with the slow persistence of manuscripts through the centuries. The second is the conservation of resources, particularly in the sustainable use and re-use of both products and by-products.[56] Of course, in practice these two concepts overlap in many ways, and as this book will show, durability provides a basis for the use, resourceful re-use and circulation of hard-wearing materials.

Fifteenth-century English craftsmen aimed to make things to last, and made things efficiently. In terms of expressing this, by the late fourteenth century, Middle English had the verb *to sustain* in a variety of spellings, such as 'sustenen' or 'susteynen', which, among a range of senses, could mean 'to keep (the world, a created thing, etc) in existence', or to perpetuate or maintain those things.[57] Around the same time, the adjective *durable* was similarly being used to describe something that was 'able to withstand change, decay, or wear'.[58] A case study, mentioned in Chapters 2 and 4, mentions exactly this kind of staunch material endurance. The case study focusses on common-profit books, which were

---

[52] J. Dagenais, 'Decolonizing the Medieval Page', in *The Future of the Page*, ed. P. Stoicheff and A. Taylor (London, 2004), pp. 37–70 (pp. 38, 40).

[53] See J. Bennett, *Vibrant Matter: A Political Ecology of Things* (Durham, 2010); and for articulation of the human/nonhuman 'mesh' see T. Morton, *Ecology Without Nature: Rethinking Environmental Aesthetics* (London, 2007), p. 175.

[54] The two other 'thing-powers' she identifies are 'porosity and contagion' and 'inorganic sympathy' in J. Bennett, 'Powers of the Hoard: Further Notes on Material Agency', in *Animal, Vegetable, Mineral: Ethics and Objects*, ed. J. J. Cohen (Washington, DC, 2012), pp. 237–72 (pp. 252–54).

[55] *OED, durable, adj.*, Senses 1, 2a and 2b.

[56] *OED, sustain, v.*, Sense 1a: 'To keep in existence, maintain', 1b: 'To maintain (a physical object) in good condition or working order'; *sustainability, adj.*, Sense 3a: 'Capable of being maintained or continued at a certain rate or level'.

[57] *MED, sustenen, v.*, Sense 4c; *OED, sustain, v.*, Sense 1a (first used *c*. 1300).

[58] *OED, durable*, adj., Sense 1; *MED, durable*, adj., Sense 1.

religious texts directed by donors to be used sequentially by a series of readers. Inscriptions in surviving common-profit books highlight the longevity of the book as a physical thing, noting that it is to be passed on for 'as long as þe booke enduriþ'.[59] Likewise, the verb *enduren* could mean to harden or fortify, though here the foremost sense is of continuation, and the sense used in relation to things that connotes their sufficiency, adequacy and ongoing serviceability.[60]

Maintaining medieval material things was closely linked to charity, as common-profit books suggest. These and other charitable second-hand exchanges of books are discussed in Chapter 4. For example, a passage in Corinthians from the Wycliffite Bible, dated to the 1380s or 1390s, notes that 'Charite [...] susteyneth alle thingis'.[61] Another Middle English sense of *sustenen* was 'to keep in good repair', and could refer to the material fabric of buildings.[62] This sense carried connotations of charity too, and was associated with the supply of lamps, candles or tapers for churches. In one case, it was noted that 'serges' for many of the sepulchres were 'sustened of charite by oder of the parishe'.[63] Sustaining things, then, was often a charitable endeavour and is evident in the donation and preservation of second-hand books (explored in detail in Chapter 4). This suggests that these Middle English words could carry positive, even worthy overtones. Most importantly, what these examples show is that the broader concepts of durability and sustainability were not alien or inexpressible in this time.

Whether or not the kind of book-centred durability and re-use explored in this study was ever precisely articulated, people would have understood and recognised different degrees of material sustainability. In addition, throughout the fifteenth century greater quantities of older medieval books than we know today were still in existence, and more books were in existence than the ancestors of fifteenth-century people would have ever known, all testifying to their own durability by their presence. The network of medieval book designers and users would have been witness to the ongoing survival and long life of manuscripts. As the inscriptions in common-profit books acknowledge, books could 'endure' but there was also a keen awareness that they might not. The goal of this study is to reveal the physical evidence in the books themselves which shows that people were interested in making things well and making them to last.

---

[59] London, Lambeth Palace Library, MS 472, fol. 260r.
[60] *MED*, *enduren*, *v.*, Senses 2a and e.
[61] Corinthians 13.7, see for example BodL, MS Douce 369; *The Holy Bible, Containing the Old and New Testaments, with the Apocryphal Books, in the Earliest English Versions Made from the Latin Vulgate by John Wycliffe and His Followers*, ed. J. Forshall and F. Madden (Oxford, 1850), p. 362.
[62] *MED*, *sustenen*, *v.*, Sense 4b, with particular application to buildings or structures.
[63] From an inventory dated 1467, from All Saints Church in Derby, in J. C. Cox, *Notes on the Churches of Derbyshire: The Hundred of Morleston and Litchurch and General Supplement* (Chesterfield, 1879), p. 87.

The discussions of re-use and durability in this study naturally precipitate a dialogue with ecocritical frameworks, especially regarding waste. Thus far, medieval literary ecocriticism has followed a similar trajectory to the wider field of ecocriticism, tracing a path from analysis of medieval landscapes and green environments, to more recent enquiries into more diverse approaches. Early criticism, beginning in the late 1960s, focussed on providing accounts of 'nature' in medieval texts and developing green textual readings.[64] Alongside key medieval ecocritical publications there have been many others with a yet wider spectrum of approaches and preoccupations.[65] I suspect that increasing attention to waste in medieval scholarship may in part derive from the focus on waste in later periods, especially in the early modern period. The focus there is both on literary texts and book history concerned with waste paper and manuscript dispersal following the dissolution of the monasteries. Nevertheless, relatively little has been done to consider ecocriticism and manuscript materiality in the late medieval context.

Medieval ecocriticism has developed beyond modes of 'green reading' to address historical attitudes towards waste and resources. The etymology of waste is Latin *vastus*, which gives the idea of wasteland, or other void spaces, but also therefore shares a root with the word 'vast'.[66] Moving away from earlier green and – relatively – pleasant readings, Susan Signe Morrison has brought a *fecopoetics* or waste studies perspective to medieval texts.[67] Waste studies have been taken up by Mary C. Flannery in an essay on the privy as a reading space in Chaucer's 'Merchant's Tale'.[68] There are also emerging fields of 'waste' and 'discard' studies, and investigations of recycling, junk, and composting, though these should be treated with caution since there is some tendency toward ahistorical conflation of modern attitudes with past approaches to waste.[69] Other commentators on medieval literature and

---

[64] L. White Jr., 'The Historical Roots of Our Ecologic Crisis', *Science* 155 (1967), 1203–07; D. Pearsall and E. Salter, *Landscapes and Seasons of the Medieval World* (London, 1973); R. Douglass, 'Ecocriticism and Middle English Literature', *Studies in Medievalism* 10 (1998), 136–63; G. Rudd, *Greenery: Ecocritical Readings of Late Medieval English Literature* (Manchester, 2007); B. A. Hanawalt and L. J. Kiser, *Engaging with Nature: Essays on the Natural World in Medieval and Early Modern Europe* (Notre Dame, 2008).

[65] Such as J. Aberth's study of the medieval environment *An Environmental History of the Middle Ages: The Crucible of Nature* (London, 2013).

[66] With thanks to Anna Reynolds for sharing her unpublished writing on this topic; definitions of waste as they apply in the early modern context are explored in the 'Introduction', in *Privy Tokens: Waste Paper in Early Modern England*, pp. 1–25 (pp. 7–14).

[67] S. S. Morrison, *Excrement in the Late Middle Ages: Sacred Filth and Chaucer's Fecopoetics* (Basingstoke, 2008); S. S. Morrison, *The Literature of Waste: Material Ecopoetics and Ethical Matter* (Basingstoke, 2015).

[68] M. C. Flannery, 'Privy Reading', in *Spaces for Reading in Later Medieval England*, ed. M. C. Flannery and C. Griffin (Houndmills, 2016), pp. 149–64.

[69] Morrison offers an overview of waste and discard studies in the 'Introduction', in *The Literature of Waste* (pp. 1–16); also, see: *Excrement in the Late Middle Ages*; and see P. Marland and J. Parham, 'Remaindering: the Material Ecology of Junk and Composting', *Green Letters: Studies in Ecocriticism* 18 (2014), 1–8.

its relationship with waste – broadly defined – are James Simpson and Eleanor Johnson. Simpson has explored the creative recycling of old literary texts in the *Confessio Amantis* and the 'complex operations of idle reading'.[70] Although also writing with a precise frame of reference, to the poetics of waste and the presentation of land use in *Piers Plowman* and *Wynnere and Wastoure*, Johnson has also argued that people were 'actively concerned [about] ecological economies of matter and energy'.[71] Though Johnson makes this statement in support of her more specific arguments, in a general sense this claim also supports this book's argument for re-use in manuscript culture.

As well as examining waste, other ecocritics have considered conceptions of matter in the Middle Ages. After all, there were wider medieval philosophical and theological concerns around the permanence and solidity of matter. Medieval thinking about matter grew out of certain strains of classical philosophy, and understanding this requires peeling back Enlightenment conceptions of materiality to rediscover premodern concepts of human and nonhuman things.[72] The previously discussed manifesto for vibrant materiality by Bennett draws on the longer history of thinking about human and nonhuman matter. However, in their study of sacred objects, Shannon Gayk and Robyn Malo caution that object-oriented ontologies such as Bennett's fail to account for the 'potential instrumentality and derivative power of objects within the sacred economy'.[73] In addition to empowering objects, theology of the medieval period also encouraged widespread belief in the doctrine of resurrection, which described what could be expected at Doomsday. It was believed that resurrection would take place as a literal bodily reality, with flesh and bone restored to long-dead bodies for their journey to the afterlife.[74]

Interdisciplinary scholarship offers diverse avenues for medieval manuscript studies, and some notably imaginative ways in which to refocus on the actual matter of manuscripts. Taking a 'media archaeology' perspective, for example, enables a radical reappraisal of the labour and resources involved in the production of manuscripts, as well as generative comparisons with more recent media technologies.[75] The intersection of the sciences and

[70] J. Simpson, 'Bonjour Paresse: Literary Waste and Recycling in Book 4 of Gower's "Confessio Amantis"', *Proceedings of the British Academy* 151 (2007), 257–84 (p. 284).

[71] E. Johnson, 'The Poetics of Waste: Medieval English Ecocriticism', *PMLA* 127 (2012), 460–76 (p. 473); reviewed, in the context of the development of medieval ecocriticism, by V. Nardizzi, 'Medieval Ecocriticism', *postmedieval: a journal of medieval cultural studies* 4 (2013), 112–23 (p. 118).

[72] See Frow, 'Matter and Materialism', pp. 25–37; K. Robertson, 'Medieval Things: Materiality, Historicity, and the Premodern Object', *Literature Compass* 5 (2008), 1060–80.

[73] S. Gayk and R. Malo, 'The Sacred Object', *JMEMS* 44 (2014), 458–67 (pp. 460–61); for another approach to holy objects, see K. M. Rudy, *Postcards on Parchment: The Social Lives of Medieval Books* (New Haven, 2015).

[74] C. Walker Bynum, *The Resurrection of the Body in Western Christianity, 200–1336* (New York, 1995), pp. 36–38.

[75] I am thinking particularly of Tom White's research project: 'Working Theories of the Late Medieval Book'; see also, for example, M. Foys, 'The Remanence of Medieval Media', in *The Routledge Handbook of Digital Medieval Literature*, ed. J. Boyle and H. Burgess (Oxford, 2017).

the humanities is producing innovative methods for analysing manuscript materiality, such as ambitious digital humanities projects. Several projects aim to image and even to reunite fragments of manuscripts from across the world (for more on this, see Chapter 2). Another, 'The Book and the Silk Roads' project, endeavours to combine 'comparative codicology' with imaging technology, such as CT scanning of bindings.[76] Perhaps most striking is the relatively new field of 'biocodicology', from which has emerged a novel non-invasive technique for analysing parchment DNA, among other highly informative research outputs.[77] These interdisciplinary approaches demonstrate the variety of techniques for investigating medieval manuscript materiality.

Though I keep in mind the differences between medieval and modern conceptions of matter, this book identifies medieval habits of manuscript making and use which foreshadow modern attempts at sustainability. Rather than understanding the past by looking back through the prism of modern-day throwaway culture, though, this book attends to how a variety of medieval people engaged with materials around them, in the specific context of late medieval book culture. For instance, the fact that parchment is itself a by-product underpins key aspects of my arguments. Moreover, most medievalist ecocriticism to date is grounded in literary criticism and representations of waste and has not looked at the actual matter of medieval manuscripts; my work extends this area of scholarship. Therefore, this book moves on from the representation of waste to the material incarnations of literary texts as themselves – sometimes – becoming waste, or resourcefully avoiding waste through sustainable practices.

* * *

In this book, manuscripts are considered using a deliberately eclectic range of approaches. Throughout there is a commitment to inclusive sampling and an openness to a variety of methods. Research in archives with plentiful fifteenth-century manuscripts, and particularly those with fifteenth-century bindings, allowed me to augment each chapter with additional case studies as the book progressed. The limitations of catalogue records sometimes hampered traditional survey techniques (for example, the search for material traces of parchment production in Chapter 1). It is for this reason that seemingly esoteric examples of manuscripts, which arose by chance, are included alongside more formally selected case studies and surveys.

---

[76] 'The Book and the Silk Roads' project (2019–21), Old Books New Science lab, University of Toronto, <https://oldbooksnewscience.com/aboutobns/lab-projects/>.

[77] S. Fiddyment, M. D. Teasdale, J. Vnouček, É. Lévêque, A. Binois and M. J. Collins, 'So You Want To Do Biocodicology? A Field Guide to the Biological Analysis of Parchment', *Heritage Science* 7 (2019), 1–35; see Chapter 1 of this book, which draws on biocodicological and zooarchaeological research; see also the Beasts 2 Craft project website, online <https://sites.google.com/palaeome.org/ercb2c/home?authuser=0>.

Each chapter takes a different line of enquiry into a different aspect of medieval manuscript sustainability. Chapter 1 considers how parchment was made in the fifteenth century, tracking the journey of parchment from its origins as animal skins, through the hands of tradesmen to craftsmen, who transformed the material into parchment writing supports. To achieve this, the hides or skins underwent a series of processes. Evidence for these processes is drawn from medieval recipes for parchment making and from tangible evidence surviving in extant parchment. In this chapter, fifteenth-century recipes for parchment making, derived from existing indexes of manuscripts, are transcribed and compared with one another.[78] Although some of these recipes have received attention previously, they have not been considered for the ways in which medieval parchment making may (or may not) have been sustainable. Each stage of production is addressed for the ways in which it enhanced or diminished parchment's durability and sustainability, and consequently its eventual re-use.

The second part of the chapter focuses on parchment damage, which was ignored, accommodated, or even celebrated, and on the ways in which parchment was sustained through repair efforts. Here, I explore case studies of extant manuscripts, with relevant examples identified either by gleaning from catalogue descriptions, or from serendipitous encounter in the archives. This strategy, as mentioned above, enabled the discovery of these otherwise uncharted features of fifteenth century manuscripts. These further examples demonstrate damage such as holes or tears, often overlooked in conventional cataloguing, and a few cases of parchment repair.

In Chapter 2, the focus shifts from the production of parchment and its repair to the re-use of parchment in books. This chapter explores case studies of parchment recycled as reinforcing strips, quire guards, flyleaves, pastedowns, limp covers and palimpsests: in short, all the materials re-used in the making and remaking of manuscripts. Some of these are scraps, like small off-cuts, whereas some pieces of parchment – in a range of sizes – were recycled, with some still bearing earlier writing. This chapter explores the hallmarks of re-use and investigates the techniques required to achieve the material recycling seen in manuscripts. In these instances of re-use, parchment is being 'transformed […] into matter' and valued for its material properties.[79]

As in Chapter 1, many of the case studies discussed in Chapter 2 are the result of chance encounter. The manuscripts included here came to my attention fortuitously either through word-of-mouth recommendations, or as the result of foraging in catalogues, handlists, textbooks, and other scholarship. The key principle guiding the search for examples was the presence of fifteenth-century bindings. Though not always watertight, and subject to the vagaries of date attribution to medieval books and book materials, the presence of a fifteenth-century binding helped to secure the date of other physically recycled

---

[78] M. Clarke, *The Art of All Colours: Mediaeval Recipe Books for Painters and Illuminators* (London, 2001); Clarke, *Crafte*; D. V. Thompson, *The Materials and Techniques of Medieval Painting* (New York, 1956).

[79] Smyth and Partington, *Book Destruction*, p. 8.

components of the book block or binding. In the fifteenth century, the binding of books that had been made recently existed side-by-side with the binding and repair of older manuscripts. The focus of this chapter, then, is upon manuscripts with fifteenth-century bindings, which enclose predominantly fifteenth-century book blocks, as well as featuring recycled parchment strips, leaves, and scraps.

Chapter 3 turns the attention away from the production, repair and recycling of parchment, to the handling of books, chiefly to the re-use of their margins as a writing surface. These written or drawn re-uses are not associated with the main text, and include marks such as doodles, alphabets, signatures and verses. Margins are defined broadly, to incorporate the extraneous writing surfaces available in the book, such as spaces around the text block on each leaf, as well as flyleaves and pastedowns. People re-used those spaces either for ephemeral purposes, which meant that they avoided wasting other materials, or as repositories for writing. Sometimes it seems that people anticipated that the marks they made in books would be read in the future: this expectation of future use depended upon the durability of the book.

A more formal, conventional selection strategy was adopted for Chapter 3. In order to address the kinds of opportunistic marginal markings that I wanted to explore in this chapter, research was limited to two of the Bodleian Library's collections, the Douce and Laud collections. Middle English manuscripts dating to the fifteenth century, which featured some form of marginal inscription, whether written or drawn, were sought in relevant handlists and catalogues.[80] Browsing large numbers of manuscripts from these collections yielded case studies of marginal annotations and drawings that did not comment directly on the main text, but rather suggest treatment of the book as a useful writing support or as a repository.

The focus of the final chapter is second-handedness and the ways in which, when books underwent transitions in ownership, people depended on books' durability. To this end, this chapter tracks the ways in which manuscripts moved between religious institutions, colleges and individuals, circulating from one owner to another, or to another custodian. Manuscripts could move between people as a result of giving, bequeathing, selling, or some specific directed forms of gift-giving such as shared common profit books. Again, in Chapter 4, manuscript examples were sourced from a combination of catalogue foraging, book lists compiled by other scholars, in addition to two substantial formal surveys. First, I drew on C. Paul Christianson's handlist of known manuscript producers who also sold works second-hand.[81] Then, focusing on accessions to the Bodleian's early collections, I limited myself to the library's *Summary Catalogue* Volume II.i. The results of this enabled closer analysis of a range of inscriptions marking ownership or exchange.

Through these four perspectives, this book reconsiders the materiality of manuscript culture, and draws attention to occasions when what might otherwise have become waste

---

[80] *IMEP* IV; *IMEP* XVI; *Summary Catalogue* IV; *Quarto Catalogue* II.
[81] Christianson, *Directory*; *Summary Catalogue* II.i.

was not treated as waste. William H. Sherman has described books as participating in a 'dynamic ecology of use and re-use, leading to transformation and destruction as well as to preservation'.[82] The focus here is manuscript materials – whether in the form of parchment fragments, or as larger pieces, or in codex form – that were transformed and preserved by being repaired, recycled and re-circulated. The sources for study in these chapters are *actual* materials, recipes, traces of production and markings in fifteenth-century manuscripts. In whatever ways they were made, handled or circulated, manuscripts were part of a wider medieval habit of re-using materials. In her beautifully illustrated study of limp bindings at the Vatican Library, Monica Langwe notes that in the medieval period 'the concept of conservation […] was more a process of extending the use of the book'.[83] Far from being wasted, scraps or leaves of parchment, margins and whole books were all valued – in a range of ways – for their materiality. In fifteenth-century manuscript culture, books sustained people, and people sustained books.

---

[82] Sherman, *Used Books*, p. 6.
[83] M. Langwe, *Limp Bindings from the Vatican Library* (Sollerön, 2013), p. 21.

1

Making Parchment For Books

Parchment, like a book, was made to be durable. Making parchment used up animal materials sustainably, and the end product could be conserved and re-used in all kinds of ways. As discussed in the introduction, parchment's hard-wearing potential relies on the intrinsic material properties of skin. Cultivated by craftsmen, skin's long-lasting durability when made into parchment provided the foundations for both uses and re-uses. Throughout, this chapter is informed by codicological studies of medieval book production, as well as extant medieval manuscripts and recipes for making parchment.[1] Fifteenth-century manuscripts provide evidence for their production in their form, and recipes offer instruction and information about book-producing crafts. Considered in conjunction with one another, manuscripts and recipes reveal efforts made by fifteenth-century people to enhance the durability of parchment, and to use resources and their by-products as efficiently as possible. There was a 'nose-to-tail' approach, which avoided waste and used the whole animal.[2]

To explore these practices, the stages of parchment production are re-evaluated here, step-by-step, from farm to writing table. Though these stages are well known to specialists, this chapter offers a new description of parchment-making as an exercise in cultivation and conservation. The discussion begins with animal husbandry in the field, and ventures through various supply chains, into the hands of slaughtermen. Then, the dead animal matter, be it as raw hide or skin, travels to parchmeners (there is no consensus on the spelling of this word, which is found as *parchmenter, parchemyner, parchminer* and *parchmyner*).[3] Here the discussion appraises the processes, time, care, skills, tools and additional resources required to turn hide or skin into usable parchment. Finally, the

---

[1] Prior to M. Clarke's excellent edition, *Crafte*, I identified relevant codicological recipes in *The Art of All Colours: Mediaeval Recipe Books for Painters and Illuminators*, ed. Clarke (London, 2001), and first-hand consultation of recipes in manuscripts.

[2] This is used in analogy with the twenty-first century phrase 'nose to tail eating', which means that the entirety or vast majority of an animal is used up to ensure as little waste as possible; the phrase was made popular by Fergus Henderson's recipe book, *The Whole Hog: Nose to Tail Eating* (London, 2004).

[3] Following Christianson, *Directory*, pp. 112–13, I prefer the spelling *parchmener*; P. W. M. Blayney lists possible spellings in *The Stationers' Company Before the Charter, 1403–1557* (London, 2003), p. 17; M. P. Brown prefers *parchmenter* in *Understanding Illuminated Manuscripts: A Guide to Technical Terms*, revised by E. C. Teviotdale and N. K. Turner (Los Angeles, 2018), p. 81.

'luxury commodity' of parchment is available for use and for re-use.[4] Alongside the main product of this process, parchment, there are by-products such as gelatine and glue made from bits of the carcass or trimmings of skin; and, furthermore, lower grade or damaged parchment could be used, or efforts could also be taken to sustain it by repair. Re-evaluating each stage of production indicates how medieval parchment production embraced and embodied sustainability.

But books could also be made from paper. Fifteenth-century paper was made from 'cellulose (flax, hemp, linen), which in late medieval Europe was usually obtained from cloth rags or ship sails (or even recycled scrap paper)'.[5] These rags were sorted, fermented, washed and beaten into a runny pulp before being shaken into shape, squeezed, set to dry, then sized.[6] In its own form, as a recycled, reconstituted substance, paper is an example of resource conservation through re-use. Though paper may in many cases be more frangible and fragile than parchment, and is not necessarily associated with durability in the same way as parchment, nevertheless many fifteenth-century paper manuscripts do survive.[7] Paper was used in a range of ways, with plentiful evidence of post-Reformation books bound with 'waste' paper pastedowns, flyleaves and linings.[8] There were special efforts taken in the fifteenth century to protect and enhance the potential of paper books for survival, such as the insertion of parchment reinforcing strips, quire guards and binding linings, among other strategies. Many of these strategies drew on the material qualities of parchment, using it as a sacrificial buffer.[9] So, paper was itself recycled, could be durable and was subject to measures designed to sustain it.

Parchment was the substance most commonly used for writing supports in the Middle Ages, until the use of paper as an alternative resource took hold.[10] Since the first records, humans always made books with the materials afforded by their environment, whether that took the form of clay writing tablets, papyrus rolls, or parchment leaves.[11] The use of parchment for writing has a long tradition and is thought to take its name from the

---

[4] H. E. Bell, 'The Price of Books in Medieval England', *The Library* 17 (1937), 312–32 (p. 332).

[5] R. Clemens and T. Graham, *Introduction to Manuscript Studies* (Ithaca, 2007), p. 7.

[6] For a short description, see C. de Hamel, *Medieval Craftsmen: Scribes and Illuminators* (London, 1992), pp. 16–17.

[7] N. Baker, *Double Fold: Libraries and the Assault on Paper* (New York, 2001), p. 7.

[8] For a study of early modern paper with a decidedly ecological approach, see J. Calhoun, 'The World Made Flax: Cheap Bibles, Textual Corruptions, and the Poetics of Paper' *PMLA* 126 (2011), 327–44, also J. Calhoun, *The Nature of the Page* (Philadelphia, 2020).

[9] These uses of parchment in conjunction with paper are discussed in Chapter 2.

[10] O. Da Rold, 'Materials', in *PBE*, pp. 12–33 (p. 25); Da Rold argues that 'by the middle of the fifteenth century [paper] had become a sturdy material of choice', 'Introduction', in *Paper in Medieval England: From Pulp to Fictions* (Cambridge, 2020), pp. 1–21 (p. 10).

[11] Many scholars draw a distinction between *vellum* (calfskin) and *parchment* (usually sheepskin). Here, the distinction will be made between calf or sheep where necessary, and the term *parchment* is used throughout. For definitions, see Muzerelle, *Vocabulaire codicologique*, online <http://codicologia.irht.cnrs.fr/theme/liste_theme/121>.

ancient city of Pergamon (or Pergamum, now Bergama in western Anatolia, Turkey), hence the Latin *pergamenum*. This writing support was 'supposedly invented [...] in the second century B.C.E'. and, after supplies of papyrus were disrupted by the invasion of Egypt, was adopted thereafter as an alternative.[12] Whether parchment was invented at Pergamon is unknown; however, it is known to be a site of early production.[13]

Then, as in the medieval period, a simplified working definition of parchment would be: untanned hide or skin that has been soaked in solution and then dried under tension.[14] This process yields a substance that has the potential to be remarkably durable. But why was parchment chosen for medieval book production? Arguably, there was little choice before the introduction of paper and, in many cases, parchment could have been chosen for its ability to hold ink well, rather than for any special consideration for its longevity. However, parchment continued to be widely used and, in many cases, there was attention to promoting its potential for long-term durability. Parchment has a range of distinctive physical properties: 'lightness and flexibility of the writing surface, [...] high tearing strength [and] exceptional long-term stability', all of which contribute to its durability.[15] People's attitudes to animals and the resources they provide sometimes rely on a 'particular functional attribute for a raw material'.[16] A combination of these distinctive properties – the 'functional attributes' – of animal hide or skin, and enhancement of these by people, ensured that parchment persisted as the favoured writing support for so long.

Parchment was made from the hides of cattle, or skins from calves, hair sheep, pigs or goats. For bookbinding, Alexandra Gillespie notes that in addition to calfskin and sheepskin, seal, deer and ox skin were made into leather.[17] Both hides and skins as leather and parchment were commonly used in book production: as leather for binding books, usually over wooden boards, and as parchment for the main writing support. Though hides were imported into England, there is some indication that choices between hide or skin used to make parchment show a geographical pattern. Research into DNA from twelfth- and thirteenth-century parchment manuscripts confirms a 'predominance of calfskin being used in France, a pronounced use of goatskin in Italy, and a more mixed pattern emerging

---

[12] R. W. Clement, 'A Survey of Antique, Medieval, and Renaissance Book Production', in *Art into Life: Collected Papers from the Kresge Art Museum Medieval Symposia*, ed. C. G. Fisher and K. L. Scott (East Lansing, 1995), pp. 9–47 (p. 13); M. L. Ryder, 'The Biology and History of Parchment', in *Pergament, Geschichte, Struktur, Restaurierung und Herstellung*, ed. P. Rück (Sigmaringen, 1991), pp. 25–33 (p. 25).

[13] Brown, *Illuminated Manuscripts*, p. 80.

[14] For a concise description, see R. M. Thomson, 'Parchment and Paper, Ruling and Ink', in *CHBB* II, 75–84 (p. 77).

[15] R. Reed, *Ancient Skins, Parchments and Leathers* (London, 1972), p. 5. Reed's comments are mentioned again in Chapter 2 for the ways in which these properties enabled parchment recycling.

[16] T. O'Connor, 'Thinking About Beastly Bodies', in *Breaking and Shaping Beastly Bodies: Animals as Material Culture in the Middle Ages*, ed. A. Pluskowski (Oxford, 2007), pp. 1–10 (p. 1).

[17] A. Gillespie, 'Bookbinding', in *PBE*, pp. 150–72 (p. 150).

from England'.[18] These national trends not only reflect preferences in meat consumption but also suggest that parchment was often a locally sourced by-product, linked to the livestock available in a region.

The lexical terms used in late-medieval England reveal the animals available for parchment making. The Latin *pergamenum* through French *parchemin* eventually became Middle English *parchemyne* or *parchement* or *parchemin* (among a range of other spellings).[19] Where parchment is mentioned in Middle English texts, it is also referred to as fell, membrane, vellum, skin or hide, some of which suggest the animal origins of the material.[20] The term 'perchemyn felle' for a writing support is used in a copy of *Guy of Warwick* written in about 1475: 'Of Guyes felawes shull we telle / As y fynde in this perchemyn felle'.[21] *Felle* descends from Old English and Old Germanic roots, with a cognate in the Latin *pellis* meaning skin, whilst *membrane* comes from the Latin *membrana* meaning an outer covering of an animal body. Also from Latin, *vitulus* or *vitellus* (calf), via French *velin*, comes *vellum*.[22] The word *skin* is an early Scandinavian borrowing, the Old Icelandic manuscripts known as *Fagrskinna* and *Morkinskinna* (fair-skin and rotten-skin) carry this sense of skin meaning parchment, implying attention to quality.[23] Skin tended to refer to integuments from smaller animals, whereas hide, from Old English *hyd*, indicated pelts from larger animals.[24] Thus, parchment was referred to by an array of terms which evoked its animality.

However, though parchment was known to be an animal product, and was sometimes implicitly referred to as such, contemporaries only rarely commented explicitly on its animality. A riddle from the Exeter Book offers an early medieval account of the essential processes of parchment making.[25] Unusually for a reference to book production, the riddle begins with the death of the animal ('Mec feonda sum feore besnyþede, / woruldstrenga binom', 'A certain enemy robbed me of my life, took my world-strength') and describes the transformation of the animal's skin into parchment and its incorporation into a decorated

---

[18] S. Fiddyment, B. Holsinger et al., 'Animal Origin of Thirteenth-Century Uterine Vellum Revealed Using Noninvasive Peptide Fingerprinting', *Proceedings of the National Academy of Sciences* 112:49 (2015), 15066–71 (pp. 15068, 15069).

[19] *OED, parchment, n.*, etymology, and Senses 1 and 2.

[20] *MED, parchemin, n.*, Senses a, b and d particularly.

[21] GCC, MS 107/176, ll. 4793–94, in *The Romance of Guy of Warwick: Edited from the Auchinleck Manuscript in the Advocates' Library, Edinburgh, and from MS 107 in Caius College, Cambridge*, ed. J. Zupitza, EETS ES 49 (London, 1887), II, 275; James, *GCC Catalogue* I, 107–08.

[22] *OED, vellum, n.*, etymology and Sense 1.

[23] *OED, skin, n.*, etymology and Sense I.1.a, but especially Sense 2.

[24] *OED, hide, n.*, etymology and Sense 1a.

[25] Exeter Cathedral Library, MS 3501 is dated 960–90; *Catalogue of Manuscripts Containing Anglo-Saxon*, ed. N. R. Ker (Oxford, 1957), p. 153. See discussions of Riddle 24 in: B. Holsinger, 'Of Pigs and Parchment: Medieval Studies and the Coming of the Animal', *PMLA* 124 (2009), 616–23 (pp. 621–22); and in S. Kay, 'Legible Skins: Animals and the Ethics of Medieval Reading', *postmedieval: a journal of medieval cultural studies* 2 (2011), 13–32 (p. 19).

book.²⁶ And towards the end of the medieval period, in William Horman's Latin textbook of 1519, schoolboys would have learned the following:

> That stouffe that we wrytte upon: and is made of beestis skynnes: is somtyme called parchement / somtyme velem / somtyme abortyue / somtyme membraan. Parchement of the cyte: where it was first made. Velem / bycause it is made of caluys skynne. Abortyue / bycause the beest was scante parfecte. Membraan / bycause it was pulled of by hyldynge fro the beestis lymmes.²⁷

This description defines each term used to describe the writing support, from 'beestis skynnes' to 'parchment', 'velem', 'abortyue' and 'membraan', culminating in a visceral image of the skin being pulled off a beast's body through 'hyldynge', meaning skinning. The riddle and Horman's textbook suggest that, across the centuries, many medieval people were well aware of the animal origins of parchment.

Curiously, as Horman's textbook suggests, fifteenth-century writers noted a peculiar kind of parchment, known in Latin as *abortivum*, or Middle English *abortyve*: so-called *uterine vellum*.²⁸ These names described especially fine, thin and white parchment, allegedly always made from the skin of stillborn calves or lambs. Uterine vellum has become associated with thirteenth-century French Bibles, which were made of superfine, extremely white parchment. A codicological recipe in BodL, MS Ashmole 750 gives instructions to use very little size when gilding an initial painted on this type of parchment: 'And ȝif þu wyll mak letter on abratif or abortyf, lai þi zyse als thyn þeron as þu may'.²⁹ Abortive was considered finickity to work with; writing on it required careful preparation. This material seems at first to be consistent with a sustainable, 'nose-to-tail' approach – even stillborn animals' skins were made into parchment.

But the use of stillborn skins in the creation of parchment is subject to debate. As Christopher de Hamel notes, 'it is very difficult to believe that thousands of cows miscarried for generations, or were deprived of their foetuses in such numbers to supply the book trade economically'.³⁰ And if calves were being stillborn naturally in such quanti-

---

26 The most common solutions are 'book', 'Bible', or 'gospel book', Riddle 24 in *A Choice of Anglo-Saxon Verse*, ed. R. Hamer (London, 1977), pp. 103–05, ll. 1–2.
27 W. Horman, *Vulgaria*, ed. M. R. James (Oxford, 1926), p. 123; cited by W. L. Ustick, '"Parchment" and "Vellum"', *The Library* 4th s. 16 (1936), 439–40 (p. 440); also cited by C. Clarkson, 'Rediscovering Parchment: The Nature of the Beast', *The Paper Conservator: Vellum and Parchment, The Journal of the Institute of Paper Conservation* 16 (1992), 5–26 (p. 5).
28 *DMLBS, abortivus, n.*, Sense 3 (first noted 1265, also examples from 1445 and 1446 noted); *MED, abortive, n.*, Sense 3: 'Parchment made from the skin of a stillborn animal' with citation of a recipe in BL, MS Sloane 2584. J. Pouzet also cites 'motlyn abortif' as part of a note written in CUL, MS Ee.4.20 by William Wyntershulle, in 'Book Production Outside Commercial Contexts', in *PBE*, pp. 212–38 (p. 218).
29 BodL, MS Ashmole 750, fol. 178r; *Quarto Catalogue* X, 357–62; Clarke, *Crafte*, p. 256.
30 De Hamel, *Scribes and Illuminators*, p.16.

ties, 'animal husbandry must have been in a very precarious condition'.[31] Yet superfine uterine vellum was known from classical times: Pliny referred to this material as *charta non nata* or *charta virginea* and claimed that *pergamenae vitulinae* (calfskins) were used because of the larger cutting area available (compared to uterine sheepskins).[32] Research into this question suggests that such fine parchment was the result of 'highly specialized craft' using both very young animal skins as well as specific finishing techniques such as splitting skins, rather than *always* only uterine vellum.[33] Skin splitting is also known from accounts of rabbinic parchment preparation.[34] And while it is a tragic outcome, there always have been and will be occasional stillbirths in the course of animal husbandry. Known as 'slunk vellum', uterine vellum continues to be used today as one of the highest grades of parchment available to calligraphers and is particularly prized for precise botanical illustration.[35]

The production of any manuscript required a remarkable range of other organic materials, some of which were also animal products or by-products. These included natural growths such as oak galls, also known as oak apples, the formation of which is triggered by the gall wasp, and which were used for making ink.[36] Many recipes for ink requiring galls are attested. One for ink of Lombardy, for example, suggests: 'Forto make ynke Lombards do þusse. Take a novnce of gallis' and another in the same manuscript, for text ink, advises: 'Text ynke þus. Take .iiij. once of galles *and* breke þam small in a morter'.[37] Another animal part needed for writing was bird feathers. Feathers were hardened and sharpened into flexible, strong quills for writing. Turkey, swan, crow, duck, and more rarely raven,

---

[31] D. V. Thompson, *The Materials and Techniques of Medieval Painting* (New York, 1956), p. 27.

[32] R. Reed, *The Nature and Making of Parchment* (Leeds, 1975), pp. 76–77.

[33] Fiddyment et al., 'Uterine Vellum', 15070; see also Thompson, *Materials*, p. 27; and C. Ruzzier, 'The Miniaturisation of Bible Manuscripts in the Thirteenth Century: A Comparative Study', in *Form and Function in the Late Medieval Bible*, ed. E. Poleg and L. Light (Leiden, 2013), pp. 105–25 (p. 115).

[34] A. Martini, 'Ritual Consecration in the Context of Writing the Holy Scrolls: Jews in Medieval Europe between Demarcation and Acculturation', *European Journal of Jewish Studies* 2 (2017), 174–202 (p. 177).

[35] The calligrapher P. Lovett discusses the use of slunk vellum on her website, online <https://www.patricialovett.com/tag/slunk-vellum/>; available from modern-day parchment-makers such as Pergamena New York, 'Manuscript Uterine Calf Parchment', online <http://www.pergamena.net/parchment-products/manuscript-uterine-calf-parchment>).

[36] Gum, gall and metallic sulphate were typical ingredients for making ink, and for a modern-day reconstruction of iron gall ink recipes using these ingredients, see S. Tohma, 'Making & Testing Iron Gall Ink', online <https://www.westdean.org.uk/study/school-of-conservation/blog/books-and-library-materials/making-testing-iron-gall-ink>.

[37] CUL, MS Dd.v.76, fol. 7r; *IMEP* XIX, 26–30; Hardwick, *CUL Catalogue* I, 285; Clarke, *Crafte*, pp. 216–17. For more examples of typical ink recipes, see also: BL, MS Cotton Julius D.viii, fol. 89v: 'To make ynk Lumbard' and 'To make tyxt ynk', and BL, MS Sloane 4, fol. 3v: 'To make ynk Lumbart'. See also the ink recipe in BodL, MS Laud misc.444 mentioned in Chapter 3.

pelican or peacock feathers could be used; however, scribes preferred goose feathers.[38] As the Goose in Lydgate's poem 'The Debate of the Horse, Goose, and Sheep' says: 'Men plukke stalkes out of my weengis tweyn, / Some to portraye, so*m*me to noote & write'.[39] To 'note and write' on parchment required feathers for quills and ink galls: additional animal by-products. Other resources required for parchment-making included chalk or similar calcium compounds for making lime solution to soak the hide or skin, as well as pumice (or a substitute, for which there were contemporary recipes), and a plentiful water supply. Additional organic materials might be necessary for other aspects of book production, for example plant juices for making ink or for tanning leather. Metal and mineral resources were also required to make pigments.[40] Each of these additional resources contributed to the book, but in terms of their sustainability, some were a product in their own right, whereas others were efficient uses of by-products. Since meat and eggs were the main products from geese, goose feathers for quills were a by-product.[41] Furthermore, some of these resources enhanced the production of parchment, or some other feature of the book, and in so doing improved its long-term durability.

But are traces of raw materials and their animal origins visible in the finished book? Today, just as they would have been then, these medieval 'beestis skynnes', as Horman previously described them, can be striking. Parchment has flesh and hair sides: the difference in texture of each side may be detectable by touch. The flesh side, once the inner side of the skin, is usually paler and smoother than the outer hair side, also known as the grain side. By this period, flesh and hair sides are usually arranged in manuscripts according to the Rule of Gregory, so that at any opening like faces like. Richard W. Clement suggests this rule was followed for 'aesthetic reasons' and argues that if the quire was 'arranged properly' the reading experience would not be disrupted by the contrasting colour and texture of each side.[42] Often manuscript leaves are speckled with follicle marks (BodL, MS Laud misc.739 and HEHL MS HM 114),[43] and occasionally some still have a few stray hairs intact on the hair side (Worcester Cathedral Library, MS Q. 93 and TCC,

---

[38] M. Finlay, *Western Writing Implements in the Age of the Quill Pen* (Penrith, 1990), p. 3; and J. I. Whalley, *Writing Implements and Accessories from the Roman Stylus to the Typewriter* (London, 1975), p. 16.

[39] J. Lydgate, 'The Debate of the Horse, Goose, and Sheep', in *The Minor Poems of John Lydgate*, ed. H. N. MacCracken, EETS OS 192 (London, 1934), II, 539–66 (p. 547), ll. 183–84.

[40] Clarke, *Art of All Colours*; Thompson, *Materials*, pp. 74–188.

[41] U. Albarella, 'Size, Power, Wool and Veal: Zooarchaeological Evidence for Late Medieval Innovations', in *Environment and Subsistence in Medieval Europe: Papers of the Medieval Europe Brugge 1997 Conference*, ed. G. de Boe and F. Verhaeghe (Zellik, 2007), pp. 19–30 (p. 27).

[42] Clement, 'A Survey', p. 25; described by J. P. Gumbert, as a 'deliberate choice' and not a consequence of folding, 'Skins, Sheets, and Quires', in *New Directions in Later Medieval Manuscript Studies: Essays from the 1998 Harvard Conference*, ed. D. Pearsall (York, 2000), pp. 81–90 (p. 87).

[43] See for example: BodL, MS Laud misc.739, fol. 161; Seymour, *Chaucer Catalogue* II, 179–82; *Quarto Catalogue* II, 524, 584. Also, see: HEHL MS HM 114, fol. 152; Dutschke, *HEHL Catalogue*, pp. 150–52.

MS R.3.22).⁴⁴ Sometimes, though very rarely, books were bound with what appears to be hairy parchment. In such cases, though the hair has not been fully removed, the skin has not been tanned like leather and appears instead to have undergone the key features of the parchment-making process. Examples include: a thirteenth-century copy of works by Bede from Byland Abbey; a thirteenth-century manuscript at Worcester Cathedral Library; a book of homilies in a sealskin binding from Iceland; and furry leaves which once wrapped a fourteenth-century treatise in reproof of worldly clergy.⁴⁵ The follicular features and hairy sheets are reminders of parchment's animal origins.

In addition to stray hairs, parchment sometimes registers other features of the body it once enveloped, even when prepared appropriately and used in a book. The contours of the skin, especially at its edges, may trace the former body. Sarah Kay notes that 'the curve of the animal's body persists in the natural curl of the pages'.⁴⁶ Denis Muzerelle refers to this curl as the *sens de la peau* (impression of the skin) and this can be seen in numerous manuscripts.⁴⁷ The outer edges of the skin were a cheaper option for making smaller manuscripts, but these sections may be either 'inadequately stretched' with 'hard and horny [parts] like rawhide', or 'weaker', softer areas.⁴⁸ These 'marginal textures' correspond with more flexible parts of the skin at the animal's armpits and groin.⁴⁹ Relatively low-grade parchment was sometimes made from 'raw, rough and almost "wild" skins' and, in the shape of such parchment 'we can recognize such animal parts as flanks, belly, legs'.⁵⁰ In manuscripts of substantial size each bifolium is a whole skin: in the Ellesmere Chaucer the spine of the animal runs from the book's head to tail,⁵¹ and in the Vernon manuscript

---

⁴⁴ Worcester Cathedral Library, MS Q. 93, fol. 67; Thomson, *Worcester Catalogue*, pp. 181–82. TCC, MS R.3.22 has hair on fol. 168; *IMEP* XI, 28; James, *TCC Catalogue* II, 602; with thanks to J. Henderson for this reference.

⁴⁵ Wormsley Library 12 (the Byland Bede), no.3, in P. Getty and H. G. Fletcher, *The Wormsley Library: A Personal Selection by Sir Paul Getty* (London, 1999), pp. 8–10; Worcester Cathedral Library, MS F.12, Thomson, *Worcester Catalogue*, pp. 13–14 notes the 'overcover of rough brown cowhide' (p. 13); an Icelandic manuscript now in Sweden, National Library of Sweden, MS Isl. Perg. 4 No. 15, online. <http://www.kb.se/samlingarna/Handskrifter/Smakprov/Nordiska-handskrifter/Islandska-Homilieboken/> with thanks to S. McDonald Werronen for this reference; BodL, MS e Mus. 198*, *Summary Catalogue* II.ii, 738–39, with thanks to J. D. Sargan for this reference.

⁴⁶ Kay, 'Legible Skins', p. 14.

⁴⁷ Muzerelle, *Vocabulaire codicologique*, s.n. sens de la peau.

⁴⁸ J. Borland, 'Unruly Reading: The Consuming Role of Touch in the Experience of a Medieval Manuscript', in *Scraped, Stroked, and Bound: Materially Engaged Readings of Medieval Manuscripts*, ed. J. Wilcox (Turnhout, 2013), pp. 97–114 (p. 103).

⁴⁹ Gumbert, 'Skins, Sheets, and Quires', p. 82.

⁵⁰ J. Vnouček, 'The Manufacture of Parchment for Writing Purposes and the Observation of the Signs of Manufacture Surviving in Old Manuscripts', *Care and Conservation* 8 (2005), 74–92 (p. 77).

⁵¹ HEHL, MS EL 26 C 9, noted in M. B. Parkes, 'The Planning and Construction of the Ellesmere Manuscript', in *The Ellesmere Chaucer: Essays in Interpretation*, ed. M. Stevens and D. Woodward (San Marino, 1997), pp. 41–47 (p. 43).

a 'dorsal stripe' runs across each bifolium, a ghostly, visceral impression of vertebrae.[52] The animal origins of parchment, therefore, register in the curl and texture of books' leaves.

The animal pre-history of the book

As these dorsal stripes, skin shapes and other surface blemishes all show, before parchment production, a considerable 'pre-history' of the book had already elapsed in the form of living animal organisms. These materials performed a rather different function as part of the animal, preserving and sustaining life long before they were used to preserve and sustain manuscripts. Animal skins have a remarkable range of functions. Skin is a complex organ, made up of highly specialised living tissue structures. These tissues operate together to 'control form, shape and size' and, individually, perform regulated physiological functions such as responding to stimuli, excreting waste, secreting enzymes and hormones, providing cohesion and assisting movement. The outer epithelial tissue also makes 'direct contact with the external environment', affording protection against 'light, water, and fluids generally'.[53] This organ has evolved to fulfil these necessary physiological functions. In a sense, then, the *re-use* of skins could be said to be any use occurring after the death of the animal, thus changing the function of the skin.

The necessary death of animals for making parchment raises ethical issues, as highlighted by Bruce Holsinger. He notes that to study parchment manuscripts 'is to be hopelessly implicated in and to constantly witness the mass deaths of countless sheep, lambs, calves, and goats for the means of literary transmission'.[54] He goes further, entertaining an imaginary scenario in which all medieval parchment is discovered to be made from human skin: in this way he dramatically foregrounds the ethical ramifications of parchment culture through a stark analogy.[55] Holsinger's essential argument is that medievalists should be mindful that – to paraphrase it – parchment is murder. Yet the slaughter of animals was everyday, familiar and readily visible in the meat markets of medieval towns. Slaughter usually took place where blood and detritus could be sluiced away, for example in the streets of butchers' stalls known as *Fleshambles*. There is a street still known as the 'Shambles' in York, which derives from *flesh-shameles*, meaning shelves or benches for

---

[52] BodL, MS Eng. poet. a. 1, as discussed by A. I. Doyle, 'Codicology, Palaeography, and Provenance', in *A Facsimile Edition of the Vernon Manuscript: Oxford, Bodleian Library MS Eng. Poet. A. 1*, ed. by W. Scase, Bodleian Digital Texts 3 (Oxford, 2012), pp. 1–19 (p. 4); Gumbert uses the term 'dorsal stripe', in 'Skins, Sheets, and Quires', p. 82; the 'dorse' is the back of the animal, from the Latin *dorsum*, this word came to be used as an alternative for 'verso', also to refer specifically to the back of charters, and developed into modern English 'endorsement', P. Beal, *A Dictionary of English Manuscript Terminology 1450–2000* (Oxford, 2008), pp. 127, 138.

[53] Reed, *Ancient Skins*, pp. 13–14.

[54] Holsinger, 'Of Pigs and Parchment', p. 619.

[55] B. Holsinger, 'Parchment Ethics: A Statement of More Than Modest Concern', *New Medieval Literatures* 12 (2010), 131–36.

meat.⁵⁶ Customarily, animals were baited into a frenzy before slaughter, due to a belief in the improved taste and tenderness of baited flesh.⁵⁷ Baiting meant of course that animals endured additional suffering and injury just before death.⁵⁸ Medievalists must be aware of the ethics of parchment, but must also engage in studies of parchment that are capacious enough to explore parchment production within wider frameworks of materiality.⁵⁹

Witnessing the animal deaths involved in studying parchment can go beyond mere hopelessness; there is hope in learning from the animal remains of a pre-industrial time. Though the frenzied deaths that prefigured book production are rightly horrifying, there are wider medieval agricultural, economic, environmental and social contexts of parchment. It is worth exploring why, in the fifteenth century as throughout the earlier Middle Ages, people were motivated to kill animals to make parchment? What else could hides and skins have been used for instead? What made parchment cost-effective, profitable, or socially desirable? Was parchment made wastefully or efficiently, and was it made to last? Paying closer attention to medieval parchment-makers and their methods might more fully and respectfully 'witness' a pre-industrial approach to these animal material resources.

Though today medieval animal slaughter is understood to be ethically problematic, this should not prevent research into the products and by-products of that slaughter. Parchment production was a trade embedded in the various interlinked agricultural and cultural economies of monastic estates, rural hinterlands, and urban centres. Lydgate's poem 'The Debate of the Horse, Goose, and Sheep', mentioned previously for the comments made by the Goose about quills, makes much of wool and mentions that 'Of Sheep al-so comyth pilet & eke fell, / Gadrid in this lond for a gret marchau*n*dise'.⁶⁰ Hides and skins took their place in a system of merchandise, and parchment has been described quite matter-of-factly as 'a standard article of commerce, prepared by specialists'.⁶¹ Parchment was, after all, part of an extensive system that depended and capitalised upon animal slaughter. There is much to learn from medieval uses – and re-uses – of animals to make products and by-products.

To source necessary raw resources, fifteenth-century parchmeners depended on the wider agricultural economy. As Ralph Hanna emphasizes, 'One must always insist on this agricultural underpinning [...] since it is always silenced at the heart of texts and

---

[56] *MED*, *shamel*, *n.*, Senses a, 'a footstool', and b, 'a bench'; *BT*, *sceamol*, *n.*, 'a bench or stool'; *Farming Glossary*, *macella*, *n.*, 'a slaughterhouse or shambles', p. 27; *DMLBS*, *macellum*, *n.*, Sense 1a.

[57] For more on the violence of humans towards animals, and its philosophical ramifications, see K. Steel, *How to Be a Human: Animals and Violence in the Middle Ages* (Columbus, 2011).

[58] L. Kalof, *Looking at Animals in Human History* (London, 2007), p. 65.

[59] See, for example, N. K. Turner, 'The Materiality of Medieval Parchment: A Response to "The Animal Turn"', *Revista Hispánica Moderna* 71 (2018), 39–67.

[60] Lydgate, 'Horse, Goose, and Sheep', ll. 356–57, p. 554; also discussed by J. Aberth, *An Environmental History of the Middle Ages: The Crucible of Nature* (London, 2013), p. 168.

[61] Thompson, *Materials*, p. 24.

substantial efforts taken to hide its existence'.[62] Domestic animals such as cattle, sheep, pigs, poultry, goats and horses were put to multiple uses by people. Primarily, animals were reared to provide meat, dairy and eggs – for food.[63] In the fifteenth century, rising living standards stimulated the urban consumption of meat and the demand for leather goods.[64] Then as now, the demand for animal-based foodstuffs gave rise to a supply of animal by-products, including hides and skins, as well as wool, glue, leather goods, tallow, lard, wax and butter.[65] For sheep, when wool was in high demand, it could be the 'main source of profit', with meat and skin as by-products.[66] The common requirement for skinning and butchery of the carcass meant that 'the respective needs for meat and skins must have had impact on one another'.[67] Once the main product, meat, had been separated from the skin, bones and other parts of the body, these could be processed into other commodities.

As well as making parchment, hides and skins were made into a range of other commodities of variable durability, such as 'clothing, footwear, bags, drinking vessels, and bone tools' which 'range from being relatively rare to virtually impossible to find today', whereas parchment survives in vast quantities.[68] However, though hides and skins were clearly widely used and rarely wasted, animals were not reared expressly to provide materials for these goods. Rather, as Umberto Albarella stresses, hides and skins 'could never be regarded as anything more than important by-products', leftovers from the core demands of butchery for meat or from the wool trade.[69] Skins were a by-product, but they were never an afterthought: making the most of each part of the animal was always important. And

[62] R. Hanna, *London Literature, 1300–1380* (Cambridge, 2005), p. 158.
[63] Albarella, 'Size, Power', pp. 19–30; and for discussion of the difficulties involved with integrating evidence, see: Umberto Albarella, '"The Mystery of Husbandry": Medieval Animals and the Problem of Integrating Historical and Archaeological Evidence', *Antiquity* 73 (1999), 867–75.
[64] M. Kowaleski, *Local Markets and Regional Trade in Medieval Exeter* (Cambridge, 2003), p. 307.
[65] Kay, 'Legible Skins', p. 18; E. M. Carus-Wilson, 'The Overseas Trade of Bristol', in *Studies in the English Trade in the 15th Century*, ed. E. Power and M. M. Postan (London, 2006), pp. 183–246 (p. 198); and for more on meat, see: K. Seetah, 'The Middle Ages on the Block: Animals, Guilds and Meat in the Medieval Period', in *Breaking and Shaping*, ed. Pluskowski, pp. 18–31.
[66] C. Dyer, *Lords and Peasants in a Changing Society: The Estates of the Bishopric of Worcester, 680–1540* (Cambridge, 1980), p. 151, and discussion of sheep products and by-products at p. 140.
[67] T. Stinson, 'Counting Sheep: Potential Applications of DNA Analysis to the Study of Medieval Parchment Production', in *Codicology and Palaeography in the Digital Age II*, ed. F. Fischer, C. Fritze, G. Vogeler (Norstedt, 2011), pp. 191–207 (p. 201).
[68] Stinson, 'Counting Sheep', p. 195. For a range of surviving artefacts, see K. Grömer, G. Russ-Popa and K. Saliari, 'Products of Animal Skin from Antiquity to the Medieval Period', *Annalen des Naturhistorischen Museums in Wien, Serie A für Mineralogie und Petrographie, Geologie und Paläontologie, Anthropologie und Prähistorie* 119 (2017), 69–93.
[69] Albarella makes this comment of hides and skins, but also 'wool fells, bones and horns', 'Size, Power', p. 27. For a discussion that comes to a radically different conclusion, see B. Holsinger, 'Ecocodicology; Or, Is The Book A Byproduct?', in *The Parchment Inheritance: Animals, Archives, and the Making of Culture from Herodotus to the Digital Age* (forthcoming).

skins for making parchment continue to be generated as by-products of agribusiness even today; for example, William Cowley parchment makers insists on the ethical sourcing of skins.[70] Taking into account the demand for meat, in addition to the demand for leather goods, it is hard to imagine that much was wasted. Hides and skins had a salvageable use-value for making other things and this helped to avoid waste and to conserve materials. And among the other things that could sustainably be made from them, parchment stands out as a particularly durable commodity.

As a by-product rather than a main product, the supply of hides and skins for making parchment took place alongside the demand for these materials for other crafts and trades. Recognising the key importance of 'staple' commodities, the Staple was instituted in 1291 by Edward I in order to regulate the supply of wool, leather and sheepskins.[71] These resources directly supplied England's largest industry, the cloth trade, and its second largest industry, the leather-related trades.[72] Others who relied on hides and skins included butchers, skinners, tanners, furriers, curriers, glovers, cordwainers, saddlers and others.[73] In support of the close affiliations between parchment producers and other trades, Peter Blayney suggests that a parchmener 'as a craftsman' had 'real affinities with the Skinners and Leathersellers'.[74] Parchmeners may well have been members of other closely related guilds and some were certainly amalgamated into the Leathersellers' Company[75] which was thriving in the fifteenth century and was granted a charter by Henry VI in 1444.[76] One known 'parchemynmaker' and stationer was Richard Colop, and while it is not known if he was involved in a guild himself, he was certainly closely associated with Peter Bylton, warden of the Mistery of Textwriters and Limners in 1426.[77] Other London parchmeners recorded between 1370–1467 include: John Corby, Roger Crane, William Fisher, John Grafton, Adam Leycestre, John atte Nashe, John Pountfreyt, Geoffrey Sprottesburgh and

---

[70] See the statement on the William Cowley website <http://www.williamcowley.co.uk/ethical/>; C. Stevens and R. Verhé, 'Primary Production of Raw Materials', *Renewable Bioresources: Scope and Modification for Non-Food Applications* (Oxford, 2004), pp. 87–90 (p. 87).

[71] T. Hoffman, *Guilds and Related Organisations in Great Britain and Ireland: A Bibliography*, online <http://www.bbk.ac.uk/lib/elib/databases/tom-hoffman/tom-hoffman-bibliography-on-the-guilds>, p. 7.

[72] M. Kowaleski, 'Town and Country in Late Medieval England: The Hide and Leather Trade', in *Work in Towns 850–1850*, ed. P. J. Corfield and D. Keene (Leicester, 1990), pp. 57–73 (p. 57).

[73] E. Veale highlights *The Libelle of Englysche Polycye* (1436–38), which comments on the extraordinary variety of furs traded in Ireland and Scotland, in *The English Fur Trade in the Later Middle Ages*, London Record Society 38 (London, 2003), p. 60.

[74] Blayney, *The Stationers' Company*, p. 17.

[75] Hoffman, *Guilds*, p. 201, notes that the 1635 ordinances of the Leathersellers refers to the various constituent trades that made up the guild, which by that time included the Fellmongers, Leatherdressers, Glovers, Pursers, and Pouchmakers, Leather-dyers, and – most importantly for this study – the Parchment-makers.

[76] J. Farrell, *The Leathersellers' Company: A Short History* (London, 2008), pp. 5–6.

[77] Christianson, *Directory*, pp. 91–93. Colop is discussed further in Chapter 4.

Ralph Tonworth.⁷⁸ The Whitetawyers guild, who received their charter in 1346, not only produced skin- and leather-based 'gloves, laces, belts, [and] bookbinding materials' but also 'superior (white) grades of parchment for writing purposes'.⁷⁹ So parchmeners were closely linked to some of these guilds, and among a range of other related products, it was a viable, profitable choice to use hides and skins to make parchment.

Hide or skin by-products were of course linked to meat production but almost 'nothing is known about the management of herds to be slaughtered in order to produce writing material'.⁸⁰ Rare evidence survives in the Beaulieu Abbey accounts (1269–70), which note the grades of sheepskin and calfskin parchment produced there.⁸¹ Specifics relating to cattle and sheep rearing for parchment production are not widely recorded, but more is known about animal husbandry in general. The archaeological and documentary evidence suggests a well-organised system of sheep farming. For example, by the fifteenth century sheepcotes were used for lambing, administration, sheltering sheep, storing fodder and as a source of manure.⁸² Detailed documentary evidence suggests the 'expansion of cattle and sheep farming' in Exeter, 'which produced a cheaper source of raw materials' for the leather trades.⁸³ After the Black Death reduced the population, numbers of animals in England increased,⁸⁴ due to a 'reduced demand for cereal crops' and the 'high price of labour', which encouraged a shift towards 'more lucrative pastoral farming'.⁸⁵ So, by the fifteenth century, there may have been some tension between keeping valuable, wool-producing sheep alive and the relative value of slaughtering younger sheep for their skins.

How were the animals that yielded these related products and by-products reared, slaughtered and distributed? How did skins get to parchmeners? Cattle or sheep could be reared in-house, or driven to market from near or far. The fifteenth-century English translation of a French hunting manual, *The Master of Game* by Edward, duke of York, details that the 'alauntes', or dogs of the butcheries, were trained to bring animals from the country into town, and are also explicitly linked with bull baiting.⁸⁶ Some aspects of the movement of

---

⁷⁸ Christianson, *Directory*.
⁷⁹ Reed, *Nature and Making*, p. 32.
⁸⁰ Thomson, 'Parchment and Paper', p. 76.
⁸¹ M. Gullick, 'From Parchmenter to Scribe: Some Observations on the Manufacture and Preparation of Medieval Parchment Based Upon a Review of the Literary Evidence', in *Pergament, Geschichte*, ed. Rück, pp. 145–57 (pp. 147–48); see also Da Rold's discussion of the Beaulieu Abbey account books, 'The Economics of Paper', in *Paper*, pp. 58–93 (pp. 88–89), see especially Table 2.7.
⁸² C. Dyer, 'Sheepcotes: Evidence for Medieval Sheepfarming', *Medieval Archaeology* 39 (1995), 136–64 (pp. 150–55).
⁸³ Kowaleski, *Medieval Exeter*, p. 307.
⁸⁴ J. Salisbury, *The Beast Within: Animals in the Middle Ages* (London, 2011), pp. 18, 44.
⁸⁵ Kowaleski, 'Town and Country', p. 64.
⁸⁶ Edward, duke of York, *The Master of Game: The Oldest English Book on Hunting*, ed. W. A. Baillie-Grohman and F. N. Baillie-Grohman (New York, 1909, repr. Philadelphia, 2005), pp. 116–18; a copy of this text survives in BodL, MS Douce 335; *Summary Catalogue* IV, 598.

hides and skins from field to market were supervised by fellmongers.⁸⁷ They operated as middlemen between farmers, butchers and tanneries.⁸⁸ Records of broken contracts between tradesmen in medieval Winchester suggest that there were close partnerships and common trade arrangements dealing in skins between butchers and local tanners and parchment-makers.⁸⁹ Consequently, in addition to the agricultural context of manuscript production, the trades that facilitated production could also organize the supply and movement of hides and skins.

Supply of skins could be achieved on a highly localised scale; for example, the husbandry, slaughter and butchery undertaken by close-knit communities such as monastic estates. Jean-Pascal Pouzet has noted cases of 'in-house' production from the thirteenth to the fifteenth centuries at Benedictine institutions, including the Cathedral Priory of Norwich, the monastic Cathedral Chapter of Durham and the Abbey of St Albans.⁹⁰ Likewise, the aforementioned Cistercian Abbey of Beaulieu in Hampshire, which was founded in 1203–04, was still thriving in 1468 when a grant of Edward III gave the monks a weekly Thursday market, and confirmed that in the nearby forests of Bere and Porchester they had the rights of pasturage.⁹¹ The Cistercian order was notable for the effective way in which members of the order conducted animal husbandry; for instance, they introduced some 'effective innovations' in breeding and farming arrangements.⁹² The basic organising unit of mixed agriculture in houses of this order was the grange. The many Cistercian houses in Yorkshire, centred around the foundation of Rievaulx in 1132, and Fountains Abbey shortly after, were 'renowned for their sheep farming'.⁹³ Many houses became wealthy from the sale, bartering and export of animals and their by-products. Most importantly for this consideration of localised, systematised animal husbandry, these resources also 'contributed to [...] self-sufficiency' and presented prime opportunities for 'in-house' production.⁹⁴ These details give a glimpse of how animal husbandry was

---

87 *MED, felmongere, n.*, Sense 3b: 'one who sells skins'; *OED, fellmonger, n.*, 'A dealer in skins or hides of animals, *esp* sheep-skins'.

88 D. Serjeantson, 'Animal Remains and the Tanning Trade', in *Diet and Craft in Towns: The Evidence of Animal Remains from the Roman to the Post-Medieval Periods*, ed. D. Serjeantson, T. Waldron, British Archaeological Reports, British Series 199 (Oxford, 1989), pp. 129–46 (p. 129).

89 D. Keene and A. R. Rumble, 'Trades and Marketing', *Survey of Medieval Winchester* (Oxford, 1985), I, 249–365 (p. 288).

90 Pouzet, 'Book Production', p. 217.

91 *A History of the County of Hampshire*, ed. H. A. Doubleday and W. Page (London, 1903), II, 140–46; Pouzet, 'Book Production', p. 217.

92 T. R. Eckenrode, 'English Cistercians and Their Sheep During the Middle Ages', *Citeaux: Commentarii Cistercienses* 24 (1973), 250–66 (p. 266).

93 Cistercians Project, 'Sheep Farming', online <http://cistercians.shef.ac.uk/cistercian_life/environment/farming/farming14.php>.

94 P. Ranft, *Medieval Theology of Work: Peter Damian and the Medieval Religious Renewal Movement* (New York, 2016), p. 138.

integral to the running of monastic communities and might have allowed for *in situ* and sustainable production of parchment for books.

The general importance or applicability of hyper-local monastic supply, however, should not be overemphasised: Pouzet writes that only cathedral chapters or the largest houses of the regular orders had the 'socio-economic conditions requisite for *in situ* provisioning of materials for book production'.[95] By the fifteenth century it seems there was some saturation in book ownership and production, with older houses already owning key texts. However, some chapters and houses still produced manuscripts, as did some newer foundations. Many of the institutions capable of 'in-house' production were already well-established and wealthy and had, in any case, a long reach and large geographic scale. *In situ* production was less about the minimum distance from field to workshop, although in some cases this was important, and more about institutional wherewithal. In contrast with the relatively localised scales of production in monastic communities, on a larger regional scale, parchmeners relied on longer supply chains.

To move hides and skins from rural areas to markets in urban centres required dynamic supply chains. This is put in perspective in a study of medieval Exeter, which, thanks to surviving records, is one of the best-documented fifteenth-century English cities for trade. Exeter's hinterland of hides and skins is described as the 'most extensive of all [trades]' and the 'marketing chain' of these raw materials reached out as far as north Somerset and Cornwall; in the thirteenth and fourteenth centuries, there was enough surplus to support a thriving export business. From field to market could be a long journey. In addition, E. M. Carus-Wilson's study of another busy port and trade hub, Bristol, highlights the supply of Irish and Welsh hides to the craftsmen of that city, such as makers of parchment and clothing.[96] These supplies were moved by sea, or animals were walked to market 'on the hoof' to urban centres along drovers' routes.

Though this understanding of the products and by-products of medieval animal husbandry and the 'nose-to-tail' use of animals helps to situate parchment more clearly in its historical economic and agricultural context, did the craft of parchment-making have other, negative impacts? Drawbacks include the environmental and ecological impacts of animal husbandry, including methane emissions from cattle. It is now known from sampling of ice cores in Greenland that production of this greenhouse gas rose between 800–1200. Emissions appear to drop following the Black Death, before rising again in the 1500s.[97] Whether animal husbandry was more or less sustainable in the fifteenth century than modern-day farming methods, given the methane emissions incurred through the rearing of animals and the differences of scale and population, is a question for another

---

[95] Pouzet, 'Book Production', p. 217.
[96] Carus-Wilson, 'Bristol', p. 187.
[97] A. Doyle, 'Romans, Han Dynasty Were Greenhouse Gas Emitters: Study', *Reuters*, 3 October 2012 <http://uk.reuters.com/article/2012/10/03/us-climate-romans-idUSBRE89212020121003>); see also: C. J. Sapart, G. Monteil, M. Prokopiou, et al., 'Natural and Anthropogenic Variations in Methane Sources During the Past Two Millennia', *Nature* 490 (2012), 85–88.

book. But as a resourceful sideline industry, parchment production at least made exhaustive use of skins and hides. Though the varied products made of meat, bone, horn and skin might not have been truly sustainable in a holistic sense, medieval animals were used in myriad ways in an undeniably efficient fashion.

Medieval parchment craftsmanship

Once separated from a living body, skins do not last in nature. Unless they are naturally air-dried or preserved in peat, they rot away. Making a skin into parchment is a way of sustaining this bodiless organ and thereby extending its shelf life. For medieval animal skins to become parchment, the energies and efforts of human bodies were required. After all, parchment-making required skin-on-skin contact between humans and animals. At first, both skins are alive, until the human kills the animal. Then the living skin, encasing a live human body, deftly crafts the dead skin, flayed from animal flesh, into a stripped back and distinct new form.

Evidently, animal bodies are transformed by parchment-making, but so too are human bodies.[98] Crafting parchment from a raw skin or hide was, and still is, difficult, involving a sequence of processes that require a range of specific tools and manual skills. Parchmeners handled chemicals, sharp knives, blunt knives, unwieldy vats, beams and frames, and needed to be skilled in several specialist techniques. How did they achieve these skilled techniques? Richard Sennett argues in *The Craftsman* that 'all skills, even the most abstract, begin as bodily practices'.[99] The bodily practices of parchment making were hard-won through what has been described by Jonathan Wilcox as 'repetition to the point of mindlessness'.[100] A group of modern-day medievalists, including Wilcox, gathered to experience parchment production for themselves, applying their own bodies to the task. The process of attaining muscle memory, through extensive, immersive repetition, resulted in skills 'wired into the fingers and joints rather than thought through the brain'.[101] Similarly, hours of repeated practice changed medieval craftsmen's bodies, attuning them to parchment-making.

It is this finely tuned craftsmanship that made possible the making of durable parchment. Parchment's physical and chemical properties are brought into being through human exploitation of the intrinsic structures of hide or skin. Many of the same properties that make skin so vital to animals – lightness, flexibility, strength, stability – are carefully enhanced by craftsmen through the process of parchment production. Evolved to sustain and protect a living animal, then removed from the dead animal, the skin's peculiar

---

[98] For reflections on the contact between human and animal bodies in such processes see S. Crane, 'Introduction: Animal Discourses and Animal Studies', *New Medieval Literatures* 12 (2010), 117–19 (p. 119); and K. L. Walter, 'Introduction', in *Reading Skin in Medieval Literature and Culture*, ed. K. L. Walter (Basingstoke, 2013), pp. 1–10 (p. 2).

[99] R. Sennett, *The Craftsman* (London, 2008), p. 10.

[100] J. Wilcox, 'Introduction: The Philology of Smell', in *Scraped, Stroked*, ed. Wilcox, pp. 1–14 (p. 7).

[101] Wilcox, 'The Philology of Smell', p. 7.

possibilities for parchment-making are only accessed through human intervention. Those properties are cultivated through the application of techniques which are designed to make the parchment last and to enhance its shelf life as a sustainable material for books.

Fifteenth-century recipes for parchment-making

Parchment production involved a number of stages, which took the material from being live tissue on the back of an animal into a supple yet robust material. Whatever the resulting quality, a series of procedures were executed: soaking in a lime solution, dehairing and stripping away the upper skin layers, before finally stretching the remaining fibre-network layer of the skin so that it dried under tension.[102] Due to the organic nature of the materials, each time the process was undertaken it produced a subtly different outcome. If these processes were undertaken with care and with reasonable resources, then the resulting product took the form of durable parchment. Both the parchment manuscripts that survive from this period and contemporary descriptions of the process are rich sources of information for how parchment was made to be durable.

Surviving manuscripts exhibit variable parchment quality. Quality parchment depended on several factors. Good, fine parchment might be expected to be smooth, evenly trimmed, consistent in colour and texture, hole- and hair-free. Achieving this required a long chain of successful processes. First, the size of the animal mattered: a bigger skin would yield more sheets, or would make it possible to cut larger, neater bifolia. But more substantial skins grew on the backs of growing, ageing animals, and there was a trade-off between the size of the skin and the age of the animal. So, second, the age of the animal was important. Younger skins were preferred, as they suffered less exposure to natural damage, especially if the animal was fast growing. As Albarella has noted, by the end of the fifteenth century animals were bred to increase the size of younger animals, resulting in improved growth and therefore yield.[103] Third, freshness made a difference: 'if the skins [...] are not quite fresh, they give a spotty product'.[104] Fourth, resulting quality depended on the type of skin selected, whether that was sheepskin, cow hide, or any other pelt. Finally, the parchment quality could be influenced by the care with which the skin was treated throughout each stage of production.[105]

Fifteenth-century Middle English codicological recipes prove valuable for understanding how parchment was made. Sequences of book making recipes are often clustered in a fashion typical of many medieval recipe collections, whether they consist of medical,

---

[102] Ryder, 'Biology and History', p. 26, describes the 'basic method'.
[103] Albarella, 'Size, Power', pp. 22, 25, 27–28; Stinson, 'Counting Sheep', p. 200 also notes the practice and development of selective breeding in the Middle Ages, such as Cistercian sheep-breeding for wool production.
[104] Thompson, *Materials*, p. 28.
[105] B. Shailor, *The Medieval Book: Illustrated from the Beinecke Rare Book & Manuscript Library* (Toronto, 1991), p. 9.

culinary, or scientific recipes, or are concerned with practical crafts.[106] These recipes took their place in manuscript collections of varied 'Fachliteratur' recipes belonging to the 'procedural genre'.[107] Usually, but by no means always, when medieval recipes have been compiled, they are grouped by topic. Collectively, the group of similar or related recipes acts as a finding aid. If one is looking for a parchment recipe, flipping through various herbal cures, culinary recipes and diagrams, lighting upon a recipe for leather or ink would suggest that a parchment recipe might be somewhere nearby. For example, in TCC, MS R.14.45, there are various recipes for making vermilion, fols. 49r–50v, recipes for verdigris, fols. 51r–52r, recipes for azure and gold colour, fols. 55r–56v, recipes for parchment and vellum on fol. 57r, followed by a recipe for cordwainers' cord fols. 57r–v, a recipe for white leather on fol. 57v and for red leather on fol. 58r.[108] Recipes may be written in Latin or English, or, occasionally, in a mix of the two languages. Discrete recipes are often marked by paraphs, rubrication and titles. There may be multiple recipes designed to produce the same result, or smaller strings of related recipes, such as one for ink followed by a series of different recipes for coloured inks, as in TCC, MS R.14.45. It is not uncommon to find recipes for dyeing kidskin leather (cheuerell or cheverel) white or red, closely followed by recipes for parchment.

It is difficult to determine whether fifteenth-century readers really used these written instructions to make parchment. It seems possible that any reader seeking out the details of book production with this level of specificity might have been professionally – or personally – interested in attempting to follow some of these recipes. The recipes are structured as lists of ingredients, actions and tools, following a temporal sequence leading to the desired result.[109] They are usually accurate, though may be vague on some details, perhaps deliberately as a strategy to protect the trade. As Mark Clarke points out, 'many of the manuscripts [...] were not for professional use' but for 'general interest for amateurs, and even on occasion for practical use by some of those amateurs'.[110] Maybe some readers did have a go, in an amateurish fashion, at making parchment. And if a reader was both literate and able to write, maybe they tried one of the more achievable recipes, such as coloured ink, size, or stanchgrain.[111]

---

[106] C. Griffin explores the scholarly consensus on recipe collections, in 'Reconsidering the Recipe: Materiality, Narrative and Text in Later Medieval Instructional Manuscripts and Collections', in *Manuscripts and Printed Books in Europe 1350–1550: Packaging, Presentation and Consumption*, ed. E. Cayley and S. Powell (Liverpool, 2013), pp. 135–49 (pp. 136–39). See also C. Griffin, *Instructional Writing in English, 1350–1650: Materiality and Meaning* (Oxford, 2019).

[107] I. Taavitsainen, 'Middle English Recipes: Genre Characteristics, Text Type Features and Underlying Traditions of Writing', *Journal of Historical Pragmatics* 2 (2001), 85–113 (p. 86).

[108] James, *TCC Catalogue* II, 331–33.

[109] Taavitsainen, 'Recipes', p. 98.

[110] Clarke, *Crafte*, p. xxv.

[111] *MED*, *staunche-greine*, *n*. 'a compound used for preparing the surface of parchment'.

Yet in manuscripts containing sequences of book-making recipes, leather and parchment seem the least feasible from a do-it-yourself point of view. While Michael Johnston and Michael Van Dussen suggest that recipes for book production are indicators of the 'decentralization and "amateurization" of book production', there was often some distance between the intended reader and working parchmeners, who presumably had some interest in protecting their trade.[112] These compilations and miscellanies may have been designed to satisfy readers' curiosity about how books were made, rather than for readers to have a go themselves. Carrie Griffin points out that 'Recipes may be performative' and 'may have functioned as fictions [...] that may or may not have been realistically accessible'.[113] Many of these instructions, particularly the leather or parchment-making recipes, required specialist resources, equipment and skills. The distance between the reader and actual parchmeners is suggested by the instruction in one recipe to 'take suche a flessyng knyf as þis *parchemyneres* vse' (Figure 1).[114] Here, the reader is not assumed to be a parchmener. All in all, it is unclear whether fifteenth-century amateur book producers really followed these practical recipes.

Either way, recipes do offer remarkable accounts of parchment production. Some recipes are short, 'telegraphic even', such as the ink recipes cited earlier in this chapter. One short recipe for vellum comes to seventy-five words.[115] To enable this relative brevity, the recipe-writer has taken advantage of the similarities between the preparation of parchment and vellum and refers back to the immediately preceding recipe on the same page for parchment: 'do þer with inne þe same maner as þov dedist wiþ þi schepis skynne'.[116] This recipe for vellum, then, mostly consists of a caution to 'schave hit [þe kalves skynne] on bothe sydys', an extra effort apparently not required for parchment. Other recipes are longer, and typically detail the key stages of parchment production. One longer recipe 'To make a *perchemyn* skyn' takes up two-thirds of a folio and comes to nearly 300 words.[117] Some are even longer, such as a recipe which takes up a full side of a folio, entitled 'They

---

[112] M. Johnston and M. Van Dussen, 'Introduction: Manuscripts and Cultural History', in *The Medieval Manuscript Book: Cultural Approaches*, ed. M. Johnston and M. Van Dussen (Cambridge, 2015), pp. 1–16 (p. 10); Clarke notes that the use of both Latin and Middle English in recipe collections is not an indication of a professional audience (as it is in the context of medical recipes): whereas an amateur book maker might know some Latin, a professional craftsman might not, in *Crafte*, p. xxxi.

[113] Griffin, 'Reconsidering the Recipe', p. 142.

[114] TCC, MS R.14.45, fol. 57r; *IMEP* XI, 46–59; Clarke, *Crafte*, p. 134. The distance between professional parchment makers and the intended audience of this text is noted by C. Griffin, 'Instruction and Information from Manuscript to Print: Some English Literature 1400–1650', *Literature Compass* 10 (2013), 667–76 (p. 669), and again in 'Texts and Textuality', *Instructional Writing*, pp. 73–109 (p. 93).

[115] Clarke, *Crafte*, p. xxvii.

[116] TCC, MS R.14.45, fol. 57r.

[117] BL, MS Cotton Julius D.viii, fol. 88r; Clarke, *Crafte*, p. 143.

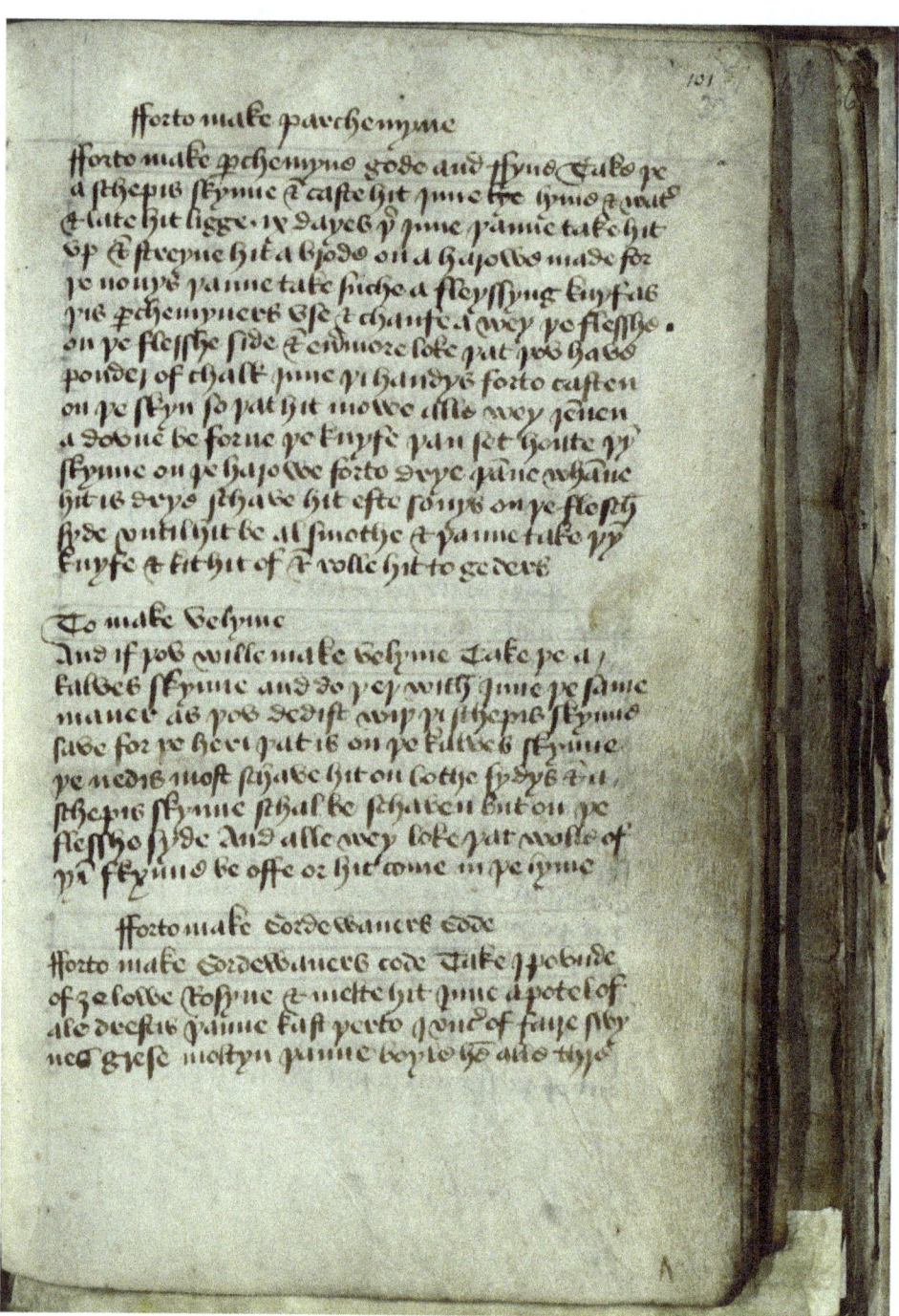

Figure 1. TCC, MS R.14.45, fol. 57r (or p. 101), recipes for parchment and vellum. Reproduced by permission of the Master and Fellows of Trinity College Cambridge.

Makyng of fyne velom', which is 462 words long,[118] and incomplete, cut off by the end of the folio. Whether long or short, these extant recipes offer suggestive details of fifteenth-century parchment craftsmanship.

In terms of making parchment well, on the whole recipes seem to offer viable directions with appropriate instructions in the right order and a reasonable level of detail about the timings, tools and skills required. Relatively carefully written recipes suggest attention by the deviser to doing a good job: strict, detailed instructions improve the maker's chances of avoiding waste, and, moreover, creating a durable product. Sometimes mention is made of particularly desirable qualities, such as the recipe (just mentioned) entitled 'They Makyng of fyne velom'. This title suggests specific interest and attention to making parchment well, to producing a 'fyne' result, set out thoroughly in what was once a lengthy recipe. The recipe for parchment in another manuscript is precise where quantities are specified: 'ii unces', 'half a pynt' and 'too ȝelkes'.[119] While the language here is accessible – not difficult or technical – it is specific.[120]

By contrast, some recipes offer instruction which is markedly vague: such ambiguous instructions risk wasting resources and making parchment that will not be durable. For instance, one recipe has an afterthought that follows the seemingly specific requirement for 'too ȝelkes' (two egg-yolks) with the modification 'or elles þre'. This afterthought perhaps assumes the ability to judge by eye, or some prior or shared knowledge of how much yolk is required. Similarly, the vagueness of 'two or three' is repeated in the recipe's approach to whether the skin should be washed again 'twyes or þryes'. The repeated 'two or three' idea gives an impression of specificity, through enumeration, while at the same time remaining imprecise, through the 'either or' construction. The recipe equivocates in other ways too, assuming the maker's ability to determine when the skin is 'clene ynoghe', how long laying it down for a 'litel while' might last, and what degree of wringing-out might be meant by 'sumwhat wryng hit' (later repeated and accompanied by the caution 'but noȝt to harde'). Therefore, due to its vagueness, trying to make parchment by taking instruction from this recipe might well result in excessive waste of resources, and poor quality, shoddy parchment.

Parchmeners also had a choice of material with which to begin the process. This meant they could develop skins into parchment with differentiated grades of quality. Nicholas Hadgraft interpreted the flock sizes of the flourishing British wool trade of the fifteenth century as providing parchmeners with a 'large stock of skin from which to select raw material' which 'enabled the craftsman more easily to offer grades of parchment related to the grade of manuscript'.[121] Recipes too sometimes pass comment on quality, describing

---

[118] TCC, MS O.8.36, fol. 22v; *IMEP* XI, 135–36; James, *TCC Catalogue* III, 437–39; Clarke, *Crafte*, pp. 289–90.

[119] BL, MS Cotton Julius D.viii, fol. 88r.

[120] Clarke discusses the language used for measurements, time, weight, and temperature, in *Crafte*, p. xxxviii.

[121] N. Hadgraft, 'English Fifteenth Century Book Structures' (unpublished doctoral thesis, University College London, 1997).

the intended result of the prescribed techniques. For example, the intended product may be described as 'fyne velom'[122] (as mentioned) or 'parchemyne gode and ffyne'.[123] Another recipe begins by calling for scab-free skin: 'perchemyn skyn of mothyn wiþouten scabbe'.[124] Taken together, these assertions suggest that parchment-makers – or at least the writers of these recipes – were concerned with parchment quality, or with giving the impression of quality, and used these terms to express this. There was an expectation of parchment-making: that it would yield a 'good', 'fine', luxury product.

Turning hides or skins into writing supports begins with flaying or skinning, the removal of the hide or skin from the body wall and from the carcass of the animal. This was achieved through mechanical means, such as tearing, pulling, or, usually, slicing with a sharp knife.[125] Like many other stages of parchment production, as we will see, the viability and integrity of the whole piece of parchment is put at risk by this tearing action. One slip and the whole skin can be torn in such a way that the later stages of dehairing and fleshing on the beam or stretching on a herse become impossible. These stages required both heavy and light knives and therefore also demanded special care. Butchers, such as those with stalls on the Fleshambles in York, were well placed to undertake this work and are known to have provided skins to other trades, although slaughtermen and hide-workers would also flay skins.[126] Wherever it took place, if the ultimate parchment product was to be of lasting strength and economic size, this early stage was as crucial as any other.

The economic viability of making parchment depended on being able to store skins. After all, the product of flaying was a barely treated raw hide or skin, which had to be worked soon after skinning, otherwise it would spoil. A pile of flayed skins, without further treatment, would quickly rot away before they could be worked into parchment. Due to the manual nature of later stages of parchment production, it was impossible to completely process a large batch of freshly flayed skins all at once without risking rot. Whether parchmeners worked solo or in a workshop as members of a team, it seems that some did take on the risk of working with large quantities of skins. This is suggested by the fact that skins were often salted, which effectively preserved them until it became possible to continue the next stages of production.[127] Jiří Vnouček proposes that this was commonplace, noting

---

[122] TCC, MS O.8.36, fol. 22v.
[123] TCC, MS R.14.45, fol. 57r.
[124] BL, MS Cotton Julius D.viii, fol. 88r; Clarke, *Crafte*, p. 430, glosses *mothyn* as sheep.
[125] U. Albarella notes that sharp cut marks on bones at the extremities of the skeleton indicate skinning (pulling off the skin in one) rather than butchery (dismembering and removing the hide), 'Tawyers, Tanners, Horn Trade and The Mystery of The Missing Goat', in *The Environmental Archaeology of Industry*, ed. P. Murphy and P. E. J. Wiltshire, Symposia of the Association for Environmental Archaeology 20 (Oxford, 2003), pp. 71–83 (p. 74).
[126] K. Seetah, 'The Butchers' Craft in Roman and Medieval Britain', in *Humans, Animals, and the Craft of Slaughter in Archaeo-Historic Societies* (Cambridge, 2019), pp. 158–83 (p. 165).
[127] Muzerelle, *Vocabulaire codicologique*, salt curing.

that 'Usually the skin is salted and dried first and stored for some time'.[128] The option to store skins must have been essential for managing workflow. In addition, it offered the opportunity to acquire skins in bulk and to manage seasonal gluts.

Animal husbandry was guided by the seasons, and there was a regular pattern of activity in the farming calendar. The skins of juvenile animals, slaughtered between April and July, were considered the best.[129] As mentioned, juvenile animals were increasingly bred for size in the late medieval period. And though it was often challenging to achieve, there was an economic imperative to select the youngest possible materials for making parchment. While a steady supply would have made it possible to use only relatively fresh, young skins, parchmeners also had to cope with gluts of raw hides and skins, which could be ad hoc but were also seasonal. Hides and skins were a by-product of other animal product-driven industries, and no matter how closely related these industries were, supply and demand were not always in balance. Sheep could be kept to produce multiple yields of wool, and cattle could be used for traction, so some animals were kept alive for many years.[130]

However, the selective cull of a herd or flock was essential for overwintering and was a traditional event. Martinmas, falling on 11 November, was known as a time for feasting because animals were selectively slaughtered. Culling resulted in a glut of animal materials, meat for feasting and through the winter, and skins – sometimes the skins of older animals. This may have presented parchmeners with the option of choosing the freshest, most suitable skins, or it may have encouraged them to store as much as possible for future use, or may have encumbered them with old, poor-quality skins. But it has been noted that farmers could still 'fit into this annual cycle' without 'enormous financial sacrifice' by slaughtering young animals a few months before Martinmas.[131] Moreover, slightly earlier selective slaughter of younger animals would have provided both fresh meat and younger skins, better for making parchment well so that it would last. Martinmas culling, therefore, managed the demands of supporting a flock through the winter and also contributed a supply of workable skins for making the most durable parchment possible.

To make parchment, freshly flayed and cured skins require an initial stage: washing in freshwater, to clean off blood, dung and any other dirt before undergoing liming. A fifteenth-century recipe mentions this, offering rather striking detail of blood being washed from calf skins: 'first lay th[em] in fayre rennyng watyr a day or ij. And ich day turne th one or ij tyll they blode be cleyne owte off them', the recipe goes on to pointedly note: 'And iff they skynnys be hard or old slayn: they most ly ther lon<g> in they water tyl þou see them nesch'.[132] So whether freshly flayed, cured, hard, or 'old slayn' skins needed

---

[128] Vnouček, 'The Manufacture of Parchment', p. 84.
[129] Salisbury, *The Beast Within*, p. 18; Reed, *Ancient Skins*, pp. 40, 126.
[130] C. Dyer, *Making a Living in the Middle Ages: The People of Britain 850–1520* (London, 2009), p. 25.
[131] Stinson, 'Counting Sheep', p. 203.
[132] TCC, MS O.8.36, fol. 22v; angled brackets here indicate letters cut off by a margin, which is only partially visible to due to tight binding.

cleaning, even soaking in water. Drenching was also essential for working cured skins – it rehydrated them and removed salts. To achieve this, skins were either immersed in tanks or baths of water, or, preferably, soaked under 'fayre rennyng watyr'. Whether immersed or left under running water, the result is a 'high degree of hydration of the skin structures'.[133] This cleaning and hydration of skins led to polluting effects. As one fifteenth-century recipe for making parchment enjoins its reader-maker: 'washe þy skyn in þat ylk water til hit wexe alle foul'.[134] A survey of medieval Winchester identifies the most prevalent recorded offences committed by parchmeners: fouling of streams. In 1396 Robert Wantlesburgh complained that the parchment-maker Richard Gay and his wife had washed foul calf and sheepskins opposite his house at Newbridge, where he was 'unable to remain because of the stench'.[135] This stage prepares the skin and promotes the next stage's chemical soaking action. The generous use of water to drench the skin improves the next stages of production and thereby the durability of the final parchment product.

Once sufficiently soaked with water, the next process is to remove the uppermost layers of the skin (Figure 2). The surface of the skin is known as the epidermis. Beneath this lies the dermis, and beneath that the hypodermis. The dermis itself has two main parts, the papillary layer and the reticular or fibre-network layer, also known as the corium, and this becomes the main component of parchment. The epidermis and the papillary layer 'intimately ramify' with one another, which makes them difficult to separate.[136] It is not possible to achieve full separation of the epidermal structures from the lower layers of the skin or hide through mechanical means. For example, hair follicles are not removed fully at the root by shaving. So, unlike the first process in the making of parchment – the mechanical flaying by hand of the whole skin from the rest of the animal body – the internal layers of the skin can only be separated through chemical action.[137] This constitutes the second stage in the parchment-making process: 'unhairing' or 'dehairing' by soaking in a chemical solution. Chemically paring the skin back to one strong layer, the corium, is a crucial step in making the skin workable into long-lasting parchment.

To make it more effectively workable, as well as dehairing the skin, it was also important to chemically swell the hide. This could be accomplished by 'changing the acidity or basicity of the skin from near neutral (pH 7) to either strongly acid (pH 1) or strongly basic (pH 13)'. The substances available to parchmeners 'rang[ed] from faeces, egg, bran and other vegetable materials for the acid dehairing of a skin, to lime (calcium hydroxide) for the basic dehairing method'.[138] The alkali liming method was the most common, as

---

[133] Reed, *Ancient Skins*, p. 51.
[134] BL, MS Cotton Julius D.viii, fol. 88r.
[135] Keene and Rumble, *Winchester Survey*, p. 288.
[136] Reed, *Ancient Skins*, p. 20.
[137] Reed, *Ancient Skins*, p. 20.
[138] J. Meyer, 'Parchment Production: A Brief Account', in *Scraped, Stroked*, ed. Wilcox, pp. 93–96 (p. 93).

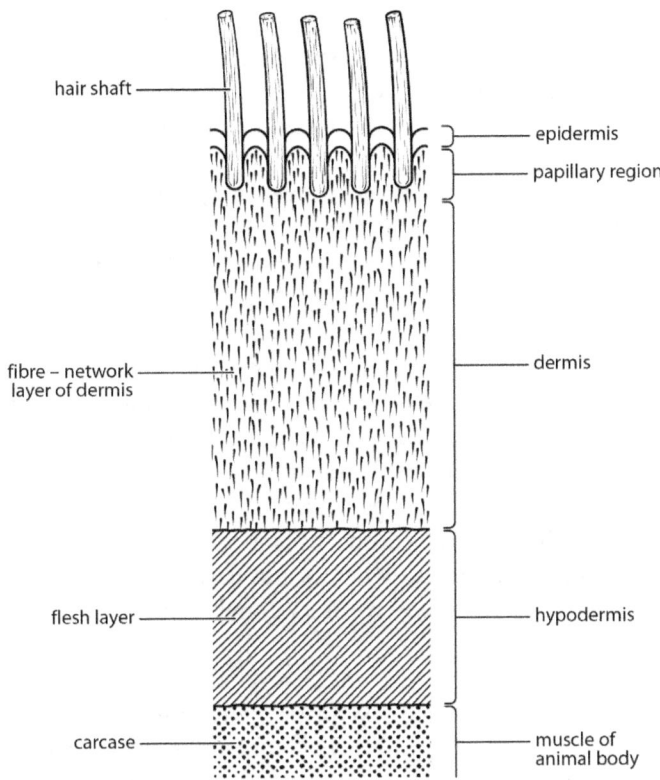

Figure 2. Diagram to show mammalian skin layers, modelled on Ronald Reed, *Ancient Skins, Parchments and Leathers* (London, 1972), p. 14, fig. 1.

detailed in the recipe entitled 'To alyme the skyn'.[139] This chemical action served to loosen the epidermis from the corium, denature certain non-collagenous proteins, and remove keratin proteins (hair), grease and fats. Within the corium itself, the solution also causes the collagen to swell and the collagen fibre-bundles to split.[140] Typically, the alkali method used to soak hides or skins was a calcium hydroxide solution. This was made from water mixed with lime or ash, or both lime and ash together. The 'suppleness' of medieval writing supports has been attributed to the 'prolonged soaking in water and lime' recommended in parchment recipes.[141] In this way, medieval parchment-makers separated the skin layers to isolate the corium and could begin to make it into a sustainable support.

Once thoroughly soaked, the swelled skin is worked further on a beam. This stage employs physical, mechanical methods to dehair the skin and to remove any remaining flesh. Both processes require beamwork: the skin is draped over a wooden beam to provide

[139] BodL, MS Douce 54, fols. 24v–25r.
[140] Stevens and Verhé, *Bioresources*, p. 89.
[141] G. S. Ivy, 'The Bibliography of the Manuscript Book', in *The English Library Before 1700*, ed. F. Wormald and C. E. Wright (London, 1958), pp. 32–65 (p. 36).

a firm surface over which it can be scraped. The unusually lengthy recipe mentioned previously offers details of exactly how this should be done: 'take on skyn an lay on they bord and þe flesch side upwards a brod'. The parchment-maker should reach forward over the skin, pushing away across the beam. The recipe goes on: 'and rub wel on þe flesch side on þat with they knyff to make hit liȝht and sowpul and tender and playn'.[142] Double-handed knives are used: for unhairing, a blunt knife; for fleshing, a very sharp knife. The blunt knife has a gently curved blade and is used to remove hair from the outer side of the skin, a process known as *scudding*.[143] The lengthy recipe also informs the reader of the ideal knife for this task: 'a knyff with ij hafts and the blade a fote and half long. and not scharp but a party blunt'.[144] In the fleshing process, the sharp knife is used to cut away from the flesh side of the skin any remnants of hypodermal or muscle tissue.[145] In TCC, MS R.14.45 (Figure 1, mentioned previously), there are two recipes for parchment. The first, for 'schepis skynne', tells the reader to 'take suche a flessyng knyf as þis parchemyneres vse and chaufe awey The flesshe on þe flesshe side'. In the same manuscript, on the same folio, a separate recipe 'to make velyme', notes that, 'on þe kalves þe nedis most schave hit on bothe sydys and a schepys skynne schal be schaven but on þe flesshe syde'.[146] Beamwork treats one or both sides of the skin to clean away debris and flesh and – though it potentially jeopardizes the skin by risking knife damage – is essential for the creation of sustainable parchment for writing.

Mechanical skin-stretching is a vitally necessary stage in the production of parchment, though it risks tearing the whole piece of skin (Figure 3). In its instructions for making parchment, one fifteenth-century recipe uses the word 'streyne' to describe the stretching action: to achieve this, the skin was attached to a frame, called a 'harowe' in this recipe.[147] Some recipes suggest that alternatively a hoop could be used, known as a *circulus*, though a square frame could also be used, a *herse*.[148] The skin should not be hooked or tacked on to the frame, as anything pushed through the skin will cause tears as soon as it is subjected to tension, rendering the skin unusable for writing. Efforts are made to avoid damage. To safeguard the skin, it is attached by means of small pebbles (*pippins*) or buttons, pushed into a pocket of skin near the edge of the sheet, pegged to the frame and pulled tight in a loop of cord. Though attaching the skin in this way renders the gathered skin at the outer

---

[142] TCC, MS O.8.36, fol. 22v.
[143] Clemens and Graham, *Introduction*, p. 10.
[144] TCC, MS O.8.36, fol. 22v.
[145] Reed, *Ancient Skins*, p. 53.
[146] TCC, MS R.14.45, fol. 57r; for discussion of these recipes, see Griffin, *Instructional Writing*, pp. 92–95.
[147] TCC, MS R.14.45, fol. 57r; *MED*, *harwe*, *n*., Sense 2a: 'A frame with pegs or spikes on which skins were stretched to dry'.
[148] *DLMBS*, *circulus*, *n*., perhaps Sense 5a; *OED*, *herse*, *n*., Sense 3; de Hamel, *Scribes and Illuminators*, p. 11; Thompson, *Materials*, p. 25; Clemens and Graham, *Introduction*, p. 11, see also Figures 1–12.

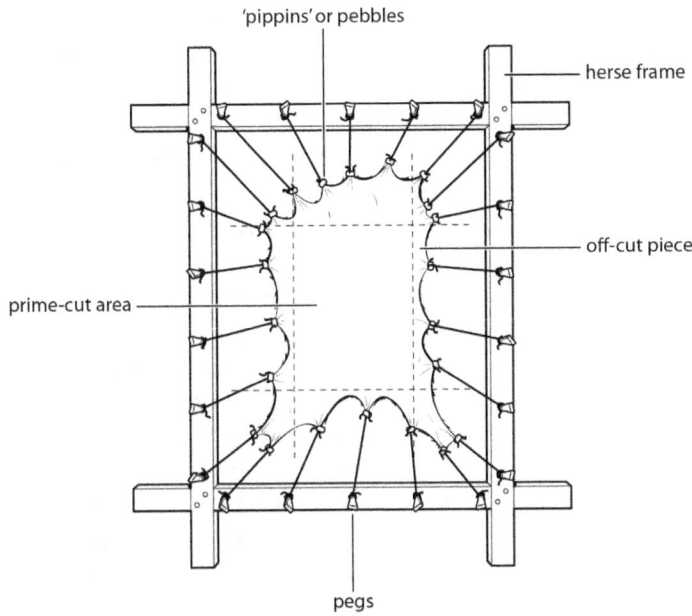

Figure 3. Diagram to show the prime cuts and off-cuts of skin, modelled on Jiří Vnouček, 'The Manufacture of Parchment for Writing Purposes and the Observation of the Signs of Manufacture Surviving in Old Manuscripts', *Care and Conservation* 8 (2005), 74–92 (p. 77) fig. 28a.

edges of the skin useless for writing, this ingenious technique makes it possible to safely adjust the tension, while simultaneously avoiding tearing and wasting the parchment.[149]

The tension provided by stretching the skin across the herse as it dries causes the parchment to form resilient structures at a deep level. The intense stretching is described evocatively in the following recipe instruction: 'then set þe skynnys on þe tent als strayte as any tabor'.[150] As Christopher Clarkson states, 'The stretching [as the pelt] dries reorganizes the fibre network of the dermal layer to a laminal structure, in which tremendous forces are locked up'.[151] The 'natural fibre weave' of the skin is changed and under tension settles into a horizontally layered structure.[152] The ground fluid dries as gelatine, locking the fibres into place. Adjacent fibre surfaces strongly stick together, and as the skin dries and water is lost, the spaces between fibres remain. Instead of the shrinking effect that should accompany drying, stretching the skin maintains a large surface area. Therefore, this essential stretching process not only provides the maximum possible writing area but also develops its size, long-term durability and remarkable resilience.

Contemporary awareness of the violence of the skin stretching process in parchment production can be glimpsed in some Middle English texts. Several texts use the image

---

[149] Serjeantson, 'Animal Remains', p. 141 notes that sometimes horns and feet were kept on skins at this stage for ease of attachment; Albarella, 'Tawyers, Tanners', p. 75.

[150] TCC, MS O.8.36, fol. 22v.

[151] Clarkson, 'Rediscovering Parchment', p. 5.

[152] C. Woods, 'Conservation Treatments for Parchment Documents', *Journal of the Society of Archivists* 16 (1995), 221–38 (p. 222).

of the stretched skin to describe Christ's crucifixion, drawing on the likeness of the skin on the frame to the way that his body was 'streyned' and 'sprede' on the cross (using the same language as medieval recipes), but also make explicit the process of strengthening through violence. In 'The Meditation on the Five Wounds of Christ', about 1410, Christ 'suffrede hym to be streyned on the harde cros. moore dispitously *and* greuously þan euer was schepys skyn streyned [...] vp on þe parchemyn makeris harowe aȝens þe sonne to drye'.[153] And in Rolle's 'Meditations on the Passion', Christ's body is 'streyned as a perchemyn skynne vpon a racke'.[154] Additionally, in the 'Privity of the Passion', from the Thornton manuscript of about 1440, Christ 'was thus sprede o-brode one þe crosse more straite þan any parchemyne-skyne es sprede one þe harowe'.[155] In these images of stretched skin there is a strong association between 'skin, parchment, pain and meaning' and to the 'memorial significance of bodily surfaces'.[156] The point of these comparisons is, of course, to highlight Christ's sacrifice on the cross. However, it is telling that all three resort to the idea of parchment to highlight the stress, strain and even pain of the stretching action. The first text describes Christ as stretched 'moore dispitously' on the cross than a 'schepys skyn' on the harowe. The comparison is employed to emphasize the Christ's pain, yet there is a tacit acknowledgement that the stretching of sheepskin is also 'dispitous'. Skin is similarly harmed – and potentially sacrificed entirely – by being violently stretched, and this duress results in strengthened, longer-lasting parchment. The death of Christ, which led to an enduring triumph and eternal life, offers a compelling analogy to the way in which parchment results from processes which strengthen through violence.

While still stretched out on the frame, the hide or skin is refined further with mechanical scraping using a knife. The surface of the taut parchment 'deflects [...] each bite of the knife' which would result in a high risk of damage should an everyday knife be used: its sharp point would puncture the skin. Punctured skin would present further risk of tearing and might reduce the writing space available. To mitigate this effect, the blade must be *lunate* (crescent or semi-circular) in shape.[157] The special knife used for smoothing parchment is thus known as a *lunellarium* or *lunellum* (little moon) and allows the necessary level

---

[153] Oxford, University College, MS 97, pp. 262–63; 'Catalogus MSS Collegii Universitatis', *Catalogus Codicum MSS. Qui in Collegiis Aulisque Oxoniensibus Hodie Adservantur*, ed. H. O. Coxe (Oxford, 1852), I, 28; *IMEP* VIII, 109; C. Horstmann, *Yorkshire Writers: Richard Rolle of Hampole and His Followers* (London, 1896), II, 440.

[154] Uppsala, University Library, MS C.494; *IMEP* X, 28; H. Lindkvist, 'Richard Rolle's "Meditatio de Passione Domini"', *Skrifter Utgifna af K. Humanistiska Vetenskaps-Samfundet i Uppsala* 19 (1917), 34–59 (p. 50), l. 24.

[155] Lincoln, Lincoln Cathedral Library, MS 91, fols. 179r–89r; Horstmann, *Yorkshire Writers* I, 198–218 (p. 206).

[156] R. Mills, *Suspended Animation: Pain, Pleasure and Punishment in Medieval Culture* (London, 2006), p. 27.

[157] Vnouček, 'The Manufacture of Parchment', p. 87; J. Bloxam, 'The Beast, the Book and the Belt: An Introduction to the Study of Girdle or Belt Books from the Medieval Period', in *Breaking and Shaping*, ed. Pluskowski, pp. 80–97 (p. 82).

of control.¹⁵⁸ The knife is also 'burred': the blade is turned over by a 'hair's breadth of steel' at its outer edge.¹⁵⁹ G. S. Ivy describes the process of wet scraping as follows: 'the blade presses the skin into a small arc at each stroke [...] squeezing out the moisture'.¹⁶⁰ The aforementioned lengthy recipe in TCC, MS O.8.36 also offers detailed information about this stage of parchment production: 'take a schavyng iron *with* dult egge and ffraye hard on þe skynne on both sydis hard and fore so long þat þou mayst bring owt no more wat*er* off þe skynne'.¹⁶¹ This recipe particularly notes the 'dult egge' of the burred shaving knife which leaves the material thinner and the surface more even, as the recipe in TCC, MS R.14.45 notes: 'schave hit efte sonys on þe flesch syde vntil hit be al smothe'.¹⁶² This specialist equipment is essential for reducing the risk of damage and for achieving a smooth piece of parchment with as little waste as possible.

Waste is limited wherever possible, but by this stage there are many trimmings and parings, and these leftovers are by-products of skins (which themselves are by-products too). Any 'rough and unwanted' areas are trimmed away, and other by-products are scrapings from the flesh side of the pelt, known as *fleshlings*,¹⁶³ and pared-off 'fluffy little peelings' from smoothing the sheet.¹⁶⁴ These scraps and scrapings could be salvaged and made into size or glue, as they are today at William Cowley's. Fifteenth-century recipes attest to this highly resourceful, 'nose-to-tail' approach to such by-products – every last scrap was used. Trimmings of parchment – and parchment only – could be boiled up to make *size*, which is 'practically pure gelatine', whereas *glue* involved boiling up the fleshlings with 'bits of cartilage, tendons [...] as well as skin'.¹⁶⁵ In addition to these waste-based glues, also popular at the time were glues made from a variety of substances, such as cheese or stockfish.¹⁶⁶ Glue and size could be used for the same purposes: as a binding medium in paint or ink, for gilding and for repairing parchment. As a result, recipes sometimes confused size and glue, for example, though it is described as 'horn glew', one recipe specifically tells the maker to 'take pec*es* of velym' only and soak them in 'stondyng watyr', before straining them through a cloth into a basin. Then, 'whan yt ys cold', the recipe instructs the reader to 'cut yt owt in pecys and put yt on a thred and drye yt in the su*nn*e'.¹⁶⁷ As it was for others involved in

---

¹⁵⁸ Clemens and Graham, *Introduction*, p. 11.
¹⁵⁹ Thompson, *Materials*, p. 26.
¹⁶⁰ Ivy, 'Manuscript Book', p. 36.
¹⁶¹ TCC, MS O.8.36, fol. 22v.
¹⁶² TCC, MS R.14.45, fol. 57r.
¹⁶³ Reed, *Ancient Skins*, pp. 53–54.
¹⁶⁴ De Hamel, *Scribes and Illuminators*, p. 12.
¹⁶⁵ Thompson, *Materials*, p. 59; Calhoun discusses animal size in *The Nature of the Page*, pp. 108–11.
¹⁶⁶ For example, two recipes for fish-based glue in BL, MS Sloane 2584, fol. 6r; Clarke, *Crafte*, p. 319.
¹⁶⁷ CUL, MS Ee.i.13, fol. 141v; *IMEP* XIX, 86–94; Hardwick, *CUL Catalogue* II, 12–14; Clarke, *Crafte*, p. 223. For another example of a glue made from parchment or hide, written in Latin, see: BodL, MS Canon. misc.128, fols. 68r-v; *Quarto Catalogue* III, 513–14.

hide and skin processing, such as skinners, butchers and tanners, the production of gelatine and glue was a convenient sideline for parchmeners. Moreover, it was a sustainable, effective and comprehensive way to use up these scrappy by-products (of by-products).

Following these efforts to smooth the parchment, a decisive moment in the production of parchment took place: the cutting-down from the frame of the stretched skin. Again, this mechanical action risked damaging the parchment or leaving it vulnerable to further injury. The skin could either be released from the frame by undoing the cord tied around the pippins and then cut to size, or it could be sliced from the frame. Whichever option was taken it seems likely that a sharp knife, shears, or scissors were the tools required to create a neat, even-sized and straight-edged prime cut (Figure 3).[168] Leftover was 'a thin and uneven outer rim' from which cheaper, smaller cuts, or off-cuts, could be made (also seen in Figure 3).[169] An illustration in a thirteenth-century account book from Beaulieu Abbey confirms that parchment could be cut with precision using scissors.[170] So cutting skin evidently necessitated especially careful, controlled cutting. Cutting could be wasteful if executed poorly; if executed well, it supported the ongoing integrity of the prime piece of parchment, as well as generating scrap that could be re-used as off-cuts, or for making size or glue.

Another refining process involved smoothing and de-greasing, which promoted ink adherence and improved the parchment's functionality as a writing support, but also risked the written skin's long-term durability. While the parchment was stretched out drying, more lime could be applied 'to facilitate the removal of moisture and grease'.[171] De-greasing powders or pastes, made from calcium compounds such as lime, chalk, or woodash, could be applied. Another option was *stanchgrain*, made from varying quantities of lime, quicklime, flour, egg white and milk. This paste was rubbed into parchment with a damp cloth and created a smooth, hard, even, white appearance. One recipe for 'stanchegreyn' is entitled 'ffor to rason parchement with owt knyffe', which emphasizes this treatment's smoothing effect.[172] Another recipe describes 'staunchegrey þat seruyth for scryveners for swagyng of letters', and suggests muddling chalk powder, wheat flour, milk and egg white into a paste, forming cakes from the paste and drying them in the sun.[173] *Swagyng* refers to the way in which these treatments 'used calcium salts to prevent the ink from running,

---

[168] J. Cowgill, M. de Neergaard, N. Griffiths, *Knives and Scabbards* (Woodbridge, 2000), pp. 106–14.

[169] E. Kwakkel, 'Cultural Residue in Medieval Manuscripts', in *The Medieval Manuscript Book*, ed. Johnston and Van Dussen, pp. 60–76 (p. 67). Off-cuts are discussed again in more detail in Chapter 2.

[170] An illustration of scissors being used to cut parchment (or perhaps cloth, according to M. de Neergaard, 'The Use of Knives, Shears, Scissors and Scabbards', in *Knives and Scabbards*, pp. 51–61 (p. 61) is available online: BL, MS Add. 48978, fol. 43r, <http://cistercians.shef.ac.uk/image_gallery/pages/C3605-03.php>.

[171] Bloxam, 'The Beast', p. 81.

[172] BL, MS Harley 218, fol. 147v. Clarke, *Art of All Colours*, p. 84; D. V. Thompson, 'Medieval Parchment Making', *The Library* 4th s. 16 (1935), 113–17 (p. 117).

[173] TCC, MS R.14.45, p. 79.

in the same manner they were used medicinally to staunch the flow of blood'.[174] On the one hand, these treatments risked smoothing the parchment unevenly or drying the parchment too much, so that it might become brittle and less resilient. On the other, such treatments helped refine parchment and promote long-term usefulness.

Rubbing with pumice powder, known as *pouncing*, could be performed to scour away any remaining unevenness, although this could also risk the parchment's durability by making it patchy and fragile. This process could be undertaken by a scribe closer to the time of writing.[175] One recipe suggests making what it calls 'stange greyne', by grinding eggshells and baked fish into a powder, and 'yf þe ynke sqwage caste þat powdyr on [...] and frete yt well w*ith* pomys'.[176] The combined effect of stanchgrain and pumice would vigorously exfoliate the parchment surface, which resulted in thin or weakened patches of parchment. An alternative exfoliant was glass bread. According to D. V. Thompson, because 'Natural pumice was an imported product in England', parchment-makers would bake 'a sort of bread largely composed of powdered glass' and use this to scour parchment smooth.[177] There was one more option for treating the appearance of parchment, which required normal bread. If a book was 'defovlyed or squaged' a 'schevyr of old brown bred' could be rubbed 'sore vp and downe' to clean it.[178] Though usually considered a method for aftercare, used to help remove dirt, this technique could feasibly be used as part of the parchment production process.[179] Though these final stages were meant to refine the product, some of these processes could also inflict damage and diminish parchment's chance of survival. The risks of weakening parchment, however, were relatively low, easily mitigated by the judicious application of these techniques by skilled, careful craftsmen.

Of course, this assumes that parchmeners would be intentionally careful and craftsmanlike and that at each stage every effort was made to produce 'gode and ffyne' parchment. There is the possibility that some parchment was made to poor and shoddy standards. Poor craftsmanship would have been far less effective in conserving resources and would have resulted in much more waste. Moreover, it would have amplified the risks to the material at each stage, thereby reducing the craftsman's chances of producing long-lasting parchment. Overall, then, the durability of parchment is dependent not only on the intrinsic properties of animal skins, but also on human agency. The craft and graft of skilled people were essential aspects of the process and indeed of the larger project of book production.

---

[174] K. Gould, 'Terms for Book Production in a Fifteenth-Century Latin-English Nominale (Harvard Law School Library MS. 43)', *The Papers of the Bibliographical Society of America* 75 (1985), 75–99 (p. 81); *MED*, *swagyng, swaginge, ger.*, Senses 3a 'cessation' and b 'stanching'.

[175] De Hamel, *Scribes and Illuminators*, p. 12, suggests that this was 'probably' the case, and that parchment was sold 'not yet buffed up and rubbed with chalk in preparation for the actual writing'.

[176] CUL, MS Ee.i.13, fol. 140r.

[177] Thompson, *Materials*, p. 29.

[178] CUL, MS Ee.i.13, fol. 141v.

[179] A. Timmerman, 'Of Dirty Books and Bread', online <http://recipes.hypotheses.org/2859>.

To create durable parchment which would survive for many hundreds of years required particular skills and a considerable measure of effort and care. As Krish Seetah notes, 'the extra preparation that went into producing these commodities' increased their value.[180] It is the subjection of animal materials to the investment of skilled labour and effort that underpins parchment sustainability, both in terms of avoiding waste as well as developing and safeguarding long-term durability.

By exploring the complexity of parchment making in more detail – and resisting a broad-brush interpretation – this discussion has shown that as well as understanding the ethics of animal materials, craftsmanship, effort and care are also important. Moreover, material by-products such as skin were transformed in ways that made them at once more enduring and less wasteful. Parchment-making was often a careful attempt to cultivate and conserve resources. After all, skin was not intrinsically long-lasting: it was the processes of parchment production that made it so. As well as mourning the animal deaths on which manuscript culture is founded, the lesson here is that medieval people took great care to sustain material resources. They valued skins, and took pains to enhance the workability, shelf life and usefulness of those skins as parchment.

The sustainable use and repair of skins

Books made of skin constituted objects of substantial added value, engendered by human effort, and were often well-respected as such: many books were considered worth sustaining by conservation and restoration long after the initial production of materials. The sustainable use of parchment in medieval manuscripts is seen especially in the use of flawed skins and in the repair of damage. Injured parchment in surviving manuscripts enables an exploration of how and why this damage came to be and how it was ignored, accommodated, and even celebrated. Others have noted in passing that 'defective' pieces of parchment were 'quite commonly' used in books, even when they bore clearly visible damage, and that anyone consulting a medieval manuscript 'almost inevitably encounters some parchment damage'.[181] The apparent tolerance of tangible damage to skin and the efforts taken to repair and occasionally to decorate it point to an ethos of sustainable parchment use. Crucially, the treatment of visible injuries exposes the expectations of makers and users of medieval books and their practical abilities in sustaining book materials. This section provides something of a handlist of various types of parchment damage.

As well as accommodating visible damage, manuscripts were also made in ways that excluded the most damaged parts of parchment sheets. Ingenious cutting, folding and discretion over the size of the sheet could help to mitigate holes when they were unwanted – sometimes by

---

[180] Seetah, 'Animals, Guilds, and Meat', p. 22.
[181] Clemens and Graham, *Introduction*, p. 12; C. Sciacca, 'Stitches, Sutures, and Seams: "Embroidered" Parchment Repairs in Medieval Manuscripts', *Medieval Clothing and Textiles* 6 (2010), 57–92 (p. 57).

excising damaged parts of the sheet. Damage could also be avoided by cutting, or folding the parchment just so, the sheet arranged so that damage lay outside the textblock.[182] Though this may seem a wasteful use of precious resources, the trimmings and off-cuts could be re-used. Aside from the aesthetic considerations at play in such cases, selecting damage-free parchment improved a book's overall durability. Choosing parchment without holes, tears or weak patches helped to prevent further splits or worsening damage from everyday use. In resource-poor contexts, or other contexts where there was little choice available, the presence of holes or other visible damage in the parchment may either be a sign of that lack of choice, or of acceptance. However, in contexts where book-producers were well supplied, the presence or absence of damaged parchment demonstrates that people could choose exactly which piece of parchment to use.

The origins of parchment injuries can be either natural or man-made. After all, animal skin or hide is an organic raw material but is also hand-crafted into parchment. Parchment is textured, with 'cracks, cuts, blots, blurs and surface irregularities' such as soft or thin parts, plaques, horny patches, scrapes, stretch marks and scars, all of which should be expected of skin.[183] When skin with any, some, or all of these features is made into parchment, these marks may be observable still, or detectable by touch. Natural or man-made imperfections are difficult to distinguish from one another and, although there are a few hallmark differences, often damage incurred naturally during the animal's life and injuries acquired during the parchment production process look similar.[184] Decay or other changes can also make differences harder to see. Damage in the written area, which the scribe works round, is definitively medieval, rather than later; but of course, other holes may be post-medieval. These damage features can occur anywhere in manuscripts where parchment is used, whether as flyleaves, wrappers, or text-bearing leaves, and they can occur in the margins of those leaves, or in the written area. The use of flawed parchment in medieval manuscripts, with visible and tangible natural or man-made damage, was widespread.

Why was this tolerable? The ideal outcome of the consecutive processes of parchment-making – the purpose that drives the entire undertaking – is the creation of material suitable for use as writing supports for the activities of scribes and limners, including ruling, drawing, gilding and painting. Of course, though parchment could have been made 'badly' to provide lower grade material for protective or ephemeral uses, or for re-uses such as wrapping food or cleaning shoes (as Chapter 2 notes), without consideration of writing requirements, this seems doubtful. Though a range of parchment quality was acceptable to medieval manuscript makers, it seems that the most desirable, deluxe parchment provided a reasonably smooth, substantial and continuous available surface area to hold ink as writing or painted illustrations. For example, one of the parchment-making

---

[182] For a discussion of possible folding arrangements when creating quires, see J. P. Gumbert, 'On Folding Skins, According to Gilissen', *Gazette du livre médiéval* 43 (2003), 47–51.

[183] Vnouček, 'The Manufacture of Parchment' p. 74.

[184] J. Eagan refers to scars incurred during the animal's life as 'natural faults' and those during parchment manufacture as 'process faults', personal correspondence.

recipes mentioned previously calls for unblemished skin 'wiþouten scabbe'[185] which suggests an awareness that other people might be willing to use scabby parchment, even if the writer of this recipe was not. In addition, the many recipes for stanchgrain also attest to an interest in creating a smooth surface. But it was not always possible to achieve ideal parchment and skins could be peppered with scabby holes incurred during the animal's life, or riddled with patchy or glassy areas, man-made holes, or slits caused during production. So, with all this in mind, though undamaged parchment was desirable in most contexts, why was damage itself a problem?

Holes or gaping tears are a problem for a number of reasons. Aside from the aesthetics and not meeting the intended grade of production, perhaps the most obvious problem caused by parchment injuries is that it reduces the space available for writing. By their very nature, holes or tears in parchment constitute non-surface and take the form of a void, negative space. Whether natural or man-made, holes or tears in the textblock area that go right through parchment affect the available space for writing on both hair and flesh sides. In a sense then, when parchment is used for writing, the adverse consequences of one mistake are doubled. A hole-free parchment leaf maximises the surface area available for writing. Damage can also result in plaques or eyes of scar tissue, and in addition to providing an inadequate surface for writing, these present the risk of unpredictable future loss if panes of ground fluid flake away. Finally, holes, tears and the vestiges of tissue damage are all of concern because they compromise the strength of the parchment sheet: they can diminish its overall integrity.

Whatever form damage takes and whatever problems it poses, it is difficult to determine whether the damage caused to the parchment was medieval. Where writing or illustration actively accommodates damage in some way, such as the bending of a written column to avoid a hole, then the injuries either took place prior to or concurrent with those phases of manuscript production. More specifically, any instances of damage or repair in the form of holes or tears that have been pulled under tension were already present before the stretching stage of the parchment-making process, or were inflicted during the process, and so must pre-date the scribal stage of production.[186] Thus, although parchment damage is usually not datable by its own form, features of binding and handwriting can suggest when parchment damage occurred at an earlier stage of production. Seemingly undatable parchment defects are often more securely identifiable as medieval phenomena than other examples of recycling, which (as we will see in Chapter 2) can be difficult to date accurately and in many medieval manuscripts may well be the result of post-medieval interventions. Wherever possible in the following discussion, damage and repairs are identifiably medieval.

---

[185] BL, MS Cotton Julius D.viii, fol. 88r. I am grateful to Dr Yvonne Bohm and Dr Martin Nicholas for inviting me to visit their lambs in the Cotswolds and for sharing with me their knowledge of scabby sheepskins.

[186] De Hamel, *Scribes and Illuminators*, p. 11; Sciacca, 'Stitches, Sutures', p. 65; R. Fuchs, 'Old Restorations and Repairs in Manuscripts', *Care and Conservation* 6 (2002), 224–41 (pp. 225–26).

As noted previously, while the form of many marks and holes makes identification difficult, some clearly originated during the animal's lifetime. Natural damage may be caused by environmental factors such as weather or climate, which can lead to excessively hot, cold, wet, or dry weather, or too much or too little sun, all of which may affect the skin's growth and its susceptibility to parasites or disease.[187] Sometimes distinctive scars, for example those caused by certain insects, mark the skin. Warble flies, for instance, burrow into the skin of animals to lay their eggs, and where they puncture the skin they leave 'characteristic holes and "pits"'.[188] If unhealed, these holes are known as 'open warbles', or when healed, 'blind warbles'. In addition, other types of fly puncture and leave lesions in the skin, which can become infected by bacteria. Mites such as the *psoroptes ovis* may also lay their larvae in the skin of parchment-producing animals, causing irritation known as mange.[189] Larger animals might also attack a cow, sheep or even a young sheep before its first shearing, as noted in *The Master of Game*: a wolf 'shal wel slee a kow' and 'shal bere in his mouthe a gote a shep or a ʒonge hogge' and wild cats were known to take sheep.[190] The ravages of flies and mites, or even wolves or wild cats, during an animal's life could leave lasting traces on skin after death as holes or tissue damage in parchment.

Likewise, human interventions may register on animals' bodies long before their skins have been transformed into books: during an animal's life, traditional animal husbandry techniques, accidents, or rough handling could all affect an animal's skin. However, human control is made most distinctively manifest on skin by the death blow. In the late medieval period, this blow was usually delivered with a tool called a poll-axe or poleaxe to the head of the animal, to stun, incapacitate, and then to kill.[191] Medieval cattle skulls discovered in Bruges feature circular fractures in the frontal bones, which confirm this method of stunning and slaughtering.[192] Before further processing, this blow must have made a significant and recognisable mark on the frontal bones still attached to the raw hide or skin. Other methods used to kill animals must also have resulted in marks on the carcass and through the skin.

---

[187] Eckenrode, 'English Cistercians', pp. 257–58, details various diseases that afflicted medieval sheep, including foot rot and murrain, however, the only disease he notes that would have damaged sheepskin was scab.

[188] C. Freeman, 'Feathering the Text', in *Rethinking Chaucerian Beasts*, ed. C. Van Dyke (Basingstoke, 2012), pp. 33–47 (p. 39); and Vnouček, 'The Manufacture of Parchment', p. 78.

[189] Reed, *Ancient Skins*, p. 36, describes the attacks of warble flies, other flies, and mange.

[190] BodL, MS Douce 335, fol. 23r (wolves), fol. 27r (wild cats); Edward, duke of York, *The Master of Game*, pp. 58, 70. Salisbury, *The Beast Within*, p. 19, also mentions the vulnerability of sheep to wolves.

[191] *Farming Glossary*, Latin *pollexa*, for 'poleaxe', and English *polmarked*, meaning marked on the head, p. 34.

[192] A. Ervynck, B. Hillewaert, A. Maes, and M. Van Strydonck, 'Tanning and Horn-Working at Late- and Post-Medieval Bruges', in *The Environmental Archaeology of Industry*, ed. P. Murphy and P. E. J. Wiltshire, Symposia of the Association for Environmental Archaeology 20 (Oxford, 2003), pp. 60–70 (p. 63).

If the carcass, known in Latin as a *cadaver*, was not properly drained of blood, some would pool in the branches of veins.[193] The *mort de sang* (death-stain) is an evocative modern term used to describe the resulting dark patches of blood retained in animal skin and still visible in parchment.[194] These marks are visible due to iron compounds in the blood.[195] De Hamel notes that, though hard to prove, such 'tree-like vein marks' were likely more common in the pelts of hunted animals than in well-bled skins.[196] Today, vein-marked parchment is made by design for modern book artists.[197] Instances of this phenomenon occur on a number of leaves in a manuscript written in the second half of the fourteenth century, deposited in an Oxford chest in the early years of the fifteenth century.[198] The vein-marks on the leaves in this manuscript are most easily seen when backlit.[199] Although it should be noted that any *mort de sang* is not a mark of the death blow itself, but rather of blood trapped in the skin, it is intriguing that a skin stain of this kind has become semantically linked with the death of the animal. It is another mark of production that leaves its traces on parchment.

Further notable and identifiably man-made damage can be inflicted upon the skin in the parchment-making process. Every stage discussed in the previous section of this chapter – flaying, dehairing by soaking in solution, stretching, scraping with a knife (either when fleshing or dehairing) and smoothing – posed a serious risk of damage. These key processes not only risk marking the skin, they can also jeopardize the overall integrity of the sheet. Many injuries are compounded by the effects of later stages of production and any imperfections – whether natural or man-made – such as punctures, thin patches, tears, scrapes or cuts, can succumb completely when subjected to tension.

The first three stages of production can cause odd colouring, or patchy weakness, cuts or nicks in parchment. During both the initial flaying and later beamwork scraping, the skin is at risk of knife damage. The Latin word used for flaying or skinning was *excoriare*, from *ex-* (out) and *corium* (hide).[200] *Excoriare* was also used to refer to the act of shelling peas

---

[193] *Farming Glossary, cadaver, n.*, carcase (or, carcass), p. 7.

[194] Muzerelle, *Vocabulaire codicologique, mort de sang*; see also Figures 1–7, in Clemens and Graham, *Introduction*, p. 10.

[195] L. Avrin, *Scribes, Script and Books: The Book Arts from Antiquity to the Renaissance* (London, 1991; repr. Chicago, 2010), p. 213.

[196] De Hamel, *Scribes and Illuminators*, p. 15; for further discussion of vein-trails in parchment, see: E. J. Johnson, 'Scarring, Tears, Veins and Hair: The Imperfections of Medieval Parchment', The Ohio State University Libraries, online <https://library.osu.edu/blogs/rarebooks/2008/12/01/107/>, with thanks to Twitter user M. Tullius Cicero (@spiritofcicero) for this reference.

[197] H. Bain, 'Binding Marvell: Form and Content in Book Arts', *Andrew Marvell Newsletter* 5 (2013), 9–16 (p. 10).

[198] The practice of depositing books is discussed in more detail in Chapter 4.

[199] BodL, MS Bodley 251, a copy of commentaries on Biblical texts by Nicholas de Lyra; *Summary Catalogue* II.i, 314.

[200] *OED, excoriate*, v., etymology.

and this range of meanings gives an impression of the delicacy of the flaying operation.[201] On either side of the skin, manual scraping with a knife endangers the writing surface to be made available in the finished parchment sheet, putting the integrity of the whole skin at risk. A slip of the knife, especially the sharper knife used for the fleshing process, can injure the skin or worsen existing imperfections. During the beamwork, when fleshing or dehairing, the knife is dragged up across the skin stretched over the beam. Damage caused by a parchment-maker at this stage can take the form of characteristic 'v-shaped' nicks, where the knife catches the skin.[202]

Between those flaying and beamwork stages, the second stage of soaking and liming can result in patchy skin damage. Too little time soaking and the solution penetrates the pelt unevenly, resulting in difficulty stretching the skin and 'variable colour and opacity', but on the other hand, overdoing the length of time or strength of the lime soak weakens the fibre network.[203] Recipes offer varying levels of precision about the ideal length of time needed to soak skin. One recipe for recycling written parchment into imitation cheverel, in BodL, MS Douce 54, advises the reader to 'wesch the skyn […] the space of a *miserere*', relying on an everyday prayer to function as a mnemonic, before then hanging the skin out to dry.[204] Another fifteenth-century recipe specifies the duration a skin should be soaked: 'Forto make parchemyne gode and ffyne Take þe a schepis skynne *and* caste hit inne lyme *and* water *and* late hit ligge ix days þer inne'.[205] These recipes suggest that processes such as washing and soaking could vary but that it always took time and care to prepare parchment.

After washing, liming, and further scraping, the skin is put under tension. When exerted on the skin, tension can exploit even the very smallest holes. Though stretching is crucial for forging the hard-wearing qualities of parchment (as noted earlier), the stretching process pulls on the whole skin structure, notwithstanding any existing imperfections, whether natural or man-made. It is this indiscriminate tension that can lead to more serious damage and put the entire skin at risk. Pre-existing flaws can develop under the influence of tension into gaping holes, or splits across the whole hide or skin. For example, even the smallest pinprick punctures may be 'pulled out into circular or oval holes' by stretching.[206] Not all skins respond the same way to the stretching process: some are more susceptible to high tension than others. Sheepskin is thinner and greasier than other skins and more vulnerable to critical tear damage whilst being stretched. As

---

[201] *DMLBS*, excoriare, v., Sense 1: 'to excoriate, flay, strip of skin', and Sense 3a: 'to pod, shell'; and *Farming Glossary*, excorio, v., 'to skin, to flay, to shell (peas)', p. 15.

[202] There are repaired v-shaped cuts, in BodL, MS Bodley 744, fols. 170, 179; *Summary Catalogue* II.i, 533.

[203] Reed, *Nature and Making*, pp. 80–81.

[204] BodL, MS Douce 54, fol. 23v; *Summary Catalogue* IV, 506; the timing is noted by Griffin, 'Instruction and Information', p. 670; also by Clarke, *Crafte*, p. xxxviii, p. 264.

[205] TCC, MS R.14.45, fol. 30.

[206] De Hamel, *Scribes and Illuminators*, p. 11.

Vnouček notes, the upper layer of the sheepskin 'tends to delaminate' and is 'liable to rip' under tension.[207] Numerous examples of pulled out holes can be seen in manuscripts, one of which is a fifteenth-century copy of *The Northern Homily Cycle*, a very large manuscript written by the Irish priest William Kame (or Thame).[208] The humble context of production and the desired size may help to explain why this scribe tolerated a variable quality of parchment. In this manuscript, notably pulled out holes can be seen in the inner margin of one leaf and the outer margin of another.[209] There is no visible attempt at further repair of these holes, so this man-made damage was tolerated perhaps because this was a book that was not valued for aesthetic purposes particularly, but more for practical use as verse preaching materials.

Sometimes holes in finished parchment appear to have scabbed over with a thin pane of translucent material, as if the dead skin has somehow repaired itself. These are known as plaques or 'delamination areas' and they are more common in sheepskin, which has a greater tendency to delaminate.[210] These *plaques* are also known as *eyes*, and Muzerelle defines the *tache vitreuse* as follows: 'Petite surface de forme elliptique ou arrondie, à l'intérieur de laquelle le parchemin s'amincit et ne forme plus qu'une fine pellicule translucide'.[211] For instance, there are many intact plaques in a large, fourteenth-century manuscript copy of works by Robert Grosseteste, given by the executors of William Fylham to Exeter Cathedral (mentioned again in Chapter 4).[212] As in this example, plaques may be slightly speckled with follicle marks, or they may be yellowish-to-nearly-clear, fill or partly fill the void, and may slightly overlap with (or flake off at) the edges of the hole. A detached plaque that is flaking away can be seen in a manuscript copy of works by Gregory the Great.[213] Where plaques have detached completely, they leave a stretched-out oval hole in the parchment.

Sometimes it is difficult to detect whether what appears to be a plaque is in fact very fine repair work, for many manuscripts do bear leaves with stitched or glued repairs. Stitched or otherwise repaired parchment leaves embody the 'stitch in time' approach to sustaining materials; simultaneously avoiding waste, conserving resources, and enhancing long-term

---

[207] Vnouček, 'The Manufacture of Parchment', p. 83. The 'propensity of sheepskin parchment to delaminate' is also noted in Fiddyment et al., 'Uterine Vellum', p. 15069.

[208] HEHL, MS HM 129 measures 217 × 145 mm, is still in a fifteenth-century whittawed binding, and the scribe signed his name on fol. 231r; discussed by D. Wakelin, 'Editing and Correcting', in *Probable Truth: Editing Medieval Texts from Britain in the Twenty-First Century*, ed. V. Gillespie and A. Hudson (Turnhout, 2013), pp. 241–59 (pp. 248–54); Dutschke, *HEHL Catalogue*, pp. 164–72.

[209] HEHL, MS HM 129, fols. 25, 170.

[210] Eagan, personal correspondence.

[211] 'A small round (or elliptical) surface around which the parchment thins and forms no more than a slight translucent film', Muzerelle, *Vocabulaire codicologique*.

[212] BodL, MS Bodley 830, fol. 174 (among many others in this manuscript); *Summary Catalogue* II.i, 509.

[213] BodL, MS Bodley 809, fol. 69, flaking away on the recto; *Summary Catalogue* II.i, 482.

durability. One of the many advantages of skin for making and sustaining parchment that is destined to be used in manuscript production is this deceptively simple affordance: that it 'allow[s] easy stitching'.[214] Repairs suggest attempts to guard against further damage and to contribute to the overall usability and longevity of the material. In whatever way holes or tears came to be present in parchment, they were highly susceptible to ripping further. Efforts to stitch and glue parchment bolstered material resilience and limited these risks. In addition, these repairs improved the integrity of the whole sheet, and, therefore, the future sustainability of the whole manuscript. As mentioned previously, glue could be fish-based, or could be made from parchment trimmings and parings. It was, then, easy and possible by a range of means to repair parchment.

Stitched repairs could be performed at any stage in the production process. Effective stitching bound the edges of a tear or hole together and protected the parchment from further damage. Such 'oversewing' of damage could be undertaken in order 'to avoid the enlargement of the hole during stretching'.[215] Parchment tear-repair was usually achieved using strong *pacthred* 'with a simple but firm stitch'.[216] Such repairs to tears or holes in parchment can be seen in many manuscripts.[217] When stitching was undertaken before the skin was put under tension on a frame, it could acquire a distinctive stretched effect. This is especially noticeable where the pin-prick holes through the parchment have stretched into ovals on either side of a tear, versions – in miniature – of the pulled-out holes described above. A good example of this can be seen in a copy Peter of Lombard's *Sentences*.[218] Around the hole in the parchment the tiny holes stabbed through by the needle have then pulled out and stretched into ovals. Sometimes these visible efforts to repair parchment could inflict further small-scale damage. Tiny stitch holes in repairs could also be compromised entirely under tension, damaging the parchment further. Sewn repairs are designed to draw together the edges of a wound in the parchment, so by necessity the small holes formed by the needle when stitching must be close to the cusp of the damage. When stitch-holes themselves are compromised under tension they collapse into and enlarge the original tear. Where these repaired holes have not collapsed, the parchment may still

---

[214] Reed, *Ancient Skins*, p. 5.

[215] Fuchs, 'Old Restorations', p. 225.

[216] *Farming Glossary*, *pacthred* or *pakthered*, pack-thread, p. 31, and *MED*, *pakthred*, n., Sense 3a, 'strong thread for sewing or tying up bundles', among several other uses; Vnouček, 'The Manufacture of Parchment', pp. 85–86.

[217] Eton College, MS 39; *MMBL* II, 672–75; *A Descriptive Catalogue of the Manuscripts in the Library of Eton Catalogue*, ed. M. R. James (Cambridge, 1895), p. 20. HEHL MS HM 19918; Dutschke, *HEHL Catalogue*, pp. 606–08. London, Gray's Inn, MS 8; *MMBL* II, 57–58. Oxford, University College MS 91; Coxe, 'Catalogus Collegii Universitatis' I, 27. Oxford, Hertford MS 4; formerly known as 'MS 2' in 'Codices MSS Aulae B. Mariae Magalenae', *Catalogus Codicum MSS. Qui in Collegiis Aulisque Oxoniensibus Hodie Adservantur*, ed. H. O. Coxe (Oxford, 1852), II, 5–6.

[218] BodL, MS Bodley 744, fol. 45.

register the pinprick stitch-holes as small but significant signs of the repair effort. Ironically, then, efforts to stitch up repairs in parchment risked exacerbating damage.

Scraps could also be glued onto parchment to patch over damage. These forms of repair required appropriately sized scraps of parchment and glue or other adhesives with which to hold them in place. It was, as described earlier, possible to make glue from parchment trimmings or parings. Patches are harder to date securely, as they may have been attached long after any medieval campaigns of production. Having said this, such repairs certainly took place during the medieval period, some of the contemporary recipes for glue specify the purpose of parchment repair, and there are surviving parchment patch-repairs, for example those bearing text or decoration.[219]

More rarely, instances have come to light of manuscripts containing decorated damage. These decorative additions go beyond the typical motivations of stitching up parchment primarily to repair it, and testify to manuscript repairers' creative flair. Though there was an earlier medieval tradition, as Robert Fuchs notes, for insular or Northumbrian scribes to use ink to 'emphasise [...] holes by surrounding them with red dots', there are also some later medieval examples of manuscripts that contain decorated holes and tears.[220] There is a fourteenth-century manuscript now held in Uppsala University Library and several manuscripts surviving from southwestern Germany and Switzerland that feature eye-catching, colourful silk thread work.[221] These repairs draw the eye to damage and make a feature of it. The neatly pricked holes, which have not pulled out, indicate that the stitching was executed after stretching. This, in conjunction with the colourful design, suggests that in these cases decoration and preservation went hand-in-hand, perhaps even functioning in concert. These fanciful, delicate embroideries draw attention to their own design, as complex needlework art, and to the holes into which they are stitched – indeed, they might encourage greater care in handling. Without organic or man-made damage, this application of skilled craftsmanship could not exist. These embroideries go way beyond

---

[219] BodL, MS Ashmole 1494, fol. 532; *Quarto Catalogue* X, 1380–86; D. V. Thompson, 'Trial Index to Some Unpublished Sources for the History of Medieval Craftsmanship', *Speculum* 10 (1935), 410–31 (p. 422). A copy of Lydgate's *Troy Book*, BodL, MS Digby 230, written in the third quarter of the fifteenth century, features a large patch of written parchment, used to repair the lower outer corner of fol. 159, *Quarto Catalogue* IX.i, 242, 99; G. Guddat-Figge, *Catalogue of Manuscripts Containing Middle English Romances* (München, 1976), pp. 257–58.

[220] Fuchs, 'Old Restorations', pp. 225–26.

[221] Sciacca, 'Stitches, Sutures', pp. 57–92, E. Kwakkel, 'Broidery on a Medieval Page', Tumblr, online <http://erikkwakkel.tumblr.com/post/52258862048/broidery-on-a-medieval-page-holes-in-the-pages-of>; and E. Kwakkel, 'Halloween (4): Stabbed, Cut and Stitched Back Together', Tumblr, online <http://erikkwakkel.tumblr.com/post/65552828979/halloween-4-stabbed-cut-and-stitched-back>; A. Strand, 'The Examination and Conservation of a Medieval Manuscript with Embroidered Repairs', *Care and Conservation*, 8 (2005), 113–22; A. Strand, Uppsala Library, 'A Medieval Book Mended with Silk Thread', online <https://web.archive.org/web/20131017052042/http://www.ub.uu.se/en/Just-now/Projects/Completed-projects/A-medieval-book-mended-with-silk-thread/>.

salvaging damaged material: in these cases, parchment damage and stitching has become a form of artistic expression. Parchment, then, can sustain other forms of creativity that exceed its usual uses.

Conclusions

Parchment, made from the skins and hides of animals, was a re-usable by-product of meat production. When crafted well, parchment had the potential to last for a long time. The supply of skins and hides from sheep and cattle depended on wider systems of medieval animal husbandry and trade networks. By exploring the 'agricultural underpinning' of parchment production in detail, this chapter has offered a fuller sense of medieval practices and processes of treating skin.[222] An ethos of efficient, resourceful production can be witnessed in medieval processes of parchment making. Fifteenth-century recipes for making parchment, which may or may not have been used by craftsmen or amateurs, express interest in making well and avoiding waste. Furthermore, surviving manuscripts demonstrate that fifteenth-century people accommodated and made efforts to repair damaged parchment in their books, sometimes with a decorative flourish. Paradoxically, repair could exacerbate damage by causing stitches to pull out or split completely. Nonetheless, both recipes for making parchment and parchment in extant manuscripts demonstrate that people in this period could and did choose to make parchment durable, so that it would last.

---

[222] Hanna, *London Literature*, p. 158; Holsinger, 'Of Pigs and Parchment', p. 619.

2

Re-using Parchment In Books

Sixteenth-century accounts describe parchment leaves that were 'reserved of those lybrarye bokes, some to serve theyr iakes, some to scoure theyr candel styckes, and some to rubbe their bootes'. Leaves were also reportedly sent 'to the grossers and sope sellers, and some they send ouer see to ye bokebynders [...] at tymes whole shyppes full'.[1] This chapter takes note of such destructive re-uses and focuses on the bits of books that came to be recycled in other books. The durable qualities of new parchment – as emphasised in Chapter 1 – enabled both the production and preservation of books, and in many instances relied on the re-use of older materials. Strikingly, medieval recycling of parchment in books is not fully explained by a straightforward evaluation of cost. In this chapter a more complex picture starts to emerge: books could impart and import recyclable parts, which were valued for their usefulness, material properties, and adaptability. As a result, these parts were re-used in myriad different ways, and possessed remarkable latent potential for multiple uses. This chapter asks: what values were associated with these varied uses and re-uses of book materials?

Recycling is ubiquitous in medieval manuscripts. After all, the very production of some book materials was predicated on recycling: as mentioned previously, medieval paper was usually made from recycled rags.[2] Although fragments of fibre are sometimes visible in the fabric of paper, this form of recycling is not necessarily discernible to the eye. Yet, in this period, paper sheets were constituted of re-used fibres which had another form and a previous life. As discussed previously, the efforts taken to process rags into paper or skins into parchment resulted in added value for those materials. This begs the question: what was the value of the uses and re-uses of those materials thereafter? To continue this discussion, this chapter explores how and why value is added – or taken away – from book-materials by recycling. Some materials in medieval manuscripts are more tangibly recycled than others, such as flyleaves that bear writing, or visibly scraped

---

[1] *The Laborious Journey and Serche of Johan Leylande, for Englandes Antiquitees, geuen of hym as a newe yeares gyfte to Kynge Henry the viii in the xxxvii yeare of his Reygne, with declaracyons enlarged: by John Bale* (1549) Sigs. A2v, A7v, cited by: A. Smyth, 'Burning to Read: Ben Jonson's Library Fire of 1623', in *Book Destruction in the West, from the Medieval to the Contemporary*, ed. A. Smyth and G. Partington (Basingstoke, 2014), pp. 34–54 (p. 47).

[2] Mentioned in Chapter 1, and widely noted by scholars who mention the materiality of paper. For the most informative account of medieval paper, see O. Da Rold, *Paper in Medieval England: From Pulp to Fictions* (Cambridge, 2020).

palimpsests. Though these particular forms are noticeable today, recycled materials did not have to be overt for those working with books to know that they were there. Materials from books were often salvaged, redeployed or even destroyed as part of efforts to sustain books.

A commonplace feature of medieval book production was the use of wooden boards in bindings. Mirjam Foot points out that 'the boards of fifteenth-century bindings were usually made of wood (oak and beech were most common)'.[3] However, where records survive it is often difficult to disentangle the value of the boards from the total cost of binding.[4] As part of a new binding, book boards themselves could be re-used, or 'cannibalised' as Michael Gullick puts it, 'from discarded bindings'.[5] Timber was widely valued in medieval culture for all kinds of applications, and boards for bindings must have represented substantial investments – as indicated by their full and partial re-use. Sometimes bindings were taken apart and the boards they yielded were rebound on to the same book; sometimes they were removed from one book and used in their entirety to bind another.[6] For example, a sixteenth-century rebinding of a Worcester Cathedral manuscript was furnished with 'ill-fitting chamfered oak boards' reclaimed from another book.[7] In the flesh, though hidden under leather covers, these uneven wooden boards render this instance of recycling markedly noticeable.[8] In addition, Exeter Cathedral Library, MS 3520 features 'late medieval' re-use of bevelled boards, which have been turned around.[9] The binder who rebound HEHL, MS HM 132 in the fifteenth century inscribed itemised costs on the back pastedown, including mention of 'ii new bordes i d'.[10] These components were an important part of medieval book production, and they held

---

[3] M. Foot, 'Bookbinding 1400–1557', in *CHBB* III, 109–27 (p. 111).

[4] H. E. Bell mentions the bindings on Cambridge, Peterhouse College MS 114 and MS 154, 'which are known to have cost 2s. each' – although, of course, this includes more than just the wood, 'The Price of Books in Medieval England', *The Library* 4th s. 17 (1937), 312–32 (p. 322).

[5] M. Gullick, 'The Bindings', in *Worcester Catalogue*, pp. xvii–xlviii (p. xli).

[6] For case studies of fifteenth-century 'upgrades' to extant bindings, see N. Hadgraft, 'English Fifteenth Century Book Structures' (unpublished doctoral thesis, University College London, 1997), p. 14 (on the Bury St Edmunds and the Gonville and Caius College campaigns); for the campaign at St Gall, Switzerland, see J. A. Szirmai, *The Archaeology of Medieval Bookbinding* (Aldershot, 1992), pp. 165–70.

[7] Worcester Cathedral Library, MS F.37; Thomson, *Worcester Catalogue*, p. 24. BodL, MS Bodley 333 has older sewing on six supports, since repaired and bound in a white sheepskin binding dated to about 1602; *Summary Catalogue* II.i, 276.

[8] M. Foot affirms that binding boards were 'frequently finished with a slight bevel' in 'English Decorated Bookbindings', in *BPPB*, pp. 65–86 (p. 66).

[9] *MMBL* II, 830–32.

[10] HEHL, MS HM 132: 'In ledd*ur* hongre ii d; In whyte threde ii d; ii new bordes i d; ii skynys of p*ar*chement viij d; A skyn of redlath*er* ii d; In blac sylke *and* greyne j d ob; In glw ob; ij claspys ij d; su*mm*a totalis xix d'; Dutschke, *HEHL Catalogue*, pp. 175–77 (p. 176); also cited by Szirmai, *Archaeology*, endnote 24, (p. 279). Chapter 4 offers a more detailed study of book prices and costs.

their value as recyclable commodities. Both boards and paper are material artefacts that provide evidence for material re-use in medieval books.

Likewise, pieces of parchment were re-used in the fifteenth century in myriad, ingenious ways.[11] Outdated, unfashionable, or simply dilapidated manuscripts that were no longer needed or wanted for their texts were taken apart for their component parts. This is evidenced in the making and re-making of bindings. Nicholas Hadgraft suggests that, 'As books ceased to be useful', many were dismantled 'and the materials re-used in bindings'.[12] Parchment leaves, taken from broken books, were amenable to re-use as flyleaves, pastedowns and spine padding in other books.[13] There have been some prior studies of this range of fragmentary material, such as Jan Brunius's studies in Swedish archives, as well as Hadgraft's own work, in addition to more recent digital humanities and union catalogue projects.[14] As Hadgraft notes, materials were also re-used in 'no doubt other ways'.[15] In addition to their use in bindings, recycled forms of parchment in books include other structural functions, smaller cuts re-used as reinforcing strips, scraps added as inserts or extensions, and larger pieces used as quire-guards, and as quasi-bindings such as wrappers. *Fragments* is the umbrella term often used to describe such material, which can be somewhat misleading. This broad category encompasses everything from the obviously fragmentary small slips of paper found in spine padding, or cut-out miniatures, to more substantial formats, like whole leaves used as wrappers.[16]

As well as in books, parchment was put to an array of other re-uses in medieval life. For example, Erik Kwakkel has brought attention to a bishop's mitre, held in Norway's Árni Magnússon Institute, constructed from four pieces of parchment dated to *c*.1270.[17]

---

[11] I previously explored several aspects of parchment re-use in books, in H. Ryley, 'Constructive Parchment Destruction in Medieval Manuscripts', *Book 2.0* 7 (2017) 9–19.

[12] Hadgraft, 'Book Structures', p. 13.

[13] Discussed in the context of manuscript and print re-use by J. Boffey, *Manuscript and Print in London c.1475–1530* (London, 2012), pp. 74–75.

[14] J. Brunius, *From Manuscripts to Wrappers: Medieval Book Fragments in Swedish National Archives*, Skrifter utgivna av Riksarkivet 35 (Växjö, 2013), p. 24; see L. F. Davis, 'Fragments and Fragmentology in the Twenty-First Century' Stanford Text Technologies webinar, 23 April 2020, online < https://www.youtube.com/watch?v=JQ-XGFZolF8>; the 'Broken Books' project <http://brokenbooks.org/brokenBooks/home.html?demo=1>; the international 'Fragmentarium' research project (2015–2022) <https://fragmentarium.ms>; and D. Rundle's 'Lost Manuscripts' project <https://www.lostmss.org.uk/project>.

[15] Hadgraft, 'Book Structures', p. 13.

[16] For a focus on cut-out miniatures, see C. de Hamel, *Cutting Up Manuscripts for Pleasure and Profit* (Charlottesville, 1996); examples of cut-out initials in a copy of *The Prick of Conscience*, BodL, MS Douce 156 (pp. 9–10, 45–46, 71–72, 120–21); and many cut-out initials in a manuscript copy of the *Golden Legend*, BodL, MS Douce 372, some of the most dramatically cut leaves at fols. 47, 62.

[17] Reykjavík, Árni Magnússon Institute, AM 666 b 4to, <http://handrit.is/en/manuscript/view/AM04-0666-b>; as cited by E. Kwakkel, 'A Love Story Hidden in a Hat', Tumblr, <http://erikkwakkel.tumblr.com/post/55554381477/a-love-story-hidden-in-a-hat-you-are-looking-at-a>.

This was designed to create a stiff parchment structure which was then covered with cloth. Written on the parchment are Old Norse translations of the Breton *lais Les Deux Amants* and *Graelent*.[18] Another intriguing example of manuscript recycling has been investigated by Henrike Lähnemann: a set of fragments sewn into the hems of dresses by nuns in Lüneberg. These ornate dresses were made to clothe religious statues, and the hems are lined with scraps from over thirty different manuscripts, including liturgy, hymns and law texts.[19] Liturgical music manuscripts were also used to line hatboxes and organ cases.[20] These examples shed light on more book-centred re-uses by demonstrating the characteristics of parchment that motivated material recycling in such diverse contexts. The mitre and dress-linings were used in circumstances in which washing or wetting could be avoided. To maintain the structural integrity of any parchment-based item (whether hat, dress or book) it is essential to keep it dry, because parchment is sensitive to changes in humidity.[21] Instances of esoteric parchment recycling demonstrate this vulnerability – and these other kinds of re-use are rare survivals – but also suggest the remarkable utility of this material. These re-uses all take advantage of parchment's strength and pliability, qualities that motivated many instances of recycling in medieval books.

Furthermore, as the sixteenth-century reports mentioned at the start of this chapter suggest, parchment leaves were taken from books and recycled for wiping, scouring, rubbing and wrapping. These destructive kinds of re-use flourished – or at least records of such re-use flourished – following the Reformation, apparently accelerated by the Dissolution of the monasteries and the dispersal of book collections. J. A. Szirmai notes the 'truly wholesale destruction' of manuscripts, particularly outdated liturgical texts, during the sixteenth century which witnessed the Peasants' War in Germany (1525); the Dissolution of monasteries in the British Isles (1537–39); the Council of Trent (1545–63); and the Huguenot wars in France (1561–89) which resulted in 'cartloads of cheap "binder's waste"'.[22] As well as humidity, heat, naked flame and liquids are damaging to parchment. Domestic re-uses tended to destroy manuscript material utterly. As Margaret M. Smith

---

[18] 'Tveggia elskanda strengleikr' and 'Grelentz saga' (Old Norse translations undertaken in thirteenth-century Norway).

[19] H. Lähnemann, 'Text und Textil. Die beschriebenen Pergamente in den Figurenornaten', in *Heilige Röcke: Kleider für Skulpturen in Kloster Wienhausen*, ed. C. Klack-Eitzen et al. (Regensburg, 2013), pp. 71–78; see also Lähnemann's talk 'Recycling Parchment: Manuscript Fragments in Medieval Dresses' for the ICON Paper Conservation group, 1 May 2020, online <https://historyofthebook.mml.ox.ac.uk/2020/05/01/recycling-parchment/>.

[20] J. Craig-McFeely, 'Digital Image Archive of Medieval Music: The Evolution of a Digital Resource', *Digital Medievalist* 3 (2007/8), §2, online <http://digitalmedievalist.org/journal/3/mcfeely/>.

[21] R. Reed, *Ancient Skins, Parchments and Leathers* (London, 1972), p. 119: 'Ideal storage conditions […] are temperatures between 0 and 20°C [and] relative humidity between 50 and 65%'.

[22] Szirmai, *Archaeology*, endnote 11 (p. 278).

notes wryly: 'fate as a pie liner probably consigned most fragments to oblivion'.[23] These early-modern household re-uses were typically ephemeral, with no consideration for parchment's longer-term durability. In contrast with the survival of carefully kept mitres, then, little physical evidence of these disposable re-uses remains – from any century.[24]

There is, however, plentiful evidence of parchment re-use in books. Recycled components of books were incorporated in the making, unmaking and remaking of books. Unfortunately, these book-centred re-uses are seldom described by fifteenth-century contemporaries, but the rationale for these re-uses can be reconstructed from physical evidence. What form does the evidence take? The material, physical form of manuscripts gives clues as to how and why they were made and remade and can also provide grounds for informed speculation. Physical structures reveal a range of medieval techniques for re-using parchment and the reasons for doing so. Normally, parchment is – almost exclusively – thought of as a writing support. When made well, the surface of parchment is exceptionally good at holding ink, whether it sits on the surface (carbon-based inks) or bonds chemically by 'burning' into the parchment (caustic ink made from iron salt and oak galls).[25] But parchment is not only good for writing; it is also an adaptable material, with a remarkable variety of potential uses and re-uses in book production. It is strong and pliable, a durable, virtually indigestible substance, with 'lightness and flexibility [...] high tearing strength [and] exceptional long term stability'.[26] That books made from parchment survive to the present day attests to this very resilience. In this chapter, the fundamental physical characteristics of well-made parchment will be seen to enable re-use and improve endurance.

Rather than addressing how or why manuscript material was re-used, previous studies have tended to emphasise fragments, wherever they turn up, as a potential treasure trove of undiscovered texts. Eric H. Reiter describes fragments as 'looking like discarded waste' which 'often [contain] unique textual treasures'.[27] Studies of flyleaves and palimpsests

---

[23] M. M. Smith, 'Preface', in *Interpreting and Collecting Fragments of Medieval Books*, ed. L. L. Brownrigg and M. M. Smith (California, 2000), pp. xi–xv (p. xii).

[24] Although I have not encountered fifteenth-century accounts of domestic re-uses of parchment, similar kinds of recycling are likely to have taken place. For example, a thorough search of the digitised corpora of documents from the Cely, Stonor, and Paston families did not provide accounts of parchment re-use: *Selections From the Correspondence and Memoranda of Cely Family Merchants of the Staple AD 1475-1488*, ed. H. E. Malden (London, 1900), online <http://www.r3.org/on-line-library-text-essays/the-cely-papers/>; *Stonor Letters and Papers 1290–1483*, ed. C. L. Kingsford (London, 1919), online <http://name.umdl.umich.edu/ACA1723.0001.001>; *Paston Letters and Papers of the Fifteenth Century*, ed. N. Davis (Oxford, 1971), online <http://name.umdl.umich.edu/Paston>.

[25] R. Clemens and T. Graham, *Introduction to Manuscript Studies* (Ithaca, 2007), p. 19; J. I. Whalley, *Writing Implements and Accessories from the Roman Stylus to the Typewriter* (London, 1975), pp. 77–78.

[26] Reed, *Ancient Skins*, p. 5.

[27] E. H. Reiter, 'Recycling the Written Word: Manuscript Fragments and Late Medieval Readers', in *Fragments*, ed. Brownrigg and Smith, pp. 189–204 (p. 189).

seem especially motivated by the desire to unearth lost texts; they consider whence the fragments came, and the texts or undertexts that they bear. In this treasure-hunting vein, David Rundle and Scott Mandelbrote justifiably describe manuscript fragments as 'valuable, tantalising shards of evidence'.[28] This chapter moves away from these preoccupations by focussing on the ways in which fifteenth-century manuscript makers went about recycling materials. It considers the various related reasons why manuscripts were re-used by addressing issues of *waste* and *value*, and, through case studies, explores how the materials of books were recycled in practice.

Before the fifteenth century, recycling had been a part of book production for centuries, and it continued to be so long after. The evidence preserved in fifteenth-century manuscripts demonstrates that there had always been access to scrap materials for initial (and any ongoing, or subsequent) campaigns of production.[29] But how that material was made available and how it then came into the hands of book producers is less clear. Several sixteenth-century records survive of book-scrap re-use, such as those by Bale and Leland mentioned earlier. These describe abundant availability of book materials, recycled in both everyday and extraordinary ways. There are later accounts, therefore, of the profitable re-use of parchment leaves in commercial settings, such as grocers' and soap sellers' shops, and even for the use of overseas bookbinders. The Dissolution provided a glut of scrap material from books. Trade and distribution of manuscript materials, which were 'sold as bulk waste to members of the book trade',[30] enabled re-use – and, particularly, the opportunity to capitalize on the value of these recyclable materials – more widely than ever before.

Taking into account the variable survival of books and the distortions inherent in the manuscript record, the trade in book-scrap before the sixteenth century was likely far smaller in scale than that described by Bale and Leland. But as this chapter argues, evidence for the re-use of such scrap in the fifteenth century can be glimpsed in the fabric and makeup of surviving books. This suggests, then, that in the centuries prior to the dramatic increase in available material around the time of the Dissolution, access to scrap was already in place in some form. As Ralph Hanna has noted 'recycling had been a routine procedure of library custodianship in the Middle Ages as well'.[31] Codicological features, such as inserted *schedules* or *schedulae*, are more prevalent in certain kinds of manuscripts, such as university notebooks or copies of standard university texts.[32] Other phenomena

---

[28] D. Rundle and S. Mandelbrote, 'Corrigenda', in N. R. Ker, *Fragments of Medieval Manuscripts Used as Pastedowns in Oxford Bindings*, 3rd s. 4 (Oxford, 2004 for 2000), pp. †1–29 (pp. †1–2).

[29] *OED*, scrap, *n.*, particularly Senses 2 and 3. *MED*, scrappe, *n.*, refers only to 'a piece of food remaining after a meal'.

[30] R. Hanna, *Introducing English Medieval Book History: Manuscripts, their Producers and their Readers* (Liverpool, 2013), p. 142.

[31] Hanna, *Book History*, p. 142.

[32] *OED*, schedule, *n.*, Sense 1; *MED*, scedule, schedule, *n.*; *DMLBS*, scheda, schedula, *n.*; mentioned by R. Beadle as one of a range of 'ephemeral' materials used for writing drafts, 'English Autograph Writings of the Later Middle Ages', in *Gli autografi medievali: problemi paleografici e filologici: atti*

include flyleaves and palimpsests, frequently recycled from liturgical manuscripts, or from outdated canon or civil law texts. These features and texts may be indicative of certain environments, such as scholarly or clerical milieu. Therefore, in the centuries preceding the Dissolution, universities or monasteries might well be places where homegrown book-scrap was commonly recycled.

In addition to individuals re-using minor quantities of scrap generated by their own institutions, there was probably also scrap exchange in book-producing centres. In the fifteenth century, Oxford and London were notable centres for book production. Scribes and bookbinders in these cities would have been well placed, like those in universities or monasteries, to enjoy access to scrap material generated by their own industry. For example, Julia Boffey describes the 'sources of supply which provided large quantities of high-quality waste' used by Robert Fabyan, a London sheriff, alderman, Master of the Draper's Company and author.[33] Given the close proximity of book producers' premises, exchange of or trade in scrap was eminently feasible. After all, even book makers who used scrap opportunistically, or only when necessary, somehow managed to acquire such material. By its very nature, whether in provincial settings or busier cities, this trade in scrap was likely to have been inconsistent, often localised, and highly informal. It is therefore exceptionally difficult to investigate. Nevertheless, patterns of trade and distribution in scrap – and, simply, access to it – did not spring up overnight in the wake of the Dissolution. During the fifteenth century, as in the sixteenth century, book-producers could and did access supplies of book materials for recycling.

Sustaining books by re-using bits of other books might appear arbitrary, but these efforts were intentional and were part of a wider culture and practice of sustaining books. As in any period, fifteenth-century book production was shaped by social, economic and technological pressures. Not only was scrap re-used in various small-scale ways to reduce the costs of book production, but it also represented an opportunity for increasing profits. This could be achieved through more organised re-use of parchment or even through trade in book-scrap. A pressing issue for any craftsman looking to make a profit from a product is the amount and kind of work that the craft entails. This was an important consideration for those who chose to repurpose material too: the effort or ease of the task. The time, intensity and skill level of labour involved varied widely between different processes of recycling. As Gillespie succinctly puts it: 'As long as people have wanted to get their hands on textual materials there have been slap-dash as well as skilled ways of getting that material into a serviceable form'.[34] In any era, skilled work, and the time and materials it takes to execute that work, usually increases the price of production, and so one of the reasons for re-using material at all was of course the financial bottom line. But that's not the only consideration: fifteenth-century people actively chose to re-use materials in books even when that involved

---

del Convegno di studio della Fondazione Ezio Franceschini, Erice 25 settembre–2 ottobre 1990, ed. P. Chiesa and L. Pinelli (Spoleto, 1994), pp. 249–68 (p. 260).

[33] Boffey, *Manuscript and Print*, pp. 171–72.
[34] A. Gillespie, 'Bookbinding', in *PBE*, pp. 150–72 (p. 172).

a great deal of effort. Accordingly, this chapter starts with cases of manuscript re-use where there was minimum input of effort and then proceeds to examples in which considerable extra effort was expended. It begins with off-cuts and other small strips, continues through several other re-uses of fragments, and concludes with palimpsests, a re-use of parchment entailing a significant input of labour. Throughout, re-use is contextualised as an endeavour to make the production of books more economically viable (whether through expediency or extra labour), and to make books themselves more durable material objects.

Off-cuts

From early in the process of production parchment is open to and available for a range of potential uses, and due to this adaptability it is also liable to be salvaged. While in the process of being made, and once dried under tension, parchment must either be cut down directly from the herse frame, or released by removing the pebbles and cords. After being cut free or released, the parchment sheet is then trimmed to the desired shape. Whichever technique is preferred by the parchment-maker, cutting or trimming necessarily results in the creation of spare slivers of material, which were typically cheaper options for making books or salvageable as scrap for uses outside books. The choice piece of parchment usually takes the form of the largest possible rectangular-shaped, centred 'prime cut' (see again the diagram, Figure 3).[35] The leftovers, remainders from this optimised cut, the off-cuts (mentioned in Chapter 1) are typically identifiable by the following features: pronounced follicle patterns; horny patches; discolouration (dark or yellow patches); edges that fall too short and elongated gaps caused by the fore and hind legs of the animal.[36] Of course, off-cuts are only identifiable where these features are visible – some books may use off-cuts that are not securely identifiable as such. Using off-cuts in the production of books was a simple way to salvage available material, and to make books in a sustainable way.

Off-cuts, in common with other oddly shaped fragmentary scraps of parchment, were put to a range of other uses: as unbound singletons, for ephemeral letters or drafts and by students for note-taking (see Figure 3).[37] These scraps of parchment were known as *schedulae*, mentioned previously. But off-cuts were also used for constructing books. Kwakkel contends that they were used for 'very small books only, with a page height of no more than 130–170 mm'.[38] Although off-cuts are just as frugal as parchment that is

[35] E. Kwakkel, 'Commercial Organization and Economic Innovation', in *PBE*, pp. 171–91 (p. 187).

[36] E. Kwakkel, 'Discarded Parchment as Writing Support in English Manuscript Culture', *Manuscripts Before 1400, English Manuscript Studies 1100–1700* 17 (2013), 238–61 (252). I am grateful to Stephanie Lahey for sharing with me insights from her research on this topic: 'Offcut Zone Parchment in Manuscripts from Later Medieval England: A Corpus-Based Study' (unpublished doctoral thesis, University of Victoria, 2021).

[37] Kwakkel, 'Discarded Parchment', p. 241.

[38] Kwakkel, 'Commercial Organization', p. 187. Lahey proposes updates to the defining features of off-cuts, such as a page height of no more than 150 mm and typically much smaller than this, 'Offcut Zone Parchment'.

cut to include the natural edge of the skin, the two should not be confused.[39] Off-cuts are a distinct category with identifying features; a particular hallmark is their small size.[40] Fifteenth-century examples of books comprising off-cuts used as leaves are relatively rare and hard to find. In a survey of thirty-five small manuscripts (using Kwakkel's definition of 130–70 mm height) selected from the Ashmole, Digby and Douce collections in Oxford's Bodleian Library, only seven could be confidently described as including off-cuts.[41] These manuscripts mostly incorporated between three to nine off-cuts, scattered throughout a much larger book block. Two date to the fifteenth century, one is of uncertain date, and the other four date to the thirteenth and fourteenth centuries. The limited examples found in this survey tentatively suggest that off-cut use may have been rare in the fifteenth century.

Like many of the re-uses discussed in this chapter, off-cuts were used both in manuscript production and in other, more ephemeral ways outside books. Perhaps they too were used for making notes, documents, drafts, or even for the destructive household tasks with which this chapter opened. It's even possible to imagine that off-cuts were sometimes added into the size or glue pot.[42] Off-cuts can be recognised by long curved edges, also known as a lacuna, at the lower corner of the leaf, which is caused by the animal's flank and represents the limits of the usable part of the skin. These edges are often accompanied by signs of stretching and other skin imperfections. Notwithstanding their visibly different quality, these leftover scraps became a real option for book production. At lower grades of production, then, cheap cuts of parchment, including off-cuts as a distinct category, could be salvaged to make small manuscripts. During the fifteenth century, off-cuts were therefore surely available for ephemeral, destructive purposes, as well as for book production.

So, how were off-cuts used to make small manuscripts? As Kwakkel notes, a translation of the *Speculum ecclesie* into English exhibits the typical features of off-cuts when used in books (BodL, MS Douce 25, see Figure 4). The suitably small size of the whole manuscript (127 × 95 mm) falls comfortably within the parameters of the off-cut 130–70 mm range. In this book, the parchment is generally consistent in quality throughout, with off-cuts used for the three final leaves of the manuscript.[43] On these folios, curved lacunae and

---

[39] BodL, MS Bodley 757 is manuscript which includes much larger pieces of parchment used sustainably (not off-cuts), this manuscript includes leaves with holes and missing corners, and measures 260 × 180 mm. *Summary Catalogue* II.i, 411–12.

[40] This is not to say that it is always clear where the boundary lies between true off-cuts and larger cuts of parchment with similar features.

[41] Manuscripts with off-cuts: BodL, MS Ashmole 1280, BodL, MS Digby 2, BodL, MS Digby 14, BodL, MS Digby 15, BodL, MS Digby 20, BodL, MS Digby 24 and BodL, MS Douce 52; survey of *Quarto Catalogue* X (Ashmole), IX (Digby), and *Summary Catalogue* IV (Douce); survey for E. Kwakkel's 'Holsterbooks and Off-cut Manuscripts', Bodleian Library Manuscript Masterclass, University of Oxford (24 February 2014); survey undertaken in collaboration with J. Henderson.

[42] See Chapter 1 for discussion of recipes for making size and glue.

[43] BodL, MS Douce 25, dating to the early fifteenth century, the text is written in bastard anglicana influenced by secretary hand, off-cut folios at fols. 70–72. In addition, fols. 40–45 are missing the

This booke was maad of þe goodis
of a certeyne p{er}sone for a wnyn p{er}[son]-
[n]e / þat þat p{er}sone þ{at} haþ þis booke
co{m}mittid to hi{m} of þe p{er}sone þat haþ
power to co{m}mitte it. haue þe vss p{er}-
of teerme of his liif. p{ra}yng for þe
soule of þe same p{er}sone of whos go-
[o]dis þis booke was maad / And i[f]
[h]e þ{at} haþ þe forseid vsse of co{m}missio{u}
whanne he occupieþ it not leene it
for a tyme to su{m} oþer p{er}sone /
[A]lso þ{at} þat p{er}sone to whom it m[ay]
[be co]mmittid for þe teerme of liif / [or]
[und]er þe forseide co{n}dicio{u}s deliuer[e]
[i]t to anoþ{er} p{er}sone þe teerme of [h]-
[i]s liif / And so be it deliu{er}ed s[o]
[c]ommittid fro p{er}sone to p{er}sone
[as lo]nge as þe booke may or wou[lde]
[as] longe as þe booke endurith /

Figure 4. BodL, MS Douce 25, fol. 72r, off-cut.

stretch marks are present around the edges of the parchment, and both indicative of the natural edge of the skin and key signs of off-cuts.[44] It is not clear whether the rest of the parchment used in this manuscript was also off-cut, as distinguishing features are seen only on the last three folios. Additionally, it is not clear whether the manuscript is small because it was made from off-cuts, or if it includes off-cuts because it was designed to be small. The use of identifiable off-cuts at the very end of this translation of the *Speculum ecclesie* suggests that the scribe may have run out of the main batch of parchment and supplemented it with off-cuts. However, given its size, it remains a possibility that the whole manuscript was made from off-cut material and later trimmed to its current format.[45] Off-cuts could constitute the entire book block or could be scattered throughout or concentrated towards the end of the manuscript.

The rationale for using off-cuts might be easier to imagine in this case than in some others, for more details are known about the making of this book. It happens to be one of a group of five 'common profit' books, financed from the proceeds of wealthy merchants' estates and identified by similar inscriptions written into the books.[46] These books for spiritual edification were typically made to relatively low grades of production.[47] As a more affordable production, this copy of the *Speculum ecclesie* was a cost-efficient charitable donation, designed to promote access to religious literature. One of the final, off-cut leaves in the book bears a statement instructing future readers that this manuscript was 'maad of the goodis of a certeyne persone for a comyn profite' and that it should be handed down from one owner to another for 'as longe as the booke enduriþ'.[48] These books represent the re-use of merchants' wealth into charitable gifts at the same time as physically consisting of re-used matter. The mention of the possible longevity of the book's existence calls

---

lower right corner of each leaf, which may be because they are off-cuts (especially fols. 40, 44, 45 which have 'natural' edges), or this may be because they have suffered later damage (see fols. 41, 42, 43 which appear injured). *Summary Catalogue* IV, 497; *IMEP* IV, 7–10. See also D. Wakelin, *Designing English: Early Literature on the Page* (Oxford, 2018), pp. 46–47.

[44] Kwakkel, 'Commercial Organization', pp. 187–89, including fig. 8.2 (p. 188).

[45] This possibility is difficult to substantiate: the margins on each side of the text block are a comfortable, 'normal' width. In comparison, the top margin seems smaller than it should be. In any case, the book has been rebound since the fifteenth century, which may have obscured original information about the size of the book and whether or not other leaves are also off-cut parchment.

[46] The four other known common-profit manuscripts are: CUL, MS Ff.vi.31; BL, MS Harley 993; BL, MS Harley 2336; London, Lambeth Palace Library, MS 472, as identified by W. Scase, 'Reginald Pecock, John Carpenter and John Colop's 'common profit' Books: Aspects of Book Ownership and Circulation in Fifteenth-Century London', *Medium Ævum* 61:2 (1992), 261–70 (p. 261); common-profit books are discussed further as a form of second-hand circulation that afforded spiritual benefits, in Chapter 4.

[47] From observation of the four known books cited above, I suspect this to be the case. For example, CUL, MS Ff.vi.31 was also made from generally low-grade material, including off-cuts with lacunae at fols. 3, 19, 31, 35.

[48] BodL, MS Douce 25, fol. 72r.

attention to its material form. Just as this common profit book was intended to work hard as an educational, spiritual resource over many years, it was also expected to endure as a material object.

Manuscripts made with these repurposed, cheaper off-cuts might lead us to anticipate that in every regard the grade of production was lower. However, as in the common profit book, other manuscripts containing visibly off-cut parchment also feature aspects of production that were well executed. Another early fifteenth-century manuscript of religious texts, BodL, MS Digby 14, which includes *The Prick of Conscience*, was constructed from scattered off-cuts.[49] Although the off-cuts might suggest that this manuscript is materially lower-grade, there is careful attention to detail in the writing and rubrication of the text itself. The scribe and bookmaker may have been the same person, or these stages of production may have been conducted in sequence. There are occasional flashes of rubrication on the letters at the beginning of each line and, in addition, rubrication of Latin lines embedded in the body of the text. There are also blue-ink letters beginning the line on occasion and bracketing of verses in the scribe's usual brown-black ink. Another book, BodL, MS Digby 15, a compilation of astrological texts, exhibits a similar juxtaposition of neat copying and attention to rubrication and initials with lower-grade writing supports: the writing is executed on parchment of variable quality, including some off-cuts.[50] This contrast between lower-grade materials and apparent investment in relatively effortful copying is typical of many kinds of recycling. This contrast suggests that choices were made to economise in some aspects of production but not in others. Opting for parchment as a writing support was a priority, even if it sometimes had to be lower grade to fit a budget. Perhaps opting for cheaper parchment off-cuts meant that more time could be spent on the labour of writing the text itself.

Yet, despite the attention to other aspects of the book's design, there was an abiding willingness to use evidently cheaper looking parchment cuts. Off-cuts were sometimes scattered throughout the book block; arranged in this way they might be more or less discernible. The previously mentioned copy of *The Prick of Conscience* features this uneven distribution. When compared with the rest of the parchment, which is cut neatly with squared-off, regular edges, the off-cuts in this book are notably conspicuous. On six leaves, scattered sporadically throughout the book, the fore-edges of the parchment are dramatically and noticeably curved.[51] The darker edges of the off-cuts are eye-catching in contrast with the other paler parchment. The collection of astrological texts features off-cuts scattered throughout the book too.[52] The last off-cut in this manuscript is a particularly fine

---

[49] BodL, MS Digby 14, which measures 160 × 110 mm, within the parameters of Kwakkel's proposed height range for off-cuts; *Quarto Catalogue* IX.i, 10; this manuscript emerged from the survey of small books in the Digby collection, but I would also like to thank Daniel Sawyer for suggesting this manuscript to me.

[50] BodL, MS Digby 15 measures 160 × 110 mm; *Quarto Catalogue* IX.i, 11.

[51] BodL, MS Digby 14, there are 160 leaves in total, off-cuts at fols. 32, 87, 109, 111–13.

[52] BodL, MS Digby 15, 135 leaves in total, with off-cuts at fols. 34, 62, 134.

example of the hue of the hide darkening towards the outer limit of the feasible parchment area: this discolouration is caused by uneven stretching at the edges of the skin.[53] Also, all three of the off-cuts in this manuscript are much yellower – almost like the colour of horn – than the creamy-coloured leaves that intersperse and surround them. Again, the effect of arranging off-cuts in this scattered way is striking.

The distribution of off-cuts in both BodL, MS Digby 14 and BodL, MS Digby 15 begs the question of whether visibly 'cheaper' material – such as off-cuts marked by lacunae, darker areas and stretch marks – was purposely arranged in this way. Was this cheaper material, by design, hidden by being strewn unobtrusively throughout the book? That may have been the intention, yet, leafing through either of these manuscripts suggests that off-cuts were and still are conspicuous. However, in any era, it is unclear whether everyone might notice, or mind, cheaper materials in books. Nevertheless, this striking difference in quality would have been immediately recognisable to anyone who came into regular contact with parchment manuscripts, and even more so for anyone familiar with the processes of making parchment.

To try to understand these cases of off-cuts in books, it is helpful to reconsider the stage at which off-cuts were used, and the immediacy of their value. Maybe these materials were available in places of book production and could be entertained as a choice for cheaper production from the beginning of a project. For example, they would be useful for people who were likely to be eking out materials to make books as frugally as possible, such as university students and amateurs copying for their own use.[54] So, rather than thinking of off-cuts as being 'discarded', or as part of a throwaway culture, off-cuts can be characterised instead as having latent potential for multiple other uses.[55] Those handling off-cuts were aware that these materials had a range of other possible functions: they could be boiled into size or glue by binders, or redeployed as writing supports for notes or drafts.[56] These possible uses, and use-values, were weighed up by people who made books, and in some cases there was forethought and a planned process of production that actively incorporated off-cuts, and in others there was an openness to the ad hoc use of such materials. Surviving examples of off-cuts show that makers of books sometimes salvaged these by-products and, arguably, did so because they were aware of their potential as recycled material for making books. This awareness also holds true for other scraps of parchment used to make books.

[53] BodL, MS Digby 15, fol. 134. Kwakkel described the discolouration at the edges of the stretched hide in 'Holsterbooks and Off-cut Manuscripts'.

[54] University students made notes of sermons and lectures, but in some places also engaged in a regulated system for copying books in parts; for a definition of the *pecia* system, see P. Beal, *A Dictionary of English Manuscript Terminology 1450–2000* (Oxford, 2008), pp. 290–91, and for more information see M. B. Parkes, 'The Provision of Books', in *The History of the University of Oxford: Late Medieval Oxford*, ed. J. I. Catto and T. A. R. Evans (Oxford, 1992), II, 407–83 (pp. 462–70); see also J. Pouzet's account of amateur book production in 'Book Production Outside Commercial Contexts', in *PBE*, pp. 212–38, especially pp. 220–21.

[55] Kwakkel, 'Discarded Parchment', mentioned in the title and at pp. 238–39.

[56] For more on trimmings used to make size or glue, see Reed, *Ancient Skins*, p. 54.

Reinforcing strips

It was relatively easy to repurpose small fragments of parchment to help protect a book's structure: layered scraps were often used as spine linings to provide padding, and thin strips could be used to strengthen and help to sustain sewing structures.[57] The use of reinforcing strips[58] in books made of paper, or of a mix of paper and parchment, suggests that some late medieval binders believed that paper was not as resilient as parchment against the tearing effect of sewing structures.[59] Up to the 1480s, sewing guards were typically used to protect every gathering in a paper book block, and by the end of the century this reduced to one or two at each end of the book block.[60] During the fifteenth century, many book producers chose to add these tough parchment strips to counteract the risk of tearing and to promote the longevity of the new book. Parchment reinforcing strips could be sliced from good cuts of new parchment, from parchment that bore writing, or even from off-cuts or other fragments or trimmings. Any of these forms of parchment could be cut relatively easily into narrow reinforcing strips; in the fifteenth century, cutting was achieved either with a penknife, or perhaps with shears or scissors.[61] The straightforward re-use of these small pieces of parchment has much in common with off-cuts. Both kinds of fragments were formed quickly and simply, with little processing beyond accurate cutting. Like off-cuts, reinforcing strips might also be generated by another customary process of making leaves: trimming the edges of sheets of parchment. When made in this way, strips should be understood as by-products.

There were possibilities for generating multiple reinforcing strips at once, either by shredding one large piece of parchment into many ribbons, or by gathering up the trimmings left over from cutting through the edges of a stack of parchment, perhaps on its way to becoming a stock of evenly sized material, or a stock for a specific book block. What may be seen in some manuscripts are identifiable batches of strips, deployed throughout a manuscript, which were likely to have been made from the same book, or document, or possibly even cut from the same leaf. For example, in HEHL, MS HM 144, a late fifteenth-century miscellany including works by Chaucer and Lydgate, there are reinforcing strips around and inside each of the paper quires.[62] This added material was mostly cut

---

[57] For a report on the conservation of fragmentary spine linings and guards discovered in 2014 in Cambridge University Library, see B. Warrington, 'Conservation Report on the Pembroke Fragments', online, <https://www.english.cam.ac.uk/manuscriptslab/conservation-report-on-the-pembroke-fragments/>, particularly figs. 7, 8.

[58] Ker refers to 'reinforcing strips' in *Pastedowns*, p. vii; these structures are also known as sewing guards, sewing stays, or quire liners, in *Bindings Thesaurus*.

[59] *Bindings Thesaurus* notes of *sewing guards* that 'it was thought that paper alone would not be strong enough to prevent the sewing thread tearing through the gatherings of bound books with paper leaves'.

[60] *Bindings Thesaurus* also notes that sewing guards are 'rarely found in the sixteenth century'.

[61] J. Cowgill, M. de Neergaard, N. Griffiths, *Knives and Scabbards* (Woodbridge, 2000), p. 60.

[62] HEHL, MS HM 144; Dutschke, *HEHL Catalogue*, pp. 197–203.

from the same source: on one side is a fourteenth-century text of liturgical directions and on the other, written upside down, are fifteenth-century documents of accounts – already a sheet used and then re-used for another purpose. Numerous details are legible on the strips in HEHL, MS HM 144, including the names of monks, dates, and the Augustinian priory Bisham Montague (in Berkshire) to which it is thought this source material once belonged.[63] The surviving reinforcing strips constitute a third re-use of this parchment. That strips of this kind were possibly made in batches, as this single-source example suggests, gives a sense of the ways in which they may have circulated. Nicholas Pickwood suggests that economies govern the making of small, recycled scraps, a principle readily applicable to the batch-production of reinforcing strips.[64]

Reinforcing strips are added to books to strengthen the binding of the whole book block by supporting the sewing of the quires (that is, the booklets or gatherings of parchment or paper). From the reader's point of view, these strips appear as narrow stubs poking out from between regular leaves. Two books that include reinforcing strips are copies of Chaucer's *Troilus and Criseyde* (BodL, MS Rawl. poet.163 and BodL, MS Selden supra.56).[65] The stubby strips either lie flat, because they have been pasted on to adjacent leaves, or they stand up separately, as can be seen in both manuscripts of *Troilus*.[66] Unfixed reinforcing strips, attached only by the sewing structures and not pasted down with adhesive, often look like the remainders of cancelled leaves. However, despite this resemblance, reinforcing strips can be distinguished from cancelled leaves by their arrangement. The strips are most commonly used to prevent thread from tearing through paper leaves, and therefore are normally located either around, or in the centre of, quire gatherings, as this is where the stress on paper is greatest. The most committed application of this protective method involved using reinforcing strips both inside each centrefold and outside each quire. In addition to the miscellany (HEHL, MS HM 144) with reinforcing strips cut from documents, this can also be seen in a fifteenth-century collection of sermons, Worcester Cathedral Library, MS F.121, still in its original binding. The parchment strips remain intact, sewn into the centre and enclosing each quire.[67] Whether or not there was in fact

---

[63] J. Pouzet has also suggested a connection with this Augustinian priory, 'Southwark Gower: Augustinian Agencies in Gower's Manuscripts and Texts – Some Prolegomena', in *John Gower: Trilingual Poet: Language, Translation and Tradition*, ed. E. Dutton, with J. Hines, and R. F. Yeager (Cambridge, 2010), pp. 11–25 (p. 17).

[64] N. Pickwoad notes this of spine linings and endleaf guards, in 'The Use of Fragments of Medieval Manuscripts in the Construction and Covering of Bindings on Printed Books', in *Fragments*, ed. Brownrigg and Smith, pp. 1–20 (p. 6).

[65] BodL, MS Rawl. poet.163, strips at fols. 14–15, 25–26, 37–38, 56–57, 64–65, 72–73, 80–81, 88–89, 101–02, 109–110; this manuscript also includes a poem by Chaucer, entitled 'To Rosemounde'; Seymour, *Chaucer Catalogue* I, 65–66; BodL, MS Selden supra.56, strips at fols. 6–7, 20–21, 34–35, 48–49, 62–63, 76–77, 90–91, 103–04; Seymour, *Chaucer Catalogue* I, 63–64.

[66] Strips are adhered to the pages in BodL, MS Selden supra.56, fols. 90–91.

[67] For example, Worcester Cathedral Library, MS F.121; Thomson, *Worcester Catalogue*, p. 83.

much risk of paper tearing, these thorough protective measures certainly reinforced the book's sewing structures.

Although they can be made from unblemished, 'new' parchment, reinforcing strips were also made from recycled material, as we have seen already. In the two copies of *Troilus and Criseyde*, reinforcing strips used at the centre of quires have traces of script on the strips used in each of these manuscripts, although the writing is not always legible. It is likely that the source for the reinforcing strips used in one of them was a document of some kind. On some of the strips what might be names, numbers and dates, perhaps the name 'John' on one strip, almost legible.[68] The length of the text running horizontally most of the way along the spine suggests that the writing was arranged in long lines, rather than columns. This was the typical layout of documents in the fifteenth century.[69] So despite the barely legible words, the format and script indicate former documentary use. Thus, documents could be repurposed as reinforcing strips to make books sustainable: rather than being disposed of, small fragments of parchment are re-used to preserve the material integrity of other texts.

Quire guards

Quire guards serve a similar purpose to reinforcing strips; it was believed that these structures helped to prevent the material in the book block from being shredded by the thread that held it together.[70] However, unlike stubby strips, guards are usually a similar size to the rest of the leaves in a manuscript. Being more substantial than strips, they offer additional protection by acting as bracketing leaves to each quire unit. In this way, quire guards act as a sort of internal flyleaf. As the fifteenth century wore on, more and more books were made of paper, and the difficulty with binding these books was their supposed liability to tearing.[71] It is true that sewing holes are weak spots where forces applied to the book are magnified. Pulling leaves away from the spine exerts considerable stress on the sewing structures that hold the book together, which can result in tearing. The task that the guards perform relies on parchment's material properties: its particularly tight structure withstands stresses well and therefore mitigated damage. Parchment's resilience and its ability to withstand rubbing and tearing made it highly appropriate for making quire

---

[68] BodL, MS Rawl. poet.163, strip at fols. 14–15.

[69] See comparable examples of documents in L. C. Hector, *The Handwriting of English Documents* (Dorking, 1980), pp. 80–83, plates XII–XV.

[70] Quire guards are also known as inner and outer parchment bifolia, and there are various possible common combinations of mixed parchment and paper in both print and manuscript books in this period.

[71] The concern that printed books would not last well, because they were printed onto paper, is particularly associated with Johannes Trithemius's *De laude scriptorum* of 1492; Da Rold discusses the frequent scholarly citation of Trithemius and other medieval paper-sceptics, and offers context for these anxieties, in *Paper*, pp. 7–9, and discusses Chaucer's references to tearing paper letters and pages, pp. 204–08.

guards. By consolidating the integrity of the quires, guards represent a way to promote the durability of the book as a whole.

Parchment quire guards are often readily noticeable in amongst paper leaves. Worcester Cathedral Library, MS Q.15, which contains a copy of the Wycliffite text *Rosarium theologie*, features such parchment quire guards, forming the centrefold and surrounding each paper quire.[72] The contrast of parchment and paper is visually striking and distinctive to the touch when handling the manuscript.[73] Endowed with the necessary material qualities, the parchment reinforcements to each quire ultimately fortify the whole book. Likewise, Worcester Cathedral Library, MS F.114, a collection of texts by Bernard of Clairvaux, Hugh of St Victor, and St Jerome, among others, is made from paper, except for the inner and outer bifolia of each quire, which are guards made of parchment leaves.[74] This is a manuscript still in its original, late fifteenth-century binding. In these examples, parchment quire guards are found in conventional formats and constitute tangible efforts to sustain the manuscript in its entirety.

Quire guards could be made from any kind of parchment; one manuscript includes quire guards recycled by palimpsesting (Oxford, Hertford MS 4). It is uncertain how unusual this example might be. A series of extracts from Wycliffite Sunday epistle sermons has been rubbed down and used to support, protect and strengthen quires in a compilation of scientific texts, including astronomical and medical texts (see Figure 5).[75] These texts were written in several scripts, ranging from neatly executed small anglicana-influenced secretary hands, to larger, sprawling secretary hands. The palimpsests were bound in either to enclose or to sit in the middle of a quire.[76] Five are complete leaves, which have been trimmed, and five are individual half leaves.[77] All the palimpsests were rotated through ninety degrees (clockwise) before being bound in, so that the columns of the undertext now appear to run across the folio. Of the fourteen palimpsests used as quire guards, traces of the previous text are legible enough be securely identified as known Wycliffite

---

[72] Worcester Cathedral Library, MS Q.15: Quires I to XVII – although XVII is made entirely of parchment, Thomson, *Worcester Catalogue*, p. 129.

[73] BodL, MS Laud misc.735 is a substantial paper manuscript copy of texts by Hoccleve and Lydgate, which has noticeably mixed-quality parchment quire guards, and the manuscript measures 305 × 220 mm; *Quarto Catalogue* II, 522–23; this manuscript is discussed in Chapter 3 for signatures inscribed in the book, and a heavily annotated back flyleaf.

[74] Worcester Cathedral Library, MS F.114, Thomson, *Worcester Catalogue*, p. 75.

[75] Oxford, Hertford MS 4. The rest of the manuscript is written on paper and has been dated to c.1400 by H. O. Coxe, known as 'MS 2', in 'Codices MSS Aulae B. Mariae Magalenae', *Catalogus Codicum MSS. Qui in Collegiis Aulisque Oxoniensibus Hodie Adservantur*, ed. Coxe (Oxford, 1852), II, 5–6.

[76] Oxford, Hertford MS 4, palimpsest quire supports are located at fols. 2, 19, 42, 43, 50–51, 58, 59, 108, 125, 138–39, 195, 196, 209.

[77] Oxford, Hertford MS 4, complete leaves around the outside of quires: fols. 43 and 58, 50 and 51, 108 and 125, 196 and 209. Complete leaves in the middle of a quire: fols. 138–39. Half leaves: fols. 19, 42, 59, 195 (fol. 2 is illegible).

Figure 5. Oxford, Hertford MS 4, fols. 49v-50r, palimpsested quire guards. With the permission of the Principal, Fellows and Scholars of Hertford College in the University of Oxford.

sermons.[78] Although they have been scraped, the shape of the undertext indicates that the parchment leaves were trimmed down to be compatible with the new setting.[79] Thoughts towards protecting the new text and its functionality for years to come can be inferred from the presence of the quire guards: in this example, both kinds of sustainability – durability and re-usability – come together.

These quire guards and reinforcing strips demonstrate how parchment could be deployed for its capacity to shield and pad out the whole book. Both 'new' and used parchment could be added to a paper book to make it more resilient. Sometimes this caused the destruction of documents or other texts on the parchment sheets in the service of protecting other book materials from sewing stresses or rubbing. Used – or re-used – because of its physical properties, parchment was the perfect material for this task. Though sewing structures were by this time well-developed, it is perhaps ironic that the sewing and binding techniques designed to preserve the book block were also believed to tear through leaves, especially those made from paper. By adding parchment, in the form of quire guards and reinforcing strips, book producers improved the durability of the whole book. In addition, quire guards helped to limit the damage caused by friction between different sections of the book, much like flyleaves and pastedowns.

Flyleaves and pastedowns

Medieval flyleaves and pastedowns (also known collectively as *endleaves*) survive in many late medieval manuscripts. Binders and other bookmakers secured material for guarding the beginnings and endings of their manuscripts from superfluous deeds, letters, superseded canon law, old liturgy or other simply worn out books.[80] Szirmai suggests that the 'large scale' use by binders of outdated or illegible manuscripts began in the fifteenth century, and cites Greek and Irish texts cut up for pastedowns at St Gall in the rebinding campaign of 1436–61.[81] Blank parchment was used only rarely for making endleaves, which were 'often of low quality' parchment or 'discarded manuscript leaves'.[82] It is usually difficult to determine the dates of such re-uses precisely, and many may well have been added during later, post-medieval rebinding campaigns. The selection of manuscripts analysed in this section is driven by the presence of flyleaves in their original medieval bindings.

Many fifteenth-century manuscripts did have contemporary or older endleaves, however, and there is a tendency to conflate the presence of flyleaves and pastedowns in

---

[78] A. Hudson, *English Wycliffite Sermons* (Oxford, 1983), I, 94–96; *IMEP* VIII, 37.

[79] Hudson proposes that 'The original leaf size must have been approximately 300 mm by 220 mm; the written frame approximately 223 mm by 152 mm' in *English Wycliffite Sermons* I, 95.

[80] G. S. Ivy, 'The Bibliography of the Manuscript Book', in *The English Library Before 1700*, ed. F. Wormald and C. E. Wright (London, 1958), pp. 32–65 (pp. 52–53).

[81] Szirmai, *Archaeology*, endnote 11, at p. 278.

[82] Szirmai, *Archaeology*, p. 178, for diagrams of endleaf constructions in Gothic bindings, see fig. 9.2 on p. 179.

medieval manuscripts with the work of post-Reformation binders because that was so large-scale and widespread. In his magisterial study *Fragments of Medieval Manuscripts Used as Pastedowns in Oxford Bindings*, N. R. Ker suggests that pastedowns found in medieval manuscripts are largely a sixteenth-century phenomenon. He points out that pastedowns were usually indicative of Oxford or Cambridge binderies, and 'were used during a longer period at Oxford than elsewhere, regularly between c.1520 and c.1570 and commonly or occasionally during the half-century on either side of these limits'.[83] That claim encompasses the period back to 1470. While this is evidently the case in the manuscript record, medieval manuscript material was re-used to make flyleaves and pastedowns earlier in the fifteenth century too. After all, as Alexandra Gillespie has emphasised, 'old books supplied handy material to binders long before the Reformation'.[84] The following case studies focus, as far as possible, on verifiably fifteenth-century re-uses of older books.

Ostensibly, the primary purpose of a flyleaf is to protect the book block. Although one single flyleaf cannot properly cushion a book block, it may at least minimise the 'rubbing [of boards] against the first and last leaves of the text', especially when those boards are heavy, as they need to be in large manuscripts.[85] Indeed, that minimising effect on wear and tear might better be understood as sacrificing the flyleaves. Weighty wooden boards were typically used for the bindings of bigger manuscripts, as significant closing pressure was required to keep the book shut and therefore to keep out dust, pests, and moisture. The flyleaves of a fifteenth-century manuscript of sermons on the Gospels demonstrate the successful reduction of wear from rubbing.[86] This is a heavy manuscript, measuring 280 × 205 mm, and is furnished with substantial boards. The flyleaves were taken from a relatively contemporary manuscript: a fifteenth-century Book of Hours, with writing executed in a large module textura. These leaves were bound in upside down. They are also – significantly – marked by pink stains, where colour has transferred from the turn-ins of the cover due to rubbing. This pigment transfer, which is quite common, indicates the success of flyleaves such as this in bearing the brunt of the potentially destructive friction between the book block and the boards.

Similar marks accumulated over years of rubbing can be seen in numerous manuscripts; one further example is a manuscript of historical and medical writings written in Canterbury in 1465 and, according to Geoffrey D. Hobson, probably bound there too.[87] The manuscript

---

[83] Ker, *Pastedowns*, p. vii; see also D. Rundle's online edition POxBo, part of the 'Lost Manuscripts' project, <https://www.lostmss.org.uk/pastedowns-oxford-bindings-online-poxbo>.

[84] Gillespie, 'Bookbinding', p. 161.

[85] Ivy, 'Manuscript Book', p. 52.

[86] BodL, MS Barlow 24, fol. 2: 'Dominus Thomas Noly est huius libri verus possessor', 'Lord Thomas Noly is this book's true owner'; *Summary Catalogue* II.ii, 1059.

[87] BodL, MS Bodley 648, inscription in the top margin of fol. 5r: 'Iste liber constat .W. Boolde monacho Ecclesie Christi Cantuarie. anno domini M°CCCC°lxviij', 'This book belongs to W. Boolde monk of Christ Church Canterbury. Anno domini 1468'; *Summary Catalogue* II.i,

remains in a late medieval binding made of dark tanned leather, decorated with stamps. Its front and back flyleaves, taken from a fourteenth-century civil law manuscript, were formerly pastedowns: the flyleaves have left offset ink on the inside faces of front and back boards.[88] In addition to faint impressions of ink, the leaf is heavily marked by stains, residues of pigment which have transferred from the abutting dark leather turn-ins. Thus, the flyleaves in both manuscripts were subjected to rubbing, which is marked by traces of pigment from the turn-ins. These traces demonstrate the successful, sacrificial, protective capability of flyleaves.

In the fifteenth century, in addition to making flyleaves with materials from relatively recent books (written in the fourteenth or fifteenth centuries), much older fragments of parchment were re-used to make flyleaves. For instance, an older leaf dating to the tenth century was taken from a Gospel book and then unevenly folded and added to the front of a fourteenth-century manuscript of texts and tables of logic, which was bound during the fifteenth century.[89] The leaf could have been added to the book block at any time, perhaps even soon after it was written, or, at any point until it was rebound in the fifteenth century. The old leaf is noticeably darker, dirtier parchment than the rest of the manuscript. It has been folded at an odd angle and sewn in lopsidedly. It is decorated with architectural designs, grotesque faces and colourful inks. Despite its casual treatment, and scrappy presentation, perhaps this leaf possessed some interest to whoever slipped it into the front of the book, as a decorative thing or an object of curiosity or even as a token of a bygone era. Nevertheless, it has acted together with the sleeves of the overcover and the pastedowns to assist in protecting the manuscript from damage.

Sometimes flyleaves were recycled from parchment that had been already partly prepared for writing. For example, in BodL, MS Bodley 731 the front bifolium (two leaves out of eight flyleaves at the front of the book) and the back bifolium and pastedown had all been ruled for writing.[90] The manuscript measures 230 × 160 mm, and on the ruled leaves the columns measure between 87–89 mm in width, with the same pattern of ruled lines across each page. The front flyleaves were ruled – but not written on – and now bear later markings such as signatures. The back flyleaves and pastedown were partly used: there is writing on fols. 107v–108r, and fol. 109r. The ruling and vestiges of writing on these flyleaves do not correspond to format or script used in the main text. Similarly, recycled parchment can be seen in a manuscript with ruled but unwritten parchment at both front and back, and another manuscript with flyleaves made from a Gradual, on which the notes

---

291–92; G. D. Hobson, *English Binding Before 1500*, The Sandars Lectures 1927 (Cambridge, 1929), p. 15.

[88] BodL, MS Bodley 648, fols. i, 129.

[89] Worcester Cathedral Library, MS F.72, fols. 1–2, Thomson, *Worcester Catalogue*, p. 46. The binding dates to the fifteenth century, although it is not thought to be this book's earliest binding.

[90] BodL, MS Bodley 731, fols. iii–iv (of flyleaves fols. iii–x), and fols. 107–08, and pastedown at fol. 109. The fifteenth-century binding is in whittawed leather. As well as these partly prepared, ruled flyleaves, the front pastedown is an upside-down fifteenth-century themata for sermons. On the front pastedown is a purchase note dated 1489 naming Robert Elyot as the owner, discussed further in Chapter 4. *Summary Catalogue* II.i, 496–97.

had not yet been entered.[91] In these examples, parchment from unfinished campaigns of production was re-used for protective purposes.

This protective function is also the main purpose of pastedowns. However, contrary to popular belief, as Graham Pollard categorically states: 'Pastedowns do not in fact strengthen a binding'.[92] Instead, they are often used to shield expensive decoration on the front page of the book block, and may even be decorative in their own right.[93] Therefore, in many ways pastedowns serve similar purposes to quire guards or flyleaves, but are adhered to the inner sides of binding boards. A typical example can be seen in a manuscript of legal texts and Royal Forest administration, which has a protective leaf pasted inside the front boards.[94] While the main texts were written in cursive hands in the second half of the fifteenth century, the crumpled pastedown was composed earlier in the same century in large module textura and is replete with red and blue ink decoration, and musical notation on four line staves.[95] The sewing structure connecting the spine sewing to the covers is apparent where lumpy knots emerge from channels in the board. These knots lie beneath the pastedown. Protecting the main text block from being rubbed into holes by knots such as these, which sit slightly proud of the board, is one of the key reasons for pastedowns, as for flyleaves.

Limp covers

Parchment can offer protection in other ways too, for instance when wrapped around the exterior of a book as a limp binding. In the most general sense, limp bindings, or more properly *limp covers*, are book coverings that do not have wooden boards, as suggested by one of the medieval terms for these structures – *libri sine asseribus*, literally, 'books without boards'.[96] Another Middle English word, 'forrels', is used in the poem *Mum and*

---

[91] BodL, MS Bodley 809, fols. i verso–v verso, fols. 103v–07v and the back pastedown, *Summary Catalogue* II.i, 482; BodL, MS Bodley 787, fols. 114–15, the variation from the Sarum use points to Tewksbury, *Summary Catalogue* II.i, 457.

[92] G. Pollard, 'On the Repair of Medieval Bindings', *The Paper Conservator* 1 (1976), 35–36 (p. 35). This statement does not include limp covers, or pasteboard bindings, which of course may be strengthened significantly by a pastedown or other parchment or paper lining.

[93] M. M. Smith, *The Title Page, its Early Development, 1460–1510* (London, 2000), p. 21.

[94] BodL, MS Lyell 32 is in a 'contemporary binding in wooden boards covered with white leather', and survives with the original sewing intact, a front pastedown and a former pastedown bound as a flyleaf at the back (fol. 86), as noted by A. C. de la Mare, *Catalogue of the Collection of Medieval Manuscripts Bequeathed to the Bodleian Library, Oxford by James P. R. Lyell* (Oxford, 1971), pp. 75–80 (p. 75).

[95] The front pastedown of BodL, MS Lyell 32 was part of a noted Gradual, and contains parts of the 'Agnus dei' and 'Credo'; identified by de la Mare, *Lyell Catalogue*, p. 80. Visible to me, on the upper side of the pastedown, are the following words of the 'Credo' visible from 'omnium et invisibilium' down to 'descendit de celis'. On the reverse, where the pastedown is lifting from the board, visible to me are staves in red ink, the word 'Agnus' (with blue ink initial **A**) and, further down, the phrase 'tollis peccata mundi' from the 'Agnus dei'.

[96] I will use the terms 'limp bindings' and 'limp covers' interchangeably, since both terms are used by scholars, *Bindings Thesaurus*, limp covers, online, <http://w3id.org/lob/concept/1423>.

the *Sothsegger* to refer to boardless pamphlets.[97] Coverings were a distinct entity: while bookbinding costs are often hard to discern, medieval notes of payments for bookbinding sometimes distinguished between the charge for binding (*ligacio*) or for binding and covering (*coopertura*).[98] Boardless books could be left uncovered, or could be covered with soft leather, fabric, paper or parchment.

Moreover, parchment wrappers were sometimes made from 'recycled older documents'.[99] Like any binding, these structures help to protect books from dust, spills, mould, insect infestation, tearing and abrasion. This can be seen in the marks of heavy wear on some extant wrappers, for example the soft parchment binding on BodL, MS Rawl. D.403, a paper manuscript of religious tracts, which is worn, dirty, and stained.[100] The cover is generally dark with wear and the build-up of grime, however, it is also marbled with lighter worn areas, due to uneven rubbing of the outer surface over the years. Like other protective formats, wrappers testify to parchment's capacity for being re-used as a resilient shield, even to the point of destruction. Like flyleaves or pastedowns, parchment wrappers (whether or not they are recycled) help to conserve other materials.

Unlike flyleaves or pastedowns, in the manuscript record, fifteenth-century limp covers are relatively rare. There is 'little doubt' according to Gullick and Hadgraft, that 'there once existed a large number of books with limp covers of parchment, tanned or tawed skin, and even textile'.[101] They note a bequest of books to Evesham in 1392 and the catalogue of a Premonstratensian house at Titchfield dating to 1400, both of which describe about a third of the books listed as being *in quaterno* or in limp covers.[102] But they go on to assert that 'there are now very few [limp covers] of British origin as nearly all of them have been rebound in modern times'.[103] Perfectly serviceable limp covers have long been at risk of rebinding, often due to a lack of interest – historically, collectors and scholars were more interested in luxurious bindings – or due to the antiquarian penchant for standardised bindings.[104] They are also, like most book components, liable to partial or complete destruction through wear and tear.

---

[97] A. Gillespie, 'Bookbinding and Early Printing in England', in *A Companion to the Early Printed Book in Britain 1476–1558*, ed. V. Gillespie and S. Powell (Cambridge, 2014), pp. 75–94 (p. 92).

[98] Bell, 'The Price of Books', p. 322.

[99] M. Langwe, *Limp Bindings from the Vatican Library* (Sollerön, 2013), p. 27.

[100] BodL, MS Rawl. D.403.

[101] *MED, tannen, v.* Sense 1a: 'to cure (skins, hides, leather, etc.) with an infusion of tanbark; *ppl. tanned*, preserved by tanning'; *tauen, v.* Sense 1a, to: 'treat (a skin or hide) with alum and salt to produce a supple white leather, taw'.

[102] M. Gullick and N. Hadgraft note: the bequest of nearly 100 books to Evesham by Prior Nicholas (d. 1392), of which 'about one third had limp covers', and a catalogue of 1400 from a Premonstratensian house at Titchfield, in which 33% of the 224 volumes were in limp covers, 'Bookbindings', in *CHBB* II, 95–109 (p. 107).

[103] Gullick and Hadgraft, 'Bookbindings', p. 107.

[104] The post-medieval fortunes of medieval manuscripts often included later disbinding or rebinding. These actions are of course part of the longer history of the book; however, due to the defined scope of this study, these post-medieval fortunes are not included here.

There are few studies of limp covers, so it is difficult to ascertain exactly how many might still survive in British collections. To give a sense of the possible numbers involved, Agnes Scholla surveyed 89 medieval limp bindings from across Europe.[105] Given the apparent scarcity of survivals, the case studies that follow are selected from the few known extant English limp covers. Surviving limp covers range from fully intact to more fragmentary examples. Whatever their physical completeness or rarity, these case studies demonstrate that limp bindings had the potential to promote the longevity of the books they bound.

A limp cover is just one type of binding among many medieval binding formats, which during the fifteenth century included leather covers over wooden boards which could be tanned leather or alum-tawed skin, and might also be decorated with blind-tooling, stamps, rolls, or cuir-ciselés; there were also treasure bindings; textile bindings; girdle-books; and chemise or overcover bindings.[106] Efforts to protect books could take other external forms, such as book bags (some of which were known as *aumônières*), satchels, or chests and shelving arrangements.[107] Amongst all these protective options, limp covers constitute a capacious category, as the name refers to a range of specific and differing forms of boardless bindings in 'a wide variety of technical constructions'.[108] The vague terminology associated with this group of bindings may have its roots in this sheer variety of forms. Medieval libraries used a range of terms, such as *libri sine asseribus* (books without boards, as mentioned), *in quaterno* (as noted in the monastic library catalogue of c.1400, mentioned above),[109] or *sine postibus* (without sewing),[110] or *in pergameno* (in parchment),[111] all of which could be used to catalogue limp bindings. In spite of the apparent specificity of these terms, when used in catalogues or inventories, in most cases the exact form of the limp cover is unclear from these phrases alone.

---

[105] A. Scholla, 'Libri sine asseribus: zur Einbandtechnik, Form und Inhalt mitteleuropäischer Koperte des 8. bis 14. Jahrhunderts' (unpublished doctoral thesis, University of Leiden, 2002).

[106] Gillespie follows F. A. Bearman's distinctions between the terms chemise, wrapper (fully detached coverings), and overcover (secondary covers without flaps), in 'Bookbinding', p. 151; F. A. Bearman, 'The Origins and Significance of Two Late Medieval Textile Chemise Bookbindings in the Walters Art Gallery', *Journal of the Walters Art Gallery: Essays in Honor of Lilian M. C. Randall* 54 (1996), 163–87.

[107] Bearman, 'Textile Chemise Bookbindings', pp. 168–69. Various kinds of chests and shelving are discussed in more detail in Chapter 4.

[108] Szirmai, *Archaeology*, p. 98.

[109] N. R. Ker defines a *quaternus* as 'usually a fairly light-weight book bound in a limp parchment cover' in 'Oxford College Libraries before 1500', in *Books, Collectors and Libraries: Studies in the Medieval Heritage*, ed. A. G. Watson (London, 1985), pp. 301–20 (p. 306); and mentions it again in N. R. Ker, 'The Books of Philosophy Distributed at Merton College in 1372 and 1375', in *Books, Collectors*, ed. Watson, pp. 331–78 (p. 358); *DMLBS, in quaterno/quaternus, n.,* Sense 4b, in a 'notebook, booklet, pamphlet'.

[110] *DMLBS, sine postibus,* 'without posts (that is, without sewing supports)'.

[111] P. R. Robinson notes that 'Many library catalogues refer to works which are said to be bound in limp parchment or *in pergameno*', in 'The "Booklet": A Self-Contained Unit in Composite Manuscripts', *Codicologica: Essais typologiques* 3 (1980), 46–69 (p. 52).

Often, scholars have assumed that fifteenth-century parchment wrappers were always intended to be temporary, and, therefore, should be understood to be throwaway. The perceived hierarchy of medieval bookbinding structures, and the relative cheapness or low grade of wrappers compared with other kinds of binding, especially compared with solid wood boards and expensive decoration, adds to this impression of impermanence. It is also true that later, particularly in the early modern period, limp bindings *were* typically used as a cheap trade or retail binding solution, to protect commercially produced books in transit, storage or on the shop floor.[112] This pervasive association between later, post-medieval limp covers and transience – even fragility – has been attributed to surviving medieval limp covers. Whether it is their similarity to trade bindings, or their liability to be rebound in more substantial bindings, or simply their relative cheapness, all too often surviving medieval limp bindings are considered merely temporary measures.

But this is not the whole story: fifteenth-century limp bindings can be highly durable. Though rare, intact wrappers do still exist. Jan Storm van Leeuwen argues (of fourth- to fourteenth-century wrappers) that wrapping books in parchment 'did not serve a very temporary purpose'.[113] For example, the parchment wrappers of a fifteenth-century confessor's manual (SJC, MS S.35) and a late fourteenth-century collection of romances (BodL, MS Ashmole 33) both still survive. As will be explored in more detail shortly, a range of wrapper-fragments have also endured. Inferior in quality though some of these surviving limp covers may look, such as the waxy, holey and stained wrapper that enfolds a fifteenth-century scientific miscellany, many had the potential to last for a long time.[114] In his study of limp bindings, Szirmai rails against the assumption that all limp covers were somehow 'temporary' and 'inferior', calling this a 'misconception'.[115] Limp bindings were not intrinsically or inevitably temporary things – indeed the earliest known medieval paper wrapper dates to 1482, and still survives today.[116] In any case, limp covers that were made for more temporary purposes, such as trade bindings in later ages, coexisted with other kinds of wrappers, which were made to be durable and sustainable.

When limp covers were not functioning as a temporary measure, why did fifteenth-century people choose to cover books in this way? Medieval book producers may have been attracted to this option because most limp bindings are easy to make. Reed emphasizes the 'remarkably simple construction' of limp bindings, which required 'little or no adhesive and hence were produced easily in large numbers'.[117] Yet, surviving examples have been recognised as

---

[112] Pickwoad, 'Use of Fragments', p. 3; Foot, 'Bookbinding 1400–1557', p. 111; and J. Raymond, *Pamphlets and Pamphleteering in Early Modern Britain* (Cambridge, 2006), p. 56.

[113] J. Storm van Leeuwen, 'Review of Agnes Scholla's Thesis: *Libri sine asseribus*', *Quaerendo* 35 (2005), 150–52.

[114] BodL, MS Lyell 36, de la Mare, *Lyell Catalogue*, pp. 92–101.

[115] Szirmai, *Archaeology*, p. 286.

[116] M. V. Cloonan, *Early Bindings in Paper: A Brief History of European Hand-made Paper-Covered Books with a Multilingual Glossary* (London, 1991), pp. 4–5.

[117] Reed, *Ancient Skins*, p. 167.

'practical bindings of sound and even sophisticated construction'.[118] So were they simple or sophisticated constructions? Reed's analysis compares limp bindings with bindings that took longer to make, or involved adding adhesive, so he concludes quite reasonably that they are comparatively simple constructions. And it is true that when compared with other more substantial and expensive bindings, most kinds of limp covers were easier to make. However, I argue that the sophistication of limp bindings lies in the very simplicity of their construction. The design of limp covers was elegant *and* economical, both simple and cheap to make.

Whether the overall design of limp bindings is regarded as sophisticated or not, makers had several options when crafting these covers. The essential stages of construction were acquiring pliable material and using it to encase the body of the book. The book to be covered might take one of many diverse possible formats including a conventional book block, or a group of booklets or quires. Surrounding that body, a limp cover might be loose, or might be attached by means of stitching. For the most basic structures, then, the cover may not have been sewn to the spine, or stab-stitched through the quire folds, at all, although if it was, the quickest, simplest method was tacketing (to be discussed shortly). In this way, some limp bindings acted less like a binding and more like a modern-day folder. There are also examples of loose, folder-like covers, but these are more susceptible to loss or destruction than other types of limp binding.

Whatever further processes were undertaken, beyond enclosing the body of the book, an appropriate piece of material first had to be sourced. This material might be too big or too small for the purpose, or might be reshaped by folding or trimming to size. Materials used for limp bindings typically included tawed skin or tanned leather, lower grade or damaged new parchment sheets, or recycled manuscript leaves.[119] An example of a soft leather limp binding is bound into the front of the fifteenth-century BodL, MS Rawl. D.1220, which contains an astrological treatise on the twelve signs and a number of full-page illustrations, one of which depicts scribes and rubricators at work (fol. 32r). This soft leather was recycled from the binding of a manuscript dating from the late twelfth century.[120] The folios which immediately follow these leather 'flyleaves' are also made from recycled parts of the same older manuscript, and may have originally functioned as pastedowns.[121] Enclosing BodL, MS Lyell 36, a fifteenth-century scientific miscellany, there is a wrapper which is similarly low in quality.[122] It is horny and thick, with follicle marks and one particularly

---

[118] Gullick and Hadgraft, 'Bookbindings', p. 108.

[119] Textiles could be considered 'limp bindings' of sorts, as mentioned earlier, but these survive very rarely, are usually studied as a separate phenomenon, and due to the limited scope of this study will not be addressed here. For more on textile bindings, see Bearman, 'Textile Chemise Bookbindings'.

[120] BodL, MS Rawl. D.1220, fols. xiv–xv; Macray notes that other leaves bound in as flyleaves by Rawlinson date to the sixteenth, seventeenth and eighteenth centuries, *Quarto Catalogue* V.iv, 356.

[121] BodL, MS Rawl. D.1220, fols. 1–2.

[122] BodL, MS Lyell 36.

Figure 6. BodL, MS Ashmole 33 outer covers.

large hole, features which made it a poor surface for writing. Because they were cheaper, these lower grade pieces of parchment, which could include salvaged material and even off-cuts for especially small books, were a viable option for making particularly 'frugal' wrappers.[123] Yet, though lower grade, this piece of substantial, resilient parchment was remarkably well-suited to its protective purpose as a wrapper. Christopher Clarkson points to other streamlined, pragmatic aspects of limp binding design, which include their 'light weight, mechanical yielding qualities, lack of distortion in varying atmospheres and the durability of their component materials'.[124]

As well as protecting the books they encased, parchment wrappers helped to promote the fragmentary survival of other books, from which they were sometimes recycled. These wrappers were not only hard-wearing, like other parchment products, but also tangible examples of re-use. For example, the cover of a roughly made paper-and-parchment manuscript of astrological tracts and tables (BodL, MS Ashmole 366) was fashioned from a leaf of a fourteenth- or fifteenth-century religious treatise in French.[125] The handwriting of the French text is still visible on the surface of the parchment. Similarly, a fifteenth-century confessor's manual written in English and Latin was bound in four leaves of canon law (SJC, MS S.35). This volume is heavily worn on the outer cover, which still features a horn button for fastening the wrapper, and bears the inscription *Confessio* in large letters. The canon law text is more legible on the protected inner lining.[126] A further example is a double-wrapper arrangement encasing a fourteenth-century collection of romances, BodL, MS Ashmole 33 (see Figure 6). The inner and outer wrappers were recycled from papal and clerical documents relating to the dioceses of Exeter and Sherborne (see Figure 7).[127] These examples will be discussed in more detail presently. Each of these wrappers display overt re-use of parchment as a covering material: there was no attempt to hide or scrape away the writing on the surface of these covers. This suggests that expedient, no-frills repurposing of material was the key aim of this kind of parchment recycling.

In the production of limp covers, all further processes beyond the acquisition of material and enclosure of the book were optional. These optional processes might include cutting,

---

[123] Gillespie uses the phrase 'frugal business' to describe cheaper strategies of bookbinding, such as restoring or repairing books, or using recycled materials, in 'Bookbinding', p. 162.

[124] C. Clarkson, *Limp Vellum Binding and Its Potential as a Conservation Type Structure for the Rebinding of Early Printed Books: A Break with Nineteenth and Twentieth Century Rebinding Attitudes and Practices* (Oxford, 1982 repr. 2005), p. 1.

[125] BodL, MS Ashmole 366. Black notes that the 'flapping cover' is a fourteenth- or fifteenth-century leaf, in *Quarto Catalogue* X, 281–82.

[126] SJC, MS S.35; James, *SJC Catalogue*, pp. 293–94.

[127] BodL, MS Ashmole 33; Black notes that 'The outer [wrapper] is a letter executor of a bull of pope Innocent VI for the presentation of Thomas de Silton to the vicarage of Columpton, in the diocese of Exeter, then vacant by the death of Peter Moleyns' and the 'The inner cover is a very long and imperfect public instrument', in *Quarto Catalogue* X, 14–15; and G. Guddat-Figge, *Catalogue of Manuscripts Containing Middle English Romances* (München, 1976), p. 245, notes that the inner cover dates to 1377 and the outer to 1357.

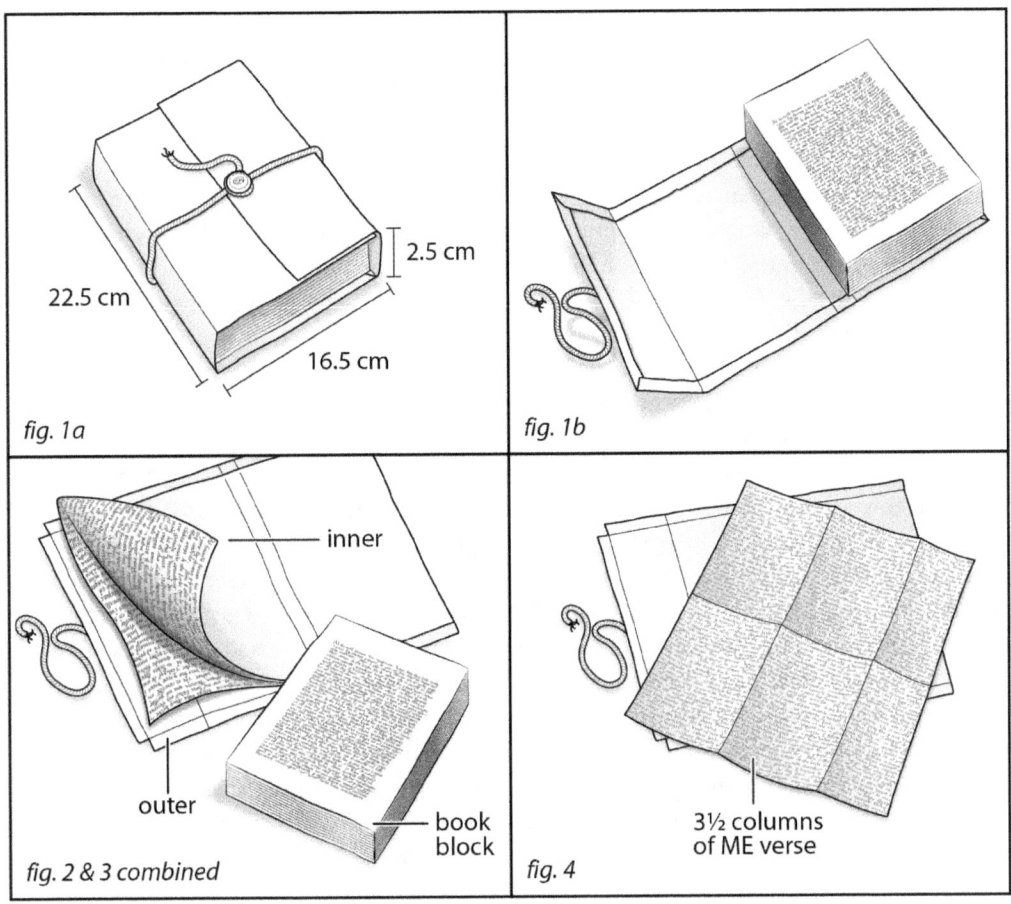

Figure 7. Diagram to show the inner and outer covers of BodL, MS Ashmole 33, modelled on Stephen H. Shepherd, 'Four Middle English Charlemagne Romances: A Revaluation of the Non-Cyclic Verse Texts and the Holograph Sir Ferumbras' (unpublished doctoral thesis, University of Oxford, 1988), p. 18.

folding, layering, trimming, making turn-ins and flaps, attaching support strips and ties, tacketing, stab-stitching, other kinds of stitching, and dyeing, writing on or decorating the cover. While limp bindings are – rightly – thought of as cheaper choices than books bound with boards, not all elements of limp binding fabrication are quite as parsimonious as they might seem. Surviving limp bindings indicate that the size of available material mattered to makers. When makers opted for extra folds, layers, turn-ins and flaps, these apparently meagre structures consumed a substantial quantity of parchment.

Makers could choose from a wide variety of methods for attaching the covers to the book block or quires. Tacketing or stab-stitching were both quick and relatively simple ways of fastening the physical contents of the book to its limp binding, demanding minimal production time.[128] The strands used to secure bindings were typically made of thread, cord, leather, or parchment.[129] To tacket, a strand of material was threaded through holes in the parts of the book to be secured together. To stab-stitch, a strand was pushed through the folded quire from front to back, so, literally stabbed through the full thickness of the quire.[130] This method was often used to attach parchment wrappers because it was simpler than other techniques, such as sewing methodically through the centre of the quire folds. The wrappers of a number of fifteenth-century manuscripts clearly show this typical technique: one is SJC, MS E.2, a stab-stitched copy of some scientific tracts, including Chaucer's *Treatise on the Astrolabe*,[131] another is the wrapper from a collection of religious tracts, BodL, MS Rawl. D.403, which has been since disbound and re-folded off-centre, making visible the lines of holes from earlier stabbed stitching.[132] Both tacketing and stab-stitching were cost and time-efficient techniques for fixing a protective wrapper onto a book block.

Sometimes extra care is taken to stab-stitch a cover and its contents. The thirteen quires of the scientific miscellany BodL, MS Lyell 36, mentioned previously for its poor-quality parchment wrapper, were held together with 'primary' (or 'quire') tackets, then secured with secondary tackets into a parchment cover. Multiple stab-holes remain, punctured through the parchment along the spine. The construction of this wrapper is particularly interesting because recycled 'twist' tackets that bear writing were used, which can be seen in the gutter between fols. 29–30 (Quire II).[133] These appear to be written in the same hand as the main text in this quire, and may have been rejected during the process of copying, or cut out later. In addition, the book block was attached to the cover with two or three thin strips of rolled parchment, used doubled-up for strength. While relatively inexpensive, and often salvaged by-products of trimming, doubling-up the thickness of these strips consumed double the resources.[134] That a tangle of knotted strips is still intact, holding the

---

[128] Kwakkel, 'Commercial Organization', p. 190. Here I follow the *Bindings Thesaurus* definition in referring to 'secondary tackets', which were 'used to attach cases of parchment or cartonnage' to a book block; see also *Bindings Thesaurus* definitions of 'tackets' and 'primary tackets' for the differences between these features.

[129] Szirmai, *Archaeology*, at p. 183, notes that white leather thongs or cords were commonly used for sewing Gothic manuscripts, and at p. 182 mentions that in parchment manuscripts 'quire tackets were regularly used in the fourteenth and fifteenth centuries'.

[130] *Bindings Thesaurus*, stitching, 'The [simple] process of holding bookblocks together by stabbing a material such as thread, textile tape, parchment or tanned or tawed skin thongs through the inner margin of an entire bookblock'.

[131] SJC, MS E.2; James, *SJC Catalogue*, pp. 138–39.

[132] BodL, MS Rawl. D.403: the limp binding is now bound into the back of the book that it once enclosed, at fols. 124–25; *Quarto Catalogue* V.iii, 292–94; there are eight or nine holes in each slightly wobbly line of stabbed holes, mirrored on either side of the spine.

[133] BodL, MS Lyell 36, fols. 29–30.

[134] Although it is not known whether these attaching strips were made of recycled material too (for they do not bear text or images or other evidence of former use), they were certainly designed to last.

wrapper in place, demonstrates the efficacy of this heavy-duty version of a standard sewing technique. A single thin strand was sufficient for other wrapper designs, so this structural feature indicates that extra care and effort was made to cover this scientific miscellany. These added efforts, which required materials and time, provide insurance for sustaining limp bindings into the future.

A striking impression of longer-term use is also suggested by limp bindings with decoration, or other markings such as finding aids. On an ostensibly ephemeral structure, decorative strategies indicate expectations of a useful future. Added markings might be as discreet as the title *Confessio* written on the outer wrapper of the confessor's manual mentioned previously (SJC, MS S.35). On the front cover of the paper manuscript of handwritten religious tracts just mentioned, BodL, MS Rawl. D.403, are two titles. The limp wrapper is marked up for identification, reference and use with the words *Mariale* and *Liber mortis et vite*.[135] Other features of some limp bindings suggest similar investment of time and effort into materials, anticipating longevity of use. These include decorative strategies such as dyeing, elaborate stitching and tooling. An example of decorative stitching is found on SJC, MS F.22, a fifteenth-century copy of *Fasciculus morum* with English texts and receipts from Foston on the Wolds in Yorkshire.[136] Long vertical and chain stitches attach the text block to the spine, and are executed in an elegant pattern.[137] Another example, this time of remarkably lavish decoration, is the 'Statutes and Inventory of Rotherham College', which is covered with a blind-tooled, red-dyed tawed limp binding.[138] This kind of decoration was more common on bindings with boards, so it is striking to find it adorning a limp binding.

Besides these noteworthy examples of effort expended on decorating limp bindings, even undecorated parchment wrappers used up surprisingly plentiful quantities of material. Far from relying on odd scraps, a binder making a parchment wrapper was likely to be using substantially more material than strictly necessary, and not just by doubling-up strands. Pickwood has identified a tendency for binders to use overlarge leaves in the construction of limp covers.[139] Advantages of this technique include the provision of multiple layers (usually double, but sometimes more), stronger turn-ins, and the option of a wrap-around flap. While this method of limp covering uses lots of material, it also wastes no time on trimming. So, the apparent extravagance of using larger pieces of parchment is

---

[135] BodL, MS Rawl. D.403.

[136] SJC, MS F.22; noted by James, *SJC Catalogue*, pp. 190–91.

[137] Gillespie, 'Bookbinding', p. 166.

[138] Hadgraft, 'Book Structures', p. 33; *A Descriptive Catalogue of the Manuscripts in the Library of Sidney Sussex College, Cambridge*, ed. M. R. James (Cambridge, 1895), pp. 2–9; Archbishop Thomas Rotherham founded Jesus College, Rotherham, in Yorkshire in 1483, *BRUC*, pp. 489–91; N. Orme writes about the college in *Education and Society in Medieval and Renaissance England* (London, 1989), pp. 61–62.

[139] Pickwoad draws this conclusion from his work with post-medieval limp bindings, however, it is readily applicable to medieval limp bindings too, 'Use of Fragments', p. 4.

mitigated by the efficiency of the whole process for the binder, in terms of both time and labour. It also results in long-term effectiveness as a robust, protective covering. Beyond fulfilling the desire to cover and protect the book block, then, these optional features required extra material and effort.

The tendency to overuse material in limp covers can be seen in six manuscripts (all discussed in more detail elsewhere in this section) which feature turn-ins of some sort.[140] Limp bindings could be made without turn-ins, but turning-in extra material is a straightforward process, and strengthens vulnerable corners and sides. Sometimes limp cover turn-ins are overspill material, where avoiding trimming has left a fold of overhanging parchment. As the soiled condition of side turn-ins in many manuscripts shows, these extra bits of fabric are often located exactly where covers are handled most. For example, the limp binding on BodL, MS Rawl. D. 403 (previously mentioned), a collection of religious texts, has two side turn-ins, which, on a generally grubby cover, are especially ingrained with dirt.[141] Although they entailed, in most cases, no more than a thumb's breadth of parchment, turn-ins offered significant advantages for the makers of limp covers keen to improve the survival of the book.

However, some turn-ins do show effortful attention, such as a cross-stitch to hold the folded parchment in place, or trimmed edges. In these cases, was there perhaps an expectation that bindings should have turn-ins? This may derive from the necessity of turn-ins on manuscripts with board bindings. These result from securely adhering overhanging edges of leather on to the inside faces of boards to maintain tension across a tightly fitted cover. The notion of what constitutes a binding might offer another explanation for why limp bindings feature turn-ins. To pick two examples of limp covers with turn-ins: the cover of BodL, MS Ashmole 366 has small turn-ins at the top, and the back cover includes a substantial flap,[142] and the wrapper of BodL, MS Lyell 36 has turn-ins on all four sides.[143] Perhaps extra effort was expended on providing turn-ins so that these covers looked as bindings should.

Moreover, turn-ins usually consume a small amount of extra parchment, proportional to the whole wrapper. Layering uses more substantial quantities of parchment and can double or triple the total amount required. Many limp bindings are single ply, yet nonetheless provide effective protection. For instance, the wrapper recycled from a French religious treatise is single thickness at the front, but double thickness at the back due to

---

[140] BodL, MS Ashmole 33; BodL, MS Ashmole 366; BodL, MS Lyell 36; BodL, MS Rawl. D.403; SJC, MS S.35; and SJC, MS S.54.

[141] BodL, MS Rawl. D.403 has no upper or lower turn-ins, though these may have been trimmed.

[142] BodL, MS Ashmole 366: 215 × 125 mm, turn-ins at the top of the front and back covers are 15 mm deep; the back cover is 125 mm wide with a folded-in back flap that measures 80 mm.

[143] BodL, MS Lyell 36: 200 × 135 mm, the large turn in at the lower edge is 115 mm at its deepest, but very uneven, there is a smaller turn in at the upper edge 50 mm approx., and overlapping these, turn-ins at the left and right edges of about 80–90 mm. Though it is unclear whether the intervention was contemporary or a later addition, there are crossed-stitches in each corner.

an extra, turned-in flap (BodL, MS Ashmole 366).[144] There is, then, something surplus to requirements in limp-bound manuscripts which feature an extra layer of parchment. No doubt the decision to add layers of parchment was dependent on the thickness, size, and quality of the parchment available, its affordability, and its perceived resilience to future wear. The cover of the copy of *Fasciculus morum* with decorative stitching is made from stiff, double-layered parchment, and the confessor's manual – as well as having turn-ins – is wrapped two-ply in canon law.[145] The extra thickness of these limp covers improved protection from dust, insect infestation, abrasion, spills, tears – all the usual mishaps that might befall a book – but also helped support the integrity of the whole structure.[146]

An intriguing example of a multiple-ply limp wrapper is found on the collection of romances previously mentioned, BodL, MS Ashmole 33, which includes *Roland and Ferragus*, *Sir Otuel*, and *Sir Firumbras* (see Figures 6 and 7).[147] This manuscript was written in the fourteenth century and although the book block is no longer bound into the wrapper, the book is still preserved together with its two-part covering. The two pieces of parchment formed a protective shell around the rest of the book. Folds made to fit the wrapper around the book generated three-ply layering (see Figure 7). The inner cover is made of thinner parchment, which is perhaps why it was folded in half, and then in half again, to provide more substantial protection and to better fit the book block, resulting in what Phillipa Hardman states is a 'very rare opportunity to see the 'foul paper' rather than the 'fair copy' state of a Middle English text'.[148] The outer cover, on the other hand, is formed from thicker, stiffer parchment, was kept single-ply and folded in three around the book block.[149] As mentioned, these covers were fashioned from papal documents and the wrapper comes from the South West of England. Extraordinarily, the material that wraps the manuscript also features a holograph draft version of 800 lines or so of the text of *Sir Firumbras*, a text that is found again, in full, in the main body of the manuscript,

---

[144] BodL, MS Ashmole 366.

[145] Respectively, SJC, MS F.22 and SJC, MS S.35.

[146] Bruce Barker-Benfield (Senior Assistant Librarian at the Department of Special Collections & Western Manuscripts at the Bodleian Library) and Nicole Gilroy (Head of Book Conservation at the Bodleian Libraries) both kindly answered my questions regarding the nature of limp bindings, especially in relation to humidity, personal correspondence.

[147] Also known as *Sir Ferumbras* or *Sir Fyrumbras*, as noted by P. Hardman, 'Bodleian Library, MS Ashmole 33: Thoughts on Reading a Work in Progress', in *Middle English Texts in Transition: A Festschrift Dedicated to Toshiyuki Takamiya on his 70th Birthday*, ed. S. Horobin and L. R. Mooney (York, 2014), pp. 88–103 (p. 88). For further discussion, see S. H. A. Shepherd, 'The Ashmole Sir Ferumbras: Translation in Holograph', in *The Medieval Translator: The Theory and Practice of Translation in the Middle Ages*, ed. R. Ellis (Cambridge, 1989), pp. 103–21; see also H. Ryley, 'Redrafted and Double-Wrapped: Binding a Medieval English Romance', *The New Bookbinder* 39 (2019), 17–23.

[148] BodL, MS Ashmole 33: the inner cover measures 450 × 415 mm. This cover has an additional overhanging flap of parchment. Hardman, 'Ashmole 33: Thoughts', p. 88.

[149] BodL, MS Ashmole 33: the outer cover measures 255 × 430 mm.

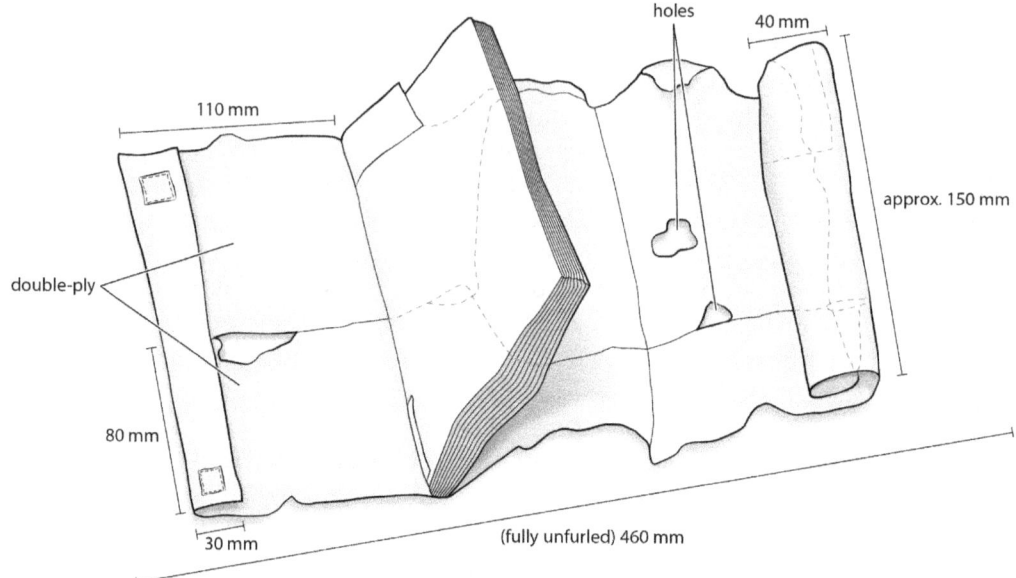

Figure 8. Diagram to show the construction of the limp cover on SJC MS S.54.

leading Nicholas Perkins and Alison Wiggins to note that that this 'suggests the composer was a clergyman of some sort with access to such materials'.[150] This is a remarkably rare survival of a draft that has survived together with the main copy of the text. The two versions continue to coexist, the draft like a sloughed-off skin. This relatively low-quality, scrappy-looking binding involves extensive use of multiple layers of material, and care was taken to fold it into a protective wrapper.

A small, late fifteenth-century manuscript of carols, SJC MS.54, possesses both an array of turn-ins and a multiple-ply wrapper (see Figure 8). In a remarkably tangible instance of the extravagant use of oversize parchment in a limp binding, this wrapper is also replete with such a long flap that it can be folded right around the manuscript.[151] Daniel Wakelin and Christopher Burlinson note the 'tattered and rather stiff vellum case-type cover' and speculate it may have been 'made from an already-damaged piece of vellum, re-used from some earlier binding or purpose'.[152] So the use of a generously sized parchment is tempered by its low grade: the material is peppered with holes and has rough edges. Yet those raw edges belie the lack of trimming of this outsize leaf. Though the paper book block

---

[150] N. Perkins and A. Wiggins, *Romance of the Middle Ages* (Oxford, 2012), pp. 64–66 (p. 65); Beadle, 'English Autograph Writings', pp. 255–60.

[151] James notes the 'vellum wrapper folding completely round' SJC, MS S.54, *SJC Catalogue*, pp. 294–96.

[152] D. Wakelin and C. Burlinson, 'Evidence for the Construction of Quires in a Fifteenth-Century English Manuscript', *The Library* 7th s. 9:4 (2008), 383–96 (pp. 384–85).

measures 146 × 105 mm, and the wrapper is a similar if wonkily variable height, the total width of the wrapper is 460 mm. The wrap-around section of the cover, when enclosing the songbook, extends from the very back, fully overlays the front leaf of the wrapper, and ends in a thick turned-in hem that hooks around the spine and rests on the back. This extensive parchment wrapper is a remarkable example of efforts to support the durability of the book, achieved by using plenty of parchment.

As well as these practical protective benefits, limp covers were relatively cheap and easy options. Across a range of forms, wrappers were not only relatively low in cost but also straightforward to produce – elegant in design. Even with 'optional extras' such as stitching, turn-ins, layers, flaps, or even decoration, limp parchment bindings were still cheaper, quicker and demanded fewer production skills than books with boards. These features made them a feasible option in a range of milieux. Amateur book production, which was an important part of book production in the fifteenth century, may well have had a significant role to play in the creation of many limp bindings. Even when these covers were made by more experienced binders or their apprentices, basic wrappers could be dashed off relatively quickly. Therefore, it was the simplicity of the processes, short amount of time, and low effort required to make limp bindings that made them such an expedient way to effectively protect a book.

As these case studies have shown, limp covers were not just used as cheaper, practical alternatives to bindings with boards. In addition to being functional, they could be decorative in their own right, dyed, tooled, or marked up in carefully executed handwriting. These features, among other less showy efforts to improve a book's chance of survival, such as multiple layers, imply a hope for longevity. As noted in the introduction, Monica Langwe's study of limp bindings in the Vatican Library emphasised the importance of conservation as a process of extending use in the medieval period.[153] Wrappers indicate that books were prepared with both everyday use and with long-term protection in mind. They were an attractive, sustainable option: not only could they be made in a sustainable way, in the sense of being made from recycled or salvaged materials, where they lasted they also promoted the sustainability of a whole book. Ultimately, even apparently frivolous details could prove functional: the aesthetic qualities of some limp covers may well have improved their chances of survival.

Palimpsests

Salvaging larger pieces of material to make a wrapper or flyleaf, or slicing it up into small strips, is relatively easy to do, but making reclaimed resources available for re-use can involve substantially more effort. This is certainly true of palimpsests. Palimpsests are pieces of parchment that bore writing which was effaced to make way – usually but not always – for a second campaign of writing. The term for this phenomenon derives from

---

[153] Langwe, *Vatican Library*, p. 21.

the Greek *palimpsestos*, meaning 'scraped or rubbed away again'.[154] In theory, if the specific piece of parchment was resilient enough to withstand it, it is possible to undertake multiple campaigns of scraping or washing and writing.[155] However many times parchment is palimpsested, it may be scarcely visible that the surface has been scraped down and re-used to the naked eye. The near imperceptibility of most palimpsests – slight scored marks and faint ink residue – signals the sheer effort taken to remove text. Palimpsests therefore represent an active and effortful choice to recycle material. Parchment that had been written on could have been repurposed relatively easily with little further effort, for ephemeral domestic purposes such as polishing, or in other ways in the production or maintenance of books as limp covers, flyleaves or wrappers (as this chapter has shown so far). In contrast with these relatively straightforward book structures, palimpsests represent more concerted resourcefulness.

Palimpsests are generally thought to be rare in fifteenth-century books. Scholarship of palimpsests focusses on a much earlier period, and is mainly concerned with the literary outputs of the early Church, and medieval Byzantine and Greek book production. It is often suggested that there is a great quantity of palimpsest material in these contexts.[156] Manuscripts of this earlier period have been subject to sustained treasure-seeking scholarship, with well known successes such as the discovery of the 'Archimedes palimpsest', which exists in only one copy as a palimpsest undertext.[157] There have been unfortunate failures too, such as manuscripts rendered illegible by nineteenth-century scholars who applied damaging chemicals, such as hydrochloric acid and potassium cyanide, in order to reveal palimpsest undertexts. Nowadays, raked light, UV light, x-ray fluorescence, colour space analysis, and multi-spectral imaging techniques are utilised to glimpse what lies beneath.[158] In her concluding remarks to a study of early medieval palimpsests, Rosamund McKitterick suggests that the 'most striking feature of palimpsests [...] is the paradox that they represent evidence preserved by destruction'.[159] That act of destruction is the focus

---

[154] OED, *palimpsest*, n., adj., etymology.

[155] Beal notes that good quality parchment can be used up to three times, in *Dictionary*, p. 279.

[156] G. Declercq counters this, warning that 'between [the years] 400 and 800 [...] often considered to be the heyday of the practice, the amount of palimpsesting should not be overestimated', in 'Introduction: Codices Rescripti in the Early Medieval West', in *Early Medieval Palimpsests*, ed. G. Declercq, *Bibliologia* 26 (Turnhout, 2007), 7–22 (p. 12).

[157] For more information, see the Archimedes Project, 'Archimedes Palimpsest', online <http://www.archimedespalimpsest.org/>; *The Archimedes Palimpsest: Catalogue and Commentary*, ed. R. Netz, W. Noel, N. Tchernetska, N. Wilson (Cambridge, 2011).

[158] C. Duffy, 'The Discovery of a Watermark on the St Cuthbert's Gospel using Colour Space Analysis', *Electronic British Library Journal* 2 (2014), 1–14, online <http://www.bl.uk/eblj/2014articles/article2.html>; again, see <http://www.archimedespalimpsest.org/> for more on the ground-breaking techniques used in that project.

[159] R. McKitterick, 'Palimpsests: Concluding Remarks', in *Early Palimpsests*, ed. Declercq, pp. 145–51 (p. 145).

here.¹⁶⁰ While these fragmentary snippets of all-but-lost texts are remarkable, and their hidden texts worthy of scholarly attention, there are other striking things about palimpsests too: *how* were they re-used? At moment of making a palimpsest, why did the value lie not in texts but in the materials on which they were written?

Scribes relied on penknives for removing mistakes.¹⁶¹ These tools were always to hand, and scribal portraits often show a quill in one hand and a penknife in the other. Kathleen Scott characterises the penknife as indispensable to scribal practice, as it was used to 'scrape away blemishes such as ink blots, to hold a page down during writing and to sharpen the pen' as well as to 'remove errors in copying'.¹⁶² With this knife, the topmost, ink-marked layer of parchment could be scraped away. This could be a fiddly job, especially with fine, thin parchment. Whatever the quality of the parchment, scraping it risked strewing scars across the surface, creating thin or rough patches, and even – when the knife slipped – holes that went right through. A series of regular inch-long slits cut into the parchment, as if someone has repeatedly tested their penknife, can be seen on a leaf in a Missal of Hereford use.¹⁶³ Furthermore, parchment scraped until it was so fragile that it disintegrated can be seen in a fifteenth-century copy of *The Prick of Conscience*, which features a number of other more successfully palimpsested leaves.¹⁶⁴ Penknives were one way, if effortful, to remove ink from parchment.

Scraping with a knife was not the only way to remove ink, and text-bearing parchment could also be ground down by repeating the final stage of production: polishing with pumice. Both the scraping and smoothing processes of parchment preparation are depicted in a fourteenth-century Italian illustration, which suggests these processes may have been undertaken in a workshop.¹⁶⁵ In addition to these mechanical palimpsesting techniques, the removal of ink could be achieved by washing. This method is considered more likely for second (or third) effacements of ink, when scraping parchment is increasingly risky.¹⁶⁶ Rather than mechanically removing the upper surface, washing involves the application of powerful chemical

---

¹⁶⁰ For my previous work on this idea, see Ryley, 'Constructive Destruction'.

¹⁶¹ For more on tools used by scribes, see Whalley, *Writing Implements*; *Pen in Hand: Medieval Scribal Portraits, Colophons and Tools*, ed. M. Gullick (Walkern, 2006).

¹⁶² K. Scott, 'Representations of Scribal Activity in English Manuscripts, c. 1400–1490: A Mirror of the Craft?', in *Pen in Hand*, ed. Gullick, pp. 115–50 (p. 132).

¹⁶³ Worcester Cathedral Library, MS F.161, although this manuscript does not contain palimpsested leaves, there is an unusual example of 'knife-trial' cuts on fols. 230, 234; Thomson, *Worcester Catalogue*, p. 110. Compare, for example, the geometric shapes sliced into a copy of Gower's *Confessio Amantis*, mentioned in Chapter 3, in BodL, MS Laud misc.609, fols. 79, 119; *Quarto Catalogue* II, 432.

¹⁶⁴ BodL, MS Rawl. C.35, fol. 28; *Quarto Catalogue* V.ii, 11.

¹⁶⁵ Bologna, Biblioteca Universitaria, MS 1456, fol. 4r; O. Da Rold, 'Materials', in *PBE*, pp. 12–33, fig. 1.1 at pp. 17–18; C. de Hamel, *Medieval Craftsmen: Scribes and Illuminators* (London, 1992), fig. 3 at p. 9.

¹⁶⁶ Declercq notes that 'it is generally agreed amongst scholars that in most cases the parchment was not subjected to a second scraping but rather [...] washing', 'Introduction', pp. 7–8.

concoctions, including ingredients such as unslaked lime, vitriol, or alum. The codicological recipe collections discussed in Chapter 1 include recipes for stanchgrain and glass bread as alternatives to pumice. However, those collections also included a recipe for palimpsesting parchment entitled: 'To done away what is ywreten in velym or parchement with out any pomyce'.[167] This recommends mixing 'rewe' and 'nettyl' into an unguent with 'chese mylke of a kow or of shepe', and letting it dry to a powder. To remove the letters, the parchment should be wetted and the powder cast over it, 'and with þi nail þou maist done awey þe lettres'. Although chemical erasure took time and effort, as well as resources and know-how, these recipes demonstrate that in the fifteenth century there were known techniques for chemically palimpsesting text-bearing parchment for re-use.

Recipes sometimes also state that the erasure is for the express purpose of writing again on the parchment.[168] And the conventional understanding of palimpsests usually incorporates this idea – that parchment was recycled to provide writing supports for a fresh writing campaign. Palimpsests of this kind can be found in a copy of Chaucer's *Treatise on the Astrolabe*, among other scientific tracts. At least six leaves are palimpsests: the only signs are rows of translucent pale green blobs underlying the Chaucerian text.[169] At first glance, it is difficult to decipher the information these folios present to the viewer. With close observation, the blotchy green-grey marks come into focus. M. C. Seymour has proposed that the leaves were 'possibly cut down from an abandoned or rejected antiphonal leaf or practice sheet of demi-vinets'.[170] Not only has this probable musical notation been almost entirely erased, but also the bifolium has been reoriented. The leaf was previously much larger, and was then turned sideways, folded, and re-used as two leaves. As a result, the staves now run vertically in the current orientation, lying crossways beneath newer handwriting. So, while in this case the musical notation has been largely destroyed, the parchment substrate has been preserved and transformed for re-use.

Numerous instances of palimpsest material can be found in the previously mentioned copy of *The Prick of Conscience*.[171] The re-used parchment is identifiable by some typical indicators of palimpsests, such as ruling schemes that do not correlate with the upper text, and traces of earlier writing which are now oriented crossways or upside down. Over fifty folios out of a total of 118 can be identified as palimpsests, though some are more visible than others.[172] In context, the non-palimpsest leaves demonstrate the generally var-

---

[167] BL, MS Sloane 1313, fol. 126v; Clarke, *Crafte*, p. 307.

[168] A recipe for stanchgrain includes detail for how to 'amende thy parchment and make hyt to [re]sseyve inke', Clarke, *Crafte*, p. 80.

[169] SJC, MS E.2, fols. 5–6, 12–13, 14, 17.

[170] Seymour, *Chaucer Catalogue* I, 118.

[171] BodL, MS Rawl. C.35; I am grateful to Daniel Sawyer for mentioning this example to me; see D. Sawyer, *Reading English Verse in Manuscript c.1350–1500* (Oxford, 2020), p. 98; see also Wakelin, *Designing English*, pp. 38–40.

[172] BodL, MS Rawl. C.35 palimpsest leaves: fols. 28r–v, 42–43, 49r, 51v, 52r, 55–56, 57r and 60v, 61–62, 64r and 69v, 66–67, 69r (and probably its partner 63, but this is not verifiable), fols. 70,

iable quality of parchment used in this book, with erratic thickness and some lacunae at the edges of folios.[173] There are a few different sources of palimpsest material, which can be distinguished from one another by several hands and inks, hazily visible beneath the new text. The sources include undertexts characterised by black ink, liturgical textura with musical notation (which will be discussed further), drypoint ruling on yellow parchment with some Latin text in brown ink, a darker brown ink in a different hand, and perhaps one more source, though it is less distinct, probably black ink in another hand. This manuscript, then, provides generous evidence for how and why palimpsests were used to make fifteenth-century English books.

In addition to this picture of variable quality and multiple sources of palimpsest material, a remarkable feature of this book is that towards the end of the manuscript one of the undertexts becomes conspicuously visible. This increasingly visible undertext is the liturgical black ink textura, which often features musical notation and red ink ruling. Several of these folios feature sections of unscraped text and notation (see Figure 9).[174] The final folio was bound in upside down, and the undertext still looks intact – it appears not to have been erased at all, comprising readings selected from Isaiah 11: 3–5 in the Vulgate Bible legible on the recto.[175] This suggests the possibility of what scraping there is elsewhere in the book having taken place after folding, as needed during the copying process. Its cognate, in contrast, was scraped down into holes.[176] This final folio forms part of an otherwise normal bifolium enfolding a quire, yet because it remains unscraped and was never re-used for more writing, it effectively acts as a protective flyleaf. This might sound fanciful, that scraping was undertaken on demand as the project proceeded. Legible traces of undertext can always be explained away as lacklustre scraping. However, upon close examination, there is a pattern: on scraped leaves, the most intact undertext is typically present in upper and lower margins, towards the fore-edge, and in the gutter crease, confirming the idea that the scraping was undertaken to fulfil only what was required for the new text.

This liturgical undertext is much used in the manuscript, and the source of all this palimpsested parchment can be identified. From some of the more legible scraps of writing, taken in conjunction with the rubricated ruling and the readily readable final folio, this source material was once a service book.[177] This particular source constitutes the majority of the material used for palimpsests in the manuscript, providing at least forty out of the

---

71–78 (Quire X), 79–86 (Quire XI), fols. 87–94 (Quire XII), fols. 95, 97–100 (Quire XIV is missing, but may have been palimpsest in part or whole), fols. 103–10 (Quire XV), and fols. 111–18 (Quire XVI).

[173] BodL, MS Rawl. C.35, lacunae at fols. 21, 75.
[174] BodL, MS Rawl. C.35, remnants of undertext are intact on fols. 104v–06r and fols. 112v–13r.
[175] BodL, MS Rawl. C.35, fol. 118.
[176] BodL, MS Rawl. C.35, fol. 111.
[177] BodL, MS Rawl. C.35, ruling especially visible at fols. 103–10.

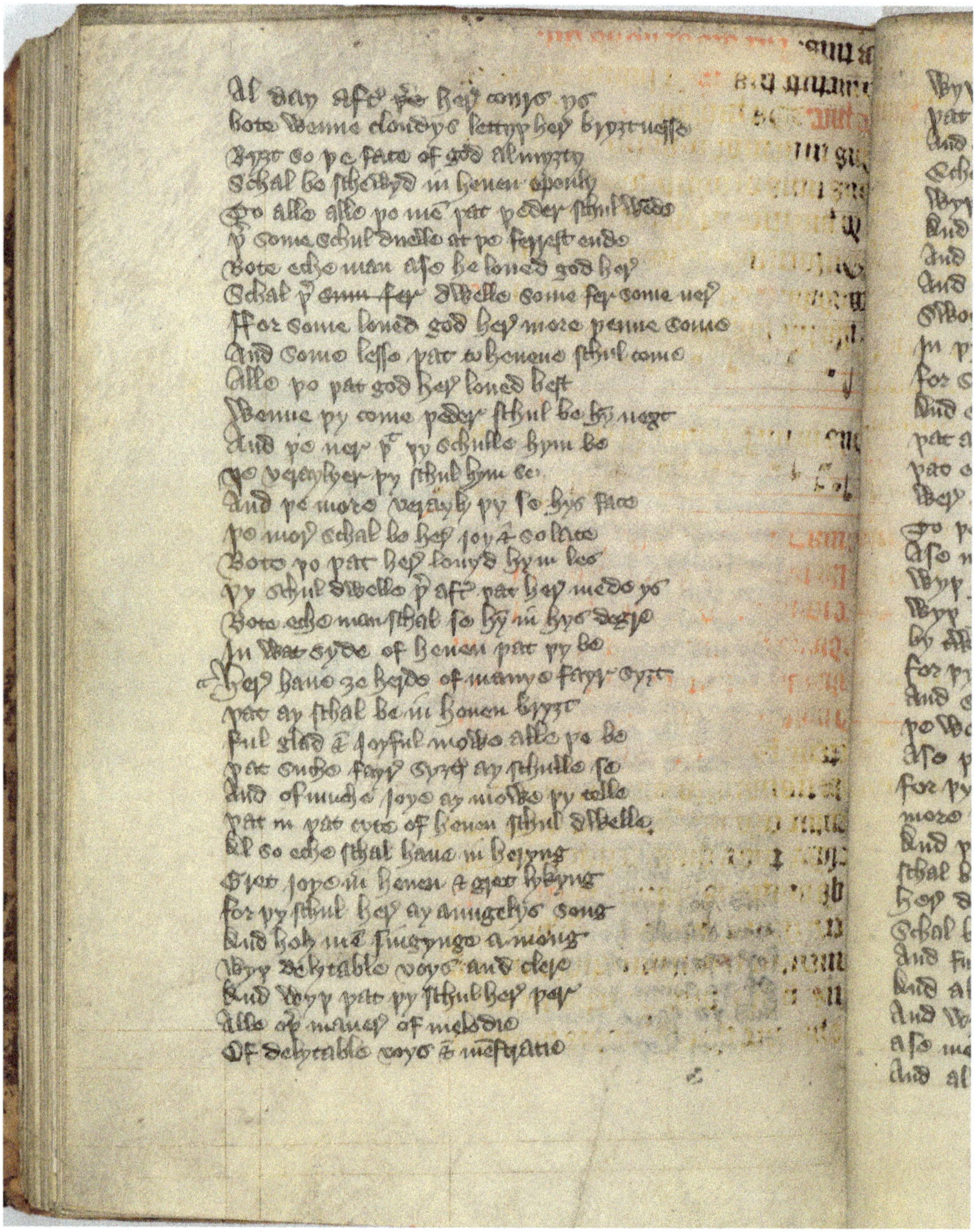

Al day aftyr þe dom comys þys
Bote wenne cloudys lettyþ hem byzt ne ſſo
Ryzt ſo þe face of god almyzty
Schal be ſhewyd in heuen opynly
To alle alſo þo men þat þeder ſchul wende
Y-come eche vn-elle at þe feyest ende
Bote eche man aſo he loueþ god hey
Schal y-ſenn hey dwelle come fey ſome neyʒ
For ſome loueþ god hey more þenne come
And ſome leſſe þat to heuene ſhul come
Alſo þo þat god hey loued beſt
Wenne þy come þedyr ſchul be þy neʒe
And þo neyʒ þ þy ſchulle hym be
To ueyþer þy ſchul hym ſe
And þe more veyaſh þy ſo hys face
Þe moʒ ſchal be hey ioye & ſolace
Bote þo þat hey louyd hym les
Þy ſchul dwelle þ aftyr þat hey mede ys
Bote eche man ſhal ſo hy in hys deʒre
In þat ſyde of heuen þat þy be
Hey haue ʒe kyde of manye fayr ſyʒt
Þer ay ſhal be in heuen byʒt
Ful glad & ioyful motte alle þo be
Þat endeleſ fayr ſyʒt ay ſchulle ſe
And of much ioye ay more þy telle
Þat in þat eyte of heuen ſchul dwelle
Al ſo eche ſhal haue in beyng
Gret ioye in heuen & gret likyng
For þy ſchul hey ay aungelys ſong
And hok mʒ ſweyngs a-mong
Þyʒ delytable voyſ and clere
And ſoyʒ þat þy ſchul hey þer
Alſo of manyʒ of melodie
Of delytable voyʒ & meſtralſie

Figure 9. BodL, MS Rawl. C.35, fols. 112v-113r, palimpsest and glimpse of undertext.

fifty identifiable palimpsest leaves.[178] What the layout of visible undertext in the margins suggests is that the palimpsest-makers were keenly aware of the spatial requirements for the new campaign of writing (again, see Figure 9).[179] That is, they knew the essential space needed for the new text, and knew exactly where on the page that area would fall. Therefore, they could tailor the preparation of the parchment accordingly, expending energy on only the most necessary scraping. It seems likely to me that this precise preparation of writing-space for the new text, bounded by such overt evidence of the old undertext, was achieved with design and efficiency in mind.

Notably, palimpsest material is re-used predominantly in the second half of this manuscript, where palimpsests become increasingly discernible, with less thoroughly scraped text. In general, the end of the manuscript gives an impression of more noticeable, legible undertexts, culminating in the intact undertext on the final leaf. Quires X–XVI are composed almost entirely of palimpsested parchment (Quire XIII is mostly but not wholly palimpsest and Quire XIV is missing).[180] Perhaps, as may be the case with some off-cuts too, makers hoped to hide away recognisably salvaged material towards the back of the book? Here, such scrappy material might be overlooked, while the aims of a new writing campaign and a new text could still be fulfilled. Or, maybe, assuming the writing of the main text was executed from front to back in chronological order, it was expedient to resort to palimpsested parchment towards the end of the book's production. A final possible reason for this distribution is that it was not only expedient but also necessary to use palimpsests as and when resources were constrained.

In contrast with these inconsistently scraped palimpsests, another fifteenth-century English manuscript, BodL, MS Ashmole 52, a copy of the same text, is comprised of exceptionally carefully executed palimpsests. On four leaves of this copy of *The Prick of Conscience*, three lines of text were assiduously scraped away from the upper margin.[181] It is quite possible that the whole manuscript was made with scraped material from the same source, and Daniel Sawyer tentatively suggests that it is 'formed from the bottom parts of single folios from a much larger and possibly liturgical manuscript, in which the text was copied in textura with a large module'[182] Overall, the book is well-produced with neat trimming. This is a very different scenario to the many palimpsests and highly variable parchment used in the copy of this text just discussed (BodL, MS Rawl. C.35). Rather, in this production, the use of palimpsests is almost surprising, given the apparently careful

---

[178] BodL, MS Rawl. C.35, Quires X, XI, XII, XV and XVI are wholly made of this material. There may be further leaves used elsewhere in the manuscript, however, these are not securely identifiable.

[179] BodL, MS Rawl. C.35, see fols. 104v–05r and 105v–06r.

[180] BodL, MS Rawl. C.35, preceding Quire X, Quires VI to IX also include a substantial number of palimpsests.

[181] BodL, MS Ashmole 52, fols. 27–30, 35–38, at fols. 27v–29r; *Quarto Catalogue* X, 91; with thanks to Daniel Sawyer for mentioning this manuscript to me.

[182] Sawyer, *Reading English Verse*, p. 98, and notes that the minim height measures 4–5mm, in n.54.

execution and general quality of the book. However, in the context of such a well-presented book, such diligent scraping might make sense as part of the plan for the design of the manuscript. Perhaps this manuscript used up material left over from an abandoned project? Whatever the source of this thoroughly scraped undertext, the emphasis in this instance of parchment recycling is more firmly on the look of the final production than the previous examples – however much effort this took.

Whether palimpsests were made carefully or inconsistently, why did people make them at all? Peter Beal confidently asserts that medieval palimpsests 'resulted […] from the high cost of parchment, which made its re-use or recycling a matter of practical economy'.[183] Certainly, practical economy is a vital motivation for many kinds of recycling, including palimpsesting. However, a consideration of the broader picture of manuscript production enables a more nuanced conclusion. After all, cheapness is not an absolute, it can only ever be relative. Palimpsests were likely a cheaper resource than new parchment, but with the craftsmanship, tools, material, know-how, labour, willingness and time required to work into parchment again in this way, they cannot objectively be described as cheap material.[184] Sparingly scraped palimpsests confirm that this process usually entailed significant effort. So, palimpsests are one of numerous cheaper choices available to book producers, many of which involved recycling.[185] This enabled some people to make books relatively cheaply for their own use, and others to improve their profits. The interaction between money, time, labour-costs and the supply of parchment are essential to understanding why anyone was willing to make a palimpsest.

That expenditure of effort – and so of time and therefore money, however limited – belies suggestions that palimpsesting was always a 'last resort', as McKitterick calls it, or a rough, desperate, even unintentional procedure.[186] On the contrary, some palimpsests were planned with care and some even formed a major campaign of production. A couple of the manuscripts discussed in this chapter strongly suggest, by the quantity and distribution of palimpsests, that the re-use of this material was carefully thought out. The Wycliffite *Rosarium theologie* (mentioned in the previous section) with effaced parchment repurposed as quire guards is a carefully planned and well-executed manuscript in which the palimpsest quire guards conform with the overall look of the book. The few palimpsests used in BodL, MS Ashmole 52 (the second copy of *The Prick of Conscience* discussed in this section) also fit the careful standards of the manuscript as a whole, and may have been left over from an abandoned project. By contrast, BodL, MS Rawl. C.35 (the first copy of *The Prick of Conscience* discussed in this section) with copious palimpsested leaves, may represent a situation in which the producer had to resort to palimpsests; moreover, the limited scraping on many leaves might indicate a time-poor scenario in which the producers were

---

[183] Beal, *Dictionary*, p. 279.

[184] Hadgraft, 'This picture of cheap labour and expensive materials seems to apply to most aspects of book production from the scribe to the illuminator to the bookbinder', 'Book Structures', p. 41.

[185] Kwakkel, 'Discarded Parchment', pp. 238–61.

[186] McKitterick, 'Palimpsests', p. 147.

rushing to finish the book. However, this manuscript may just as well suggest a campaign of production that depended financially upon palimpsests for its completion. Therefore, taken collectively these examples of palimpsests demonstrate that some fifteenth-century book producers actively chose to use these recycled materials, and not just as a last resort.

Conclusions

This chapter explores a wide range of parchment recycling. Rare texts on manuscript fragments are a customary focus of recycling scholarship, however, instead this chapter concentrates on physical features of parchment re-used in books. Parchment recycling is made possible by its particular material qualities: resilience, pliability, high-tearing strength, resistance to rubbing, and long-term stability when kept dry. Book producers understood how to salvage parchment, and how much effort it might take to repurpose parchment for various functions in books. Many of the processes of re-use explored in this chapter required limited skill or labour. However, limp bindings and palimpsests likely took more time and effort than off-cuts or reinforcing strips. Therefore, these examples of book-material re-uses are part of an equation which strikes a balance between necessity, resource availability, frugality, profit-margins, the relative cheapness of labour, and the time and effort taken to recycle parchment. The ramifications of this balancing act are different for each and every manuscript.

3

Making Marks On Books

Surviving markings on books testify to manuscript durability and to the rich potential of books for re-use as writing supports. The marks depicted in Figure 10 are clustered together on the final flyleaf in a collection of religious works by 'Jon þe blynde Awdelay' dating from the second quarter of the fifteenth century.¹ There are two upside-down doodles of faces, calligraphic flourish practice, the name 'John' scrawled twice, floating letters and squiggles, and various lines of writing in Latin and English, including a late fifteenth-century rhyme about a licentious friar named Andrew.² As this busily re-used medieval flyleaf suggests, various kinds of written and drawn re-uses took place on the manuscript page. Medieval manuscript markings could take diverse forms and serve diverse purposes. These markings were not always and not only idle space-fillers, as this chapter will show. Such markings are remarkably common survivals from the long history of human mark-making.

This chapter focuses on how the book is re-used as an object for writing on. This study assumes the conventional use of books to be as carriers of a main text, used primarily for reading and responding to that text. Throughout this chapter I employ the words *use* and *re-use* in the senses explored by William H. Sherman, who invokes a language of 'use' around books, rather than the language of 'reading'.³ Accordingly, this chapter also passes over the standard use of margins, that is, those markings that engage with and complement the main text, usually referred to as marginalia. Marks in margins have been described eloquently as 'the human presence' in books, but also as 'a farrago of abstrusities, [...] human baggage weighing down the books on our stacks'.⁴ This chapter privileges particularly 'abstruse' re-uses of marginal space.

---

[1] BodL, MS Douce 302, fol. 35v; 'John Audelay the blind' is named in the colophon ('Audelay's Epilogue') and is named repeatedly elsewhere in this manuscript; *DIMEV* 3698; S. Fein notes that it is on fol. 34ra–b in *John the Blind Audelay: Poems and Carols (Oxford, Bodleian Library, MS Douce 302)* (Kalamazoo, 2009), p. 1.

[2] BodL, MS Douce 302, fol. 35v, my description; quote from *Summary Catalogue* IV, 585; Fein writes that fol. 35v 'looks like an original outside cover' in *John the Blind Audelay*, p. 338; the manuscript measures 270 × 200 mm; further details of the main texts in *IMEP* IV, 70–71 and *DIMEV* (61 entries).

[3] W. H. Sherman, *Used Books: Marking Readers in Renaissance England* (Philadelphia, 2008), pp. xiii, 4.

[4] D. F. McKenzie, *Bibliography and the Sociology of Texts*, The Panizzi Lectures (Cambridge, 1999), p. 29; R. E. Stoddard, 'Looking at Marks in Books', *The Gazette of the Grolier Club* n.s. 51 (2000), 27–47 (p. 41).

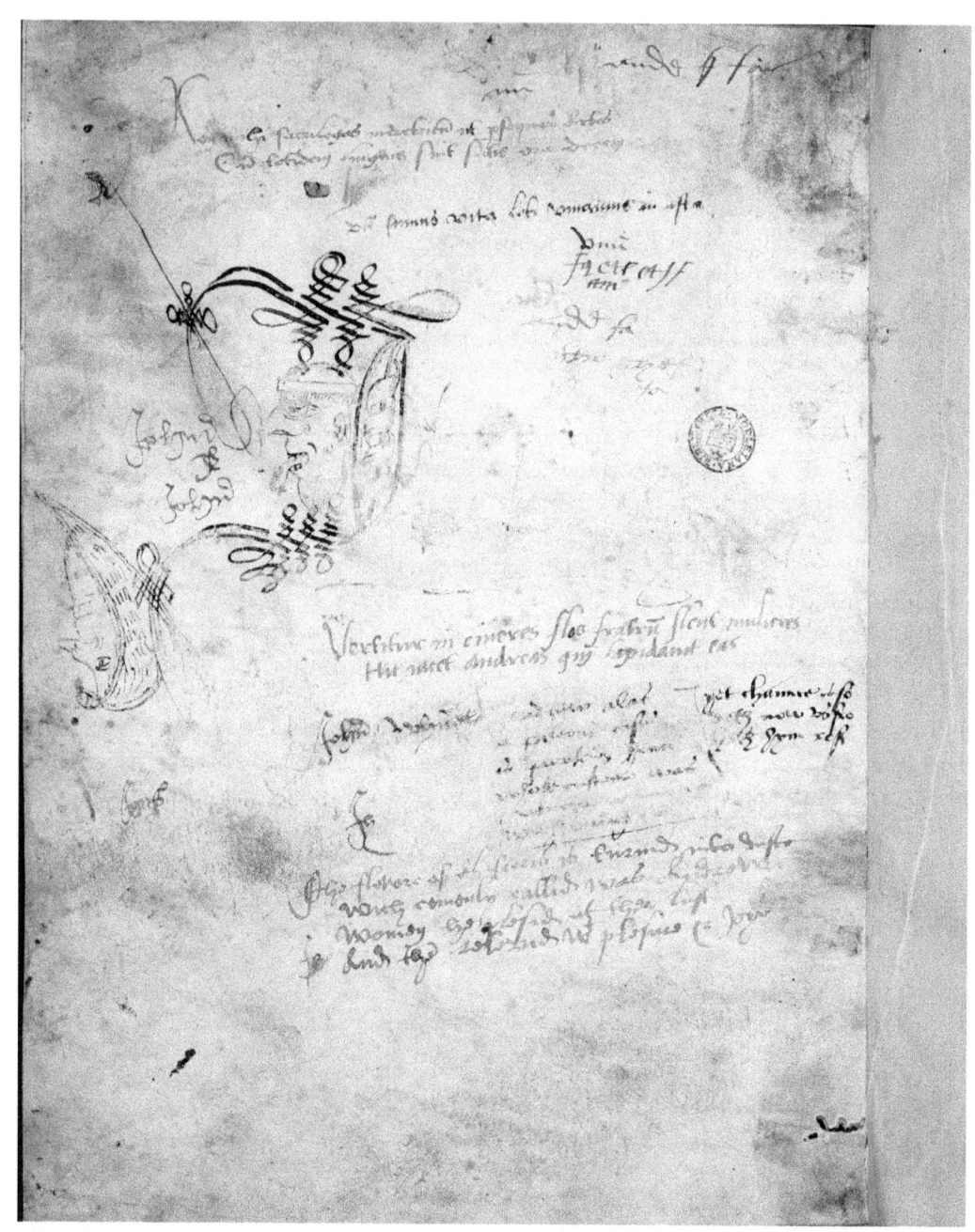

Figure 10. BodL, MS Douce 302, fol. 35v, markings on a back flyleaf.

Abstruse marginalia are part of a long history of mark-making and are found throughout the ages in books and on other surfaces. From rock art, inscribed clay tablets, papyrus scrolls and stones, to contemporary graffiti art, humans have made marks on the materials and things that they find in the environment around themselves. The habit of marking books of course continues to this day, and the popular fascination with marginalia has gained currency.[5] This chapter investigates a wide-ranging variety of non-verbal and verbal marks in fifteenth-century books. It is generally difficult to capture exactly how or why people made these marks. However, possible methods and motivations are explored here, as well as the literacies and layouts that inform the ways in which people went on to make marks in books. Both non-verbal and verbal markings are present on the last flyleaf of John Audelay's poetry collection and this thought-provoking case study clusters together a range of characteristic markings found in the marginal spaces of medieval manuscripts. As this example suggests, this chapter explores book re-use in the form of doodles, squiggles, written letterforms, names, and short phrases.

So far, this study has revealed shifts in the use-values attributed to books and their materials. The use-value of animal skins was transformed through human agency and craftsmanship into parchment available for use as a writing support (as explored in Chapter 1). Skins were useful for many other things in fifteenth-century culture, such as making glue, leather, and other goods. People could choose to improve the durability of parchment in a range of ways, and to avoid waste. While people protected and repaired their books, and put them to predictable uses, such as reading, there are also abundant re-uses of books that are perhaps more surprising. The use-value of parchment as a writing support was sometimes usurped by its use-value as a protective or practical material for other bookmaking purposes, recycled as reinforcing strips, quire guards, flyleaves, pastedowns, and palimpsests.[6]

Further change in use-values took place when manuscripts were re-used in the fifteenth century as supports for mark-making. There were of course other things that people made marks on, and there were other re-uses of books, too, which could be destructive or transformative in different ways, but the focus here is on the re-use of fifteenth-century books for further instances of writing, drawing, and other forms of mark-making, beyond the original scribe or scribes. The value of books as re-usable supports therefore draws on the same use-values of parchment that made it so appropriate and desirable for book production in the first place: it is a good, durable surface for mark-making. And, although writing into books is not directly equivalent to writing on loose pieces of scrap parchment, the evidence suggests a similar mentality behind both kinds of re-use: convenience and the avoidance of waste. It is this enduring durability and re-usability that made books a common location for many kinds of mark-making.

The varied forms of marks made in books reflect the fact that the fifteenth century was a period of mixed literacy. The idea of literacy today tends to conflate the skills of reading

---

[5] M. O'Connell, 'The Marginal Obsession with Marginalia', *The New Yorker*, 26 January 2012 <http://www.newyorker.com/books/page-turner/the-marginal-obsession-with-marginalia>.

[6] As discussed in Chapter 2.

and writing. But medieval literacies were spoken, visual, aural, and written, and varied widely across a growing and changing society.[7] For many in the medieval period, the ability to recognise or repeat the words of familiar prayers was the main aim of acquiring even a limited ability to read.[8] Reading in the late medieval period need not have had a textual basis for all, and Joyce Coleman has emphasised the importance of orality as a mode of literacy in late medieval England and France.[9] On the other hand, Malcolm Richardson has shown that middle-class professional experience of written material in the fifteenth century was widespread, and that pragmatic literacy was more common than previously appreciated.[10] Furthermore, in addition to this nuanced understanding of access to texts, the 'ability to write' and the 'ability to compose and comprehend' are skills that should be distinguished from one another.[11] Interactions with books ranged from visual or oral experiences of the text, through to a fully developed synthesis of reading and writing ability, a spectrum of literacy that will be demonstrated by case studies of re-uses in this chapter.[12] Given this range of literacies, it is not surprising to find that in the fifteenth century there were people taking up pens to write or draw in books, and that they made use of marginal spaces of various shapes and sizes in different ways.

The mark-making activities that medieval book users undertook were diverse, and included scribbling, doodling, drawing, and writing. One kind of well-attested and studied marginalia takes the form of annotations written into the margins around the main text space. However, here I am not seeking out instances of engaged reading or intellectual commentary on the main text; instead, my focus is upon re-uses that recycle the manuscript as a writing support in other ways. While evidence of engaged reading does intersect with some of the following re-uses of books, and this is acknowledged where it occurs, I focus upon habits of re-use which generally disregard the original use of the book to carry a text. For instance, this chapter considers case studies of scribbled lines, simple patterns and doodles of faces and flowers, as well as writing that takes the form of familiar combinations of letters, such as alphabets and signatures, and useful or popular combinations of words, such as recipes and short verses. So, the kinds of written marginalia explored here are not necessarily or

---

[7] B. Stock has explored the interdependence of oral and textual cultures in earlier centuries in *The Implications of Literacy: Written Language and Models of Interpretation in the Eleventh and Twelfth Centuries* (New Jersey, 1983), pp. 1–11.

[8] In his study of orality and developing literacy during an earlier period, M. Clanchy states that 'More people could read than write', *From Memory to Written Record: 1066–1307* 3rd edn (Oxford, 2013), pp. 1–20 (p. 13).

[9] J. Coleman, *Public Reading and the Reading Public in Late Medieval England and France* (Cambridge, 1996).

[10] M. Richardson, *Middle-Class Writing in Late Medieval London* (London, 2011).

[11] M. J. Carruthers, *The Book of Memory: A Study of Memory in Medieval Culture* (Cambridge, 2008), p. 11.

[12] H. J. Jackson rightly cautions, 'Annotators are readers who write. Annotation combines – synthesizes, I should say – the functions of reading and writing', in *Marginalia: Readers Writing in Books* (Toronto, 2001), p. 90.

primarily activated by or engaged with the main text of the book, and include 'opportunistic' markings inspired by a range of motivations and with a variety of purposes.[13]

To give a sense of the flavour and diversity of these opportunistic markings, this chapter surveys a wide range of manuscripts. The books selected for study are mostly vernacular texts, whether prose or poetry, and some contain texts in a mix of languages. As with all chapters in this book, the manuscripts under discussion here are all dated or datable to the long fifteenth century. These manuscripts were made to varying production values: they come in different shapes, sizes and scripts, and were adorned with differing decorative strategies. The following examples of mark-making in books are drawn from the Douce and Laudian collections in the Bodleian Library, Oxford, with additional selected examples from elsewhere for comparison or contrast. Most importantly for the purposes of this chapter, the Douce collection 'constitute[s] a representative sample of books read by a wide cross section of English society during the fifteenth century'. Although Douce did not collect his books with the aim of achieving such representation, 'by fortunate chance his random acquisitions provide [...] a microcosm of nearly every type of Middle English prose from this period'.[14] Of the relevant fifteenth-century manuscripts in these collections that contain some English, the most interesting examples or the best comparisons were picked for focussed close analysis.

Arguably, because marks are abundant in many late medieval manuscripts, approaching these collections with almost any selection strategy would have provided plentiful examples of opportunistic book re-use in the form of mark-making in marginal spaces. After all, as discussed in the introduction to this study, in the fifteenth century there was a widespread culture of writing on things. Books were also open to re-use in this way and the marginal spaces in these books were no exception. Casual writing supports were not necessarily easily or widely available and many people existed in resource-poor environments, so it makes sense that some of the functional, practical jottings of day-to-day life were made on the material that was to hand in some households, such as books. Marks in books might be usefully compared with those made on scraps such as off-cuts, loose leaves, or those inscribed into notebooks. Scraps were often used for drafts, letters, or for other practical notes: scrap parchment could be more mobile and more transient than parchment in notebooks or books. Normally, but not always, books provided relatively non-mobile surfaces for writing, and could act as stable repositories for mark-making. As will be seen in examples from the Douce and Laudian collections, readers, owners and other mark-makers were willing to treat the margins of books as jotters, and not only for practical notes to aid memory, but also for testing their pens and an array of other everyday purposes.

---

[13] P. Hardman, in defining her own rather different focus, has expressed the re-use I am concerned with here as 'opportunistic use of blank writing space for new purposes', in 'Domestic Learning and Teaching: Investigating Evidence for the Role of "Household Miscellanies" in Late-Medieval England', in *Women and Writing c.1340–c.1650: The Domestication of Print Culture*, ed. A. Lawrence-Mathers and P. Hardman (York, 2010), pp. 15–33 (p. 18).

[14] *IMEP* IV, xi.

Thus, the first section of this chapter explores occasions when books were treated as if they were like scrap parchment or paper, notebooks, or wax tablets, which were used for everyday purposes such as drafting or practising writing. Wax tablets were used as the primary tool for learning to write, or for working out personal or literary texts, as well as for teaching and composition throughout the Middle Ages.[15] The basic model of a wax tablet consisted of a wooden frame, which would have been filled with wax and the surface smoothed.[16] A stylus was then used to impress letters or markings onto the surface. Although occasionally marks were impressed onto the surface of parchment, using a stylus on wax is of course a different skill to writing with pen and ink and requires the writer to push the tool quite firmly into the surface of the wax. However, the transience associated with using wax tablets – which could be quickly smoothed over or warmed over a flame to erase the scratched-in writing – meant that it was thought of as a place for practice, for exploring ideas and for composition, with a 'necessarily ephemeral' quality.[17] It was an important tool for students to develop their writing with impunity. The marginal spaces of books were convenient for similar writing practice of this sort.

Studies of marginalia

Marginalia in books are the subject of a long-established field of study. However, the focus in this chapter represents a turn from usual studies of marginalia. Hitherto, studies have tended to prioritise marginal writing or images which are related to the text in some way; the goal is often to track reading, or other traces of intellectual interaction. For example, the art historian Michael Camille and others following him take as their focus the dialogic relationship between the book's main text and its marginal material, especially where that relationship freewheels into carnivalesque grotesques and other more provocative domains of illumination.[18] Research is usually devoted to more polished or prepared writing – and, in Camille's case, imagery – found in the margins of medieval books. Further examples of marginalia studies include Kathryn Kerby-Fulton's vital work on scribes as professional readers, Jane Griffiths' work on experimental practices of glossing, and the work of

---

[15] R. H. Rouse and M. A. Rouse, 'The Vocabulary of Wax Tablets', in *Vocabulaire du livre et de l'écriture au Moyen Age: Actes de la table ronde, Paris 24–26 septembre 1987*, ed. O. Weijers (Turnhout, 1989), pp. 220–30 (p. 220).

[16] J. I. Whalley, *Writing Implements and Accessories from the Roman Stylus to the Typewriter* (London, 1975), p. 12.

[17] R. Chartier, *Inscription and Erasure: Written Culture from the Eleventh to the Eighteenth Century*, trans. A. Goldhammer (Philadelphia, 2007), p. 4.

[18] M. Camille, *Image on the Edge: The Margins of Medieval Art* (London, 1992); the seminal importance of Camille's work is summed up by S. L. Keefer and R. H. Bremmer Jr., 'Introduction', in *Signs on the Edge: Space, Text and Margin in Medieval Manuscripts*, ed. S. L. Keefer and R. H. Bremmer Jr., Mediaevalia Groningana n.s. 10 (Leuven, 2007), pp. 3–6 (p. 3).

Christopher Baswell, Maidie Hilmo and Phillip Pulsiano, among many others.[19] Their investigations tend to focus on the relationships between marginalia and the main text. But as Deborah Thorpe has noted, 'pen doodles – neither part of the text nor an elaborate scheme of decoration – can slip through the cracks of codicological scholarship'.[20] It is these 'pen doodles' and other seemingly wayward markings in margins that are the focus of this chapter.

For later periods, there are instructive examples of scholarship that take a broader view. In the context of early modern printed books, and in books from about 1700 to the present, two key studies have considered a much wider range of marks in books. In his work on early modern used books, Sherman characterises the transition of the book from text repository to writing support. As mentioned at the very end of the introduction to this book, he describes books as being involved in a 'dynamic ecology of use and re-use, leading to transformation and destruction as well as to preservation'.[21] This, in a nutshell, expresses how mark-making as re-use is part of the life of manuscripts. These entities are sustainable, yet at the same time always changing, whether at a rapid or slow pace. In her work on readers making marks in books, Heather J. Jackson suggests that the enduring physical features of books, historical development of annotation practice and a range of common motivations give rise to marginalia in books. Books, in Jackson's study, are a 'silent witness' to historical interactions with their texts precisely because they are durable objects.[22] The durability emphasised by Jackson, and the possible outcomes described by Sherman, which may augment the potential of the manuscript by adding new uses and purposes, or lead to mutation or mutilation, underpin my understanding of how manuscripts come to be re-used as supports for more esoteric forms of marginalia.

As Sherman and Jackson have shown, the scholarship that considers intellectually engaged marginalia can be expanded and extended productively and inclusively to consider a much more diverse array of marks in books. Moreover, as Jason Scott-Warren states, such markings are 'not merely [...] evidence of reading but also and more broadly part of

---

[19] *The Medieval Professional Reader at Work: Evidence from Manuscripts of Chaucer, Langland, Kempe, and Gower*, ed. K. Kerby-Fulton and M. Hilmo (Victoria, 2001); J. Griffiths, *Diverting Authorities: Experimental Glossing Practices in Manuscript and Print* (Oxford, 2014); C. Baswell, 'Talking Back to the Text: Marginal Voices in Medieval Secular Literature', in *The Uses of Manuscripts in Literary Studies: Essays in Memory of Judson Boyce Allen*, ed. C. C. Morse, P. R. Doob, and M. C. Woods (Kalamazoo, 1992), pp. 121–160; M. Hilmo, 'The Power of Images in the Auchinleck, Vernon, Pearl, and Two Piers Plowman Manuscripts', in *Opening Up Middle English Manuscripts: Literary and Visual Approaches*, ed. K. Kerby-Fulton, M. Hilmo and L. Olson (Ithaca, 2012), pp. 153–205; P. Pulsiano, 'Jaunts, Jottings and Jetsam in Anglo-Saxon Manuscripts', *Florilegium* 19 (2002), 189–216.

[20] D. E. Thorpe, 'Young Hands, Old Books: Drawings by Children in a Fourteenth-Century Manuscript, LJS MS. 361', *Cogent Arts and Humanities* 3:1 (2016), 1–18 (p. 12).

[21] Sherman, *Used Books*, p. 6; Sherman, 'The Reader's Eye: Between Annotation and Illustration', Keble Medieval and Renaissance Research Cluster, Keble College, Oxford, 8 February 2013.

[22] Jackson, *Marginalia*, p. 100.

what we might call the anthropology of the book'.²³ The notion of the 'anthropology of the book' has deeper roots in book history, and builds on the foundations for a 'sociology of texts' laid down by D. F. McKenzie.²⁴ If the book is considered not only as a repository for literature and a space for intellectual response, but also as an object and artefact with a social history, there is a great deal that it can say about relationships between people and about attitudes towards book materials.²⁵ As part of their concern for the durability and recycling of manuscripts, medieval users reshaped the materials of those objects as a result of reimagining the sustainable uses that they might serve.

The examples of book re-use explored here are marks made in fifteenth-century manuscripts' marginal spaces. But what constitutes a 'marginal space'? There are 'hundreds of thousands of fragmentary written elements that occupy the margins, flyleaves, and textual and interlinear spaces of the medieval page'.²⁶ Sometimes these markings are found in the margins that surround the text block on each page (the conventional location for marginalia engaged with the text) and sometimes on blank, or partly blank leaves, such as flyleaves or pastedowns. Of course, the size and shape of page margins, flyleaves and interlinear spaces vary from one another, as indeed individual instances of page margins differ from other page margins, sometimes even within the same quire or book. As a result, they might invite different kinds of markings. Other odd spaces in manuscripts, for example on interleaved folios or where the main text finishes short of the lower margin, are also re-usable as supports for mark-making.

In many medieval manuscripts, the text area and margins tend to conform to remarkably consistent proportions, where the relative width is between 0.67–0.72, and this tends to be loosely in accord with the Golden Section or Rule.²⁷ Whatever their precise proportions, margins are never central, like the main text, but peripheral and exist in relation to the centre.²⁸ While they do visually define the central text, at the same time, margins

---

²³ J. Scott-Warren, 'Reading Graffiti in the Early Modern Book', *Huntington Library Quarterly* 73 (2010), 363–81 (p. 380).

²⁴ See McKenzie's full development of this idea in *Bibliography and Sociology*.

²⁵ Chapter 4 also explores these relationships between people and their books.

²⁶ J. Dagenais, 'Decolonizing the Medieval Page', in *The Future of the Page*, ed. P. Stoicheff and A. Taylor (London, 2004), pp. 37–70 (p. 39).

²⁷ C. Bozzolo and E. Ornato, *Pour une histoire du livre manuscrit au Moyen Âge: Trois essais de codicologie quantitative* (Paris, 1983), pp. 307–10; J. P. Gumbert, 'The Sizes of Manuscripts: Some Statistics and Notes', in *Hellinga Festschrift / Feestbundel / Mélanges: Forty-Three Studies in Bibliography Presented to Prof. Dr. Wytze Hellinga on the Occasion of his Retirement from the Chair of Neophilology in the University of Amsterdam at the End of the Year 1978* (Amsterdam, 1981), pp. 277–88 (p. 279); J. Tschichold notes that manuscript pages tend to be proportioned 2:3 (width: height), with the 'text area proportioned in the Golden Section', in *The Form of the Book* (London, 1991), p. 45.

²⁸ For more on centre and periphery, see R. Arnheim, *The Power of the Centre: a Study of Composition in the Visual Arts* (Berkeley, 1988).

offer opportunities for 'expansion, contest, subversion' of that text.[29] Even marks which do not comment on or interact intellectually with the main text may nevertheless disturb the *mise-en-page* from their marginal position, by drawing attention away from the centre, either with an occasional isolated doodle or piece of writing that catches the eye, or – at the extreme – with a cluttered, busily re-used margin. In many of the examples that follow, marks in the margins represent a total diversion from the main text. Moreover, the edges of pages are some of the most exposed parts of the structure of the book, as vividly demonstrated by Kathryn Rudy's analysis of dirty books.[30] Margins do not simply designate the outer perimeter of the page. Together, these edges form the bridge between the manuscript and the outer world, or 'the paginal world's encounter with the world of the reader'.[31] The hands of producers, viewers, and readers turn the pages by gripping these borders. Their exposed nature made them accessible for handwriting and other mark-making.

Pastedowns and flyleaves also offer space for re-use of the book as a writing support.[32] Books' physical forms may limit the space available: for example, pastedowns still adhered to boards or limp bindings present only one face of a leaf to write on, whereas flyleaves that can be turned and lifted pastedowns provide two surfaces. In addition, there may be multiple flyleaves one after another in sequence, which present a run of available writing supports in sequence. What is more, once someone opens a book, the front pastedown, flyleaf or flyleaves are the first part of the book to be encountered. If these leaves are relatively blank, then they are also the first available spaces inside the book on which marks can be made. Likewise, at the back of the book there may be pastedowns or flyleaves just as accessible for mark-making; after all, books can be opened from the back as easily as the front, depending on where the user of the book wishes to begin. In whatever ways fifteenth-century people approached these parts of books, pastedowns and flyleaves typically provide more substantial spaces than page margins for mark-making.

An inclusive approach is taken here, and the 'marginal spaces' studied in this chapter encompass a range of available areas in manuscripts, whatever their size or shape. Carl James Grindley corroborates this strategy, and in his own work defines margins liberally and conceptually to include flyleaves, which he describes as 'the *ur*-margins of books', as well as 'blank leaves'.[33] So marginal spaces are understood here in this extended sense to refer not only to marks made in margins, but also those inscribed on pastedowns, flyleaves, and other supplementary or otherwise erstwhile blank spaces found in books.

---

[29] Baswell, 'Talking Back', p. 122.
[30] K. M. Rudy, 'Dirty Books: Quantifying Patterns of Use in Medieval Manuscripts Using a Densitometer', *Journal of Historians of Netherlandish Art* 2:1–2 (2010), 1–26.
[31] Dagenais, 'Decolonizing the Medieval Page', p. 62.
[32] See Chapter 2 for definition and discussion of these book parts.
[33] C. J. Grindley, 'Reading *Piers Plowman* C-Text Annotations: Notes toward the Classification of Printed and Written Marginalia in Texts from the British Isles 1300–1641', in *Professional Reader*, ed. Kerby-Fulton and Hilmo, pp. 73–141 (p. 77).

Physical forms of marginal spaces

As previous chapters have already shown, the re-use of books was influenced by social, economic and religious contexts and considerations. And as the preceding discussion of margins and flyleaves suggests, the physical forms of marginal spaces are highly variable in size and shape. Though there were undoubtedly expectations about how margins bounding the text on each page should look, their size and shape was subject to the availability of parchment, the costliness of that grade of parchment, and to production processes such as trimming. Indeed, the status of a book could be signalled through the size of margins, which were a potentially costly design choice. Luxurious books were a performative symbol of prestige: opulence or significant size tends to signal that a book was intended for use in a public, social arena.[34] However, the large marginal spaces in many large books do not necessarily lead to more or more frequent marginal re-uses than is found in books with smaller margins. While expansive margins can certainly be understood to present some kind of invitation to mark-making, the general pattern in the manuscripts surveyed is that those with larger margins feature less repurposing.

While there were certain expectations of how a manuscript might look, books were made in a wide range of formats, and this affected the shape and size of margins. Book formats ranged from tiny books to *coucher* books, and from lighter girdle or holster books and limp-bound books to chained books bound in heavy wood.[35] With such diverse options available, the choices made by patrons and book producers could profoundly affect the shape and size of marginal spaces. Those purchasing or commissioning a book in the fifteenth century likely had a reasonable range of options to choose from in terms of quality, cost, and size.[36] As suggested by Chapter 1's consideration of parchment production, and Chapter 2's discussion of salvaged parchment recycled in books, many medieval book producers were prepared to make books with damaged, repaired, or otherwise 'imperfect' pieces of parchment. They could offer these options to their patrons. While peculiarly shaped edges or variable surfaces in parchment manuscripts indicate that a range of choices were available, perhaps most attractive to budget-conscious patrons or makers, in turn those choices also affected the shape and size of marginal spaces available for future re-uses of books as writing supports.

The size and design of a book affected its use: very small books with proportionally small margins made writing in those margins extremely difficult. BodL, MS Douce 1 is a mid-fifteenth century manuscript, filled with prayers, hymns and devotional texts,

---

[34] R. Perry, 'The Material Text: Reading, Identity, and the Late Medieval Book', London Medieval Society Colloquium: 'Who Read What in the Middle Ages?', Queen Mary University London (17 November 2012).

[35] *MED*, *couchour*, *n*. Sense 3b 'large service book'; for a good overview, see: R. Clemens and T. Graham, *Introduction to Manuscript Studies* (Ithaca, 2007), pp. 50–61.

[36] A. Gillespie and D. Wakelin, 'Introduction', in *PBE*, pp. 1–11 (p. 3); E. Kwakkel, 'Cultural Residue in Medieval Manuscripts', in *The Medieval Manuscript Book: Cultural Approaches*, ed. M. Johnston and M. Van Dussen (Cambridge, 2015), pp. 60–76 (pp. 65–70).

which measures only 70 × 50 mm, small enough to fit into the palm of the hand.[37] It is beautifully produced, with a full-leaf miniature at the beginning, pen-and-ink drawings, and some coloured initials.[38] However, compounding its already diminutive size, many of the leaves have been trimmed in a haphazard fashion. A consequence of the size and trimming of the book is that in order to hold the book open, parts of the text block – and certainly the margins – are inevitably obscured by one's fingers or thumbs. This of course would have made marking the margin in any way, whether scribbling, drawing or writing, virtually impossible. In this case, the size and trimming of the margins have resulted in minimal space for re-use, and this explains why there are no marks in its margins.

Most manuscripts have more spacious flyleaves than this extreme example, and margins are typically both more substantial in size and more consistent in shape. An example of a large manuscript that has particularly generous margins is BodL, MS Douce 269, a copy of the Wycliffite Bible, which dates from the first quarter of the fifteenth century. This book's dimensions are 370 × 240 mm and the text block measures 250 × 155 mm.[39] Handling this Bible is physically demanding, but in stark contrast with the challenge of handling of the small devotional manuscript, this is due to the Bible's exceptionally large format and weight. Unlike the miniaturised margins in the devotional book, the margins in the Bible provide (theoretically) generous space for re-use as a writing support, though in this case future users did not take advantage of the wide margins available to them for mark-making.

Margins may be consistent throughout a manuscript, as in the well planned small devotional book, or the equally neatly executed Wycliffite Bible just mentioned, but in less well-produced manuscripts, the layout of margins may vary. BodL MS Douce 228, a holster book written in the fifteenth century, containing a copy of the Middle English romance of *Richard Cœur de Lion*, provides an example of total loss of the original margins.[40] The margins in the manuscript are narrow for two reasons: because it was designed and made as a holster book, with typically narrow margins, and because of additional trimming of those margins. Holster books are said to be designed to enable portable usage of the manuscript and may have a relative width as low as 0.3.[41] While the margins of holster books are thus narrow in any case, the margins in this manuscript are even narrower than usual due to additional trimming of the margins. The margins were then further narrowed

---

[37] BodL, MS Douce 1; *IMEP* IV, 1–2; *Summary Catalogue* IV, 489.

[38] BodL, MS Douce 1, full-leaf miniature at fol. 1v.

[39] BodL, MS Douce 369. I use 'theoretical' advisedly, because there is a relatively low presence of marginalia inscribed in this manuscript, *IMEP* IV, 88–90; *Summary Catalogue* IV, 609; E. Solopova, *Manuscripts of the Wycliffite Bible in the Bodleian and Oxford College Libraries* (Liverpool, 2016), pp. 113–27.

[40] BodL, MS Douce 228; *DIMEV* 3231; *Summary Catalogue* IV, 562; dimensions: 290 × 100 mm; G. Guddat-Figge, *Catalogue of Manuscripts Containing Middle English Romances* (München, 1976), pp. 263–64.

[41] Kwakkel, 'Cultural Residue', p. 71.

by being cropped – or more likely torn – close to the text block on the fore-edge on every single folio, although it is hard to determine why.[42] The margins of more deluxe books than this one were washed or removed by later collectors, to excise marginalia and return the book to a 'pristine' state. However, it seems unlikely that this is the explanation in this case. The option to make marks in many of the margins has been eliminated and replaced, at some stage, with heavy repair work, upon which no later markings were entered. As this example indicates, the space available for re-use in margins can be drastically reduced.

Composite manuscripts' page layouts can change from booklet to booklet: booklets may have dramatically different amounts of planned marginal space. Haphazard later trimming may take place without regard to the existing layouts in the book, and though this may standardise the overall book block, it can denude the margins, leave large or irregularly sized margins, and can even cut through the text block. For example, there are variable margins in BodL, MS Douce 60, a composite paper manuscript from the second half of the fifteenth century, which contains a copy of John Mirk's *Festial*, as well as other texts such as a sermon and a treatise on the seven deadly sins.[43] This manuscript as a whole is neatly trimmed into a regular, rectangular book block measuring 195 × 130 mm. However, it comprises several booklets; in some later, prose-filled sections, the close trimming leaves little to no margin. Between fols. 189–215 and fols. 216–28, for instance, the trimming has impinged on the margins of the text to different degrees, from leaving virtually no margin at all, to a margin measuring at most 10 mm.[44] Earlier in the manuscript the margins are generally more consistent and more substantial: in this section the margins measure about 20 mm.[45] In contrast with these prose margins, those booklets filled with bracketed poetry tend to have wide margins, such as fols. 147r–60v. Therefore, the availability of marginal writing spaces in this composite manuscript is highly inconsistent, as is the re-use of that space in this case.[46]

As a feature of *mise-en-page*, catchwords also influence the shape of the margins. They were used to guide the production of the manuscript and many catchwords can still be seen in manuscripts.[47] A substantial paper manuscript, BodL, MS Douce 323, which comprises

---

[42] BodL, MS Douce 228; the catalogue refers to the damage – somewhat euphemistically – as 'some edges injured': narrow strips of paper have been supplied to create a false fore-edge, held in place on each folio with thinner repair tissue which extends translucently over the main text block, *Summary Catalogue* IV, 562.

[43] BodL, MS Douce 60; *IMEP* IV, 25–30; *Summary Catalogue* IV, 508.

[44] BodL, MS Douce 60: fols. 189r–92v is a Sermon for All Saints' Day (not from the *Festial*); fols. 193r–213r is Richard Lavynham's *Litil Tretys on the Seven Deadly Sins*; fols. 213r–27v is a long form of confession, mostly in English, followed by English and Latin pastoral notes, fols. 227v–28r; *John Mirk's Festial*, ed. S. Powell, EETS OS 335 2 vols. (Oxford, 2009–2011), II, 544–45.

[45] BodL, MS Douce 60, fols. 1–146: this section includes Mirk's *Festial*.

[46] Marginalia in these trimmed spaces in BodL, MS Douce 60 have also been affected in a number of places, although the manuscript as a whole is not heavily annotated.

[47] Clemens and Graham, *Introduction*, pp. 49–50.

copies of the prose *Brut*, *Piers Plowman* and the moral treatise *The Abbey of the Holy Ghost*, features eye-catching decorative catchwords in the margins.[48] They are festooned with faces, a castle and scrollwork, among other decorative marks: all fall squarely in the middle of the large lower margins, aligned towards the gutter.[49] These catchwords are not re-use in their own right, of course, because they were a part of the scribal campaign of production. Their decoration suggests that scribes were willing to lavish time on them, whether or not they were likely to remain intact or be trimmed. This notably decorative example is a reminder that in many other manuscripts – where catchwords are not visible – margins and the catchwords they once contained are likely to have been trimmed off. Either because they have been trimmed, or because they are still present and take up room, in any book catchwords therefore affect the marginal space available for future re-users.

Organising tendencies

Marks themselves may accrue over the years, made by many different hands, often interacting or jarring with one another.[50] Successive re-users may add to the space available, even on a crowded flyleaf or margin. The leaf mentioned in BodL, MS Douce 302, the collection of Audelay's poetry, cited at the start of this chapter, is a prime example of amassed written and drawn marks (again, see Figure 10).[51] Within the jumble, individual marks are placed near other marks – there is little apparent 'deference' to other markings – but there are also large gaps. This casual, higgledy-piggledy approach to the layout of the page also includes two small patches of erasure, one of which has rendered the first line of a verse illegible. While it is quite possible and plausible to imagine someone creating more space for their own marginalia by scraping away other marks, in this case the erased spaces remain blank, leaving no indication of the reason for this act.

---

[48] BodL, MS Douce 323; *Piers Plowman* A text, *DIMEV* 2458; this manuscript is dated to the second half of the fifteenth century in *IMEP* IV, 85–86; *Summary Catalogue* IV, 595; dimensions 285 × 210 mm.

[49] BodL, MS Douce 323, fols. 12v, 24v, 36v, 48v, 60v, 72v, 84v, 96v. The first text, the prose *Brut* Chronicle, begins fol. 1r and ends at fol. 101v. Thereafter catchwords are less elaborate through *Piers Plowman*, which runs fols. 102r–40r, catchwords at fol. 110v (possibly torn out at fols. 112v, 122v, 138v). It is worth noting that where each text ends, the written area is followed by drawings, and the remainder of the leaf is left empty. So, following the end of the prose *Brut* on fol. 101v are the words 'deo gracias' and 'the arms sable a saltire engrailed ermine between four roses' with the name 'Iohannes tubantisville' in a scroll, drawn in a similar design to some of the catchwords, *Summary Catalogue* IV, 595; then, following *Piers Plowman* on fol. 140r is the phrase: 'explicit liber petri plouman' in very large red and black lettering with a decorative bird-shaped initial **e**; likewise at the end of *The Abbey of the Holy Ghost* is a red and black ink illustration of an abbey.

[50] B. Watson, 'Oodles of Doodles? Doodling Behaviour and its Implications for Understanding Palaeoarts', *Rock Art Research* 25 (2008), 35–60 (p. 42).

[51] BodL, MS Douce 302, fol. 35v.

Similar leaves, which are particularly busy with markings, are found in at least four other manuscripts from survey of the Douce and Laudian collections. First, the front flyleaf in a copy of *Mandeville's Travels*, BodL, MS Douce 109, which was formerly a pastedown, but is now lifted, features a jumble of activity, including the floating letter **a** repeated multiple times, a further row of letter **d** shapes, lines aligned to form staves, squiggles and longer pen strokes; there is also a repeated Latin phrase 'Ego sum bonus puer que*m* deus amat', and a practice alphabet (see Figure 11).[52] Second, one of the final flyleaves in BodL, MS Laud misc.735, a copy of works by Thomas Hoccleve and John Lydgate, features phrases, notes, signatures, and an initial shaped like a fish, all of which are dispersed across the folio in generally upright orientation.[53] Third, the final parchment flyleaf in BodL, MS Douce 126, a copy of *The Prick of Conscience*, includes writing in Latin in different hands, calligraphic pen strokes, an elaborate initial **h**, floating letters, zigzag lines, a face, loose knot patterns, the name 'Thomas' and the name 'John', all generally in conventional orientation; the layout is otherwise random, with spaces between markings highly uneven.[54] Finally, in a copy of the Wycliffite translation of the four gospels, BodL, MS Laud misc.36, the front and back paper pastedowns are both littered with scrawled, secretary-hand annotations.[55]

Aside from these examples of densely clustered markings on flyleaves, there were other rather more dispersed re-uses of marginal spaces. Some flyleaves or margins may have only one or two isolated markings. Books may contain markings scattered throughout, as will be seen later in this chapter in examples of signatures in margins. In addition, the makers of these markings sometimes had to reorient the manuscript in order to write, particularly in narrow margins bounding the main text. Evidence for this can be seen in writing that was inscribed sideways, for example running either up or down the vertical margin. One instance of this appears in a copy of *The Prick of Conscience*, BodL, MS Douce 156. A rubricated line midway down the text block has been copied out in the left-hand margin. The writer turned the book through ninety degrees anti-clockwise, so that the writing now runs down the page towards the lower edge. The marginal note

---

[52] BodL, MS Douce 109, fol. iv verso, Latin phrase and alphabet are both discussed in more detail later in this chapter; *IMEP* IV, 109; *Summary Catalogue* IV, 524; M. C. Seymour, 'The English Manuscripts of Mandeville's Travels', *Edinburgh Bibliographical Society Transactions* 4:5 (1966), 169–210 (p. 191); *The Defective Version of Mandeville's Travels*, ed. M. C. Seymour, EETS OS 319 (Oxford, 2002), pp. xxi–xxiii.

[53] BodL, MS Laud misc.735, fol. 135r; *IMEP* XVI, 94–95, dates the manuscript to the second half of the fifteenth century; *Quarto Catalogue* II, 522–23; *LMES*; the manuscript measures 305 × 220 mm.

[54] BodL, MS Douce 126, fol. 93v. *A Descriptive Guide to the Manuscripts of the 'Prick of Conscience'*, ed. R. E. Lewis and A. McIntosh, Medium Ævum Monographs, n.s. 12 (Oxford, 1982), pp. 99–100, mentions a 'note with the date 18 August 1499 in it' on this folio; *DIMEV* (6 entries); *Summary Catalogue* IV, 529; dimensions: 230 × 170 mm.

[55] BodL, MS Laud misc.36; *IMEP* XVI, 15, dates this manuscript to *c*.1430; *Quarto Catalogue* II, 71.

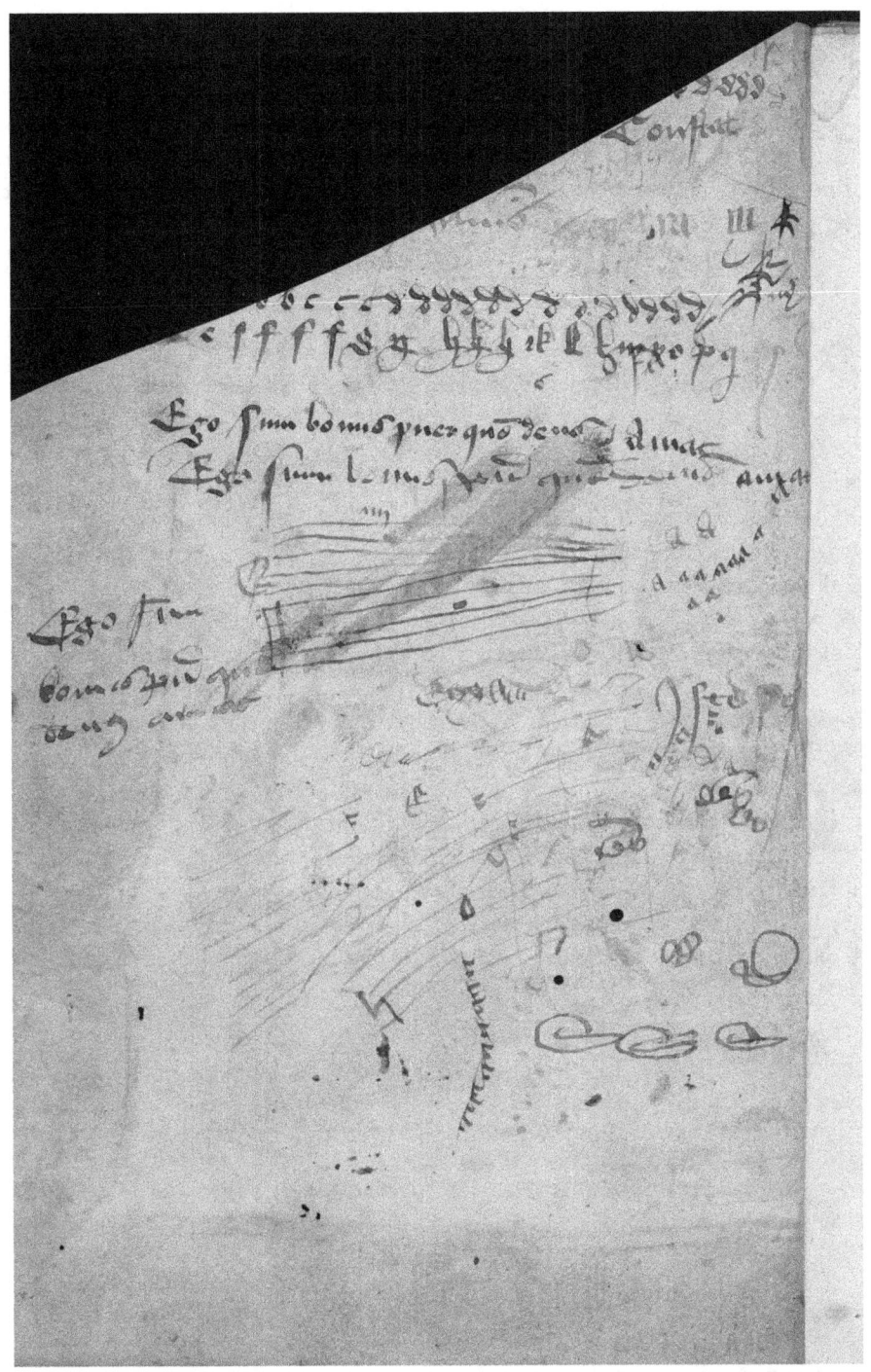

Figure 11. BodL, MS Douce 109, fol. iv verso, markings on a front flyleaf.

reads: 'Homo cum in honore esset non intellexit comparatus est iumentis insipientib*us* […]' breaking off at the leaf edge. The full rubricated line translates to the following as: 'And man when he was in honour did not understand; he is compared to senseless beasts, and is become like to them'.[56] This apparently 'senseless' annotation merely imitates the main text and does not add anything to it, or comment on it. In this way, the person who made this mark treated the book as a scrap writing surface, whether for idle, distracted copying, or as a pen trial.

Books re-used for ephemeral mark-making

Scribbles, doodles, sketches, and other drawings that are not part of a formal decorative scheme constitute significant non-verbal re-uses of marginal spaces. They may occur when books are treated like scrap parchment or paper, or wax tablets, surfaces that were valued for typically ephemeral mark-making such as draft compositions. Although marks can be scratched or impressed into the surface of parchment, which does bear some comparison to using a stylus to press into a wax tablet, marks made in manuscripts are mostly laid down with pen and ink – a different skill entirely. In scholarship about marginalia, many marginal non-verbal marks made in ink are lumped together and referred to collectively as *probationes pennae*. A 'pen test' refers to the writer's act of checking that the quill was functioning and that the ink was flowing smoothly, which was especially important if the nib had been freshly cut, before starting to write in earnest.[57] The long, wiggly lines that snake around the margins of at least three leaves in BodL, MS Laud misc.739, a manuscript of *The Canterbury Tales*, might well be pen trials, marks made to encourage ink to flow through a newly cut nib.[58]

It is equally possible that these are doodles without the purpose of preparing for writing. In the broadest sense, since we cannot ever really know how consciously or with what intention any of these marks were made, almost any marginal mark could well be considered a pen trial or an idle doodle.[59] After all, doodles are generally characterised as absent-minded, spontaneous 'scrawls' commonly featuring both figurative and apparently

---

[56] BodL, MS Douce 156, p. 16; the full rubricated line reads: 'Homo, cum in honore esset, non intellexit, comparatus est iumentis insipientibus, *et* similis factus est illis', lines 602–03, Psalm 48:21, in *Richard Morris's Prick of Conscience: A Corrected and Amplified Reading Text*, ed. R. Hanna and S. Wood, EETS OS 342 (Oxford, 2013), p. 19; *DIMEV* 1953. Lewis and McIntosh, *Descriptive Guide*, pp. 101–02, date this manuscript to the last quarter of the fourteenth century; *Summary Catalogue* IV, 540; dimensions: 250 × 150 mm.

[57] Clemens and Graham, *Introduction*, p. 45.

[58] BodL, MS Laud misc.739, scribbles on fols. 74r, 86r, 134r, drawn in an ink which is difficult to date: this caveat applies to many of the ink marks cited in this section (in contrast with datable styles of handwriting); Seymour, *Chaucer Catalogue* II, 179–82; *Quarto Catalogue* II, 524, 584.

[59] McKenzie puts this neatly: 'To venture into distinctions between conscious and unconscious intentions would be to enter upon troubled waters indeed' in *Bibliography and Sociology*, p. 18.

abstract patterns.[60] Doodle forms recur in human mark-making through the ages. Ben Watson has identified many of these common patterns among these forms in his work on palaeoart. Many forms found in marginal spaces in fifteenth-century manuscripts correlate with the recurrent patterns identified by Watson, and these include spiral patterns, squiggles, jagged lines, parallel lines, and cross-hatching.[61] There is an example of abstract strapwork in the manuscript of Audelay's works (again, see Figure 10).[62] Numerous pale ink doodles of geometric shapes sporadically appear in the margins of a copy of John Gower's *Confessio Amantis* on parchment, BodL, MS Laud misc.609, dating from the first quarter of the fifteenth century, as do similar shapes sliced with a knife through the parchment.[63] These abstractions may all qualify as pen tests, or may reflect efforts to avoid meaning on the part of those re-using the book.

While it is impossible to ascertain the intentions behind all doodles, the 'relief of boredom' or 'amusement' does seem to motivate the creation of some doodles.[64] It is quite conceivable that whimsy was a motivation for the drawing of a bearded, bandy-legged man, doodled with his hands on his hips, in BodL, MS Laud misc.739, the copy of *The Canterbury Tales* with long wandering scribbles on it. Distinctive features common to children's doodles indicate that this man may well have been illustrated by a bored child.[65] The playfulness of doodles has been traced in early modern books by Stephen H. Goddard, and I contend that similar motivations were just as likely in earlier centuries. Pleasingly, Goddard also notes that 'the English term "to doodle" derives from the Slavonic and Germanic term "to play" – usually to play the bagpipes (German *dudelsack*, Dutch *doedelzak*)'.[66]

---

[60] *OED*, *doodle, n.*, Sense 3: 'An aimless scrawl made by a person while his mind is more or less otherwise occupied'; O'Connell describes marginalia as 'spontaneous' in 'The Marginal Obsession with Marginalia'.

[61] Watson cites the following common abstract patterns (drawn from his longer list of recurrent doodle forms, including anthropomorphic and organic forms), 'cross-hatching/ lattices, multiple straight (parallel) lines, zigzag lines, [...] meandering lines, multiple "waves" [...] spirals' in 'Oodles of Doodles', p. 37.

[62] BodL, MS Douce 302: the strapwork on fol. 35v is significantly calligraphic and controlled; it is reminiscent of the flourishes commonly found under post-medieval signatures and may be a trial run for exactly this purpose.

[63] BodL, MS Laud misc.609, shapes in the margins on fols. 93r, 144r, and shapes cut through the parchment on fols. 79, 119; *DIMEV* 4226; *IMEP* XVI, 76; *Quarto Catalogue* II, 432; *LMES*; dimensions: 410 × 270 mm.

[64] P. Beal notes that 'whether actually engaged in testing a pen or else relieving the boredom of a tedious copying task by adding [...] unrelated text, doodles, or drawings for their own amusement', in *A Dictionary of English Manuscript Terminology 1450–2000* (Oxford, 2008), p. 294; Thorpe notes the 'playful aspect' of doodles by adults in 'Young Hands', p. 12.

[65] BodL, MS Laud misc.739, fol. 54v. I draw here on indicative features outlined by Thorpe in 'Young Hands'.

[66] S. H. Goddard, 'Probationes Pennae: Some Sixteenth-Century Doodles on the Theme of Folly Attributed to the Antwerp Humanist Pieter Gillis and His Colleagues', *Renaissance Quarterly* 41 (1988), 242–67 (p. 244).

Erik Kwakkel has described some medieval Russian doodles on birchbark as the work of bored children.[67] It is an oft-stated but also oft-ignored fact that scribes sometimes succumbed to boredom: marginal doodles take us into 'the world of modest play, of readers and scribes seeking distraction'.[68] While doodling may be starkly abstract in form, manuscripts also incorporate a range of doodling behaviours, including shapes reminiscent of anthropomorphic and organic forms.[69] Organic forms are also found in the same copy of *The Canterbury Tales*; there are leaf patterns on a folio midway through 'The Cook's Tale' and flowers on a folio in 'The Franklin's Tale'.[70] Perhaps these doodles are evidence of playfulness, of whimsical mark-making?

Intriguingly, of the anthropomorphic doodles encountered, faces were most common (except for the hands-on-hips posed doodle of a man already cited). Many heads drawn in the margins of medieval manuscripts were 'used for the same indicative function' as manicules.[71] While drawings of faces might be merely idle doodling, then, they do echo familiar aspects of book production and use by scribes and readers. For example, a scribe drew a face in red ink in the left margin of a paper manuscript written in the third quarter of the fifteenth century, which contains various prayers to Christ and the Virgin, medical recipes, poems and the romance *Titus and Vespasian*, also known as *The Destruction of Jerusalem* (BodL, MS Douce 78).[72] The adornment of tall ascenders with small faces is a further example of anthropomorphic decoration that might or might not be intended to serve an indicative function. Such adornment was added by scribes themselves, and these marks may represent a momentary diversion from the main text, a glimpse of a scribe 'sidestep[ping] seriousness'.[73] Instances of these little faces drawn by scribes were also found where ascenders reach into the upper margins in two copies of *The Prick of Conscience*

---

[67] E. Kwakkel, 'Medieval Kids' Doodles on Birch Bark', Tumblr <http://erikkwakkel.tumblr.com/post/67681966023/medieval-kids-doodles-on-birch-bark-heres>.

[68] Pulsiano, 'Jaunts, Jottings', p. 190; also brought to the fore by S. Justice in 'Inquisition, Speech, and Writing: A Case from Late Medieval Norwich', in *Criticism and Dissent in the Late Middle Ages*, ed. R. Copeland (Cambridge, 1996), pp. 289–322 (p. 318).

[69] BodL, MS Laud misc.739 features more substantial abstract doodles, shaped like loose trellis work with dots in the gaps, at fols. 15r, 164r; similar doodles are in BodL, MS Douce 126, fol. 93v, on the final flyleaf.

[70] BodL, MS Laud misc.739, leaves on fol. 73v, flowers on fol. 186v.

[71] It is unclear whether Grindley means to refer only to the *Piers Plowman* C-Text at this point, or whether he is making a general classification point; he also notes that heads used for the same function as manicules 'so far remain[s] unnamed' in 'Classification of Marginalia', p. 91.

[72] BodL, MS Douce 78, fol. 63v, in the same red ink that the scribe used to rubricate the main text; *Titus and Vespasian* runs fols. 19r–75v; *DIMEV* 3107; *IMEP* IV, 30–31; *Summary Catalogue* IV, 513; dimensions: 200 × 100 mm.

[73] E. Kwakkel, 'Party Time', Tumblr <http://erikkwakkel.tumblr.com/post/107251005026/party-time-the-first-and-last-text-line-on-the>.

(BodL, MS Douce 141 and BodL, MS Douce 156), and all wistfully look away from the text into the side margins.[74]

Some drawings of heads and faces by other later re-users are more obviously not being used for indicative purposes but are, like many other marginal drawings, apparently 'absent-minded' or observational. While they are not incorporated into the design of ascenders, these faces do fit the broader expectations of acceptable forms found marked into books. Perhaps more formal uses of head-maniucles or ascender-faces by scribes may prime others to make comparable marks in the margins of books, even without the same formal purpose. There is a small, simple line drawing of a head and shoulders, with popping, round eyes, which appears on the final flyleaf in BodL, MS Douce 126, a different copy of *The Prick of Conscience*.[75] This face does not indicate anything in the main text, located as it is adrift on a flyleaf.[76] Neither do the two profiles of faces drawn in black ink, on fol. 38r and fol. 182r in the copy of *The Canterbury Tales* with various other doodles already mentioned (BodL, MS Laud misc.739).[77] These profiles were drawn complete with rolls of fat, perhaps for grotesque comic effect. These examples show that in addition to drawing faces that engage with the main text, or which support a reader's navigation through the text, both scribes and readers might doodle without any particular purpose directly in relation to the text too.

Simple doodles may well be idle or even comic, but some drawings in marginal spaces are finely executed. Watson defines sketches as 'unfinished drawings [that] are usually depictive', in contrast with other non-verbal mark-making.[78] The aforementioned copy of *The Canterbury Tales*, MS Laud misc.739, contains a pencil sketch of a bearded man in an ornate hat that exemplifies this depictive quality.[79] Likewise, in BodL, MS Douce 257, a composite manuscript from the late fourteenth century, a deft ink sketch depicts a mournful-looking man's face.[80] This is drawn in the lower third of the final leaf, next to a coloured drawing of a book draped with a cloth. The layout of the page is such that

---

[74] BodL, MS Douce 141 features some abstract, curly marks in ascenders, and a couple of small faces, one face in profile peers out from under an elaborate ascender-turban, which unfurls above an **h** on fol. 13r, and on fol. 123r another profile – this time bearded – looks out from the backwards-looped ascender of a **d**; *DIMEV* 5398; *IMEP* IV, pp. 44–45; Lewis and McIntosh, *Descriptive Guide*, pp. 100–01, dates this manuscript to the first half of the fifteenth century; *Summary Catalogue* IV, 535–36; dimensions: 245 × 160 mm; BodL, MS Douce 156.

[75] BodL, MS Douce 126, fol. 93v, the drawing is in the top right corner of this heavily marked leaf, surrounded by written and drawn markings.

[76] BodL, MS Douce 126, fol. 93 sits after two flyleaves: fol. 91 on which there are Latin verses, and fol. 92 on which there is a hymn to the Virgin, and before a modern paper flyleaf at fol. 94.

[77] BodL, MS Laud misc.739, fol. 38r and fol. 182r.

[78] Watson, 'Oodles of Doodles', p. 39,

[79] BodL, MS Laud misc.739: on fol. 199v the sketch is only faintly visible.

[80] BodL, MS Douce 257, fol. 99r; *IMEP* IV, 51–52; *Summary Catalogue* IV, 569–70; dimensions: 180 × 135 mm.

the two drawings do not seem connected to one another – there is no indication that the man should be understood to be reading the book. The two illustrations, although they are adjacent, are so different that they give the impression of being here by coincidence. The survey of Middle English prose manuscripts in the Douce and Laudian collections yielded only these two examples of sketching, as distinct from more basic or abstract doodling. The various drawings and sketches of faces explored here have little in common in the ways in which they have been rendered. Nevertheless, they suggest that when people randomly doodle, whether to test a pen or to alleviate boredom, they sometimes follow shapes they may have seen marked onto other books, or other typical patterns of mark-making such as realistic sketching.

Doodling might, then, be a behaviour that is chiefly about gentle entertainment: boredom is apparently its core rationale. But doodles function as an aid to memory.[81] In practice then, these abstract or organic shapes marked on books might also be aids to reading the main text. Not only can we picture scribes doodling while at their work, but also later re-users interacting with the book by reading and concurrently doodling, or even ignoring the main text and just using the margins as a surface for doodling. In her modern study of doodling habits, Jackie Andrade advises that 'doodling while working can be beneficial', and that doodling may perhaps 'aid cognitive performance [in a dual task scenario] by reducing daydreaming'.[82] Thus, even apparently unrelated, informal doodles in margins may aid other work or aid recall of the main text by staving off distraction. Paradoxically, then, the most abstract of doodles in medieval manuscript margins, normally deemed irrelevant to textually engaged memory-work, might well be traces of a user in fact actively participating in the intellectual work of understanding the main text. Moreover, Andrade's work is a reminder of the difficulty of disentangling the various uses and re-uses of books and their texts, especially complex in the context of doodling behaviour.

Alphabets

Re-users practised everything from rudimentary to polished writing skills in the margins of manuscripts. As well as non-verbal pen tests and doodles, marginal spaces in manuscripts provided space for developing penmanship through writing out lettering and basic verbal markings. This practical re-use goes way beyond the expected or intended use of the book for reading. By re-using the book like this, people made the most of the material available in the book. In so doing, they presumably avoided having to source or use other materials

---

[81] Here, I am considering the results of modern studies into the cognitive psychology of doodling in the context of late medieval minds, which of course I cannot know or test; J. Andrade, 'What Does Doodling Do?', *Applied Cognitive Psychology* 24 (2010), 100–06. The benefits of doodling have become popularised, see S. Heller, 'The Cognitive Benefits of Doodling', *The Atlantic*, 9 July 2015 <http://www.theatlantic.com/entertainment/archive/2015/07/doodling-for-cognitive-benefits/398027/>; for more on medieval memory work and the conscious, formal making and use of visual imagery, see Carruthers, *The Book of Memory*.

[82] Andrade stresses that this final hypothesis requires further investigation, in 'Doodling', p. 106.

for writing. For example, in the copy of the *Confessio Amantis* with abstract markings in its margins (BodL, MS Laud misc.609), the lower margin of the final leaf of the book block is strewn with single letters, including the letters **a, o, p, s,** in addition to several odd shapes. These isolated letters and shapes were inscribed onto the page at a range of angles, well-spaced from one another, and do not seem to conform to any sequence or pattern.[83] In this period, writing skills were exercised through writing out simple patterns of familiar letters, such as signatures, short phrases and alphabets.[84]

A partial alphabet has been written – in a practical re-use of marginal space – on a blank half-page in BodL, MS Douce 78, a manuscript including prayers, medical recipes, and the romance *Titus and Vespasian*. In the lower margin of fol. 71v the letters **a** to **o** are set out as follows: 'a a a b b c c d dd e e f ff g g h h j / i k k l ll m n o oo', written in the space after the main text ends.[85] A couple of extra **o** graphs, and what might be **g**, or just a squiggle, float above the 'g g h' section of the alphabet. It is odd that the scribe stopped writing the main text (*Titus and Vespasian*) halfway down this page before resuming on the next page.[86] In this partial alphabet, the writer has recorded both anglicana and secretary forms of the letter **a**, and seems interested in the shapes resulting from the doubling of letters, which were an alternative to marking majuscules or upper-case letters, as well as representing two individual letters.[87] The doubles **dd** and **ll** are held together by looped cursive strokes and a long crossbar. The letters display varied levels of calligraphic effort, some of them spiky with broken strokes, particularly **b** and **h** with ascender flourishes that flick out to the right and back in sharply, and the second **e**, with a pronounced horn. These careful strokes suggest some attention to the prestige of the hand; however, the overall impression is of an unfinished alphabet, dashed off in haste. The stylish script that is being practised does not seem to be related to the campaign of production that generated the main texts of the book in which it is found. So, despite its relative lack of polish, this alphabet appears purposeful, and is perhaps a rehearsal of letter forms to be used in other acts of writing. The evident effort in these attempts at a more sophisticated style of writing suggest that, rough though this alphabet might appear, the shapes will be used once mastered. This is a notably purposeful re-use of spare spaces in the book for writing practice.

[83] BodL, MS Laud misc.609, fol. 170v.

[84] For more on alphabets and early learning in class and at home, see N. Orme, *Medieval Schools: From Roman Britain to Renaissance England* (New Haven, 2006), pp. 56–57.

[85] BodL, MS Douce 78, fol. 71v, there is plenty of space available for a full alphabet, should the writer have wanted to continue; this folio is only four folios shy of the end of the unfinished romance, and sits as part of a rather erratically trimmed book block: the limited shapes and sizes of other nearby margins may have made this available half-page of space particularly appealing for a pen trial or practice.

[86] BodL, MS Douce 78, fol. 71v. *DIMEV* 3107 notes that *Titus and Vespasian* 'ends imperfectly because of loss of folios. Last folio is damaged. A leaf is lost after fol. 70. On fol. 71v the text breaks (half of the folio is left blank) and resumes on fol. 72 with "And when all þis wes ydoo."'

[87] A. Derolez, *The Palaeography of Gothic Manuscript Books from the Twelfth to the Early Sixteenth Century* (Cambridge, 2003), p. 146.

Another near-complete alphabet appears among the educational drills, pen trials, and jottings of musical notation that fill the re-used parchment flyleaf of the mid-fifteenth-century copy of *Mandeville's Travels* (BodL, MS Douce 109) previously mentioned (again, see Figure 11).[88] The alphabet runs over two lines, from **b** to **d**, with **d** repeated thirteen times, and then from **e** to **q**. It is incomplete, the top left corner of the folio having been cut off at an angle. Notably, the alphabet was written onto a parchment flyleaf, whereas the rest of the manuscript is paper, and dates to the middle of the fifteenth century. While the parchment flyleaf had a copy of a short letter added to the recto, which is dated 1746, and a couple of lines beneath this written by the eighteenth-century antiquarian Francis Douce (who owned the book), the parchment itself had been either with this manuscript or another manuscript for some time; it is marked by discolouration around the edges on the verso, suggesting a significant interval spent as a pastedown. In amongst the mix of markings on the verso, this near-complete alphabet demonstrates re-use of a marginal space in a book for the rehearsal of letter forms.

Whereas the alphabets in BodL, MS Douce 78 and BodL, MS Douce 109 were added into the margins by later re-users, conversely, the main text of BodL, MS Douce 103 re-uses space around a 'specimen alphabet' noted into an upper margin (see Figure 12).[89] The margin on this leaf is slightly larger than the smaller upper margins on surrounding folios, and indeed on the verso of the very same folio. This small detail, in conjunction with the difference in script in the main hand and the alphabet, suggests that the alphabet may have been written before the main texts on this recto. There is an exhaustive range of letters, with many repeated letters, in an upright, prickly secretary script, with a few anglicana forms: there are instances of round **a**; 2-shaped **r**; long **r**; short **r**; kidney-shaped **s**; round **z**. This alphabet includes variant forms of different letters and ligatures from both styles of handwriting, and is rendered in a controlled, upright style with close attention to broken strokes. It is followed by a few additional words to test different letter shapes. This carefully executed alphabet suggests it may be the work of a well-trained writer trying out forms of stylish penmanship, rather than a novice tentatively practising newly learned letters. This manuscript – which includes educational texts – is an unsurprising context in which to find such accomplished and conscientious handwriting practice in the margins.

This fragment of writing may well have been set down by a professional scribe, and someone who perhaps had this quire of paper to hand whilst working on another. Multiple scribal hands contributed to this manuscript,[90] and the writer of the alphabet may have

---

[88] BodL, MS Douce 109, fol. iv verso.

[89] BodL, MS Douce 103, fol. 15r, this manuscript is datable to the middle of the fifteenth century, *IMEP* IV, 36–37; *Summary Catalogue* IV, 522–23; D. Thomson, *A Descriptive Catalogue of Middle English Grammatical Texts* (London, 1979), p. 277, describes it as a 'specimen alphabet' and dates the manuscript to the middle to end of the fifteenth century.

[90] BodL, MS Douce 103, Thomson identifies six different hands, using anglicana, secretary, and mixed styles of handwriting, to varying quality of execution, in *Grammatical Texts*, p. 277.

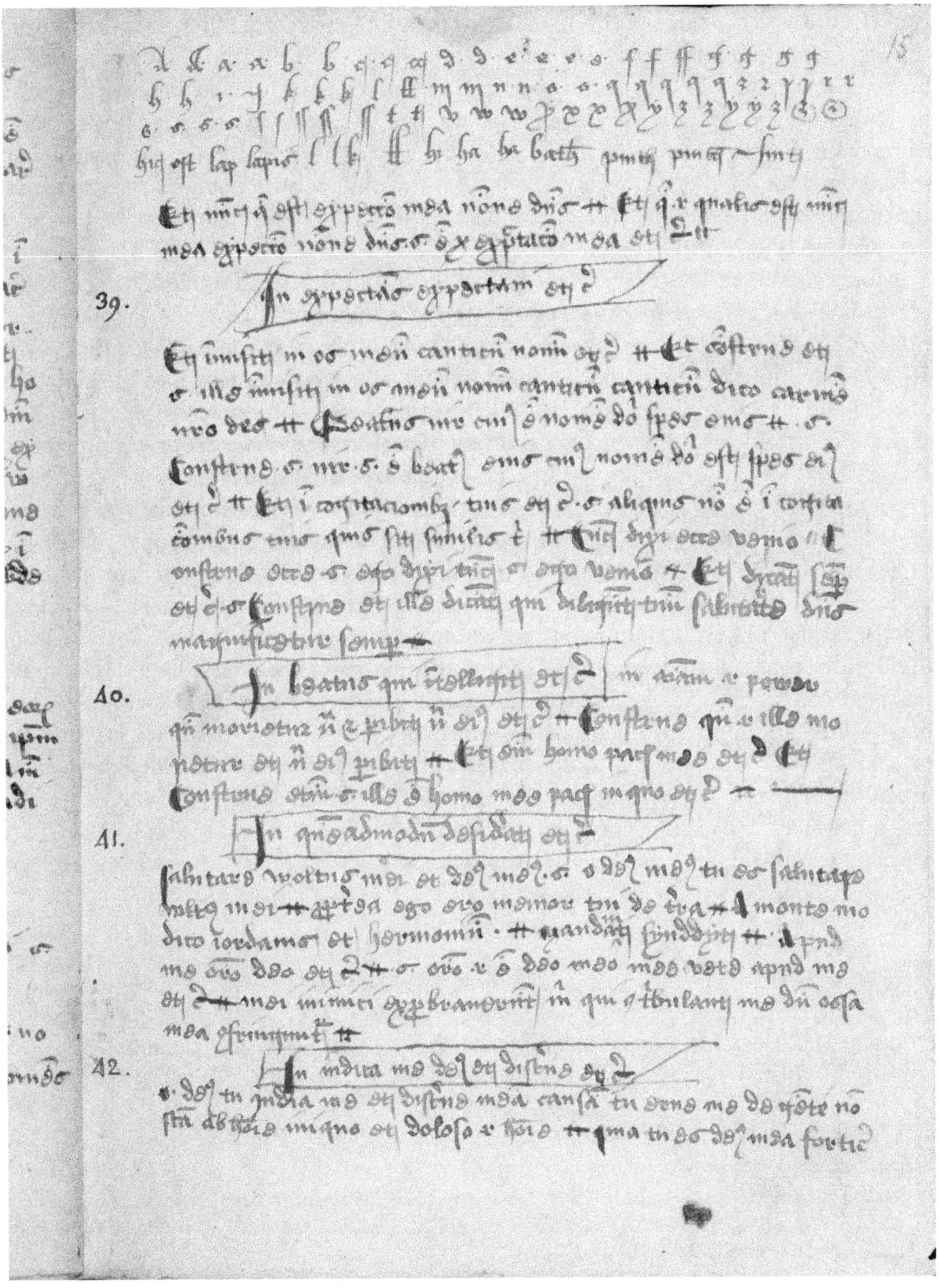

a a a b b b g g g d d e e e e f f f ff ff ff
h h i j k k k ll ll m m n n n o o p p q q q r r r r
s s s s ſſ ſſ ſſ ſſ t t v w x x x x y z z z z ⁊ ⁊ ↄ ↄ
hic est lapis lapis l l li ll ll hi ha ba bath pmit̃ pnt̃ꝰ sint

Et mĩerʒ est exp̱tio mea nõie dñi ++ Et q̈ꝛ q̈ratio eſt mĩi
mea exp̱tio nõie dñi · ⁊ exp̱tatio mea est ꝑ—

39. ¶ In exp̱tatio exp̱tatũ est e

Et inuisit̃ m os meũ cantieñ noui oy d ++ Et cõstring eſt
· illo inuisit̃ in os meũ noui cantieñ cantieñ dico ateñs
uo deo ++ Exaltauit me c̃ui ꝯ nõie dõ spẽs eius ++ ⁊
Constring · me · ꝯ · ꝯ beati omẽs c̃ui noĩe dõ est spẽs ẽs
est e ++ Et i cõſtitũõibꝰ tuis eſt d · ⁊ aliquo nõ ꝯ i tota
cõmũis tuis qṁos sitꝯ similis ẽ ++ Vide dign̷ oro uero ++ Et
cõstans oro · ⁊ ego dign̷ tuaꝰ · ⁊ oro uerus + Et dicat̃ ſp̃
eſt e · ⁊ cõstring eſt illa dicaꝰ qm dilexisti ruri Salueto dnõ
magnificabitur sompꝰ—

40. ¶ In beatus qm tollenti est e | In ĩim · ⁊ pow̃
qm morietur n · a ꝑbit n es est e ++ Constans oro · illo mo
naturꝰ est n · a es ꝑbit ++ Et oĩs homo p̱hendo est e ++ Et
constans oĩus · ⁊ illo ꝯ homo mẽs pact̃ in quõ est ꝓ —

41. ¶ In quoadmodũ dſid̃aẽ est e
Salutaꝛe uoltuꝰ mei · ⁊ deꝰ meꝰ · ⁊ · ꝯ deꝰ meꝰ tu es salutat̃ꝰ
uult̃ mei ++ Aptea ego oro memor tui de tr̃a ++ A monte mõ
dico iordanũ et hormonũ · ++ Mandauit̃ fund̷tit̃y ++ Apud
me eſt deo est e · ++ · ꝯ oro · ꝯ deo meo meo uoto apud me
est ꝓ ++ mei inimici exꝓbrauerũt in qm p̱tbulaneꝛ mo dn̄ cõſa
mea gfringunt̃ ++

42. ¶ In dicia me deꝰ est distnʒ est e
· deꝰ tu indica uos est distnʒ mea causã tu oras me dõ rete nõ
sta de t̃a iniquo et doloso · reoꝛ ++ q̈ma tu eſ deꝰ meã fortis

Figure 12. BodL, MS Douce 103, fol. 15r, alphabet.

been a different scribe from the one who completed the main text at this point, or, they could be one and the same.[91] This manuscript therefore presents a different scenario from the other two alphabets already discussed. Whoever the scribes of the main text were, and however the scribe working on this particular quire related to this alphabet, that writer has opted to work around the fragment of writing. Whatever the precise circumstances of production, this case presents a tolerance of existing marginal markings, rather than re-appropriation of the margin by a later user. In this unusual example, it is therefore the writing of the main text that constitutes re-use, an addition of 'proper' text around a marginal alphabet, rather than the other way around.

More common re-uses of marginal spaces for writing include short, familiar sequences of words as well as familiar sequences of letters like alphabets. These might include brief extracts from the Bible, from prayers, verses, songs or phrases from early-learning exercises. For example, Clemens and Graham describe a 'sequence of letters of the alphabet, a well-known verse from the psalms or some other source, or a prayerful invocation of divine aid' as some of the most typical forms of *probationes pennae*.[92] An example of an excerpt from an early-learning exercise is seen on one of the busy flyleaves mentioned previously (see Figure 11: BodL, MS Douce 109, fol. iv verso). On this lifted former pastedown, in the front of a copy of *Mandeville's Travels*, there is a haphazard jumble of accumulated markings, and in this mix of doodles and writing a phrase has been repeatedly inscribed.[93] The Latin phrase reads 'Ego sum bonus puer que*m* deus amat', which translates to as: 'I am a good boy whom God loves'.[94] This has been written out in full three times, dotted around the page and enmeshed in other markings. The phrase is a common school exercise.[95] Like other brief jottings, or non-verbal markings, this may well be an impromptu pen test by someone who knew how to write in Latin, or by someone who was learning to do so. But it might also be reminiscent of the 'proper' use of the main text for learning. As this chapter has shown, doodles of faces may emulate other faces drawn into books by scribes, and so, in a similar fashion, perhaps this repeated marginal inscription conforms to a schoolboy's expectations of what should be written in books.

---

[91] BodL, MS Douce 103, fol. 15r, the text here is the words of the Psalms, Canticles and Athanasian Creed 'rearranged for easy understanding', fols. 9v–33v, Thomson, *Grammatical Texts*, pp. 277–82 (p. 278).

[92] Clemens and Graham, *Introduction*, p. 45.

[93] BodL, MS Douce 109, fol. iv verso.

[94] D. Wakelin discusses this phrase in '"Thys ys my boke": Imagining the Owner in the Book', in *Spaces for Reading in Later Medieval England*, ed. M. C. Flannery and C. Griffin (Basingstoke, 2016), pp. 13–33 (pp. 22–23).

[95] BodL, MS Douce 109, fol. iv verso. For more on Latin/English *vulgaria*, see Orme, *Medieval Schools*, p. 112.

Signatures

Medieval people could test their pens and practise penmanship by writing other simple, familiar sequences of letters. It makes sense then that a common piece of handwriting was the signature. Signatures were one of the first things people learned to write. As Scott-Warren notes of signature practice, found in abundance throughout medieval manuscripts in both medieval and early modern hands, 'These are the endless dry-runs of people learning to write their names; they are thus of a piece with the practice alphabets that frequently crop up on flyleaves and around the edges of texts'.[96] Two of these 'dry-run' signatures can be seen in a manuscript (BodL, MS Laud misc.739, already cited) containing works by Hoccleve and Lydgate, with a heavily marked back flyleaf. The self-conscious assertion 'Thomas Ceryks hand' and the clumsily insistent 'Thomas creyke [*sic*] ys my nyme' are both written in the same awkward fifteenth-century handwriting, modelled on secretary script.[97] Both examples display a tentative grasp of the convention of signing one's own name. Signatures, phrases and alphabets all suggest the stages of development necessary in the gradual process of acquiring literacy through practice, which might involve exercises written in marginal spaces.

Sometimes entire pastedowns or flyleaves were inscribed by multiple hands, to the extent that they are swarming with doodles, inscribed names and notes, as mentioned in a select group of examples from the survey (BodL, MS Douce 109, BodL, MS Douce 126, BodL, MS Laud misc.735).[98] The front or back leaves in a book are the places traditionally occupied by fuller statements of ownership.[99] Despite the typical use of these prominent places at the front or back of the book for formal declarations of ownership, scrappier signatures can build up here too. Perhaps new writers responded to the presence of other markings by joining in, huddling their names in a tangle, sometimes embellishing them with flourishes. And perhaps, to go a step further, the blank space available on flyleaves or pastedowns attracts, even invites these markings. What begins as possibly whimsical re-use quickly becomes a new convention, patterning further re-uses, and encouraging other re-users to make their own marks.

As well as clusters of signatures on flyleaves or pastedowns, names scattered throughout books provide compelling evidence that users of the book wanted to assert their presence and contact with the book. After all, as Jackson notes, 'the first impulse of any [book]

---

[96] Scott-Warren, 'Reading Graffiti', p. 368.

[97] BodL, MS Laud misc.735. These signatures are both in the wide right margins of fol. 1r and fol. 71r respectively; while varied spelling (even in a signature) is not unusual, the spelling of 'nyme' is odd, without the vowel 'a' – this adds to the impression of the writer as a new learner of written English.

[98] I am referring to a general pattern of flyleaf re-use, but particularly to BodL, MS Douce 109; BodL, MS Douce 126; BodL, MS Laud misc.735; BodL, MS Laud misc.36, cited previously in this chapter.

[99] Jackson, *Marginalia*, p. 19; Wakelin, 'Imagining the Owner', pp. 13, 18. This placement on front or back leaves is typical of many inscriptions discussed in Chapter 4.

owner appears to be the impulse to stake a claim' and this could be achieved more or less formally.[100] But, notwithstanding re-use of marginal spaces for practising one's signature already discussed, and excluding formal statements of ownership, signatures scattered through the book block – however many of them there might be – do not necessarily fulfil such an obvious function.[101]

Whether they represent a claim of ownership or less purposeful scribbling, BodL, MS Laud misc.609 bears several signatures on its leaves. 'Symon Chimyton' appears twice on the same folio, found approximately halfway through the manuscript, and the names 'Elizabeth Makwellam' and 'Thomas Elrinten' are both written on the last folio of the text.[102] Whatever the motivations behind these signatures, they operate differently to those that make overt statements of ownership. Perhaps the people who made these highly personal marks were just asserting their presence; the spirit of this individual self-assertion is akin to graffiti-tagging. Cedar Lewisohn defines contemporary graffiti writing as 'essentially a text-based art form, with tagging (the act of writing one's personalised signature) at its core'.[103] Wax seals are a rarer mark of someone's physical contact with a book – another manuscript, BodL, MS Rawl. C.299, features an intact wax seal impression, adhered to f. 51v.[104] Another unusual example, of someone extremely keen to tag their book repeatedly, is a copy of the prose *Brut* written in the 1460s (HEHL, MS HM 136), in which Dorothy Helbarton's name was inscribed more than sixty times, in what has been described by Anthony Bale as an act of 'belligerent literacy'.[105] While Helbarton's tagging is insistent and extreme, many other names tagged in manuscripts function much like contemporary graffiti. These scattered signatures leave a mark somewhere relatively out of the way, in margins throughout the book, yet are still visible to others privileged enough to access the book.

Why did these writers take the time to jot down their signatures onto the leaves of books? Sometimes they must have been just testing a pen, as is so often the assumed motivation of any odd markings in margins, but sometimes they were rehearsing writing forms by inscribing their signature, sometimes they were adding to a jumble of other signatures, and sometimes they were tagging their contact with the book onto its pages.

---

[100] Jackson refers to books of the eighteenth century and later; however, her comments on signatures in books are also applicable to those found in other periods, including late medieval manuscripts, *Marginalia*, p. 19.

[101] Scott-Warren, 'Reading Graffiti', p. 380.

[102] BodL, MS Laud misc.609: fols. 89r, 170va and 170vb; Ogilvie-Thomson, in *IMEP* XVI, 76, suggests 'Makwellam' and 'Elrinten'; *LMES* suggests 'Mabwesham (???)' and 'elrinton (???)" [question marks theirs]; although both signatures are difficult to decipher, I am inclined to agree with Ogilvie-Thomson's suggestions.

[103] C. Lewisohn, *Abstract Graffiti* (London, 2011), p. 7.

[104] BodL, MS Rawl. C.299; *Quarto Catalogue* V.ii, 132. With thanks to S. Rajabzadeh for referring me to the wax blob she noticed in this manuscript.

[105] A. Bale dates the hand to *c.* 1500–1550, in 'Belligerent Literacy, Bookplates and Graffiti: Dorothy Helbarton's Book', in *Book Destruction in the West, from the Medieval to the Contemporary*, ed. A. Smyth and G. Partington (Basingstoke, 2014), pp. 89–111 (p. 92).

In each of these possible scenarios, the durable book presented an appropriately reliable and re-usable writing support. These re-uses depend upon the enduring physical presence of the book – with room for writing available on flyleaves, pastedowns, margins and interlinear spaces.

Books re-used as repositories for writing

Verses and recipes are other sequences of words also found jotted into marginal spaces. The writers who added these texts often treated the book as a repository, as a store for information. These forms of marginalia may have been noted down because they were practical instructions, such as recipes, which might be required for future reference, or because the act of writing things down itself assists memorisation. As Mary J. Carruthers states: 'writing depends on and helps memory'.[106] Unlike the codicological recipes in larger collections (discussed in Chapter 1) which are typically found arranged sequentially in the main body of text, these recipes are found in the marginal spaces of the book. When inscribed in margins, recipes could be transmitted singly, or clustered together, and may take surprisingly substantial forms. As Carrie Griffin has noted of the transmission of recipes more generally, these texts often 'survived and [were] consumed […] independently of the collection'.[107] Both recipes and verses treat the book as a repository for writing. By writing these short forms into books' margins, their writers drew on similar use-values to those that motivated book producers.

Recipes may be inscribed individually into the margins and endleaves of books for record and for reference. For example, on the final pastedown of BodL, MS Laud misc.444, a fourteenth-century copy of commentaries on religious texts, is an isolated recipe for ink.[108] The recipe is written in a fifteenth-century hand and does not seem to have anything to do with the texts in the rest of the manuscript. The sprawling secretary handwriting near the top of the page reads: 'To make Inke . take of Gumme j d weyght / of coperose ij d weyght of galle iiij penny weyght'[109] and, as is more common in verse, the two lines of writing are bounded by a bracket to the right. These ingredients – gum, gall,

---

[106] Carruthers, *The Book of Memory*, p. 34; see also her discussion of Quintilian's literal and metaphorical suggestions that writing should be performed carefully and frequently 'as an aid for storing memory', p. 252.

[107] C. Griffin, 'Reconsidering the Recipe: Materiality, Narrative and Text in Later Medieval Instructional Manuscripts and Collections', in *Manuscripts and Printed Books in Europe 1350–1550: Packaging, Presentation and Consumption*, ed. E. Cayley and S. Powell (Liverpool, 2013), pp. 135–49 (pp. 144–45).

[108] BodL, MS Laud misc.444. The manuscript is from the late fourteenth century, *IMEP* XVI, 45; the manuscript measures 315 × 210 mm.

[109] BodL, MS Laud misc.444, fol. 157r. The recipe is written in a fifteenth-century hand (*Quarto Catalogue* II, 319–20, 562); this side of the flyleaf also contains a note of ownership and there is one other note at the top of fol. 156v; this otherwise blank leaf is roughly scraped on both sides, and sits after two flyleaves which are ruled but unwritten, and before a blank, now-lifted

and metallic sulphate – were conventionally used to make ink for writing.[110] Perhaps the inclusion of this recipe on the pastedown suggests that the manuscript was in an environment where there was regular writing activity requiring ink. Although we cannot know whether this recipe was ever actually used to guide the making of ink, it seems more likely to be a practical aide-mémoire than something dashed off as a pen test. This recipe makes it clear that people re-used marginal spaces to record useful material that they wanted to remember, and that in this case someone may have anticipated returning to this recipe to prepare ink for further textual production. This example reveals a titbit of knowledge being sustained, and someone treating the book as a sustainable place to store that knowledge.

Other slightly longer sequences of words designed for practical purposes were also jotted into marginal spaces. Another recipe, this time a charm to staunch blood, was inscribed into Bodl, MS Douce 84, a late fourteenth-century collection of medical texts (see Figure 13).[111] In this case, the added note is of the same genre as the main texts but is written in an unusual format. The charm is written neatly across the double-page spread of an open bifolium, and on the back of the bifolium is a table of contents to the main texts of the manuscript. Widely attested elsewhere, the charm reads as follows:

> Lord god as þou were borne in Bedleem an folued in <?> Jurdan thou comandeste the flom ^flode^ to stonde and hit witstode so do this blod that this body .N. here blest þorow the vertue of the blod that thou bledeste whan thou sholdest deye as thou ert fadir and sone and holigost.[112]

This pious charm for staunching blood is sandwiched between an orderly array of other annotations, all of which are in a similarly neat script with both secretary and anglicana forms. One of these other notes is a recipe for spiced and sugared wine: '1 vnce sugre half vnce frankensence ij quart wyn and seth hem to a pynte and braie the forsayd sugre and ensence to gedre'.[113] Though these recipes for apparently utilitarian purposes might seem convenient, jotted onto a flyleaf together, it would be difficult to pick out the relevant one in an emergency, for example when suffering heavy blood loss. It seems likely that these recipes were written down not just for future reference but also for activating and exercising the memory through the act of writing. This example presents a strongly suggestive

---

pastedown; *MED, coperose, n.*, a 'metallic sulphate, as of iron (green), of copper (blue), or of zinc (white); vitriol [used in tanning, dyeing, and medicinally]'; Clarke, *Crafte*, p. 286.

[110] For more on ink recipes, see Chapter 1.

[111] BodL, MS Douce 84, fols. ii verso–iii recto.

[112] BodL, MS Douce 84, fols. ii verso–iii recto. *IMEP* IV, 31–35, dates this composite manuscript to the end of the fourteenth century and the middle of the fifteenth century; *Summary Catalogue* IV, 515; another version of this charm is in BL, MS Sloane 88, noted in *Index of Printed Middle English Prose*, ed. R. E. Lewis, N. F. Blake and A. S. G. Edwards (New York, 1985), p. 149; the widespread popularity of the 'Flum Jordan' charm in the late medieval period is mentioned by D. C. Skemer, *Binding Words: Textual Amulets in the Middle Ages* (Philadelphia, 2006), p. 208.

[113] BodL, MS Douce 84, fols. ii verso–iii recto.

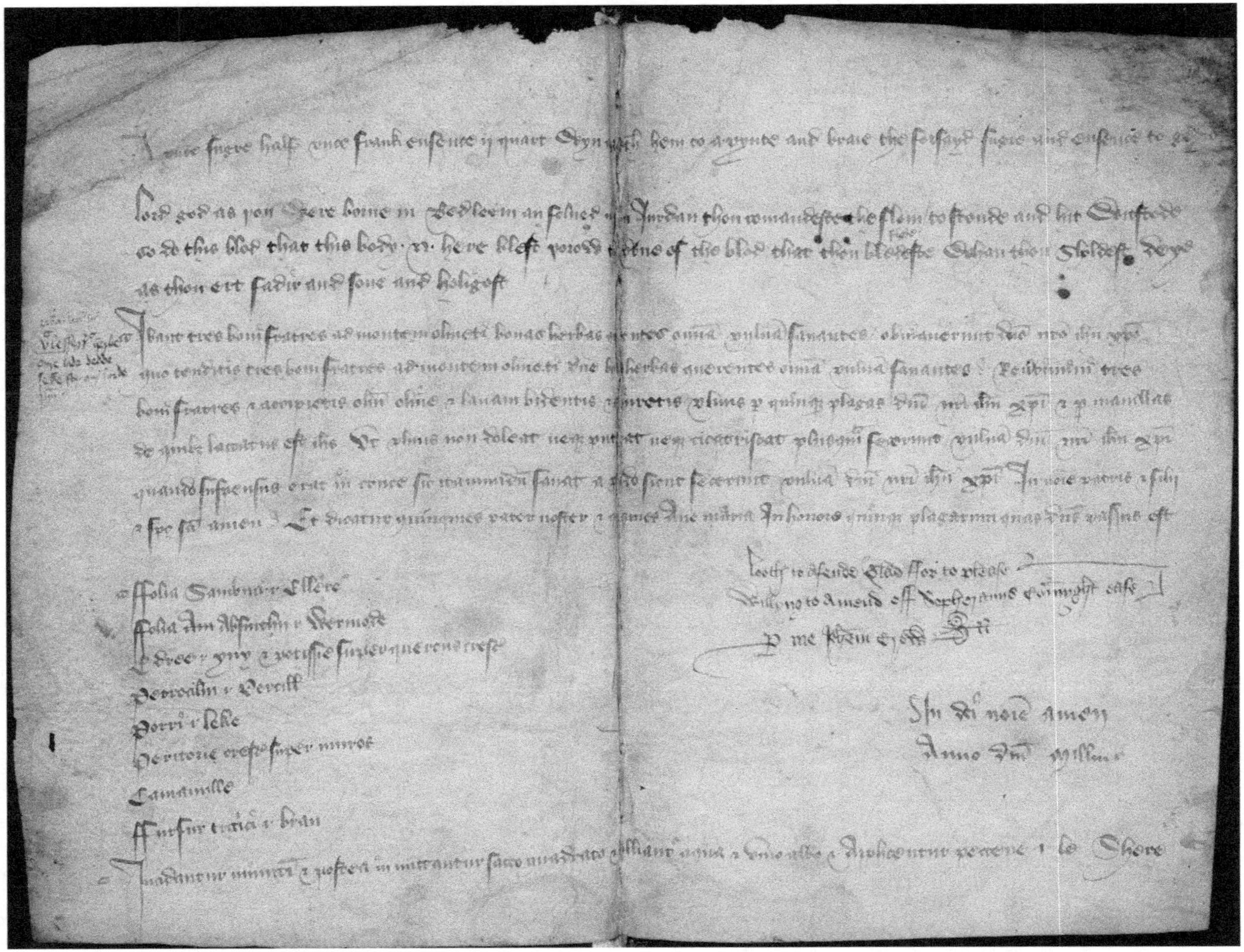

Figure 13. BodL, MS Douce 84, fols. ii verso–iii recto, recipes written across front flyleaves.

case for the acts of writing out and re-reading recipes as facilitating memorisation. In this way, by acting as repositories for written records of recipes, marginal spaces in books also sustain memory culture outside the book.

Verses

In addition to practical re-uses of marginal spaces for writing, such as the recipes or charms above, marginal spaces could also provide space for more frivolous and amusing verses. Like the other examples of marks made in books explored throughout this chapter, verses also convert the book's use-value from being an object for reading to being a space for writing. This is widely attested; as Julia Boffey comments, 'many late Middle English lyrics are found on fly-leaves or squashed into odd spaces in copies of unrelated works'.[114] And, in common with more practical or everyday verbal inscriptions, verses written into the marginal spaces of manuscripts demonstrate treatment of the book as a repository. The writing supports used to make books are therefore recycled and made available for further additions of writing. Rather than using up other resources elsewhere, these verses are written onto spare spaces in books. Sometimes verses are neatly recorded, perhaps in anticipation of others reading these entertaining marginal inscriptions, and sometimes verses seem to be written without regard for legibility or future use.

Again, a verse might be jotted in the margins to jog the memory of the writer, but perhaps not necessarily for anyone else's use. An example of this is found in the composite manuscript BodL, MS Douce 84; along with a uroscopic treatise and various medical recipes, this manuscript also contains Latin texts, including Psalm 134, and at this point in the manuscript, there is a substantial verse written in the lower margin.[115] These verses refer to the kings of England, beginning 'kyng harry þe verst' and running on for four lines. On these leaves a single scribe wrote the main text in a secretary hand. The verses are in a particularly scruffy, scrawled secretary script, and are unrelated to the main texts at this point. The main text on this folio features guidance on how to pray, written in English, which directly precedes the Latin text of Psalm 134. Therefore, this verse is clearly distinct from the adjacent texts, as well as being distinct from the general tenor of the collected works in this composite manuscript; the hand is notably different and the verses are haphazardly inserted in the lower margin. The script is significantly less disciplined than the main hands found throughout the rest of the manuscript, implying that marginal spaces were being re-used in a casual way.

A diverting extra text is added onto the damaged final leaf of another composite manuscript, BodL, MS Douce 257, which dates from the late fourteenth century and comprises an ecclesiastical calendar, texts on arithmetic and grammar, recipes for cooking chicken and instructions for conducting an exorcism. Written at the end of this mixed array of texts

---

[114] J. Boffey, 'Manuscript and Print: Books, Readers and Writers', in *A Companion to Medieval Poetry*, ed. C. Saunders (Oxford, 2010), pp. 538–54 (p. 540).
[115] BodL, MS Douce 84, fols. 33v–34r; *IMEP* IV, 31–35 (p. 34).

is a short verse about the apparent tribulations of marriage, comprising several misogynist adages about bothersome wives.¹¹⁶ Images of a man's face and a cloth-draped book were mentioned earlier in this chapter and these are on the other side of the same leaf. The verse is on the lower third of the page beneath another, more substantial piece of writing, a charm in French for curing wounds.¹¹⁷ The charm and the verse about marriage are distinct specimens of script and ink, with the charm above in a faded brown-toned black ink, and the verse below in black ink with a split nib. The parchment is visibly scuffed where the top line of this verse has been scratched away, and only the faintest vestiges of ink remain.¹¹⁸ Nevertheless, beneath this partially erased line the following lines remain:

A‹n old wife and an empty cu›p
þer ys no merth yn noþir
A man þat haþ y teyd ‹hy›m vp
May nawte chese an‹oþ›ir
A yong wyf and an arvyst gos
Moche gagil wiþ boþe
A man þat haþ ham yn his clos
reste schal he wroþe.¹¹⁹

In addition to the partly damaged and partly scraped quality of parchment on which this verse has been inscribed, the script in which this verse is written is scrappier than the one used for the text above it on the same page. Both the charm for staunching blood and the recipe for spiced wine were written to run on in prose form, whereas this verse is lineated by sound pattern. In this, it is typical of the verses and prayers used as space fillers in marginal spaces. While it could not be said to be a neat copy, the verse is set out with the poetic form observed carefully. There is even some diligent bracketing of the rhyme scheme (in an ababcdcd pattern). It shares the same kind of frivolous whimsicality and humour seen in some of the doodled non-verbal markings discussed previously. Perhaps this verse was intended to be shared with future readers, for their amusement. And in the context of motley miscellanies which already contain diverse, even highly discontinuous texts, marginalia of this kind are – to some extent – welcome. Nevertheless, while this verse

---

[116] BodL, MS Douce 257, fol. 99v. The manuscript also includes 'tricks' for cooking chicken and conducting an exorcism (*Summary Catalogue* IV, 569–70); *DIMEV* 496; R. H. Robbins entitles the verse 'The Tribulations of Marriage' and suggests that this was a popular song, *Secular Lyrics of the XIVth and XVth Centuries* (Oxford, 1952 and 1961), p. 38.

[117] BodL, MS Douce 257, fol. 99v. This sixteen-line charm is in French and explains how to cure wounds by putting a charm on a piece of lead and reciting various Latin prayers.

[118] BodL, MS Douce 257, fol. 99v. It is unclear when this line might have been removed – the top line may have been rubbed off when some marks above the verse, perhaps including signatures, were scraped off.

[119] BodL, MS Douce 257, fol. 99v. *DIMEV* 496 supplies both the first line 'An old wife and an empty cup', which is erased in the manuscript, and the words 'hym' and 'anoþir', where there is a hole in the parchment.

may be in the spirit of this composite manuscript, it was an afterthought, not part of the main production of the book. The writer of this verse was engaging with similar use-values to the book producer but supplements the initial campaign of production by claiming marginal space for an opportunistic, hastily annotated verse.

Flyleaves seem to be a standard location for humorous verse. In a copy of *Mandeville's Travels*, BodL, MS Douce 33, a verse occupies the first of three parchment flyleaves at the back of the book.[120] The book is small enough to be held comfortably in the hands, and measures 130 × 90 mm.[121] The verse reads:

> Love ys had whyll monney
> doth lest when monney ys gone
> love ys paste ~~~
> Thogh somme women be blamyd all
> hath nott offendyd please theym that
> be good the beste may be amendyd
> Better yet ys smale howsold for to
> hold then to ly yn presons fetteres
> of gold
> [amen].[122]

This verse articulates enduring, if cynical, sentiments about love and money. It is set out on the flyleaf with gaps between each of the three short stanzas. Intriguingly, though the verse is set out into stanzas the lines are written out as prose, running over lines without starting a new line at the rhyming word. The main hand in this manuscript is a consistent, neat anglicana with some secretary forms, which contrasts noticeably with this verse, written in a sprawling secretary script. When the layout is considered in conjunction with the extremely scrawly hand, this written verse suggests that the aim of the writer was to note down the verse, rather than to reflect the sound of the verse in the layout or to make it especially legible to future readers.

Another version of this verse exists elsewhere, so it seems that it was not an original composition. In the other version, BodL, Douce BB 200, the verse is noted onto the back of a flyleaf in a print copy of the Sarum Breviary of 1519, this time set out as poetry.[123]

---

[120] BodL, MS Douce 33, fols. 152–54, with verse at fol. 152r. *IMEP* IV, 10, dates it to the first quarter of the fifteenth century; *Summary Catalogue* IV, 499; Seymour, *Manuscripts of Mandeville's Travels*, p. 182; Seymour, *Defective Version*, pp. xvii–xix.

[121] BodL, MS Douce 33. Seymour notes that the book is one of two surviving copies of *Mandeville's Travels* that are 'of small octavo size, held easily in one hand' and states dimensions of 125 × 90 mm, in *Manuscripts of Mandeville's Travels*, pp. 173, 182.

[122] BodL, MS Douce 33, fol. 152r.

[123] BodL, Douce BB 200, as noted by W. A. Ringler Jr., *Bibliography and Index of English Verse in Manuscript 1501–1558*, prepared and completed by M. Rudick and S. J. Ringler (London, 1992), p. 151.

The verse itself is one of a number of short texts that have been neatly written in secretary script onto a flyleaf that directly follows the main text.[124] It reads:

> Love . ys hade . whyll sylver dothe laste
> Whene . sylver ys gone . Loue ys paste
> Who . no . thing . kepeth ys. ande more . nede.

There are no further stanzas in this copy. Taken together, these examples confirm that in its time this verse was popular enough to have existed in at least two loosely related forms, among other versions, for example it may have also circulated in song form. It may be significant that this version, in the back of a printed book, reflects the rhyme scheme in its lineation in a way that the other version does not. This could have been noted down from an aural exemplar, or from a different visual exemplar that followed this conventional layout. It is possible, too, that each instance of this verse was meant as a personal aide-mémoire, as with the recipe for ink or the pious charm for staunching blood, rather than as a 'neat copy' that others might later read. Though sometimes scrawled for future reference, like the instructions for making ink or staunching blood, verses sometimes appear to have been written with more care. In a copy of the *Confessio Amantis*, BodL, MS Laud misc.609 (mentioned previously for abstract markings and a few signatures) there is a verse added onto the final leaf of the poem, which contrasts 'driery' thoughts with May-time merriness (see Figure 14). It is a unique version of a *Bele Aeliz* poem in Middle English.[125] The verse reads:

> In Aprell and in May when hartys ⌐be all mery ¬
> Besse buntyng the myllaris may ⌐with lyppes so red as chery ¬
> She cast in hyr remembrance
> to passe hyr tyme in dalyaunce
> And to leue hyr thowth driery
> Rygth womanly arayd in a petycote of whytt
> She was nothyng dysmayd
> Hyr cowntenance was ffull lygth.[126]

Here, this smartly executed verse is written in a textura script on the final leaf. Textura script was used outside books for church inscriptions in stone and brass: textura inscriptions in

---

[124] BodL, Douce BB 200. Stains on the paper flyleaf on which it is written indicate that the page may have previously been adhered to, or perhaps just in contact with, a backboard, but not necessarily the current binding; the binding also includes two later paper flyleaves at the front and at the back of the book.

[125] P. J. Frankis, 'Two Minor French Lyric Forms in English', *Neuphilologische Mitteilungen* 60 (1959), 66–71 (p. 70).

[126] BodL, MS Laud misc.609, fol. 170va; *DIMEV* 2475; Coxe, in *Quarto Catalogue* II, 432, omits the added secretary hand on lines one and two and transcribes some lines differently: line two 'Hesse huntyng', line six 'peticote', line seven 'dymayd' and line eight 'countenance'; 'with lyppes so red as chery' supplied by R. T. Davies, who entitles the poem 'Besse Bunting', and transcribes several details slightly differently from Coxe, in *Medieval English Lyrics* (London, 1963), p. 212.

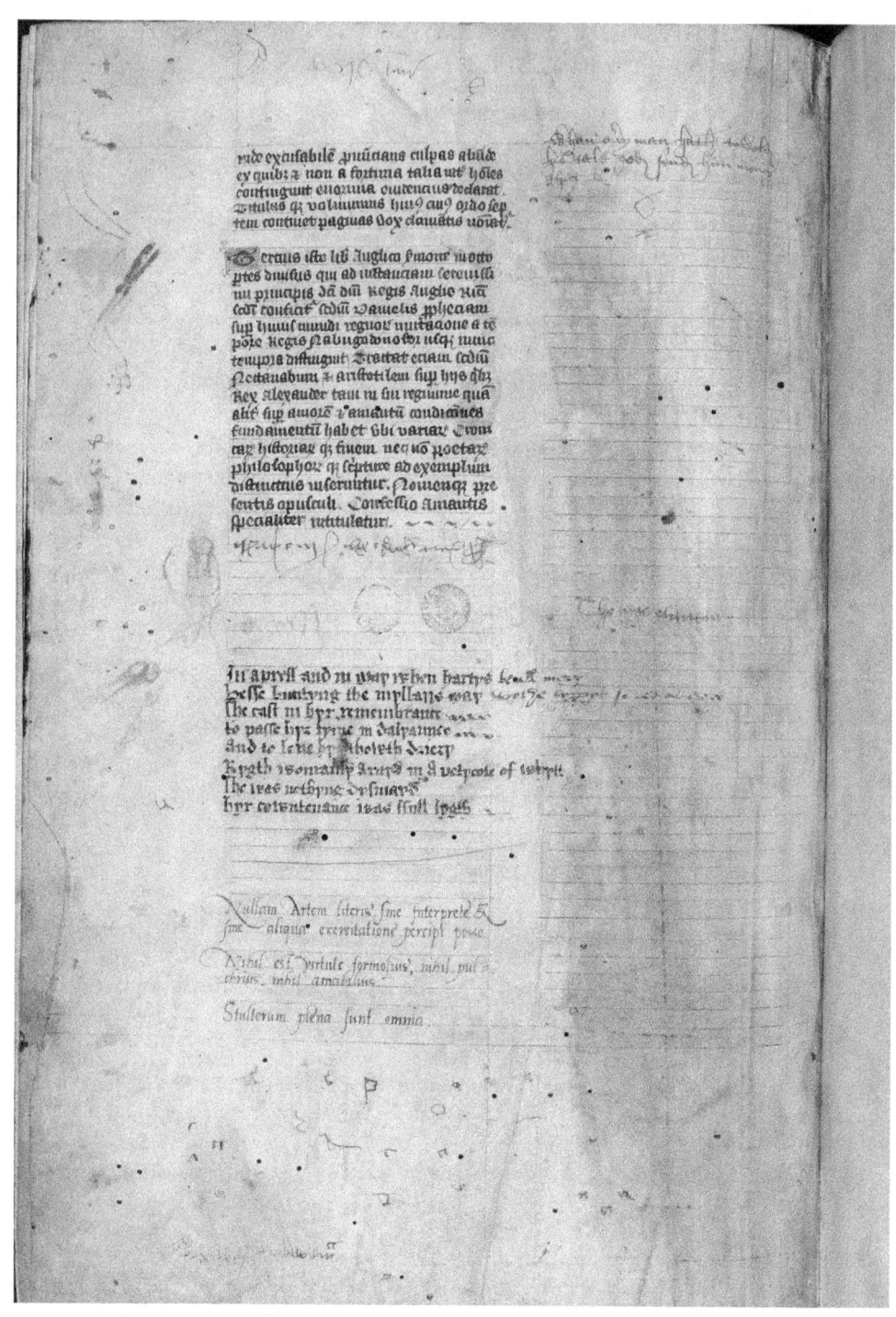

Figure 14. BodL, MS Laud misc.609, fol. 170va, verse added to the last leaf.

books were typically intended to give the impression of gravitas and were expected to last. The main text ends just above the verse, and the handwriting of the main text is gentler in execution than the spiky script used for most of the verse; the two hands are also in different inks. The rest of Column a is mostly empty, as is Column b. A later, sprawling secretary script was at some point added to complete the first two lines of the poem. This literary verse, which plays on the May-time trope, switches from serious 'remembrance' to invoking a woman's light-hearted 'cowntenance'. Moreover, it demonstrates that margins were re-used for literary verses. This example was written out so neatly that the writer made it possible for many generations of future readers to access the text, to read it with ease and to enjoy the lyric.

Conclusions

The markings explored in this chapter show that fifteenth-century books were subject to use-values that prized their surfaces as writing supports for making marks. A riot of mark-making took place in the marginal spaces of manuscripts, and these included non-verbal scribbles, doodles and drawings, as well as verbal markings such as alphabets, signatures, recipes, charms, and verses. Re-use of the manuscript for verbal and non-verbal markings alike was in part due to utility, and the recycling of books' marginal spaces is part of a wider context of writing on things. Some of these markings were pen tests, some treated manuscript leaves more like wax tablets or scrap parchment, some were early-learning exercises, and some were distractions. There were pragmatic motivations, such as re-uses that treated the book as a repository for recipes or other notes, in addition to more playful, even apparently meaningless re-uses of books. Diversion and amusement – the sheer enjoyment of spaces in books – therefore constitute another dimension of book re-use. While marginal markings are usually clearly separate endeavours from the main texts, literate writing in marginal spaces, such as recipes, charms, and verses can appear to continue the purpose of the book as a carrier of texts.

But the use-values have subtly shifted: these markings were made in such a way that they re-use the surfaces available in the manuscript as a writing support for two kinds of writing. As this chapter has shown, one kind of writing or doodling was ephemeral, treating books like scrap parchment and paper, or like the erasable surface of a wax tablet. This kind of marginal marking was sustainable in the ways in which it salvaged space in books and avoided wasting other writing supports. Modern psychological studies suggest that those scribbles and doodles – which may appear wholly unrelated to the main text – may have, surprisingly, played an active part in helping readers to concentrate on the main text by staving off daydreaming. The second kind of writing treated marginal spaces in books as places for recording information, and for future reference. Writing out recipes, charms, and verses may have had an impact outside the book, even by cultivating memory. Whether the book was being treated as an ephemeral surface or as a repository, the material presence of the marginal spaces of the book were essential supports for mark-making.

Ultimately, both kinds of marginalia explored here depended upon the physical durability of the manuscript.

As already indicated by the proprietary potential of signatures in manuscripts, which in this chapter were for practising penmanship or tagging books, markings in books could also represent significant relationships between people, and between people and their books. Chapter 4 explores many kinds of markings in books that explicitly state such relationships. In turn, these relationships suggest that books were sustained through ongoing second-hand circulation, and by further dimensions of re-use.

4

Second-Hand Books

> the slow long-term dance,
> temporary ownership, possession and loss.
> Roy Kelly, 'Another Slice'[1]

This chapter explores the second-hand movement of medieval manuscripts between people in the fifteenth century, paying attention to what they wrote about that circulation on to the leaves of books. A book was an 'artefact for reading' that could be converted into an 'artefact for owning', and the ownership of that artefact could change.[2] Kelly's poem captures this, describing things moving second-hand as a 'slow long-term dance'. In the fifteenth century, manuscripts became second-hand by a range of mechanisms: they might be sold, resold, bought, given, received, bequeathed, inherited, shared, even used as collateral for a loan. Manuscripts were 'typically produced to outlive their first users [...] an ambition made thinkable by the durability of medieval books'.[3] That durable materiality was acknowledged by donors of common-profit books: the books they gave were to be used and re-used by an ongoing sequence of worthy recipients, but they also acknowledged that books might not last forever. This chapter understands fifteenth-century books to be durable commodities with use-values that resulted in their movement between people. Inscriptions in books offer glimpses of how books passed from one person to another, and sometimes give explicit indication of how the book was being valued at that moment.

Marginal annotations express aspects of second-hand book ownership or various forms of giving, or various forms of receipt. These notes offer an insight into contemporary medieval ideas about manuscripts, expectations of them and conventional modes of recording information about second-handedness. Of course, almost any fifteenth-century manuscript-book might qualify as being second-hand: to approach this topic, this chapter is informed by surveys of manuscript collections, which yielded examples of inscriptions that

---

[1] R. Kelly, 'Another Slice', *The Spectator*, 30 January 2016, online <https://www.spectator.co.uk/article/another-slice>. Reproduced here with the permission of the poet.

[2] A. Bale, 'Belligerent Literacy, Bookplates and Graffiti: Dorothy Helbarton's Book', in *Book Destruction in the West, from the Medieval to the Contemporary*, ed. A. Smyth and G. Partington (Basingstoke, 2014), pp. 89–111 (p. 9).

[3] M. Johnston and M. Van Dussen, 'Introduction: Manuscripts and Cultural History', in *The Medieval Manuscript Book: Cultural Approaches*, ed. M. Johnston and M. Van Dussen (Cambridge, 2015), pp. 1–16 (p. 7).

note the second-hand movement of books. From these surveys arose a sense of what second-hand book transfers typically looked like, as well as examples of specific inscriptions written into books. The notes are both historical record and historical practice and testify to contemporary modes of book re-use.

Here, *second-hand* refers to any later possession of books, after the first phase of ownership. The modern understanding of second-hand goods today includes not only things previously owned by others, but also the resale of those things for profit, sometimes for the benefit of charitable causes. In their study of modern-day second-hand consumption, Nicky Gregson and Louise Crewe show that the distinction between 'the market' and 'the gift' are notably complicated in this context.[4] The market and the gift intersected in the fifteenth century too: while second-hand books were traded, charity often motivated the giving and sharing of books. The basic meaning of second-hand here is simply sequential ownership by two or more people.[5] Also, communal or collective forms of ownership are explored for the ways in which they might also qualify as second-handedness. So, second-handedness might look like individual ownership of a book by a student, or corporate ownership by a university college, or a cathedral community. Shared use of books might muddle the distinction between individual or corporate forms of ownership. Formalised versions of this mixed ownership include the handful of books donated for the 'common profit' of a designated group, or the yearly *electio* system and chained libraries of medieval colleges. Transfers in the ownership of books, then, could make books second-hand in various ways, and, in turn, those books could be re-used in various ways.

Second-hand circulation depended on both the book's material durability and on opportunities for it to pass through multiple owners. Throughout, this study finds the re-use of medieval manuscripts to depend on the durable, resilient qualities of parchment and manuscripts, in concert with organised systems for re-use. Both are in play here. First, second-hand book circulation depended on the physical resilience of books. Every purchase, gift, or pledge of a manuscript expressed expectations that the books themselves would last. Pledges to loan chests are perhaps the most explicit embodiment of belief in books' durability. Second, medieval books changed hands, and sometimes passed through several transfers of ownership. This too suggests dependence on the persistent, durable nature of books. Furthermore, sharing books (whether in a casual sense or in the sense of sequential or communal ownership) suggests efforts to pool resources, and instructions about the storage or use of books indicates attention to their ongoing conservation. In signalling these hopes, inscriptions could enable second-hand re-uses of books.

The financial corollary of the expectation that books would last was that, in fifteenth-century society at large, books were treated as a form of capital. As R. A. B. Mynors states, books were 'like plate, one of the recognized ways of holding capital', and M. B. Parkes describes books as 'not merely [...] instruments for study' but also a 'portable form

---

[4] N. Gregson and L. Crewe, *Second-hand Cultures* (Oxford, 2003), p. 8.
[5] *OED, hand, n.*, Sense VI 25a(b); *OED, second-hand, adj.*, Sense 2a.

of capital'.⁶ The sale, purchase or pledge of books usually involved financial valuation of the price that the book could command. So how did fifteenth-century people go about valuing books? Value could be attributed to the materials required for production, to the skilled artisanal labour and effort involved in its production, to the finished artefact, to the text a book carried, or to its educational, religious or social cachet. However they were derived, such valuations could be noted down in books themselves, or in other documents such as wills, inventories, booklists, donors' lists, registers, accounts, and in library catalogues.⁷ Though some reference is made to evidence external to books, like wills, the focus in this chapter is notes written into books, and how those suggest expectations that books would last.

The values attributed to books were not just economic, they were also social and spiritual. As briefly mentioned already, charity often motivated the second-hand movement of books. In his comments, Mynors goes on to point out that books held capital 'in portable and *negotiable* form'.⁸ At any given time, a book may be subject to a range of actual, perceived, and as-yet-unknown or untapped values. The potential value of a book can be enhanced by the popularity of the text it bears, or by the grade of materials used in its production, by the later addition of costly materials, such as a binding, or even by prestigious second-hand movement. A valued provenance depends on ownership by notable people, especially where this is visibly recorded in the book itself. The potential value of a book can also be diminished by the passing of time, by the changing cultural capital of a text, by the vagaries of fashion, or by wear and tear, amongst other things. In all these ways, the values attributed to a book can rise and fall. Nevertheless, many transfers of ownership represent faith in the resilience of medieval books' material forms and values.

While the value of a book could fluctuate, conventions for notating ownership are somewhat more predictable. Almost all the inscriptions surveyed for the present chapter were written at the front or back of books. Anywhere in the front of a book was regarded as the 'traditional' place for a bookplate or other assertion of ownership, and it was the first space a reader encountered upon opening the book from the front.⁹ Also, inscriptions

---

[6] *Catalogue of the Manuscripts of Balliol College, Oxford*, ed. R. A. B. Mynors (Oxford, 1963), p. xi; M. B. Parkes, 'The Provision of Books', in *The History of the University of Oxford: Late Medieval Oxford*, ed. J. I. Catto and T. A. R. Evans, 2 vols. (Oxford, 1992), II, 407–83 (p. 409).

[7] For example, see S. H. Cavanaugh, 'A Study of Books Privately Owned in England 1300–1450' (unpublished doctoral thesis, University of Pennsylvania, 1980); for the inventories of books owned by Sir Simon Burley and William de Walcote, see V. J. Scattergood, 'Two Medieval Book Lists', *The Library* 5th s. 23:3 (1968), 236–39; and for a list of medieval British library catalogues, see *MLGB*, Bodleian Libraries, University of Oxford, online <http://mlgb3.bodleian.ox.ac.uk/authortitle/medieval_catalogues/>.

[8] Mynors, *Balliol Catalogue*, p. xi.

[9] H. J. Jackson, *Marginalia: Readers Writing in Books* (Toronto, 2001), p. 19; D. Wakelin, '"Thys ys my boke": Imagining the Owner in the Book', in *Spaces for Reading in Later Medieval England*, ed. M. C. Flannery and C. Griffin (Basingstoke, 2016), pp. 13–33 (pp. 13, 18).

which observe the second-hand movement of books often adopted conventional phrasing. Sometimes inscriptions were heavily abbreviated, to function as a quick note of the price or cost of a book, or the name of a new owner. But people also wrote more extensive inscriptions to indicate whether the book was sold, purchased, given as a gift, pledged, bequeathed or donated for common profit. These longer inscriptions may name previous owners and new owners, and may locate the book in a place or community. This chapter explores a range of notes written into books for the ways in which the ownership of books transferred between people. To do so, it offers two surveys: the first focusses on second-hand booksellers, and the second gives impressions about the kinds of inscriptions that typically mark the movement of medieval books. The chapter begins with an overview of the fifteenth-century trade in new books, because the second-hand circulation of books existed within and alongside it.

Unfortunately, thanks to a 'paucity of explicit narrative or documentary evidence about book production and acquisition', exploring the trade in books at any time during the Middle Ages is difficult.[10] Nonetheless, although there is only 'fugitive' surviving evidence, scholars have developed impressions of the nature of the trade, especially in the later medieval period.[11] What is clear is that over the course of the long fifteenth century the trade changed dramatically, growing, diversifying, and becoming more organised. C. Paul Christianson has described the century that elapsed between the 1390s and the 1490s as 'the period of greatest commercial activity in making and selling manuscript books'.[12] Books were made in growing numbers as the century wore on, with 'something like a tenfold increase in vernacular book production between 1350 and 1475'.[13] The growth in production served diversifying markets, and accompanied increases in rates of literacy. The availability of books was further enhanced by imports and by continuing developments in paper and print technology.

While it is possible to characterise the book trade as undergoing these overall shifts, it may be imprecise to refer to a single book trade at all. As A. I. Doyle notes, the term encompasses three different activities: first, the 'practice of various handicrafts' towards making books, second, the 'provision of texts' and the 'coordination of the crafts to produce copies' and, third, the 'selling of books, old or new, and of the requisite materials'.[14]

---

[10] A. I. Doyle, 'The English Provincial Book Trade Before Printing', in *Six Centuries of the Provincial Book Trade in Britain*, ed. P. Isaac (Winchester, 1990), pp. 13–29 (p. 13); A. S. G. Edwards concurs that 'The nature of markets for manuscripts in the Middle Ages in England is generally not easy to understand', 'Medieval Manuscripts, the Collector, and the Trade', in *The Cambridge Companion to the Medieval English Manuscript*, ed. O. Da Rold and E. Treharne (Cambridge, 2020), pp. 284–94 (p. 284).

[11] C. P. Christianson, 'Evidence for the Study of London's Late Medieval Manuscript-Book Trade', in *BPPB*, pp. 87–108 (p. 89).

[12] Christianson, 'Manuscript-Book Trade', p. 89.

[13] J. Raven, *The Business of Books: Booksellers and the English Book Trade, 1450–1850* (New Haven, 2007), p. 13.

[14] Doyle, 'Provincial Book Trade', p. 13.

Doyle's definition shows how recycled materials and second-hand books might both fit into different parts of this wider market. Second-hand book sales constituted just one of several book trade activities.

The trades involved in making, distributing, and selling books were carried out on local, regional, national, and international scales. During the fifteenth century, Oxford and London were both hubs for the production and trade in books. Evidence from archival documents situates book artisans in Catte Street, Oxford, and around St. Paul's churchyard in London.[15] Other provincial sites of book production included Leicester and various precincts of York, among other locations.[16] Throughout the fifteenth century, the book trade, or rather, the cluster of trades and crafts collected under that term, became increasingly cooperative and organised. For example, in London the eventual incorporation of the 'Stationers' Company' in 1557 was preceded by well over a hundred years of gradual efforts towards professionalisation among textwriters and scribes, limners and binders.[17] As will shortly be seen, some of the same people involved in the trade in new books and in professionalising these collective trades were also involved in selling second-hand books. Though this has been described as 'a widespread trade in second-hand manuscripts',[18] records of book sales are relatively rare, described as 'the subject more of speculation than of clear documentation'.[19] However, several notes found jotted into surviving manuscripts identify booksellers by name, and occasionally give further particulars, which may include names and what was paid. In due course this chapter will explore some other instances of purchases and prices discovered in a thorough survey. But first it will consider a smaller group of manuscripts connected with men known to have worked in the second-hand book trade.

Christianson identified twelve known book artisan-stationers associated with twenty surviving books that were sold second-hand. Their names, using the most common spellings, are Peter Bylton, Robert Chirche, Edmund Cok, Richard Colop, John Elys, Thomas Lokton, David Lyonhill, Thomas Marleburgh, William de Nessefylde, John Pye, John Sampson and Thomas Veysey.[20] These individuals were linked to books as either owners or sellers, mostly by information in inscriptions written on to their leaves. Of those twelve

---

[15] M. B. Parkes, *Their Hands Before Our Eyes: A Closer Look at Scribes*, The Lyell Lectures, Oxford, 1999 (Aldershot, 2008), p. 52; G. Pollard, *Notes for a Directory of Cat Street: Oxford Before A.D. 1500*, Bodleian Library Archive, Catalogue of the Papers of Graham Pollard, compiled by E. Potter (1937/1988); see Christianson, 'Manuscript-Book Trade', p. 90, especially for the map of 'Bookmen's London in the fifteenth century'.

[16] Doyle, 'Provincial Book Trade', pp. 13–29; S. Gee, 'The Printers, Stationers and Bookbinders of York before 1557', *Transactions of the Cambridge Bibliographical Society* 12:1 (2000), 27–54; J. Hinks, 'The Beginnings of the Book Trade in Leceister', in *The Moving Market: Continuity and Change in the Book Trade*, ed. P. Isaac and B. McKay (New Castle, 2001), pp. 27–38.

[17] P. W. M. Blayney, *The Stationers' Company Before the Charter, 1403–1557* (London, 2003), p. 9.

[18] Johnston and Van Dussen, 'Manuscripts and Cultural History', p. 7.

[19] Christianson, 'Manuscript-Book Trade', p. 87.

[20] Christianson, 'Manuscript-Book Trade', p. 108, n. 45.

artisan-stationers, eight were 'involved with the sale of older manuscripts that were not of their own making' and four with 'sale or possession of fifteenth-century books'.²¹ The books they dealt were probably sold for profit. Some records of sales cited by Christianson are less explicit than others about whether the book is second-hand.²² Though Cok, Lokton, Elys, Veysey and Colop are all rightly recognised as members of the London book trade, in these instances they were not necessarily selling books for profit – or at least the inscriptions are not precise or informative on this matter.

Common-profit books

While it was not a sale for profit, the stationer Richard Colop was involved in the common-profit model of second-hand book exchange, mentioned in the introduction and in previous chapters. His probable relative John Colop was the executor of the grocer John Killum's estate.²³ Both Colops were stationers, and can be linked to London, Lambeth Palace Library, MS 472, a surviving example of this book exchange system, though I focus here on the link to Richard Colop. Another extant common-profit book is BodL, MS Douce 25, previously mentioned in Chapter 2 for the off-cuts at the back of the book. There are five known common-profit books, which form a unique group of second-hand manuscripts.²⁴ These books were small-scale, relatively cheaply made, portable manuscript copies of devotional religious texts. They were funded by bequests and came with conditions attached, with the aim of maximising shared use of the book by deserving readers.

---

21 Christianson, 'Manuscript-Book Trade', p. 101, does not state which stationers fall into each category, and some seem to fit both; the eight are presumably Bylton, Chirche, Lyonhill, Marleburgh, de Nessefylde, Pye, Sampson, and Veysey, and the four possibly Cok, Colop, Elys, and Lokton.

22 BL, MS Harley 641, fol. 115v: 'Edmund Cok ligavit librum istum', 'Edmund Cok bound this book'; *British Library Illuminated Catalogue*; Christianson, *Directory*, pp. 89–90. GCC, MS 23/12, fol. 1v; *GCC Catalogue*, ed. James, I, 17; Christianson, *Directory*, p. 129. There is an inscription on fol. 2v which reads 'liber <…>emptus pro x s', though this cannot be assumed to be associated with the *ex dono* inscription relating to Lokton on fol. 1v. CUL, MS Dd.viii.2, for example on fol. 2v. The manuscript was written by Katerine Moleyns, Prioress of the Monastery of Kyngton in Wiltshire; Hardwick and Luard, *CUL Catalogue* I, 334–36. BodL, MS Auct. D. 4. 5. No folio reference is given by Christianson, *Directory*, pp. 168–69; Veysey is not mentioned at all in *Summary Catalogue* II.i, 94. London, Lambeth Palace Library, MS 472; *A Descriptive Catalogue of the Manuscripts in the Library of Lambeth Palace*, ed. M. R. James and C. Jenkins (Cambridge, 1932), V, 648–50; Christianson, *Directory*, p. 100; *IMEP* XIII, 36–38.

23 W. Scase, 'Reginald Pecock, John Carpenter and John Colop's "Common Profit" Books: Aspects of Book Ownership and Circulation in Fifteenth-Century London', *Medium Ævum* 61:2 (1992), 261–70 (pp. 261–62). See also C. M. Barron, 'What Did Medieval London Merchants Read?', in *Medieval Merchants and Money: Essays in Honour of James L. Bolton*, ed. A. Martin and D. Matthew (London, 2016), pp. 43–70 (p. 50).

24 As noted in Chapter 2, in addition to BodL, MS Douce 25, the four other known common-profit manuscripts are: CUL, MS Ff.vi.31; BL, MS Harley 993; BL, MS Harley 2336; London, Lambeth Palace Library, MS 472. Note also R. Perry and S. Kelly's project: 'Whittington's Gift: Reconstructing the Lost Common Library of London's Guildhall' (Leverhulme Trust 2020–23).

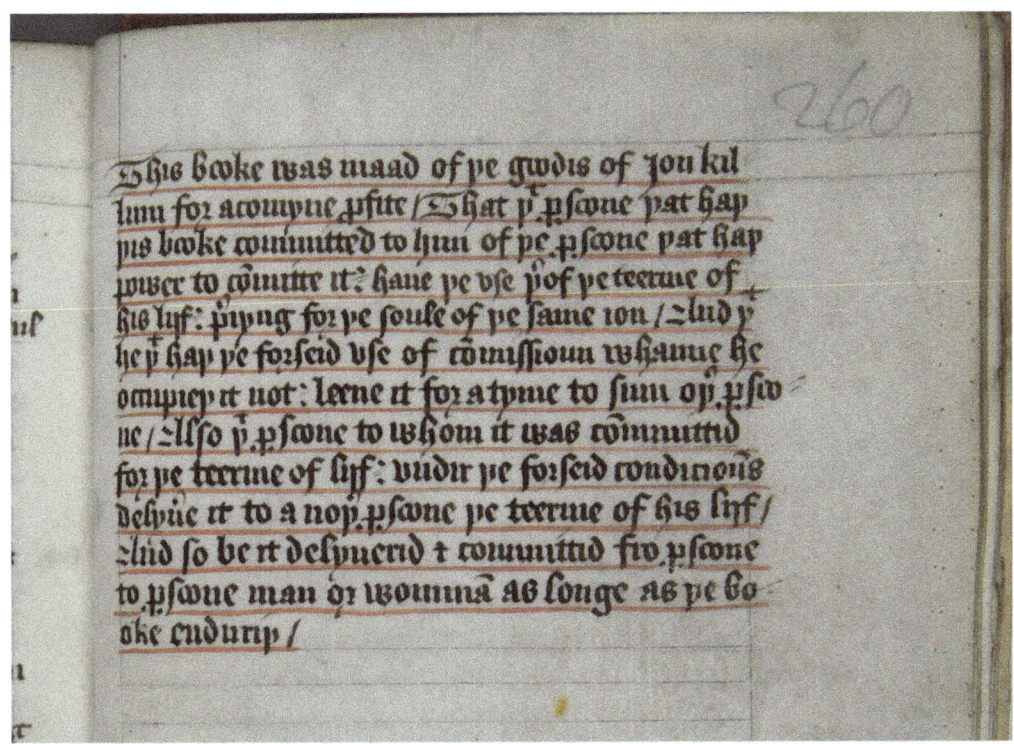

Figure 15. Lambeth Palace Library, MS 472, fol. 260r, common-profit inscription.
With kind permission of Lambeth Palace Library.

Execution of the arrangements for one of these books was entrusted to John Colop. A note towards the end of the volume details that it was funded by Killum's estate, and prescribes its future use after his death as a common-profit book. Such arrangements were signalled and stipulated by inscriptions written into each of the other common-profit books, which followed a similar form. As noted in the introduction to this book, the inscriptions call attention to the book's durability. The inscription in Killum's book is as follows (see Figure 15):

> This booke was maad of þe goodis of Jon killum for a comyne profite / That þat persoone þat haþ þis booke committed to him of þe persoone þat haþ power to committe it : haue þe vse þerof þe teerme of his lyf : praiyng for þe soule of þe same ion / And þat he þat haþ þe forseid vse of commissioun whanne he occupieþ it not : leeue it for a tyme to sum oþer persoone / Also þat persoone to whom it was committid for þe terme of lyf : vndir the forseid conditiouns delyuere it to a noþer persoone þe teerme of his lyf / And so be it delyuerid and committid fro persoone to persoone man or womman as long as þe booke enduriþ /[25]

[25] London, Lambeth Palace Library, MS 472, fol. 260r.

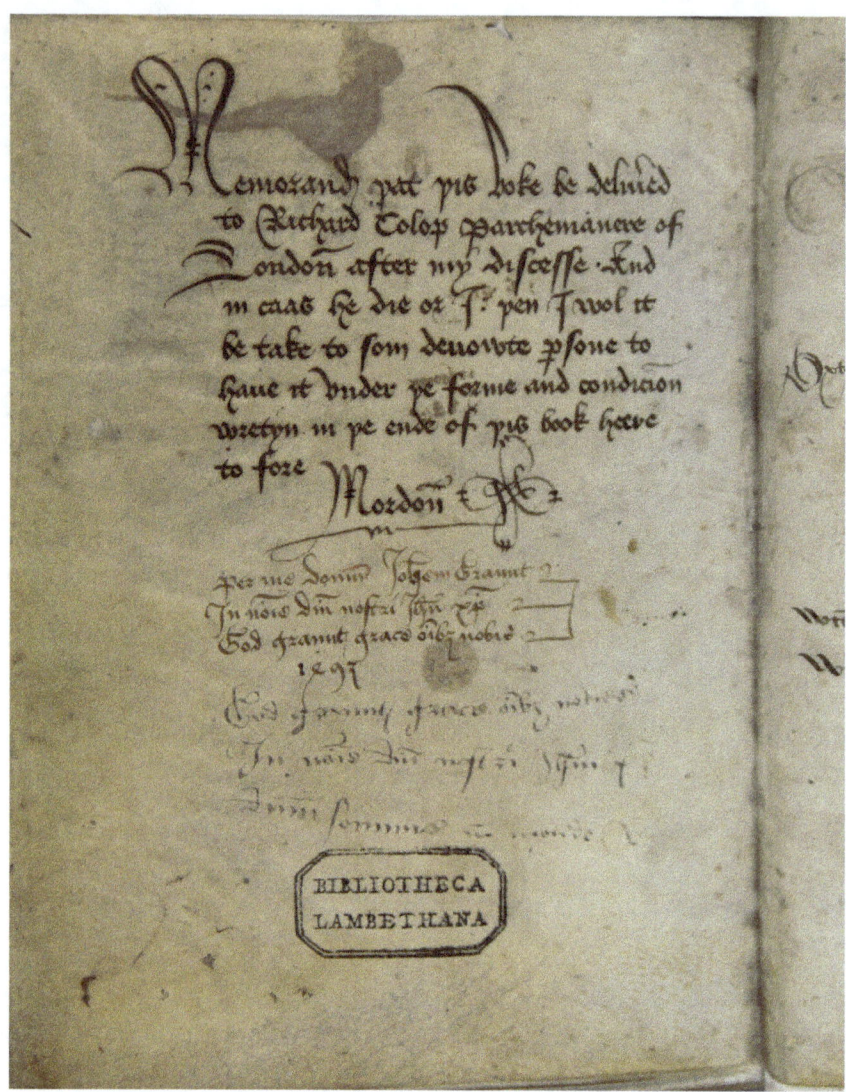

Figure 16. Lambeth Palace Library, MS 472, fol. 265r, memorandum.
With kind permission of Lambeth Palace Library.

In this inscription, there is an awareness of the passing of human lifespans in contrast with the longevity of the book itself. There is careful attention to how the book should be shared with others 'leeue it for a tyme to sum o*per per*soone', and 'delyuerid and committid' from person to person, and that 'vse' is limited to the temporary owner's 'teerme of lyf'. Therefore, the book's stipulated use-value, as an ongoing resource, absolutely depended on its physical durability. There is a clear acknowledgement that the book might not last forever but also a hope that it will be shared and passed on for 'as long as the booke enduriþ'.

Moreover, the appropriate use of common-profit books was meticulously outlined in written inscriptions in an effort to safeguard future re-uses. While common-profit inscriptions certainly suggest awareness of and concern for the ongoing sustainability of particular books, in Killum's book, an additional note a few leaves after the typical common-profit inscription specifies other practical considerations for ensuring the book's ongoing re-use, and links the book to Richard Colop by name (see Figure 16). In this memorandum, located at the back of the book, he is designated the initial recipient of Killum's manuscript:

> Memorand*um*. Þat þis boke be deliu*e*red
> to Richard Colop Parchemanere of
> London after my discesse. And
> in caas he die or I : þen I wol it
> be take to som deuowte p*er*sone to
> haue it vnder þe forme *and* condicion
> wretyn in þe ende of þis book heere
> to fore
> Mordon.[26]

Where the common-profit note is typical of its kind, this note is even more careful and elaborate in the way it has been written. The writer used a large-module, formal secretary script, and arranged the body of writing in a neat square on the page. On the page, the **M** of 'Memorand*um*' and 'Mordon' are oversized and decorated, as are various other capital letters, and following the inscription there is a decorative knotted device. The handwriting is precise, with broad strokes on stems and descenders. There are elegant sharp flicks and angular points throughout the broken shapes of the hand. The care taken over making this inscription attractive suggests that it was expected to be seen and to stay with the book. The people involved in common-profit books, such as both Colops, were involved in the London book trade. The individuals associated with common-profit books were known to each other in various ways, some still not fully established, and they drew on an awareness of the second-hand book trade to administer ongoing re-uses of their manuscripts.[27]

Other inscriptions are found in the remaining fifteen second-hand manuscripts from Christianson's list connected with eight London booksellers.[28] The most forthcoming

---

[26] London, Lambeth Palace Library, MS 472, fol. 265r.

[27] F. Somerset summarises scholarship concerning the network of connections between figures such as John Colop (likely related to Richard Colop), John Carpenter, Richard Whittington and others in '"No Man May Serue to Two Lordis": The Lollard Glossed Gospels as Spiritual Advice in John Colop's Common-Profit Book, CUL Ff.6.31', *JEBS* 22 (2019), 73–92 (pp. 73–74); see also Barron, 'Merchants', p. 66.

[28] The inscriptions in fourteen of these manuscripts are consistent with fifteenth-century hands; however, the inscription in the thirteenth-century manuscript copy of Ulpian's *Soluto matrimonio*, bought from William de Nessefylde, GCC, MS 17/133, dates to 1309–10, and so falls

notes in these manuscripts either clearly label the sellers as stationers, for example, 'J. Pye stacionario Londoniensis', or that the book was bought from someone known to be a stationer from other historical records, for example 'emptus a dauid lyenel'.[29] A few of the inscriptions offer both details. Some are therefore more comprehensively informative; others remain enigmatic. Three manuscripts, sold by two different stationers, feature only the names of their sellers. In a fifteenth-century miscellany, the stationer John Sampson's name appears,[30] and John Pye's name, without further qualification, is noted on the front leaves of two of the manuscripts that he sold. In one of these, Lancashire, Stonyhurst College, MS *Summa de Officiis Ecclesiasticis*, is inscribed 'Ion Pye'.[31] In the other, London, Gray's Inn, MS 8, rather than his full name, his surname appears with his first initial alone: 'I. Pye'.[32] It is not clear what these jotted names were for. Perhaps they were designed to indicate the stationer's temporary ownership of the book as stock before sale, or maybe they were an early form of commercial branding.

Other manuscript inscriptions are significantly more forthcoming, and in addition to naming the bookseller, offer further information about second-hand sales. An inscription with all the hallmarks of the most precise proof-of-purchase notes is found in a complex composite manuscript containing Ranulf Hidgen's *Polychronicon*, amongst other works, which was bought by John Gunthorpe in 1492. The book is in various parts, datable between the thirteenth and fifteenth centuries. The buyer saw fit to note down his own name, 'Joha*nn*is Gunthorp', his rank and role 'decani wellens*is*', the name of the bookseller 'dauid lyenel', the date of purchase '13 Julii a*nn*o vijo h*enrici* vijmi', and the book's worth 'pro iiij s iiijd'.[33] This inscription is detailed, and is symptomatic of the buyer's interest in

---

outside the long fifteenth-century focus of this study: *GCC Catalogue*, ed. James, I, 14–15; Christianson, *Directory*, p. 138.

[29] BodL, MS Bodley 110, fol. 1r: 'John Pye, London stationer', *Summary Catalogue* II.i, 135–36; and CCCC, MS 164, fol. 1r: 'bought from David Lyonhill'., *A Descriptive Catalogue of the Manuscripts in the Library of Corpus Christi College, Cambridge*, ed. M. R. James, 2 vols. (Cambridge, 1912), I, 370–74.

[30] BodL, MS Rawl. C.86, fol. 51v, Christianson, *Directory*, p. 157; *Quarto Catalogue* V.ii, 28; J. Boffey and C. M. Meale, 'Selecting the Text: Rawlinson C. 86 and some other books for London readers', in *Regionalism in Late Medieval Manuscripts and Texts: Essays Celebrating the Publication of A Linguistic Atlas of Late Medieval English*, ed. F. Riddy (Cambridge, 1991), pp. 143–69. Wakelin mentions this manuscript for an elaborate ownership inscription on fol. 30v in 'Imagining the Owner', p. 20; and K. L. Scott lists John Sampson as a 'citizen and salter of London' in 'Past Ownership: Evidence of Book Ownership by Merchants in the Later Middle Ages', in *Makers and Users of Medieval Books: Essays in Honour of A. S. G. Edwards*, ed. C. M. Meale and D. Pearsall (Cambridge, 2014), pp. 150–77 (p. 163).

[31] Lancashire, Stonyhurst College, MS *Summa de Officiis Ecclesiasticis*, now Stonyhurst Boardman MS XXVII: fol. 1r: 'John Pye'; *MMBL* III, 397–99.

[32] London, Gray's Inn, MS 8, fol. iir; *MMBL* II, 57–58.

[33] CCCC, MS 164, fol. 1r: 'dean of Wells', 'David Lyonhill', '13 July in the seventh year of the reign of Henry VII', 'for 4 s and 4 d'; Christianson, *Directory*, p. 130.

his many books – and particularly in his acquisition of them – throughout his life.[34] He is known to have recorded details of acquisition frequently in his books: there are at least twenty-four volumes with his name in them, and his name is included in notes written in a similar fashion to this purchase of 1492. A year later in 1493, an inscription states that another of his books was a second-hand purchase from 'I Barrett'.[35] The order of the details recorded in this note is identical to that jotted down in the book bought from Lyonhill, and both inscriptions serve to emphasise Gunthorpe's proof of purchase.

Equally informative, and perhaps more revealing of the weight accorded apparently insignificant details in such inscriptions, is the note in a manuscript sold by Thomas Veysey to William Palmer: 'Liber M. Will*e*h*mi* Palm*er*, ^ quo*ndam* prec*ent*or*is* eccl*es*ie Criditon ^ empt*us* a Thoma Veysey, stacion*ario* London. pro xxxiij. s. iiij. d Anno *Christi* 1433, in mense octavo'.[36] This inscription was dashed off in a current, cursive hand on a front flyleaf, and was subjected to an insertion which sits just above the line. These inscriptions are accompanied by other jottings on the flyleaf. The buyer Palmer was from Exeter diocese and studied at Exeter College in Oxford.[37] He went on to bequeath this copy of William Peraldus's *De viciis septem capitalibus et de peccato lingue* to the dean and parishioners of Crediton in Devon, as explicitly indicated by another inscription, in the same hand and ink as the insertion, set just beneath the purchase note. Having bought the manuscript for himself was important to Palmer, and, like Gunthorpe, he noted the purveyor, place, worth, and date of purchase. This inscription was then tinkered with by a later hand, to emphasise Palmer's relationship with Crediton. Presumably, Palmer's executors, or the dean and parishioners, were more interested in highlighting Palmer's role in relation to them and their shared place of worship. This gives a glimpse of the vested interests of purchasers, and of other parties involved in transfers of second-hand books.

Sometimes book artisan-stationers mentioned in the sale of manuscripts were involved as executors, which demonstrates that commercial and charitable activities around books were intertwined. Enlisted in this way, stationers were responsible for carrying out the wishes of the testator after death. Perhaps stationers, situated at the heart of London and able through their trade to develop contacts with learned individuals, and with one another, were well placed to disburse books, but also accustomed to dealing in valuable

---

[34] On John Gunthorpe, see *BRUC*, pp. 275–77, and D. Wakelin, 'England: Humanism Beyond Weiss', in *Humanism in Fifteenth-Century Europe*, ed. D. Rundle (Oxford, 2012), pp. 265–305 (pp. 267, 269, 281, 299–303).

[35] BL, MS Cotton Tiberius A.ix, fol. 2r; D. Wakelin, 'Recording Ownership, Recording the Self: Gunthorpe's Example', unpublished paper, 47th International Congress on Medieval Studies, Kalamazoo, Michigan (May 2012).

[36] Oxford, University College, MS 91, fol. 3*b: 'The book of Master William Palmer, once precentor of Crediton Church, bought from Thomas Veysey, London stationer. For 33s. 4d. In the eighth month of the year of our Lord 1433'; 'Catalogus Codicum MSS Collegii Universitatis', *Catalogus Codicum MSS. Qui in Collegiis Aulisque Oxoniensibus Hodie Adservantur*, ed. H. O. Coxe (Oxford, 1852), I, 27; Christianson, *Directory*, pp. 168–69.

[37] Palmer, *BRUO*, pp. 422–23.

goods. Though he was not selling it, this familiarity with books could account for Colop's role as the first recipient of Killum's common-profit book. Three inscriptions in three different manuscripts mention executors in relation to London book artisans. For instance, at the back of a large, beautifully decorated fifteenth-century manuscript of works by Augustine is a note which reads, 'Iste liber Al<…> ex empcione de Py stacionario *et* co-executorib*us*'.[38] This inscription clearly refers to John Pye in both his role as a stationer and, on this occasion, as co-executor. He is known to have been appointed as an executor for at least two others: for Richard Okewell in 1446 and in 1452 for Richard Broune, archdeacon of Rochester.[39] The nature of books as gifts, especially those bequeathed by a testator and managed after their death by executors, will be explored later. This inscription shows that stationers worked together to move second-hand books in a nexus of people and possessions. Thanks to their connections and expertise, stationers could act as important functional members of this network, as executors. In this role, they ensured and sustained the ongoing movement of books between people.

Two other manuscripts bring together two more London book artisan-stationers: Peter Bylton and – again – Richard Colop. The bookbinder and stationer Peter Bylton was active 1404–54 and worked on Paternoster Row, working from shops rented from London Bridge or, after 1450, in his own building 'le Petre et Poule' on the corner of Panyer Alley.[40] The two manuscripts associated with him suggest that in addition to bookbinding he may have 'dealt in older books'.[41] After Bylton's death, his books were sold off according to his wishes: as Alexandra Gillespie notes, his will of 1454 'instructs his executors to "selle all my bokes", which they did'.[42] One book, a fourteenth-century copy of works by St Augustine, went for 56s., the other, a thirteenth-century copy of works by St Bernard, for 20s., and both were bought by Richard Hopton. Hopton was head master of Eton College 1447–53 and at the time of buying these books, he would have recently demitted his post, and possibly bought them with a view to later donating them to the College, which he went on to do.[43] Hopton's purchases were documented on the final flyleaf of each manuscript, and in addition to the value of the book, the inscriptions carefully note that the book was 'em*it* ab executorib*us* pet*ri* Bylton'.[44] Furthermore, Colop and the textwriter

---

[38] GCC, MS 247/473, fol. 187r: 'This book Al<…> bought from Py, stationer, and the co-executors'; *GCC Catalogue*, ed. James, I, 297–98.

[39] Christianson, *Directory*, pp. 145–48 (p. 146).

[40] Christianson, *Directory*, pp. 79–82.

[41] Eton College Library, MS 39, fol. 213r, and Eton College Library, MS 101, fol. 182r; *A Descriptive Catalogue of the Manuscripts in the Library of Eton College*, ed. M. R. James (Cambridge, 1895), pp. 20, 40; Christianson, 'Manuscript-Book Trade', p. 101.

[42] Alexandra Gillespie, 'Bookbinding', in *PBE*, pp. 150–72 (p. 171).

[43] Hopton gave the books to Eton College in or before 1492–93, although his *ex dono* inscription is now missing; *BRUO*, pp. 960–61 (p. 961).

[44] Phrase common to both inscriptions: 'bought from the executors of Peter Bylton'; in Eton College Library, MS 39, fol. 213r; and in Eton College Library, MS 101, fol. 182r; *MMBL* II,

John Taillour were Bylton's executors, and are likely to have handled these sales.[45] These examples show that fellow stationers, as well as those outside the trade, drew on stationers' professional expertise when transferring second-hand books, and imply their expertise in dealing in older books.

These stationers' executorial roles, sometimes for one another, hint at the small scale of their working community, and the ways in which its highly interconnected nature aided the flow of books between people. Identified hubs of the London book trade suggest that many of these individuals would have worked in close proximity in 'the area immediately surrounding St Paul's'.[46] The development of the second-hand book trade depended on this group of people working together. There were certainly close ties between many of these book artisan-stationers, socially, professionally, and geographically. Some took on roles of responsibility in the nascent Stationers' Company and had a sprawling web of connections to other book artisans. This is true, for example, of Robert Chirche,[47] who, at some point during the fifteenth century, sold a composite manuscript, in which, towards the top of the second flyleaf, is a note written in black ink in a deliberate hand: 'precium .xx.s. emptus de cherch a pater noster rowe'.[48] This note also confirms that Chirche rented property in one of the areas of London most closely associated with the book trade, Paternoster Row. Similarly, Thomas Marleburgh is recorded as active in the business of the Stationers' Company alongside several other of his colleagues. He sold second-hand a book inscribed with a record of his activity: 'Memorandum quod liberaui Thome Marlburgh stacionario', and with the price, 'xxx s.'[49]

The bookselling activities of John Pye are recorded on the leaves of no less than seven books.[50] The books linked to him are all copies of theological or religious texts.[51] Two of the three manuscripts that identify Pye by name only have been mentioned already; they are inscribed with his initial and surname, or first name and surname. The third inscription to refer to Pye by name, but not occupation, also cites the price paid, and takes the form of

---

672–75 and 713–14 respectively.

[45] Scase, 'Common Profit Books', p. 52.

[46] Christianson, 'Manuscript-Book Trade', p. 90.

[47] Christianson, *Directory*, pp. 87–88, 99.

[48] BL, MS Sloane 3481, fol. 2v: 'Price 20s., bought from Cherch on Paternoster Row'; *British Library Catalogue*.

[49] Christianson, *Directory*, pp. 131–32; *DIMEV* 4911; HEHL, HM 744, fol. 36r; Dutschke, *HEHL Catalogue*, pp. 247–51; art. 6b, in *Thomas Hoccleve: A Facsimile of the Autograph Manuscripts*, ed. J. A. Burrow and A. I. Doyle, EETS SS 19 (Oxford, 2002), p. xvi; GCC, MS 492/261, fol. 148v: 'Memorandum. Thomas Marlburgh, stationer delivered [...]', '30 s'; *GCC Catalogue*, ed. James, II, 563.

[50] He was a presence in the London book trade, was made warden of the Mistery with Chirche, and was engaged routinely with legal proceedings on behalf of many other members of the trade during the 1440s–50s, Christianson, *Directory*, pp. 145–48 (p. 146).

[51] Christianson, 'Manuscript-Book Trade', p. 101.

a brief note on an endleaf: 'Iste liber emptus fuit de Joh*an*ne Pye p*recio* – xxvj s.'[52] Another inscription which indicates the price paid to Pye for a book is a short note: 'Istu*m* libru*m* emi*t* London a pye stacyonario. p*recium* xx s.'[53] Clearly, this also describes Pye specifically as a stationer, as do GCC, MS, 247/473 (already mentioned in relation to Pye's role as an executor) as well as BodL, MS Bodley 110. A named purchaser was W. Cleue, named as part of the longer inscription in BodL, MS Bodley 110: 'Hunc librum emit W. C*leue* de J. Pye stacionario Londoniensis xo die Augusti anno regni regis Edwardi iiijtl tercio *1463*, coram Roberto Paling'.[54] The other purchaser, 'T. Eyburhale' (Thomas Eborall), an Oxford graduate and a London preacher, was also named in a lengthy note, which is now lost.[55] These inscriptions pertaining to Pye may suggest that this bookseller branded his books with annotations declaring his name, or successful sales. They certainly indicate the variable combinations of details found in proofs of purchase associated with stationers. Moreover, they collectively attest to the flow of books through second-hand booksellers and on into the hands of new owners.

A survey of second-hand books

In addition to economic imperatives for sales, other motives could occasion the second-hand transfer of books. The examples of the stationer-executors and common-profit books have already indicated the re-use of books as gifts – presented to affirm status, charitably donated out of piety, or passed down as bequests. When records were made about books moving in these ways, they could be proudly recorded, inscribed into the books themselves.

To study these other motives, I surveyed one volume of the Bodleian Library's *Summary Catalogue* (Volume II.i) for fifteenth-century inscriptions that noted how books changed hands. To do this, the survey focussed on names written into books and inscriptions that explicitly cite a moment at which a book became second-hand, such as a purchase, pledge, gift, or bequest. Volume II.i of the *Summary Catalogue* records Bodleian Library accessions before 1660, and some miscellaneous manuscripts acquired in the first half of the seventeenth century. In practice, manuscripts in this catalogue typically entered the library between 1600–46, and are now mostly included in the Bodleian Library's Auctarium or Bodley collections.[56]

---

[52] BodL, MS Laud misc.414, fol. 100v: 'This book was bought from John Pye – 26 s'; *Quarto Catalogue* II, 303–04; dimensions: 250 × 170 mm.

[53] BL, Royal MS.8.D.x, fol. 206r: 'This book bought from London, from the stationer Pye. Worth 20 s'; *British Library Catalogue*.

[54] BodL, MS Bodley 110, fol. 1r: 'This book W. Cleve bought from J. Pye, London stationer, in the third year of King Edward on the tenth day of August 1463, before Robert Paling'; *Summary Catalogue* II.i, 135–36. Though it may not be linked to the Pye inscription, at the top of the same folio is a note of the price: 'precium xx s.' ('worth 20s.'). If this is the price Cleve paid Pye, it would bring the number of manuscripts to cite prices up to four: Cleve, *BRUO*, pp. 437–38.

[55] BL, Royal MS.5.C.iii, Eborall bought a manuscript of theological texts from Pye for 27s. 6d.; inscription 'at end, now lost', *British Library Catalogue*. Eborall, *BRUO*, pp. 622-23.

[56] 'Preface', *Summary Catalogue* II.i, v–x (p. v).

Wherever possible, the catalogue offers accounts of the medieval provenance of these early accessions. The following categories were documented: date of production, the date of the note recording book movement, and the mode and names associated with that movement. Some books were left out entirely, such as manuscripts written after 1530, those with an abbreviated entry, Oriental manuscripts, and manuscript fragments. Even these exclusions resulted in 837 manuscripts to be surveyed.

Dates of production, names and book movement were rendered as in the catalogue – often by century, but also as more specific dates or date ranges. For the following survey results, conclusions are drawn about inscriptions that are dated to the years 1400–1500. The catalogue did not identify which fourteenth-century or sixteenth-century datings of inscriptions were thought to fall between 1375–1400 and 1500–30, so the longer time span of this study was not relevant here. And these dates were often guesses on palaeographical grounds, by expert but not infallible cataloguers.[57] Undatable names, or those of uncertain date, were added to the database but not included in the final tallies.[58]

How representative is this survey? Whatever its own flaws, which have been minimised as far as possible by the method, the survey's record of names and notes of exchange depends on the catalogue's own levels of inclusivity. The following tallies represent the characteristics of only one cluster of books, which were subject to selection strategies by patrons, owners, collectors and donors, and eventually, by donors to the Bodleian Library. The nature of some large donations to the Bodleian Library by the libraries of Exeter Cathedral and St George's Chapel, Windsor may skew the sample to some degree.[59] Of all donors in this catalogue, the Dean and Chapter of Exeter gave the largest quantity of books to the Bodleian Library in 1602 from the Cathedral Library. Ian Philip notes that this gift was received 'through the influence of Bodley's brother Lawrence, a canon of Exeter, who was also a donor in his own right'.[60] And, whatever the source, the overall selection of manuscripts available for donation in the 1600s had been already distorted by the variable nature of manuscript survival.[61]

In addition, the categories of names and notes of exchange are particularly susceptible to bias by the way in which the catalogue presents this information. First, the legibility of written names or inscriptions can be challenging; the ink fades, or rubs away, or is erased. Second, some inscriptions and names were never recorded in the catalogue at all, despite their apparent legibility. This less-than-exhaustive approach is most apparent where some manuscripts' inscriptions are noted as containing one name, with the remaining names referred to collectively, or as 'others'. The catalogue records, for instance, names appearing in a paper manuscript of short theological works written in the 1480s–90s as simply

---

[57] *Summary Catalogue* II.i was compiled by F. Madan and H. H. E. Craster.
[58] Uncertainty about date is clearly denoted by (?) throughout the *Summary Catalogue* II.i.
[59] *Summary Catalogue* II.i, v.
[60] I. Philip, *The Bodleian Library in the Seventeenth and Eighteenth Centuries*, The Lyell Lectures, Oxford, 1980–81 (Oxford, 1983), p. 18.
[61] The vagaries of survival rates are discussed in the introduction.

'"Jacobus Caryngton", and others'.[62] Despite these shortcomings, analysing the catalogue suggests patterns in how people exchanged books across the late medieval period, and offers extant examples of how they marked those exchanges in writing.

Dated transfer of ownership inscriptions

So how were books shared, and how did they fare in the hands of other owners? The first volume of the *Summary Catalogue* offers more detail about the transfer of books to other owners. Where names alone do not necessarily help to accurately identify ownership patterns, names that form part of longer inscriptions, that were designed to record details of ownership or transfer of possession, tend to say much more about the movement of second-hand books. In the survey from the *Summary Catalogue*, there were sixty-seven discrete inscriptions that could be dated precisely or approximately to the fifteenth century, contained in fifty manuscripts. While many of these manuscripts have been rebound since the fifteenth century, most of this group have reasonably intact flyleaves, pastedowns or lifted pastedowns, on which these inscriptions occur. Some inscriptions provided exact dates, for example, the day, month and year a book was pledged. Many, however, were only vaguely datable by the style of handwriting.

Following the survey, further consultation of the fifty fifteenth-century manuscripts with inscriptions revealed more about the content, location and nature of the inscriptions. The notes were inscribed almost exclusively into either the front or back of books, usually on flyleaves or pastedowns. In the survey, there were thirteen books with fifteenth-century inscriptions only at the back and thirty books with inscriptions only at the front. Six books had inscriptions at both the front and back, and one had a third inscription about halfway through the manuscript, due to being formed from two book blocks. There were trends in the wording too: popular phrases were used to describe typical modes of movement or valuation conducted between people and institutions. These common phrases can be grouped into five clusters according to the kind of movement they described: purchases (*emptus*), valuations (*precium*), pledges (*cautio*), gifts and bequests (indicated by a range of terms, including *ex dono*). In practice, sometimes these clusters overlap, with a few books recording multiple kinds of transfer.

Alongside second-hand books that were valued, pledged, given as gifts or bequeathed, were those with annotations which expressly describe their purchase. Beyond second-hand booksellers, inscriptions of this kind could be written into a book by anyone. The *emptus* inscriptions considered here cite individuals not known to have been involved in the London book trade. A wider range of people purchasing books second-hand acknowledged the second-hand nature of their books in writing. These purchase inscriptions (*emptus*) appear in four manuscripts (6%) of the sample. Of course, many simpler valuation inscriptions, usually consisting of just a figure and currency, may well have referred to the price of a book for sale,

---

[62] BodL, MS Bodley 123, fol. 205v; *Summary Catalogue* II.i, 147. Much of the ink is faded or otherwise illegible.

or for that matter, the value of a book as security for a loan; these highly abbreviated notes will be discussed shortly. Combining all the unspecified valuations with explicitly noted purchases would boost this group to 24% of the inscriptions in the survey. However, though we can imagine what such brief valuations might have been for, the clearest evidence for acquisition comes from inscriptions that spell out the fact of a book's purchase.

Though books bearing an *emptus* inscription were bought, these manuscripts do not always state their price. In the survey, there were two examples that did. The first is a manuscript of logical and grammatical treatises from the early fifteenth century with an inscription that it was bought for 26s. and 8d. (*precium* xxvj s. viij d.).[63] The second is an eleventh-century copy of works by Ambrose, which was given for six coins known as shields ('detur pro sex scutis').[64] Putting a number on the cost – and, moreover, actually writing it into the book itself – suggests that the inscription acted as a receipt or proof of purchase. Neither party could easily claim wrongdoing if the details were agreed upon and committed in writing into the object itself.

Sometimes, where prices are not supplied, the inscription yields other details. These might include the names of individuals involved in the transaction. In another manuscript, written prominently at the top of the front pastedown is a purchase note: 'Liber Ro*ber*ti Elyot empt*us* London de m*agistro* Wille*l*mo Menyman anno gr*acie* . 1489 . 4 . die Nouembris'.[65] The manuscript was both written and bound in England in the fifteenth century, and includes a Sarum calendar, the *Martyrology of Usuardus*, and various other religious treatises and commentaries. Robert Elyot was the vice-provost of Eton from 1482 until his death in 1498.[66] By 1489, when he purchased this manuscript, he was a powerful – and quite wealthy – man. He bought the manuscript from Manyman, of Bath and Wells diocese, who had been a fellow at Lincoln College during the 1470s.[67] Elyot was a generous donor: he gave silver or books to Syon Abbey; to All Souls, Merton, and Eton Colleges and to a few individuals.[68] But why did he inscribe his name into this purchase? He may have been keen to inscribe his name and assert his ownership of his possessions. Or perhaps

---

[63] BodL, MS Bodley 643, fol. iir: 'Constat domini de motynden ordinis S*anc*te Trini*tatis*, emptus p*er* fr*atrem* Ricard*um* de Lansyng a*nno* d*omi*ni M*i*llesmo cccc^{mo}lxvij^{mo}. / *precium* xxvj s. viij d.', 'Owned by the lord of Motynden St Trinity, bought from Brother Richard de Lansyng year of our lord 1467. Worth 26s. 8d.' There is another note on fol. 256r: 'Iste liber pertinet m*agistro* domini de motynde', *Summary Catalogue* II.i, 281–82; dimensions: 210 × 140 mm.

[64] BodL, MS Bodley 866, fol. iii verso; *Summary Catalogue* II.i, 523–24; *DMLBS*, scutum, scutus, Sense 2.

[65] BodL, MS Bodley 731, top of front pastedown: 'Robert Elyot's book, bought in London from Master William Menyman (or Manyman), in the year of grace 1489, on the fourth day of November'. This flyleaf is recycled from a fifteenth-century manuscript of themata for sermons, which has been pasted in upside down, *Summary Catalogue* II.i, 496–97.

[66] Elyot, *BRUO*, p. 638.

[67] Manyman, *BRUO*, p. 1218.

[68] N. R. Ker, 'Robert Elyot's Books and Annotations', *The Library* 5th s. 30 (1975), 233–37; see also R. Beadle, 'Robert Elyot – Another Manuscript', *The Library* 5th s. 32:4 (1977), 371–72.

this munificent donor liked to keep track of the movements of his books, to account for his purchases as well as his gifts, and to record details of them in writing.

Other purchasers note even more information. For example, a manuscript written and bound in England in the fifteenth century carries an inscription dated to 1477 which details that it was bought from a carpenter named Sproxton: 'Liber fratris Johannis Gillyng monachi Bellalande . emptus a quodam carpentario . nomine sproxton . Anno Domini . 1477º . septimo kalendas junij'.[69] This inscription is written on two lines on the first folio of the manuscript, tucked above the beginning of the main text. It not only names both the buyer and the seller of the book, but also notes location, occupations and date of purchase. Two more examples from the survey typify purchase notes of the most exacting kind. Jotted in the back of a three-part manuscript of English Legatine and Provincial Ecclesiastical Constitutions, sandwiched into a column adjacent to the index, is a note of purchase by a vicar from Northbourne in Kent: 'Iste liber emptus anno domini m^{mo}. cccc^{mo} lxº 2º, et constat magistro Thome Langlay vicario de Norbourne [...]'.[70] Here the statement of purchase is used in conjunction with a robust statement of possession, reinforced by Langlay's assertion of his role as vicar. Langlay left many notes in the margins of his manuscript, and the vestiges of tabs remain on some folios. In the other manuscript, a Vulgate Bible written in about 1300, an inscription indicates that Richard Swan bought the book from a vicar in Somerset: 'Liber Ricardi Swann quem emit a domino Matheo vicario de Mudford vijo die Marcij Anno domini millesimo cccc lxxv^{to}'.[71] These proofs of purchase are explicitly located in time and place, and reference names and roles of the individuals involved. The high degree of detail and precision lends these notes an almost legalistic tone, and they may have acted as the equivalent of modern-day receipts.

The majority of *precium*-type notes are rather less precise. These are usually brief and are often found scribbled on the most accessible spaces in the book. In the survey, there were fifteen inscriptions (22% of all sixty-seven inscriptions) that denoted that a book was valued at a particular sum (see Table 1, which shows the list of manuscripts and *precium* inscriptions).[72] This kind of inscription may be as simple as a hurried note in secretary handwriting on the front pastedown of a book, for example as found on a fourteenth-century

---

[69] BodL, MS Bodley 842, fol. 1r: 'Book of Brother John Gillyng, monk of Byland. Bought from a certain carpenter named Sproxton. Seventh day of June, year of our Lord 1477'; *Summary Catalogue* II.i, 433; dimensions 220 × 140 mm. The manuscript also includes a fifteenth-century note that it belonged to Byland, a Cistercian abbey in Yorkshire (fol. ii verso), see D. Knowles and R. N. Hadcock, *Medieval Religious Houses: England and Wales* (London, 1953), p. 106.

[70] BodL, MS Bodley 794, fol. 205r: 'This book was bought in the year of our Lord 1460 and is owned by Thomas Langlay vicar of Norbourne [...]'; *Summary Catalogue* II.i, 535–36; dimensions: 295 × 190 mm.

[71] BodL, MS Auct. D.5.11, fol. 1r: 'The book of Richard Swan, which he bought from Matthew vicar of Mudford on the seventh day of March in the year of our Lord 1475'; *Summary Catalogue* II.i, 577; dimensions: 130 × 90 mm.

[72] Only *precium* notes in manuscripts that could be dated to the fifteenth century are included. This number includes one of the above *emptus*-type inscriptions which mentions a *precium*: BodL, MS Bodley 643; BodL, MS Bodley 866 was not included, because the inscription did not use

textblock, in a fifteenth-century binding: '*precium* xiijs. iiij' ('worth 13s. 4d.').[73] Often these take the abbreviated form of simply 'pcm' for *precium* followed by a number and indication of currency. In BodL, MS Bodley 750, a fifteenth-century hand jotted on to the final leaf of the book the value '*precium* v s.' (with another valuation of £1 16s. 8d.)[74] Why such an enormous discrepancy in value? These read as cryptic, isolated numbers. Perhaps these expedient jottings were a shorthand for booksellers, and in fact did refer to pledge or sale values, even where this was not explicitly noted? Where a note of the value of a book goes unqualified, its purpose can only be conjectured.

Table 1. The values of *precium* inscriptions in books (from the survey of the Bodleian Library *Summary Catalogue* II.i).

Manuscript Shelfmark	Value
BodL, MS Bodl. 251	18 marcis[75] = £12
BodL, MS Bodl. 753 (first price)	5 marcas = £3 6s. 8d.
BodL, MS Bodl. 753 (second price)	40 s. = £2
BodL, MS Bodl. 750 (pledged price, also bequeathed)	36s. 8 d. = £1 16s. 8d.
BodL, MS Bodl. 750 (*precium* price)	5s.
BodL, MS Bodl. 858	30s. 4d. = £1 10s. 4d.
BodL, MS Bodl. 721	30s. = £1 10 s.
BodL, MS Bodl. 643	26s. 8 d. = £1 6s. 8d.
BodL, MS Bodl. 830 (also bequeathed)	25s. = £1 5s.
BodL, MS Bodl. 809	13s. 4[d.] = £1 1s. 4d.
BodL, MS Bodl. 812	20 sol*idi*[76] = £1
BodL, MS Bodl. 516 (also bequeathed)	20s. = £1
BodL, MS Bodl. 689 (also given as a gift)	6s. 8d. (a gold noble)
[BodL, MS Bodl. 866	6 *scutis*]
BodL, MS Auct. F. 5. 30	8s.
BodL, MS Bodl. 676	8d.

the term *precium*; the survey indicated at least nine more *precium* notes, left out here because the dates of inscription are uncertain or omitted in the catalogue.

[73] BodL, MS Bodley 809, front pastedown; *Summary Catalogue* II.i, 482; dimensions: 250 × 170 mm.

[74] BodL, MS Bodley 750, fol. 129r, 'worth 5s.'; *Summary Catalogue* II.i, 478; dimensions 235 × 170 mm.

[75] Marks and pounds were used primarily as units for accounting; the value of marks varied across the medieval period; however, marks were worth two-thirds of a pound, or 13s. 4d., 'Money', online <https://www.nottingham.ac.uk/manuscriptsandspecialcollections/researchguidance/weightsandmeasures/money.aspx>; *DMLBS*, *marca, marcus*, Sense 2: (as measure of commodities) and Sense 3: mark (as unit of exchange or money).

[76] *DMLBS*, *solidus*, Sense 3: made of the same substance throughout; coin, originally made of one metal throughout, shilling.

The results of the survey demonstrate the sheer range of *precium* figures attributed to books in the fifteenth century: the table shows examples recorded in inscriptions. However, as Jill Mann explains 'Medieval thought on the questions of price and value was in no doubt that the process in which value is determined, both relatively and absolutely, is exchange'.[77] Since valuations did exist, in what follows I have tried to correlate them with other significant aspects of codicology, such as age, size, number of leaves, and the presence or absence of decoration. The whole group of manuscripts with *precium* inscriptions was relatively large, with numbers of leaves ranging from 109–399. The mean average height of this group of books was 287 mm, with an average width of 201 mm (ratio 0.7, average surface area 61775 mm^2.) Other than an impression of substantial size, none of the other comparisons revealed any significant patterns. So how might these figures be productively analysed?

The value of money itself was variable throughout the fifteenth century, so accurately dated inscriptions are useful when comparing financial values. Only three of the *precium* inscriptions can be dated to a particular year. The inscription in BodL, MS Bodley 251 marks it as a gift from a wealthy uncle to his nephew, who then pledged it to a loan chest in 1403, when it was valued at 18 marks (or £12). BodL, MS Bodley 750 was pledged along with other items in 1423/4 for 36s. 8d. (£1 16s. 8d.), and was valued again on another occasion at 5s. Finally, BodL, MS Bodley 643, which was bought in 1467 for 26s. 8d. (£1 6s. 8d.).

One way to try to make sense of these figures is to compare them with other records from the fifteenth-century detailing the value of books. In 1397, for example, a group of 126 books was recorded as having a value of £113.[78] This works out to a mean average of 18s. per book, though of course it is likely that there were considerable discrepancies between the values of individual books. This figure dates to only six years before the pledge-value of BodL, MS Bodley 251 was inscribed on to its pages. Yet, this makes the £12 raised against this book worth just over 13 times the average value of each of those 126 books. Other recorded values discovered by Christopher Dyer enable a rough comparison between seven books, worth £5 in 1479 (or a mean average of about 14s. each), and BodL, MS Bodley 643, worth £1 6s. 8d. in 1467.[79] BodL, MS Bodley 643 is worth almost double the average value of those books.

So, were these examples special books? In addition to their material qualities, these books of course contain texts, but these are unexceptional. BodL, MS Bodley 251 dates from the first half of the fourteenth century and consists of Nicholas of Lyra's *Postillae* on the Bible, from Genesis to Ecclesiasticus. BodL, MS Bodley 643 is made up of logical and

---

[77] J. Mann, 'Price and Value in Sir Gawain and the Green Knight', *Essays in Criticism* 36 (1986), 294–318 (p. 298).

[78] C. Dyer, *Standards of Living in the Later Middle Ages: Social Change in England c.1200–1520* (Cambridge, 1989), p. 77.

[79] Dyer, *Standards of Living*, p. 76.

grammatical treatises written by two scribes, one of whom is identified in the colophon as John Esteby.[80] BodL, MS Bodley 750 is a fourteenth-century manuscript copy of Hugh of St Victor's treatise on Noah's Ark, which also comprises sermons and other religious texts. The price jottings suggest that while these texts may not have been bestsellers, they were certainly not unwanted, and could command serious valuations. So was BodL, MS Bodley 251 an exceptionally lavish production? It is the largest of all the books that feature *precium* inscriptions, at 460 × 325 mm, with the most leaves, at 399.[81] It is also the manuscript that most noticeably signals its value through high-grade production: very fine, large-scale parchment, border decoration, illustrations, ornate initials and ample gilding. Though this helps to explain the vast difference between the value annotated into this book and the lower figures in other books, it demonstrates the difficulty in assessing the relationship between the price, cost, and value of medieval books.

In stark contrast with the high prices in other *precium* inscriptions, BodL, MS Bodley 676 seems to be very cheaply valued indeed. At 8d., this book cost 12 times less than the next lowest recorded price: BodL, MS Auct. F.5.30, at 8s., a manuscript of medical treatises written in the second half of the thirteenth century.[82] BodL, MS Bodley 676 is relatively small at 155 × 110 mm, at least compared to the average height of 287 mm, and average width of 201 mm. There is a possible off-cut amongst the parchment used, which may point to generally low-grade parchment.[83] Yet, when compared with others in the survey, this manuscript still seems almost inexplicably cheap. The text is the *Proportiones breves* and was copied in Oxford by the scribe John Buxhale or Boxhole.[84] He was a Carmelite who, at some point in his career, wanted to move from Hitchin to a more rigorously spiritual life as a Carthusian at Sheen in Surrey.[85] Perhaps this desire for a more austere life is matched in the frugal value – in both material terms and attributed value – of this manuscript? The mention of the book's price is embedded in a longer inscription: 'Codex iste at*t*inet ad Will*elmu*m Cahyssy prec*iu*m est 8d'.[86] It is unclear what this low value signals – was this book a bargain?

Another way to try to make sense of the price notes in books is to assess books with comparable valuations, checking whether books with similar values have any similar characteristics. Two pairs of manuscripts stood out as having like values: BodL, MS Bodley

---

[80] BodL, MS Bodley 643: Esteby, vicar of Banbury, 1436?–70?, wrote fols. 127–255, except fol. 134v, colophon at fol. 255v: *Summary Catalogue* II.i, 281–82.

[81] BodL, MS Bodley 251; H. M. B, 'Documents and Records II: The Wanderings of a Manuscript', *The Bodleian Quarterly Record* 2:17 (1918), 118–20.

[82] BodL, MS Auct. F.5.30; *Summary Catalogue* II.i, 528–29.

[83] BodL, MS Bodley 676, fol. 72; *Summary Catalogue* II.i, 441–42.

[84] S. J. Livesey, 'Proportions in Late-Medieval Universities: An Examination of Two Treatises', *Revue d'histoire des textes* 16 (1986, 1988), 283–310 (p. 291).

[85] F. D. Logan, *Runaway Religious in Medieval England, c. 1240–1540* (Cambridge, 2002), p. 48.

[86] BodL, MS Bodley 676, fol. ii recto: 'This book belongs to William Cahyssy, worth 8d.'

721 was 30s. (or £1 10s.) and BodL, MS Bodley 858 at 30s. 4d. (or £1 10s. 4d.); BodL, MS Bodley 812 and BodL, MS Bodley 516 were both exactly 20s. (or £1).[87]

Materially and textually, the first two are largely comparable with one another. BodL, MS Bodley 721 was written in the fourteenth century and is part of a commentary on the Epistles of Paul, and BodL, MS Bodley 858 was written in the first half of the fourteenth century and contains a copy of the *Sentences* of Peter Lombard, which has been carefully annotated in the margins. BodL, MS Bodley 721 is 350 × 250 mm, whereas BodL, MS Bodley 858 is slightly smaller at 300 × 180 mm. Yet BodL, MS Bodley 858 is thicker, and has considerably more leaves (373) compared with BodL, MS Bodley 721 (270). Then again, BodL, MS Bodley 721 has consistently finer quality parchment, with decorated borders in addition to red and blue ink initials. BodL, MS Bodley 858 was made with less consistent parchment quality and has only blue and red ink initials and occasional rubrication. It is not possible to compare the bindings, as BodL, MS Bodley 721 was rebound after the medieval period, whereas BodL, MS Bodley 858 is still bound in English fifteenth-century red leather over oak boards.[88] In this case, as we might expect, similar manuscripts were valued at a similar price.

By contrast, the second pair, BodL, MS Bodley 812 and BodL, MS Bodley 516, are much less comparable. Both were written in Latin and are concerned with religion, but the first consists of sermons, the second of religious texts such as works by Augustine. They differ significantly in age, with the former dating to the early fourteenth century and the latter to the tenth century. They also differ in physical size, having 246 and 108 leaves, and measuring 280 × 185 mm and 225 × 170 mm respectively. Some comparable manuscripts can of course be valued at comparable prices, as suggested by the previous examples. However, despite their similar valuation, this pair of manuscripts displays few comparable features.

Often medieval price tags frustrate a simple interpretation in terms of financial value. The values attributed to second-hand books are looser and more capacious than these terse *precium* inscriptions might suggest. Second-hand books could stand for much more than a financial value: they operated as tokens in relationships. The valuations may exaggerate or depress the attributed value of a book. Sometimes the price of a book may contain a grain of truth that relates to the costliness of its production. Mann has noted that medieval people distinguished value determined by exchange as opposed to 'assay', which was 'the process by which the value of precious metals is ascertained'.[89] Medieval books are not

---

[87] BodL, MS Bodley 721, fol. 269v; *Summary Catalogue* II.i, 469; BodL, MS Bodley 858, fol. 373r; *Summary Catalogue* II.i, 513; BodL, MS Bodley 812, fol. 245v; *Summary Catalogue* II.i, 490–91; BodL, MS Bodley 516, fol. vi verso; *Summary Catalogue* II.i, 430–31.

[88] BodL, MS Bodley 721 has flyleaves, though these were perhaps not originally bound with this textblock: fol. iii is part of a German deed of 1384, and also bears part of a fifteenth-century Latin prayer in a German hand, fols. iii–iv were perhaps a former wrapper: *Summary Catalogue* II.i, 469.

[89] Mann, 'Price and Value', p. 296.

known to have been valued in this way, but perhaps an element of weighing up the evident level of investment in the quality and grade of execution took place and contributed to the ongoing possible valuations of a book. Some high-grade books may have held their value better than lower grade productions. Yet it is quite feasible that fifteenth-century booksellers, looking to make a profit on a book, asked inflated prices. The inflation of valuations has also been suggested in the *cautio* system, as people sought to maximise loans.[90] On the other hand, in case a borrower defaulted on their loan and the book had to be sold by a stationer, it has also been contended that 'the tendency would naturally be rather to undervalue the pledges deposited'.[91] Conversely, the sum of a pledge written into a book may once have taken into account other valuables, pledged with the book as supplements. A book often stood as a token of circulating value, which may have had little or no relevance to the cost of its production.

Book pledges

This looseness of valuation is especially true in the case of book pledges to loan chests. The survey results demonstrate that the most common inscriptions in this sample were pledges of books to university chests (19 individual inscriptions, or 31% of all the datable inscriptions). This was a system whereby scholars could leave a book in a chest as security against an interest-free loan. Formulaic pledge inscriptions almost always begin with the word *cautio* (sometimes spelled *caucio*), they usually go on to name the loan recipient, then may note the date, details of any supplements, and finally the value, including any supplements, of the whole pledge. The order of these details may vary. The inscriptions in this survey referred to a number of chests in Oxford, including the Celton (or Selton), Dunken (or Duncan), Langton, Robury (or Roubury), Vienna (or Vienne), Waugham (or Vaughan and Hussey), and Winton chests, and to a 'Byllyngforth' chest.[92] This last chest is a Cambridge University chest, endowed by Richard de Billingford in 1432.[93] Only a few loan chests survive; what is thought to be the Billingford college chest is still in Cambridge, at Corpus Christi College.[94] Of the chests mentioned, most were

[90] R. Lovatt, 'Two Collegiate Loan Chests in Late Medieval Cambridge', in *Medieval Cambridge: Essays on the Pre-Reformation University*, ed. P. N. R. Zutshi (Cambridge, 1993), pp. 129–65 (p. 162).

[91] H. E. Bell, 'The Price of Books in Medieval England', *The Library* 4th s. 17 (1937), 312–32 (p. 326).

[92] See T. H. Aston and R. Faith, 'The Endowments of the University and Colleges to *circa* 1348', in *The History of the University of Oxford: The Early Oxford Schools*, ed. J. I. Catto (Oxford, 1984), I, 265–09 (pp. 276–77).

[93] There were two chests endowed by Billingford; G. Pollard, 'Medieval Loan Chests at Cambridge', *Bulletin of the Institute of Historical Research* 17 (1939–40), 113–29 (p. 123); Billingford, *BRUC*, pp. 61–62. For an example of an extant Cambridge University loan chest, see 'A Chest for Treasures (and Books)', online <https://exhibitions.lib.cam.ac.uk/linesofthought/artifacts/a-chest-for-treasures-and-books/>.

[94] As distinct from the University chest, just noted; Lovatt, 'Loan Chests', pp. 164–65.

set up during the fourteenth century, with the exception of the Duncan chest, which was founded in 1457. Universities were places where there was a ready market for books, sold new and second-hand. In these academic towns, stationers (*stationarii*) were specially commissioned booksellers, agents appointed by the University to supply books.[95] They traded in both new and second-hand books. Widely attested in European universities in the early thirteenth century, *stationarii* are first recorded in 1262 in Oxford and 1275 in Cambridge.[96] University stationers were not just booksellers; they were often also capable of making and repairing books, and stationers also worked for the loan chests as 'official valuers of manuscripts and other valuables offered as security'.[97] A catalyst for the foundation of the University chests was the expulsion of the Jews in 1290. Jewish people had long acted as moneylenders to scholars, and in response to the financial crisis that resulted from the expulsion, the University encouraged benefactors to finance loan chests.[98] A book could be 'pledged to a chest as security (*cautio*) for a loan of cash'.[99] Many students used this system and went on to redeem their pledge or pledges. Even if some of these books reverted to the same hands, and were not at any point second-hand per se, this system caused books to be redeployed for a time to represent a different kind of value-status.

If a student defaulted on a loan, however, the bursars tasked with administering the chest were ordered by statute to sell the book to realise its potential value, releasing it back on to the market for wider circulation. As both Alan Cobban and Roger Lovatt have suggested, loan chests were essentially 'endowed pawnshops'.[100] The system was designed to provide means by which chests could replenish their losses. Though the initial cash loan was related to a stationer's valuation of the book to be pledged, there were limits on how much money could be lent. This was pegged to the rank of the borrower or borrowers, so that different members of the college hierarchy were entitled to borrow tiered amounts. Therefore, the *cautio* arrangement was a mechanism by which books often became temporarily redeployed by being deposited in a chest, but also a way in which they could go on to become second-hand. For example, in 1454 two university stationers, John Doll and John More, sold off a backlog of unredeemed books.[101] This put books back into circulation, as could a redeemed pledge. Traces of unredeemed books sold on to others can be seen in erasures of pledge inscriptions, though this might well also indicate a later owner obliterating evidence of the manuscript's sojourn in a loan chest.

[95] E. Leedham-Green, 'University Libraries and Book-sellers', in *CHBB* III, 316–53 (pp. 328–30).
[96] Blayney, *The Stationers Company*, p. 15, traces the origin of the term.
[97] G. J. Gray, *The Earliest Cambridge Stationers & Bookbinders, and the First Cambridge Printer* (Oxford, 1904), p. 9.
[98] Aston and Faith, 'Endowments', p. 275.
[99] Parkes, *Their Hands Before Our Eyes*, p. 84.
[100] Lovatt, 'Loan Chests', p. 130; A. Cobban, *English University Life in the Middle Ages* (London, 2002), p. 26.
[101] *The Register of Congregation, 1448–1463*, ed. W. A. Pantin and W. T. Mitchell, Oxford Historical Society n.s. 22 (Oxford, 1973), p. 193.

In Oxford, it was common for stationers to write in the books that they valued. The hand and mark of Thomas Hunt, an Oxford University stationer, was identified in inscriptions in the survey. Outside the limitations of this survey, his 'initials are to be found in a number of books', five of which were identified by Parkes, and a further seven appraisals by Hunt have been added by Jenny Adams.[102] In one example from my survey, Hunt wrote on the front pastedown of a work by Hilary of Poitiers that the book had been pledged to the Robury chest. The earliest known pledge to this chest was in 1321, and it had been very generously endowed by Gilbert Robury, a judge.[103] The inscription in the manuscript states that Richard Gardyner deposited it on 18 November 1491, with four supplements, for 40 s (£2).[104] Gardyner was a fellow of Oriel College and held various college and church posts until his death in 1518.[105] The stationer added to the usual details included in the 1491 inscription by writing his mark: the letters **T** and **H** intertwined. Elsewhere in the survey, another manuscript of sermons and theological pieces features a long *cautio* note which also refers to '**T. H.**' in a simpler fashion, in the body of the inscription.[106] Outside the survey, another stationer's mark can be seen in the pledge of a manuscript to the Duncan chest. The initials are either '**I. G.**' for John Godsond, or perhaps '**I. D.**' for John Doll.[107] Oxford stationers were required to use their 'special sign' or 'monogram' to mark books once they had been officially valued.[108]

Some books in the survey seem to have been deposited only once, as is suggested by a note on one of the front flyleaves of a late thirteenth-century copy of Acts, Epistles and Apocalypse. The manuscript is large and the text well executed in differing textura hands

---

[102] Parkes, 'The Provision of Books', p. 420; Parkes notes that Hunt's valuation and monogram survive in five books: Oxford, Lincoln College, MS lat.113; BodL, MS Bodley 563, fols. 192r–97v (fragmentary evidence); BodL, MS Auct. D.inf.2.4; BodL, MS Bodley 442; BodL MS Bodley 87, in †M. B. Parkes, 'Thomas Hunt and the Oxford Book-Business in the Late Fifteenth Century', *The Library* 7th s. 17:1 (2016), 28–39, (pp. 29–30). For another seven manuscripts, see J. Adams, 'Thomas Hunt's Monograms', *The Library* 22:2 (2021), 376–82. See also F. Madan, who notes that a list of books, which seem to be printed books valued by Hunt in 1483, survives as the pastedown in BodL, MS Auct. R.sup.1, fols. i–ii, in 'Day-Book of John Dorne, Bookseller in Oxford, A.D. 1520', in *Collectanea*, ed. C. R. L. Fletcher, Oxford Historical Society 1st s. 5 (Oxford, 1885), pp. 73–177 (pp. 141–43).

[103] Aston and Faith, 'Endowments', p. 276.

[104] BodL, MS Bodley 442, top of front pastedown; *Summary Catalogue* II.i, 340–41. For an image of this inscription see fig. 2 in Parkes, 'Thomas Hunt', p. 32.

[105] Gardyner, *BRUO*, pp. 742–43;

[106] BodL, MS Bodley 87, fol. 185r, the final flyleaf, which used to be pasted down; *Summary Catalogue* II.i, 92. For an image of this inscription see fig. 1 in Parkes, 'Thomas Hunt', p. 30.

[107] Eton College Library, MS 117, fol. 211v; *Eton Catalogue*, ed. James, pp. 49–50; *MMBL* II, 726–28.

[108] Pollard notes, in total, five fifteenth-century stationers and their monograms: **IG** (John Godsond, 1435–58), **JM** (John More, 1438–70), **ID** (John Dolle, 1447–57), **TH** (Thomas Hunt, 1473–91), and the initials **C. C.** (Christopher Coke, 1493–1501), in 'Loan Chests at Cambridge', p. 117.

for the main text and the commentary. The note itself is in small, mixed secretary-anglicana handwriting and includes typical details: the manuscript was deposited in 1432, by Thomas Holgate, in the Selton chest, spelled 'Celton' in the inscription, and was valued at 6s. and 8d.[109] This chest was founded in 1360 by William Selton, canon of Wells.[110] The note was written on the edge of a lifted pastedown, and – probably since the rebinding of the book – is now upside down at the very foot of the page. Even leaving aside the effects of reorientation and rebinding, this small inscription was probably always unobtrusive. Like many books in the survey, there is no evidence to show what happened to this book in the years between this deposit and its accession to the Bodleian Library collections two centuries later: its provenance during this time is unknown. However, this note of deposit demonstrates that even one pledge might cause a book to move physically and to circulate into new terms of ownership.

Similarly, another single deposit of a book took place on 10 March 1450, by John Dorman. This time the chest was not indicated in the inscription. Dorman pledged a relatively small, thick book, made to a high grade of production, which contains a thirteenth-century copy of the Bible. The note recording his deposit takes the form of an almost illegible, scrawled inscription at the foot of the page after the end of the main text.[111] It records that the book was deemed to be worth 30s. This seems a high amount, relative to the value of the book pledged by Holgate. Though there may well be other variables involved in the valuation of these books, what is still evident today is that these books are materially very different. Although this Bible is small in scale, presumably designed to be held comfortably in the hand, it is a luxury item. The parchment is thin, consistent and fine in quality, and written on to this surface the script of the main text is tiny and precisely executed. Throughout Dorman's little book, there are delicate miniatures and illustrated capitals. By contrast, Holgate's large book is not decorated, and its parchment is of less consistent quality, occasionally repaired, with some rough corners and lacunae. The inscriptions in these two manuscripts, pledged by Dorman and Holgate, suggest that the value of pledged books may be – at least in part – related to their material quality.

Sometimes books were pledged more than once by the same person; that is, they were knowingly recycled again through the pledge system. Adams cites Graham Pollard's assertion that the practice of pledging books repeatedly was 'peculiar to Oxford'.[112] This

---

[109] BodL, MS Auct. D.1.11, fol. ii verso; dimensions: 300 × 210 mm; *Summary Catalogue* II.i, 216 notes in error that the book was deposited in the Lincoln chest: the inscription has been partly torn on the name of the chest, but it certainly ends '-lton', therefore it can only be the Selton chest.

[110] Aston and Faith, 'Endowments', p. 277.

[111] BodL, MS Auct. D.5.13, fol. 671r, it looks as though the inscription was washed, which has caused the ink to fade, inscription details supplied by *Summary Catalogue* II.i, 84–85; dimensions: 140 × 95 mm.

[112] Adams cites Pollard's papers: BodL, MS Pollard 263, fols. 39–40, in 'Hunt's Monograms', p. 381 n. 21.

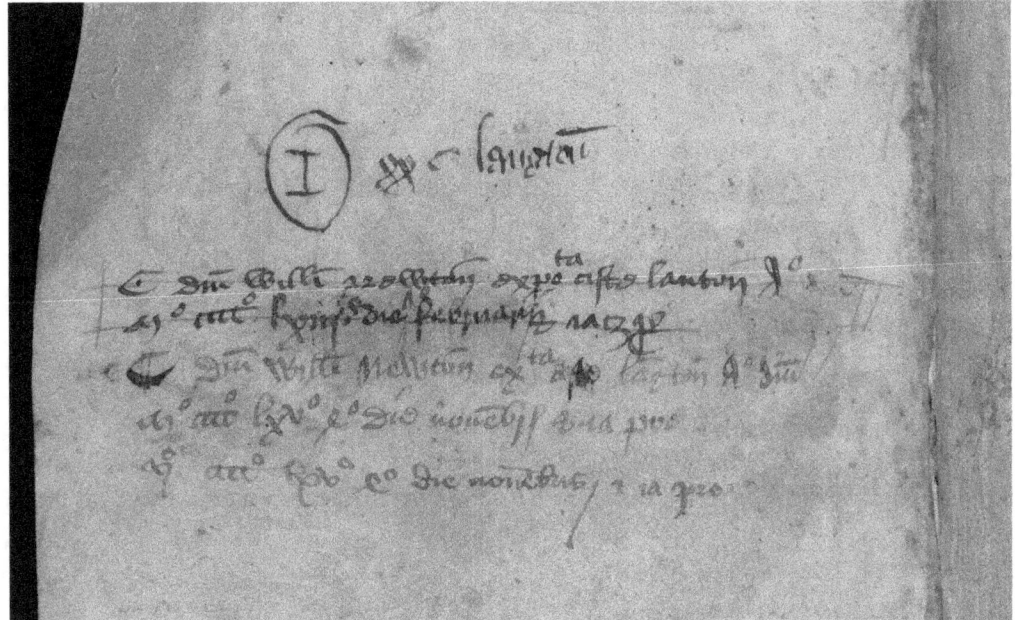

Figure 17. BodL, MS Auct. D.5.14, fol. 578v, cautio inscription and stationer's mark.

confirms further the importance of the durability of books, and, given that these pledges were enacted by the same person, also supports the notion that people had vested economic interests in maintaining their books. Fifteenth-century notes at the back of a beautifully illuminated Bible, which was written in the late thirteenth century, state that it was deposited by William Newton in the Oxford Langton chest in 1463 and again in 1465 (see Figure 17).[113] It bears John Godsond the stationer's mark.[114] The chest was endowed by John Langton, chancellor of England and Bishop of Chichester.[115] The pledger Newton was a Bonhomme, and a few leaves before this inscription there is a note that connects the manuscript to the House of Bonhommes at Edington in Wiltshire.[116] This small, independent institution was a 'colony' of the earlier House of Bonshommes of Ashridge in Buckingham: both followed the Augustinian Rule.[117] Intriguingly, in the year 1424, which

---

[113] BodL, MS Auct. D.5.14, fol. 578v; *Summary Catalogue* II.i, 83; dimensions: 145 × 105 mm.

[114] BodL, MS Auct. D.5.14, fol. 578v 'I. G.'; compare with Plate 15, and discussion of Godsond's mark in Oxford, Lincoln College, MS lat.113, fol. 218v, in Parkes, *Their Hands Before Our Eyes*, p. 84. Adams identifies ten manuscripts with Godsond's mark in 'Hunt's Monograms', p. 377, n. 8.

[115] Aston and Faith, 'Endowments', p. 277.

[116] BodL, MS Auct. D.5.14, 'Edyndon liber' is jotted at the top of fol. 576v and the *Summary Catalogue* II.i, 83 suggests that the volume belonged to the house of Bonhommes; Newton, *BRUO*, p. 1359.

[117] D. Knowles, *Religious Orders in England* (Cambridge, 1962), I, 202; Knowles and Hadcock, *Medieval Religious Houses*, p. 179.

fell between his two pledges to the Langton chest, Newton was instituted as warden of the Chantry at Edington.[118] Perhaps he experienced problems with cashflow during this period of change, and turned to his book – twice – in order to raise some ready money.

Another manuscript was also deposited twice. This thirteenth-century manuscript of homilies features two crossed-out fifteenth-century notes, written in the back.[119] These notes suggest that the book was successfully redeemed at least once. One inscription records the first date the book was deposited, on 5 July 1427. It attests that Thomas Chace pledged the book as a *cautio*, along with four supplements for £8, in the Winton chest in Oxford. Chace was a fellow at Balliol College at this time. The Winton chest was endowed long before by John of Pontoise, Bishop of Winchester, in 1306.[120] The other note in the manuscript records the second time that Chace deposited it, on 14 May 1434. This time it was pledged with five supplements, together valued at £6. In the same year, Chace became Chaplain to Humphrey, duke of Gloucester, which was likely a lucrative appointment.[121] Yet these inscriptions suggest that Chace needed cash: Mynors notes that 'his name is found constantly in pledge-notes'.[122] It was commonplace for those associated with the university to realise capital through the pledge system by treating their books as movable, reliable, re-pledgeable assets.

Towards the end of the fifteenth century, supplements like Chace's were increasingly required to top-up the value of a pledge to a chest. Lovatt argues that there was a 'shift across the period in the character of the pledges, away from books and towards other precious objects' because some books held their value less well towards the end of the century, due to the 'growing affluence of the borrowers' and the 'advent of printing'.[123] A typical example of a pledge with supplements is found in BodL, MS Bodley 750, the manuscript of a treatise on Noah's Ark, sermons, and other texts, which contains one of the three specifically datable *precium* inscriptions (and another, undatable, much lower valuation). The overall value of this pledge was 36s. 8d. in 1423–24. Though the original inscription is now illegible, the pledge listed this book 'with two other books and a silver belt &c'.[124]

---

[118] *Victoria History of the County of Wiltshire*, ed. R. B. Pugh and E. Crittall (London, 1956), III, 320–24.

[119] BodL, MS Bodley 252, fol. 228v; *Summary Catalogue* II.i, 400–01. These notes are arranged on the page so that they follow on, one after another, in the space left at the end of the main text. The manuscript is large 430 × 320 mm and heavy, made of quality parchment, and features decorative initials in red, blue and green inks.

[120] Aston and Faith, 'Endowments', p. 276.

[121] Chace, *BRUO*, pp. 379–80.

[122] Mynors, *Balliol Catalogue*, p. xvii.

[123] Lovatt, 'Loan Chests', pp. 151–52.

[124] BodL, MS Bodley 750, fol. 128v, now erased and illegible, perhaps by washing because the parchment is now puckered. The transcription is supplied by *Summary Catalogue* II.i, 478.

Figure 18. BodL, MS Bodley 251, fol. iii verso, front flyleaf with two inscriptions.

Some of the items listed as part of Chace's pledges were books, in addition to a 'covered cup' and 'six silver goblets weighing 20 oz.'[125]

As well as individuals pledging a book repeatedly, and with additional items, sometimes books were pledged on several occasions by different people. This perhaps even more plainly demonstrates fully recycled transfers of ownership, as books moved in and out of chests as surety for different owners, and sometimes then moved on into new hands. For example, a note on the final flyleaves of a thick manuscript copy of the Vulgate Bible, made in the early fourteenth century, records that it was pledged at least four times during the second half of the fifteenth century: in 1454 to the Langton chest, in 1457 to the Duncan chest, in 1472 by Lewis Neath to an unknown chest and in 1496 by Jacob Ottes to the Robury chest.[126] The pledge in 1457 is the earliest recorded note of deposit to the Duncan chest, which was endowed by Thomas Duncan.[127] A few additional inscriptions have been erased, so there were likely to have been even more pledges of the same book, to the same or other chests. The sustained potential value of this book enabled a series of owners to draw on it as a resource, providing them with financial support time and again.

Likewise, there are at least three *cautio* inscriptions in another manuscript, one of which states that it was a joint deposit by six people. The book is Lyra's *Postillae* on the Bible (BodL, MS Bodley 251, mentioned previously for the high value in one of these pledge-inscriptions; see Figure 18).[128] Two of the inscriptions, dated 1401 and 1403, are

---

[125] BodL, MS Bodley 252, *Summary Catalogue* II.i, 400–01.

[126] BodL, MS Auct. D.3.6, fols. 494v, 495r, both of which are smaller parchment folios than the main textblock; dimensions: 300 × 210 mm. 'Lodowyci Neth (?)' is unknown in the *Summary Catalogue* II.i, 504, but known to *BRUO*, p. 1340; 'Jacobi Ottes', or 'James Ottes', was sued in the Chancellor's court for debt in 1498, only two years after he pledged this book for a loan, *BRUO*, p. 1410.

[127] Aston and Faith, 'Endowments', p. 277; Duncan, *BRUO I*, 605.

[128] BodL, MS Bodley 251, fol. 398r, which is the final flyleaf; three of the inscriptions are located two-thirds up the page, just to the right of centre, the other at the foot of the page; *Summary Catalogue* II.i, 314.

almost illegible but still serve to indicate that this book was deposited multiple times. Not only was it used to secure loans on multiple occasions but also a more legible inscription indicates that in one instance at least six people were involved in using it to secure a loan. On 18 March 1402, the book was the surety of 'Johannis Blew, Ricardi Courtenay, Roberti Newby, Wilelmi Oldeni, Philippi Morgan, magistri Thome <...>' who deposited it in the 'Waugham Hussy' chest.[129] Richard Courtenay is the key figure in this group. He led an ambitious, successful, but relatively short life, and enjoyed the 'special regard' of Henry V.[130] Richard's influential uncle, William Courtenay, Archbishop of Canterbury, had bequeathed the book to him for his lifetime only.[131] In short order, Richard pledged it to the loan chest with his friends. The cash raised by this joint pledge was 18 marks.[132] Lovatt explains that one reason for two or more people to deposit a joint pledge was in order 'to borrow more than the statutory limit' from the chest, by combining their entitlements.[133] This would have been necessary for pledges of especially valuable items. In the fifteenth century, then, pledge-inscriptions make it clear that sustainable books could and did circulate through many hands.

This treatment of books for their exchange value seems tangential to the use-value of books as vehicles for learning. The *cautio* system converted a book's valuation into cold, hard cash. Furthermore, the system took books out of circulation and kept them temporarily static, locked in a chest, apparently unread and unused. The pledge chests certainly met a financial need and were likely to be genuinely inspired by well-meant pious motives. At the same time, this was an exclusive system and could hardly be said to benefit the many, the truly deprived or the unfortunate. Rather, the cash loans from chests were reserved for members of the University, men who were already learned and possibly well-off by most standards. Even then, they could only withdraw a certain amount, limited by their status. In Oxford, only the St Frideswide Chest was limited by statute to indigent scholars.[134] In the main, pledges were a form of charity that utilised books, alongside other objects as supplements, as assets of value.

But the value attributed to books was both financial and, as previously discussed, spiritual, especially for the donors who endowed loan chests. Like most donors, the wealthy individuals who endowed the chests wanted to be recognised in some way for their good works. To this end, chests were often named after their founder, such as some of the chests mentioned here, which were named after Selton, Langton, Duncan, and Vaughan. Apart

---

[129] BodL, MS Bodley 251, fol. 398r. Blew and Morgan were both from St David's diocese; Newby held benefices around Oxford; the others are unknown. See *BRUO*, pp. 201, 1312, 1353. This chest, now known as the Vaughan and Hussey chest, was endowed by Sir Thomas Vaughan in 1317–27, Aston and Faith, 'Endowments', p. 277.

[130] Richard Courtenay, *BRUO*, pp. 500–02 (p. 501).

[131] William Courtenay, *BRUO*, pp. 502–04.

[132] BodL, MS Bodley 251, fol. 398r, 18 marks is £11 19s. 4d.

[133] Lovatt, 'Loan Chests', p. 146.

[134] Adams, personal correspondence.

from reminding students of their name and their munificence, founders of loan chests also expected spiritual returns. It was especially appropriate for donors concerned for their souls to target university students, as this maximised the heavenly return on their investment. As Miri Rubin points out, since the students they were assisting were clerics 'engaged in academic pursuits with a spiritual value' many of whom were to go on to roles within the Church, 'their prayers could be highly valued'.[135] It was believed that after death, prayers would hurry the soul on to Heaven. Medieval salvation involved 'a complex amalgam of strategies to speed progress through Purgatory to eternal bliss'.[136] The wider range of strategies included the creation of monumental tombs and chantries, amongst other more modest testaments. These strategies requested prayers, in sometimes startling numbers, such as Richard's uncle William Courtenay, Archbishop of Canterbury, who provided in his will for 15,000 masses and 2,000 matins of All Saints.[137] Though donors who endowed chests did not ask for prayers in quite these quantities, 'the receivers of loans were obliged by the statutes regulating them to pray for the soul of the founder'.[138] Therefore, prayers were, however indirectly, one of the use-values of pledged books, and donors relied upon the sustained existence of books to receive their spiritual return.

Due to the poor survival of statutes relating to the Oxford chests, little documentary information exists about these intentions for sustaining prayer in perpetuity. However, the extant records at Peterhouse College, Cambridge demonstrate the chantry function of loan chests. The Peterhouse Chest was founded by Thomas of Barnard Castle and later additional endowments were provided by John Holbroke. Both benefactors enjoyed substantial spiritual benefits in return for their generosity. But neither left the form or nature of these benefits to chance: each stipulated the types and quantities of prayers required. Thomas required that all those who borrowed from the chest were to say the *Pater Noster* and the *Ave Maria* five times, the *De Profundis* once and the three collects, *Deus cuius misericordie*, *Miserere*, and *Fidelium*. Holbroke gave twenty marks in 1436, and in return every borrower was also obliged to say the *Pater Noster* three times, for the souls of Holbroke and his own benefactors.[139] Such requirements are likely to be typical of loan chest statutes. Thus, the Peterhouse Chest records show how the need for cash brought about the indirect quantification of a book's value in numbers and types of prayers. As Swanson sums it up, the quest for salvation 'functioned with two currencies: money (or goods or labour

---

[135] M. Rubin, *Charity and Community in Medieval Cambridge* (Cambridge, 1987), pp. 273–74; see also F. Pegues, 'Philanthrophy and the Universities of France and England', in *The Economic and Material Framework of the Medieval University*, ed. A. L. Gabriel (Indiana, 1977), pp. 69–80.

[136] R. N. Swanson, 'Praying for Pardon: Devotional Indulgences in Late Medieval England', in *Promissory Notes on the Treasury of Merits: Indulgences in Late Medieval Europe*, ed. R. N. Swanson (Leiden, 2006), pp. 215–40 (p. 215).

[137] J. Dahmus, *William Courtenay Archbishop of Canterbury 1381–1396* (London, 1966), p. 267.

[138] Rubin, *Charity and Community*, p. 285.

[139] Lovatt, 'Loan Chests', p. 134.

with cash value), and prayers'.[140] Books therefore acted as material tokens in a system of exchange which ultimately rewarded founders of loan chests with prayers of intercession.

Gifts and bequests

As hinted at by the book given by William Courtenay to his nephew Richard, second-hand books could also change hands as gifts or bequests. Almost as common as pledges in the survey were inscriptions stating that a book was given as a gift.[141] Phrases such as *ex dono* or *dono dedit* (gift from or gave as a gift) typically denote such donations (eighteen discrete inscriptions, or 27% of the total). Taken literally, these notes suggest that books were simply given as gifts. However, the notes may not always distinguish gifts in general from bequests in particular. For the purposes of this survey, notes that did not explicitly refer to a bequest, normally indicated by phrases such as *post obitum* or *executores dederunt* (after death or given by executors), were counted as gifts. This is probably an over-conservative approach. To rectify this, if all inscriptions classified as gifts are added to those that stipulate bequest, this combined group becomes the most common form of inscription by far (thirty-two notes, or 48% of all inscriptions). And in some ways, the differences between non-specific gifts and bequests are less important than what they share. So, however they are categorised, books that were given, rather than pledged, bought or sold, are a key part of the medieval gift economy. Book exchange, in all of these forms, depended absolutely on material resilience.

The medieval understanding of gifts was rooted in both a spiritual conception of all things as divinely given, and a worldly understanding of the necessity for the exchange of things. Natalie Zemon Davis describes an early-modern belief, inherited from medieval tradition, in the inextricable link between human and divine gifts.[142] In addition, and on a more mundane level, there was also an understanding of the human need for proportionate exchange. This drew on Aristotelian thought, as Mann has noted.[143] These tandem spiritual and worldly perspectives also existed in the context of widespread gift exchange, which has been explored by anthropologists and economists in different times and places. The characterisation of gift-giving more generally as 'an essential relational mode, a repertoire of behaviour, a register with its own rules, language, etiquette, and gestures' prompts the question: what repertoires of behaviour guided medieval book exchange?[144] Communal or ongoing sequential use, and any indication of these as a priority on the donor's part, are considered here as an indicator of medieval attitudes towards re-using books, in the sense of enabling multiple uses or lengthy future use. My question here, then, is whether books were given in ways that acknowledged the material longevity of books and their potential for re-use.

[140] Swanson, 'Praying for Pardon', p. 1.

[141] Indeed, in some manuscripts there are both *ex dono* and *cautio* notes – in this survey, only BodL, MS Bodley 251 featured both of these types of inscription.

[142] N. Z. Davis, *The Gift in Sixteenth-Century France* (Oxford, 2000), p. 17.

[143] Mann, 'Price and Value', p. 298.

[144] Davis, *The Gift*, pp. 14–15.

There were, of course, certain expectations of what could be given and how it was proper to give it, including such practical considerations as noting one's name or any conditions attached to the gift. Books were common gifts for the noble and educated classes, alongside others such as merchants who were increasingly engaging with literary culture, as already attested by many of the preceding examples. But as H. J. Chaytor has noted, books were still 'scarce and expensive' at this time and were 'bequeathed in wills with other property of value'.[145] The fact that the financial value of manuscripts was recorded in this way at all indicates that they commanded a high price, were desirable, and were considered alongside other property as significant assets. As noted in the introduction, Thorstein Veblen's critical appreciation of excess, expressed in the phrase 'conspicuous consumption', neatly encapsulates the sumptuousness of high-grade manuscripts given as gifts.[146] Moreover, the inscriptions written into these books can declare a very worldly concern with controlling consumption. Although the valuation of the book was not included in the inscriptions in all gifts, this proprietary treatment of books highlights how they carried value. Like pledges, people who gave such precious gifts often wanted to be acknowledged, and there was a real need for the book to survive, so that it might fulfil donors' desires for prayers.

Many inscriptions in the survey named donors and recipients, whether people or institutions, and insisted the books remain with those named recipients. This could provide a badge of recognition for those familiar with the individuals concerned, and, if the manuscript lasted, could continue to build a reputation even after death. Many, especially those of means, were assiduous in ensuring the remembrance of their name. Commemorating a family name was a way of seeking 'a kind of temporal immortality'.[147] This was not just for vanity; it also ensured that one would be prayed for. As Anne Scott notes, 'religious motivations and practical considerations are not so easily separable during this period'.[148] This is seen in inscriptions in Bishop Edmund Lacy's manuscripts, in which care was taken to state the name and role of the donor, as well as mentioning the 'bone memorie' – the good or fond memory of him.[149] Significantly, one inscription insists that the book is to remain in the library, using the phrase: 'in libraria remansurum'.[150] Inscriptions in medieval

[145] H. J. Chaytor, *From Script to Print: An Introduction to Medieval Vernacular Literature* (London, 1974), p. 108.

[146] T. Veblen, *Theory of the Leisure Class* (New York, 1967), pp. 60–80.

[147] P. W. Fleming, 'Charity, Faith and the Gentry of Kent 1422–1529', in *Property and Politics: Essays in Later Medieval English History*, ed. T. Pollard (Gloucester, 1984), pp. 36–58 (p. 53).

[148] A. M. Scott, 'Experiences of Charity: Complex Motivations in the Charitable Endeavour, *c.* 1100–c.1650', in *Experiences of Charity, 1250–1650*, ed. A. M. Scott (Farnham, 2015), pp. 1–14 (p. 10).

[149] Books given by Lacy, with similar inscriptions noting his name, role, and fond memory: BodL, MS Bodley 463, fol. 1r; BodL, MS Bodley 720, fol. 1r; BodL, MS Bodley 786, fol. iv verso; BodL, MS Bodley 829, fol. ii verso.

[150] BodL, MS Bodley 463, fol. 1r: 'Hunc librum disposuerunt *et* dederunt executores test*amenti* recolende bo*ne* memorie d*omini* Edmundi Lacy dum vixit Exonien*sis* Epi*scopus* de bonis eiusdem Edmundi Ecclesie Cath*edrali* Exonien*si* Cathenaudu*m* ibid*em* in libraria remansurum ibi*dem* in eadem q*uam* diu durau*er*it Orate pro eo', 'The executors of the testament of lord Edmund

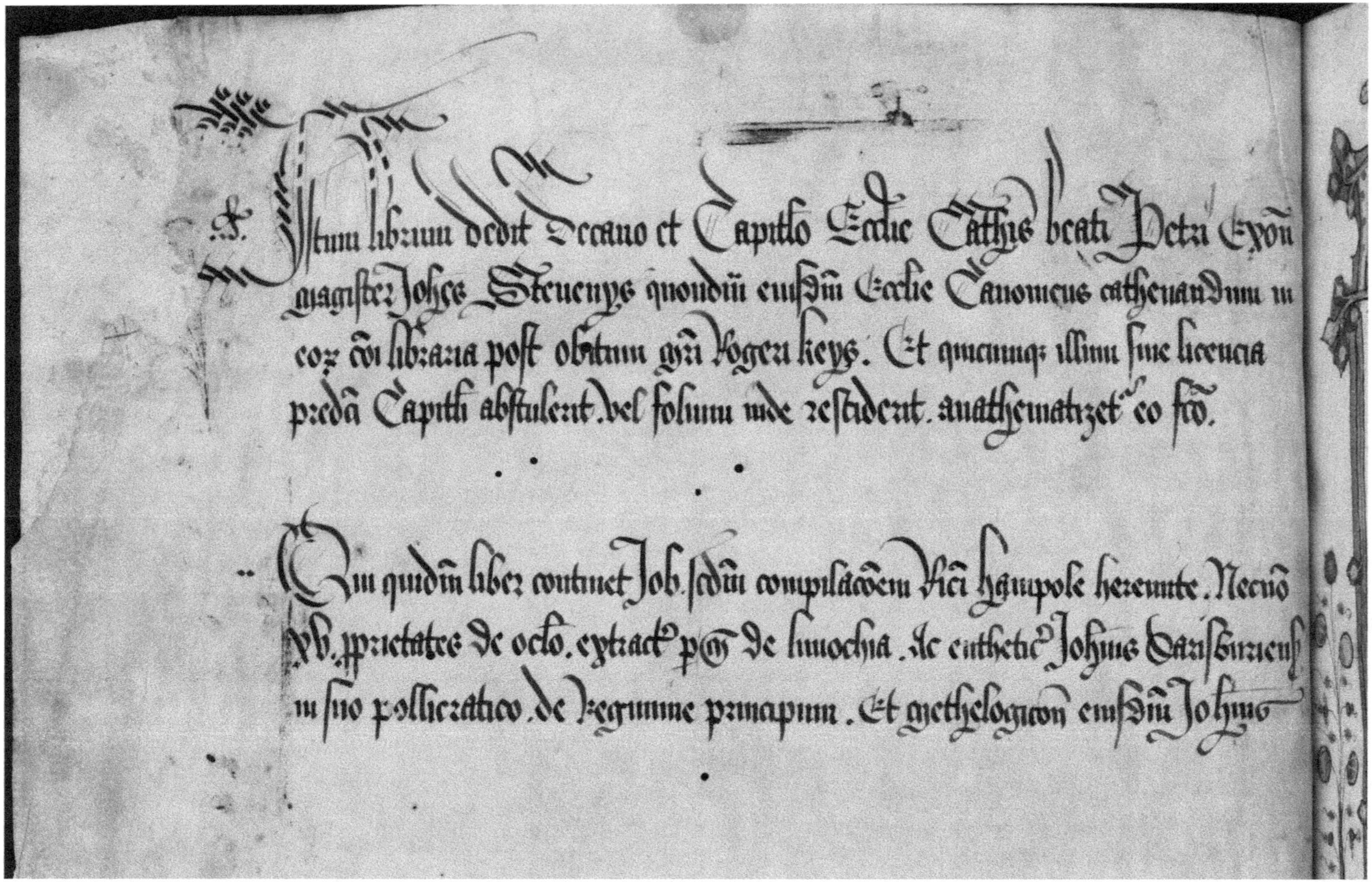
Istum librum dedit Decano et Capitulo Ecclie Cathis beati Petri Exon
magister Johes Stevenys quondam eiusdem Ecclie Canonicus cathenandum in
cor cōi libraria post obitum mri Rogeri keys. Et quicumque illum sine licencia
predcā Capituli abstulerit vel folium inde resciderit. anathematizet eo facto.

Qui quidem liber continet Job secundum compilacionem Rici hampole heremite. Necnon
xv. proprietates de oclo. extract' p[o] de lunochia. Ac enthetic' Johis Sarisburiensis
in suo polliceratico de regimine principum. Et methelogicon eiusdem Johis

Figure 19. BodL, MS Bodley 315, fol. iii verso, front flyleaf with donation inscription.

manuscripts, which often emphasise status, location, and family names, are all part of a more widespread culture of reputation-building and memorialising, which depended on – and sometimes demanded – the enduring presence of those books.

Inscriptions explicitly detailing the bequest of a book can be ostentatious, as seen in a group of books that came to the Bodleian Library from Exeter Cathedral. Elaborate inscriptions signal the esteem in which the donor and recipients were held, as well as the status of the gift itself. The handwriting of these inscriptions is extremely smart: they are written in carefully executed high-grade textura, and many are placed prominently in the book, either on front flyleaves facing the start of the main text[151] or beneath it.[152] The words of an inscription, placement in the book, layout on the page, and style of handwriting all work together to give an impression of the status of a bequest. One of the Exeter Cathedral manuscripts carries a particularly spectacular inscription: it was dedicated by Canon John Stevens, initially to Roger Keys, then upon his death to the communal library of the cathedral, and pronounces an anathema against anyone who removes the book from the library (see Figure 19).[153] Stevens, who died in 1459, gave this large manuscript, which includes copies of various commentaries and treatises by Rolle, Grosseteste and others.[154] Keys, mentioned in the inscription, was a precentor at the Cathedral, and died in 1477.[155] The book's trajectory, from Stevens after his death, through the individual ownership of Keys, and on into the collective ownership of the Cathedral, seems to be assured by the declaration made by this smart, ornate inscription. The dedication note is prominent, displayed on the verso facing the start of the main text, which is itself elaborate, with colourful decoration and gilding. The hand is textura, executed elegantly and with a great deal of flourishing. The ostentation of the handwriting demonstrates and displays Stevens's gift, as well as proclaiming his concern that the book should never be alienated from the library.

An inscription connected with a Cambridge college suggests that these kinds of details did not always need to be stated. In a fifteenth-century manuscript of treatises on astrology, music, and other subjects, there is an inscription which proves that sometimes the link

---

Lacy, of good memory and worthy of remembrance, Bishop of Exeter while he lived, assigned and gave this book from the good of the same Edmund to the cathedral church at Exeter, chained there in the library, to remain there in the same [library] for as long as it should last. Pray for him'; *Summary Catalogue* II.i, 374–75; dimensions 290 × 220 mm; also, Exeter Cathedral Library, MS 3513, *MMBL* II, 821–22.

[151] BodL, MS Bodley 315, fol. iii verso; BodL, MS Bodley 859 (two parts), inscriptions at fol. iv verso and fol. 59v; BodL, MS Bodley 333, fol. iii verso.

[152] BodL, MS Bodley 463; BodL, MS Bodley 268, fol. 2r.

[153] BodL, MS Bodley 315, fol. iii verso: '[…] anathematize*tur eo facto*', '[…] let there be an anathema on him who takes me from here' the manuscript measures 350 × 250 mm, and has 271 leaves; *Summary Catalogue* II.i, 508–09; R. Lovatt mentions chaining and anathemas in 'College and University Book Collections and Libraries', in *CHLBI* I, 152–77, 159.

[154] I. Maxted, *Exeter Cathedral Library: A Concordance of Medieval Catalogues and Surviving Manuscripts* (Exeter, 1987), p. viii.

[155] Maxted, *Exeter Concordance*, p. vii.

to a community was not explicitly noted, because it was deemed unnecessary to do so. In the front of this manuscript a parchment fragment has been preserved and pasted on to later paper flyleaves. Tantalisingly, on that fragment is written the following inscription: 'Ex dono magistri yngham quondam huius collegij socius'.[156] The omission of the college's name indicates a high level of trust in the community and in the security of the book gift. At the time of inscription, the book was probably in situ in 'this college', which is most likely to have referred to Clare Hall, Cambridge, where Yngham was a fellow in 1402–03,[157] so that naming the college was judged to be superfluous. The information in the inscription is his name and his relationship with the college, reiterated to consolidate the gift from person to institution, and the assumption that the college is known suggests the strength of that link. Whoever inscribed this note also assumed that the book would not move from the college. What this gift note implies more generally is that books circulated through networks of relationships, charged with memories of people and places – which sometimes did not need to be stated.

By contrast, another manuscript shows that manuscripts could be subject to explicitly stated, directive conditions. The late fourteenth-century compilation of texts from the Bible, already mentioned for the four *cautio* notes left by Archbishop William Courtenay to his nephew Richard (again, see Figure 18).[158] However, his will stipulated that if Richard left the church, or when he died, the book's ownership should revert to Canterbury Cathedral.[159] Inscriptions in the book demonstrate that William's wishes were carried out. The first is noted prominently in the front of the book, and relates to William's ownership: 'Prima pars Lyre Willelmi Cowrtenay. Cantuariensis archiepiscopi'. The next inscriptions are the *cautio* notes at the back of the book. The last is a brief note at the front, which copies out William's earlier inscription in small, cursive writing above the original inscription, and adds: 'quam <...> dedit ecclesie Christi Cantuariensi'.[160] Though the inscriptions themselves do not designate the bequest to Richard, they do show both that he received it, and that it was returned to Canterbury as directed. William's double-gift of the book (to Richard, and then to Canterbury) confounds a simple dichotomy of solo or shared use of manuscripts and demonstrates that this book was expected to be durable enough to be given twice.

---

[156] BodL, MS Bodley 300, written on a fragment pasted on to a later paper flyleaf fol. i verso: 'From the gift of Master Yngham, once a fellow of this college'; *Summary Catalogue* II.i, 386–88; dimensions: 380 × 250 mm.

[157] John de Ingham (or Yngham), *BRUC*, p. 326.

[158] BodL, MS Bodley 251, William Courtenay was appointed archbishop in 1381, his term ended in 1396. Dahmus, *William Courtenay*, p. 162.

[159] For details of the will, see Dahmus, *William Courtenay*, p. 269; the books were valued at about £300 in the obituary of Christ Church, in J. Stevenson, *The Church Historians of England* (London, 1853), IV, 309.

[160] BodL, MS Bodley 251, fols. iii verso, 'The first part of Lyra [of his *Postillae*], of William Courtenay, Archbishop of Canterbury', 398v, iii verso (again), 'which he gave to the church of Christ at Canterbury'; *Summary Catalogue* II.i, 314.

Specificity in a book's inscription could attempt to limit the charitable and spiritual benefits of a gift to an individual. Like those who donated common-profit books and endowed Oxford and Cambridge loan chests, testators could also spell out their request for prayers. This channelled a book's spiritual potential towards the salvation of an individual. Four books, one given by John Tillney and two by Edmund Lacy, all feature inscriptions which ask for prayers in conventional ways.[161] Tillney's book requests the reader to 'Orate specialit*er pro* ani*m*a m*agistri* Joha*nn*is Tillney', while longer inscriptions in Lacy's books conclude: 'Orate pro eo'.[162] Like other Exeter Cathedral manuscripts mentioned, the inscriptions in Lacy's books were written in large, carefully executed textura display script. Unambiguous though the wording in each of these inscriptions may seem, the writer of the note in Tillney's book used two styles of handwriting to drive home the point. Drawing on the hierarchy of scripts, the scribe wrote 'Orate specialit*er*' in a larger textura hand, before moving into secretary hand. In this case, then, handwriting was the most important component of the inscription, imbuing this request for prayers with added significance, and limiting the spiritual benefit of those prayers to one named individual.

By contrast with those efforts to circumscribe charitable benefit, gifts of books could also forge social bonds. Social bonds included relationships within a family, such as the familial bond of William and Richard Courtenay, and with friends and colleagues, such as fellow members of a college or cathedral community. Scott describes the contemporary medieval understanding of charity as the 'idealised love of one person for another following the Gospel precept: "A new commandment I give unto you: that you love one another as I have loved you"'.[163] Thus, charity was a way of expressing one's Christian love for others. Bequests of books, whether they were dedicated to individuals or to a community, were also a way of expressing this 'idealised love' through charity, a form of testamentary piety, especially where prayers were expected in return. This shared expression of fellowship and brotherhood had benefits for both the living and the dead: it strengthened the community's understanding of itself as a corporate body, at the same time as it symbolised the donor's commitment to that community, even after death.

In some communities, one form of gift-giving set a precedent for others. Many manuscripts that went on to become part of the Bodleian Library collections carry detailed records of medieval donations to Oxford colleges. During the fifteenth century, giving to one's college became increasingly fashionable. Lovatt notes that 'the more lowly associates

---

[161] BodL, MS Bodley 750, fol. 129r, given by Tillney; BodL, MS Bodley 463, fol. 1r, BodL, MS Bodley 720, fol. 1r given by Lacy.

[162] BodL, MS Bodley 750, fol. 129r 'Pray especially for the soul of Master John Tillney'; BodL, MS Bodley 463, fol. 1r: '[...] Pray for me'; BodL, MS Bodley 720, fol. 1r, 'Hunc libr*um* dederunt E*cc*lesie Cathe*drali* Exon*iensis* executors testament. b*on*e me*morie*. Edmundi Lacy nuper Exonien*sis* Epi*scopali* de bonis eiusdem Orate pr*o* eo.'; *Summary Catalogue* II.i, 461; dimensions: 360 × 225 mm.

[163] Scott, 'Experiences of Charity', p. 9.

of a college founder tended to follow his example'.¹⁶⁴ William Bygonell (or Byconyll) followed this pattern in his gift of books to All Souls College. Archbishop Henry Chichele, who cofounded the college with Henry VI in 1437, donated 370 manuscripts for its new library.¹⁶⁵ Bygonell was a lawyer in the Canterbury administration, and he acted as Chichele's executor. Bygonell's own gift to All Souls College was a pair of manuscripts, copies of Ludolphus de Saxonia's *De vita Christi*, written by the scribe John Chestur in 1444, which, among other books, he had borrowed from the college library.¹⁶⁶ The books were to be given to the named recipient, John Byrkhed (or Birkhede), and then restored to All Souls College Library.¹⁶⁷ In giving his books in this way, Bygonell relied on books as valuable, durable tokens in order to emulate the founder's book giving habits.

Often inscriptions strongly affiliated donors with their alma mater. For example, there is an *ex dono* note in a twelfth-century copy of St Gregory's homilies, which was given to Merton College in 1463 by Thomas Balsalle (or Balsall).¹⁶⁸ Balsalle was from the diocese of Worcester, and became a fellow of Merton in about 1448.¹⁶⁹ Other fifteenth-century donations to Merton that also happened to be in the sample were given by Richard FitzJames and Henry Sever, both of whom were wardens of Merton in their time. FitzJames gave BodL, MS Bodley 751, a substantial, twelfth-century manuscript that was probably written in France, which is decorated with illuminated capitals and initials. On the flyleaf facing the start of the main text is a short note of donation. This follows on from a list of contents; both are written in secretary handwriting. It gives details of FitzJames' roles as bishop and as warden: 'Ex dono d*omini* Ric*ardi* Fitz James nup*er* Cices*trensis* Epis*copi et* Custod*is* ist*ius* Collegij. Cuius a*ni*me propicie*tur* deus Amen'.¹⁷⁰ In 1468, Sever gave two manuscripts to his college: BodL, MS Bodley 689, a twelfth-century French manuscript of Latin works attributed to St Ambrose, and BodL, MS Bodley 757, a copy of

---

¹⁶⁴ Lovatt, 'Book Collections', p. 155.
¹⁶⁵ Leedham-Green, 'University Libraries', p. 320.
¹⁶⁶ BodL, MS Bodley 741 and BodL, MS Bodley 742, fol. 2r in both; the manuscripts are a series of discourses on Gospel texts; *Summary Catalogue* II.i, 529–30; dimensions of both: 320 × 220 mm; Leedham-Green, 'University Libraries', pp. 328–29.
¹⁶⁷ BodL, MS Bodley 741 and BodL, MS Bodley 742, fol. 2r in both, erased in both: '<Liber Collegii Animarum Omnium fidelium defunctorum Oxonie ex dono magistri Willelmi Bygonell post mortem magistri Byrkhed>', 'Book of All Souls College given by Master William Bygonell after the death of Byrkhed', N. R. Ker, *Records of All Souls College Library, 1437–1600* (Oxford, 1971), pp. 106, 160; Bygonell or Byconyll, *BRUO*, p. 330.
¹⁶⁸ BodL, MS Bodley 696, fol. 152v: 'Liber Collegij de Mertone ex dono magistri Thome Balsalle [...]', 'Merton College's book, given by Master Thomas Balsalle [...]'; *Summary Catalogue* II.i, 404.
¹⁶⁹ Balsall, *BRUO I*, 100; *The Medieval Books of Merton College*, ed. F. M. Powicke (Oxford, 1931), p. 219.
¹⁷⁰ BodL, MS Bodley 751, fol. v verso: 'Given by Richard FitzJames, Bishop of Chichester and warden of this college. May God bless his soul Amen'; warden of Merton 1483–1507, *BRUO*, pp. 691–92; *Summary Catalogue* II.i, 406–07; dimensions: 295 × 195 mm.

commentaries attributed to St Ambrose, written in Latin in England in the first half of the fifteenth century.[171] In the front of both manuscripts are discreet, secretary script notes on the verso of the leaf before the main text, which outline the conditions of the gift, and begin with a statement of affiliation to Merton: 'Liber domus scolarium de Mertone ex dono magistri Henrici Seuer sacre pagine professoris ac Custodis eiusdem, incathenatus in libraria ad communem vsum ibidem studere volencium, anno domini Millesimo ccccm° lxviij°'.[172] This clearly states an intention that the book should be 'incathenatus' (chained) in the library 'ad communem vsum' (for the common use) of Merton students. Though the inscription might seem preoccupied with Sever's role and relationship with Merton, it also expresses an emphatic communal sentiment and commands preservation of the book by means of chaining.

Books could be made available for the common use of college members in two ways: inscriptions in books 'frequently specified' that donated books should be kept in a chained library, like Sever's, or 'more rarely' that the book should be made available for borrowing.[173] In Oxford's fifteenth-century college communities, as in other religious communities, it was customary to divide the institution's book collection into two parts. One part was distributed to the college community annually (known as the *electio* system), and the other was reserved in the library for reference only, and was usually chained.[174] The library at All Souls was set up in exactly this way, following the model of the library at New College founded by William of Wykeham in 1379, where Chichele himself had studied.[175] Several fifteenth-century lists for the *electio* system survive from Merton College.[176] This was a yearly ballot for lending out the unchained books from the college collection to fellows, organised by order of seniority.[177] FitzJames, just mentioned, was elected warden of Merton on 20 March 1483. The next year he 'instituted an oath' for students admitted to the Library of the college, which obliged

---

[171] BodL, MS Bodley 689, *Summary Catalogue* II.i, 412; dimensions: 390 × 280 mm and BodL, MS Bodley 757, *Summary Catalogue* II.i, 411–12; dimensions: 260 × 180 mm; both given by Henry Sever, warden 1456, 'a considerable benefactor' to Merton, *BRUO*, pp. 1672–73.

[172] BodL, MS Bodley 689, fol. i verso, and BodL, MS Bodley 757, fol. ii verso: 'Merton College's book, given by Henry Seuer, a professor of holy writ, and warden of the same, chained in the library for the common usage of students of the same place, in the year of our Lord 1468'.

[173] Lovatt, 'Book Collections', pp. 158–59.

[174] C. Ferdinand, 'Magdalen College and the Book Trade, 1450–1550', in *The Book Trade and Its Customers 1450–1900: Historical Essays for Robin Myers*, ed. G. Mandelbrote, A. Hunt, and A. Shell (New Castle, 1997), pp. 175–87 (p. 180); see also J. Willoughby, 'Universities, Colleges and Chantries', in *A Companion to the Early Printed Book in Britain, 1476–1558*, ed. V. Gillespie and S. Powell (Cambridge, 2014), pp. 207–24 (pp. 208–09).

[175] *A History of the County of Oxford: The University of Oxford*, ed. H. E. Salter and M. D. Lobel, III (London, 1954), 173–93.

[176] N. R. Ker notes two *electio* lists for Merton from 1410 and 1457, in 'Books of Philosophy at Merton College in 1372 and 1375', in *Books, Collectors and Libraries: Studies in the Medieval Heritage*, ed. A. G. Watson (London, 1985), pp. 331–78 (p. 332); Powicke, *Merton Catalogue*, pp. xxii–xxiii.

[177] Leedham-Green, 'University Libraries', p. 323.

students to swear that they would not remove or damage the books, and that they would report others who did so.[178] Though none of the books in the survey featured inscriptions suggesting that they were once distributed as *electiones*, Sever's instructions to chain his book and to make it available for the common use of students at Merton indicates that donors not only had expectations about how their books would be used, but also could insist on provisions to ensure their books' long-term safe-keeping.

The corporate bonds of ecclesiastical or college communities exerted significant power, especially since such communities were home to those religious who could pray most effectively for the soul. Exeter Cathedral's own library accumulated volumes from various named donors: John Stevens, Henry Webber, Edmund Lacy, William Fylham, Walter Gybbes, Robert Rygghe and John Snetesham.[179] Each of these men is identified with his role – and with Exeter – in book inscriptions, as already seen in the case of Edmund Lacy. Nicholas Orme has noted that influential dignitaries like these men, in addition to more minor members of the clergy, were often resident in and around Exeter.[180] This was an active, engaged community, working to worship God through their lives and their actions, and many of their acts of bequest suggested this community's concern to safeguard and sustain books given to the Cathedral. Minor clergy were sometimes bequeathed books to support their religious education. Henry Webber gave a book dedicated to the 'com*m*uni librarie Ecclesie Cath*edra*lis Exon*iensis*'.[181] The manuscript now is made up of two parts: the first includes copies of works by St Augustine, while the second is an early fifteenth-century copy of Wycliffe's *De mandatis*. He also bequeathed breviaries to Alan Clerk, William Martyn and William Wolf, and a Bible and a quire of miracles to John Symon.[182] Due to the particular make-up of Exeter Cathedral's community, which included many natives of the area, 'relations between the lesser cathedral clergy, the parish clergy, and the city laity were close and often cordial'.[183] In giving such spiritually supportive presents to

---

[178] Powicke, *Merton Catalogue*, p. xxxi.

[179] BodL, MS Bodley 315, 'Johannes Steuenys', a canon; BodL, MS Bodley 320 and BodL, MS Bodley 333 given by 'Henry Webber', who was a dean (and who also gave Exeter Cathedral Library MS 3516, still there today); BodL, MS Bodley 268, BodL, MS Bodley 463, BodL, MS Bodley 720, BodL, MS Bodley 786, and BodL, MS Bodley 859, given by 'Edmundi Lacy', a bishop; BodL, MS Bodley 830, 'Willelmi Fylham', a chancellor (manuscript mentioned previously for a *precium* inscription); BodL, MS Bodley 810, 'Walterus Gybbys', a canon (who also donated Exeter Cathedral Library MS 3512, still there today); BodL, MS Bodley 749 'Roberti Rygghe'; BodL, MS Bodley 744 and BodL, MS Bodley 748, both given by 'Johannis Snetesham', a canon and chancellor (who also gave BodL, MS Wood empt.15).

[180] N. Orme, *Minor Clergy of Exeter Cathedral Biographies: 1250–1548* (Exeter, 2013), p. 2.

[181] BodL, MS Bodley 333, fol. iii verso: 'The communal library of Exeter Cathedral'; dimensions: 335 × 230 mm; Maxted, *Exeter Concordance*, p. viii; *Summary Catalogue* II.i, 276.

[182] For details of these other books given gifts see Orme, *Minor Clergy*, pp. 80, 191, 298, 244.

[183] H. Kleineke, 'Civic Ritual Space and Conflict in Fifteenth-Century Exeter', in *Ritual and Space in the Middle Ages: Proceedings of the 2009 Harlaxton Symposium*, ed. F. Andrews (Donington, 2011), pp. 165–78 (p. 169).

Clerk, Martyn, Wolf, and Symon, who were minor members of his community, Webber was consolidating his relationships with these men at the same time as maintaining an involvement in their ongoing spiritual instruction. The movement of books affirmed and sustained Webber's expression of both social and spiritual values, even after death.

Conclusions

In many of these case studies, books became carriers of potential prayers which required the preservation of the book. Worldly value was ultimately entailed to the glory of God, and both financial and spiritual value depended on physical material. This led people to make stipulations about the long-term endurance of their bequests. For instance, a lengthy inscription by William Wey, near the beginning of a manuscript authored by him and later given to the house of Bonhommes at Edington, which he joined towards the end of his life, makes a robust statement of his 'wyl' in donating his 'goodys'.[184] He had strong ideas about what should happen to his book, as well as to the other gifts he made to the chapel at Edington. Wey itemised his donations – hangings, vestments, relics and three books – before going on to stipulate that 'My wyl ys that thes afore wret be nat alyened fro the chapel of the Sepulke nether fro the holy monastery of Edyngdon'.[185] Ultimately the book came into the Bodleian Library collections, so at some point during the book's history, Wey's injunction was ignored. Although donors like him were evidently proud to hand over ownership of such 'goodys', they also insisted on conditions that were intended to govern the future location and re-use of their books.

People involved in these systems of transfer were invested in the sustained existence of books. What the foregoing manuscript inscriptions show is that the material sustainability and durability of books were often in close alignment with other fifteenth-century concerns, such as conducting oneself piously and charitably by giving a common-profit book, ensuring cashflow by pledging a book to a loan chest, commemorating relationships with others through gifts of books, and eliciting prayers for the soul by various means involving books. Whether a gift was given in the form of a common-profit book, funding for a loan chest, or a bequest, donors could expect prayers in return. In this way, as Jamieson Weetman has suggested, 'books were like chantries, and presented tangible benefits for founders and for the community at large in both a material and a spiritual sense'.[186] Through inscriptions, donors ensured that the conditions of future use could be understood. All these

---

[184] BodL, MS Bodley 565, fols. 2r–2v; *Summary Catalogue* II.i, 323–24; dimensions: 230 × 170 mm. For more on Wey's pilgrimage narratives, and more on the codicology of this manuscript, see M. Boyle, 'William Wey's Itinerary to the Holy Land: Bodleian Library, MS. Bodl. 565 (c.1470)', *Bodleian Library Record* 28:1 (2015), 22–36 and M. Boyle, *Writing the Jerusalem Pilgrimage in the Late Middle Ages* (Cambridge, 2021). Wey, *BRUO*, pp. 2028–29; for more on Wey's life, see F. Davey, *The Itineraries of William Wey* (Oxford, 2010).

[185] BodL, MS Bodley 565, fol. 2r.

[186] J. Weetman, 'Testamentary Piety and Charity in London, 1279–1370' (unpublished doctoral thesis, University of Oxford, 2013), p. 120.

modes of book circulation, and the benefits that could be derived from them, depended on the ongoing existence of manuscripts.

Books are a feature of the wider fifteenth-century culture of gift-giving, which was 'part of the symbolic articulation of social and personal relations', and is 'at any time an act of self-expression, of the presentation of one's innermost values'.[187] The 'innermost values' of the fifteenth-century individuals (and their communities) encountered in this chapter were religious, and the movement of books in these contexts reflect the key concerns of their milieux. Those making careful provision for material possessions were mindful of books' chances of survival. In this chapter, explicit attention to how long the book might endure was seen in common-profit inscriptions and in expectations that second-hand ownership inscriptions in books would survive to be read and heeded on into the future. Stipulations insisted that books be chained, stored in chests, and forbade the alienation of books from their nominated location, all of these strictures were intended to improve the survival chances of books. Such commands enabled ongoing book re-use for as long as the material fabric of the book held out.

---

[187] Rubin, *Charity and Community*, p. 1.

Conclusions

Medieval common-profit books were available to future users, but only for 'as longe as þe booke enduriþ'.¹ Today, hundreds of years after common-profit inscriptions like this were written into manuscripts, what it acknowledges still resonates: books don't last forever. Yet what these inscriptions also demonstrate is that people in the past could and did acknowledge the durability of their books. The foremost achievement of this book is to refocus attention on moments like this, when we can witness late medieval manuscript re-use in action.

Throughout, this book articulates the story of medieval manuscripts from the users' and re-users' perspectives by asking what motivated their habits of engagement with their books. Why did they value books in particular ways? Did they prioritise use-values over other kinds of value? The novelty of my approach is to reconsider production, conservation, and repair efforts from the perspectives of the medieval people who made, used, and worked with books, to imagine the affordances and obstacles to those activities presented by the material fabric of medieval books. I have accomplished this by scouring the archives and literary texts that survive from the late medieval period in unusual ways, by transcribing and making available otherwise inaccessible information and by redefining the possibilities of source study for book history. All this adds significantly to what is known about parchment and its uses in medieval books, as well as suggesting that it is worth reconfiguring our vocabulary to better reflect what we actually see in surviving manuscripts.

The long fifteenth century was a time that saw intense development in the production of books, and while there were innovations, certain practices and processes endured. Books were made, remade, and re-used in myriad ways, many of which were known in the centuries before this period, and many of those ways of doing things continued in the centuries that followed. As indicated in the introduction, re-uses of book materials (both in books and outside books, for example in domestic settings) and second-hand circulation in England have been studied in the context of the Dissolution of the monasteries and the Reformation.² The emphasis on this particular episode of book-recycling activity has been highly informative for book historians in all periods. But recycling also happened long before medieval books were rendered culturally suspect in this way. The choices to make

---

[1] BodL, MS Douce 25, fol. 72r.
[2] See for example, as cited previously: N. R. Ker, *Fragments of Medieval Manuscripts Used as Pastedowns in Oxford Bindings*, 3rd ser. 4 (Oxford, 2004 for 2000); A. Smyth, 'Cutting and Authorship in Early Modern England', *Authorship* 2:2 (2013), online, <http://dx.doi.org/10.21825/aj.v2i2.790>; A. Reynolds, *Privy Tokens: Waste Paper in Early Modern England* (unpublished), pp. 1–25.

and re-use books in the fifteenth century should be understood in the context of their own time. As this book demonstrates, late medieval book re-use was well established and it engaged in a diverse range of practices. While there are continuities, and many of the ways of recycling books did persist, late medieval manuscript culture should be understood on its own terms, and not only as foreshadowing what came about in the following century.

This book argues that fifteenth-century English manuscript culture is best explained by a narrative of re-use. The preceding chapters present a range of evidence to support this claim, drawing on innovative methods to bring together the results of manuscript surveys, detailed case studies of individual manuscripts, as well as historical records, codicological recipes and other literary texts. This evidence comes together to tell a story of manuscripts as durable, re-usable – even repeatedly re-usable – objects. As acknowledged in the introduction and elsewhere in this book, the starting points for these arguments are not new: previous studies mention that recycling occurred in medieval books and this has been enough to satisfy most scholarly endeavours. What is newly revealed here is *how* medieval books came to contain re-use as well as to be re-used. This book explores in detail the practices and processes of that re-use.

Throughout, this book addresses the span of manuscript time as fully as possible. It extends attention deep into parchment's prehistory and considers manuscripts to be fluid and ever-changing entities. Here, the dynamic life cycle of manuscripts is understood to incorporate everything from medieval animal husbandry in the field (in Chapter 1) to manuscripts chained in college libraries (in Chapter 4). But a life cycle must conclude: what happens at the end? Arguably, the manuscript record as we know it today provides a far richer account of loss than survival. Most medieval manuscripts are conspicuously absent.[3] Another way of putting it is that an estimated survival rate of something like 2–5% can also be expressed as a loss rate of 95–98%.[4] Where this book focusses on *extant* fifteenth-century manuscript culture, it is worth highlighting again the demise of so many medieval books. Whatever the actual rate of survival or loss might prove to be, only a fraction of what once existed now remains.

That partial record can be a drawback for evaluating what surviving manuscripts mean for understanding medieval manuscript culture more generally, or for any attempt to reconstruct what those remains might tell us about the reality of the past. From the outset, this book made clear the challenge of determining the wider representativeness of the findings. The surveys and case studies of manuscripts presented here can offer only a fractional insight into the limited body of surviving material. Yet, I contend that it is exactly those enduring, extant materials – the resilient, repaired, recycled, ingeniously repurposed books – that matter most for this study. The continued existence of these manuscripts lends weight to the findings. This research presents one of the rare occasions on which the

---

[3] Others address the question of how to study manuscript losses, such as: D. Rundle, 'Lost Manuscripts' project; and D. Sawyer, 'Practical Ideas of the Book: Books Present and Absent in Medieval Catalogues', unpublished conference paper (Harlaxton, 2019).

[4] As summarised by A. Bale; discussed in the introduction to this book.

partial survival of medieval manuscripts does not undercut the arguments. However low the overall survival rate, extant manuscripts demonstrate durability by their very survival and in many cases also exhibit concomitant forms of re-use. As this book demonstrates through discussion of an extensive array of examples, the potential for re-use was widely realised in late medieval manuscript culture.

The evidence I draw on throughout this study to make the case for re-use has, on occasion, been read in an alternative way, which focusses on destruction. While this study has identified specific features of manuscripts such as pulled holes in parchment, recycled flyleaves, and marginal doodles as examples of sustainable re-use, it could well have interpreted the same case studies as damage, decay, discard or destruction. In many ways, these themes were central to late medieval experience, manifested in *memento mori* culture, the popularity of the *Ars moriendi*, the *Danse macabre* and the three dead kings in varied media, as others have detailed.[5] As medievalist ecocritics and others concerned with the literary representation of waste note (cited previously in the introduction), many medieval social, cultural and religious behaviours in this period are antithetical to re-use. For example, investment in lavish material culture paradoxically proclaimed personal spiritual humility by displaying the fruits of exploitation and excess. While it is true that fifteenth-century people took care to safeguard book materials, as I have demonstrated, it is also true that they destroyed and wasted resources. In contrast to other studies, then, this book offers a generative new narrative by interpreting manuscripts as objects that embody and enact a diverse range of medieval practices of re-use.

In any case, alongside late medieval preoccupations with death and destruction, the interest in preserving and sustaining old ideas in material form was also a typical part of the contemporary mindset. As is well known, medieval writers regarded the re-use of ideas as essential to the art: literary recycling was a way of venerating earlier authors and was considered a virtue in its own right. This form of literary creativity was cherished in intellectual culture of the period. Although such bookish recycling is, of course, not the same as recycling physical books, medieval literary activity depended upon the varied kinds of manuscripts – from scholarly ones in cathedrals, to practical ones with marginal notes and doodles – explored in this study. Parchment was the substrate that enabled literature's very existence, as well as its longer-term survival. Moreover, fifteenth-century experiences of writing and reading books were conditioned by the materiality of manuscripts. The interactions between people and their books brought about these unique, specific cultural artefacts.

Fifteenth-century people were not victims of their material world: they actively shaped their environment, including their manuscripts. As Krish Seetah writes in his zooarchaeological study of butchery cut-marks: 'the residual traces of human cognition remain on the recovered materials themselves'.[6] This applies too in the context of late medieval manuscript

[5] See P. Binski, *Medieval Death: Ritual and Representation* (London, 1996); see also A. Kinch, *Imago Mortis: Mediating Images of Medieval Death in Late Medieval Culture* (Leiden, 2013).
[6] K. Seetah, 'A Constellation of Activity Embedded in Society', in *Humans, Animals, and the Craft of Slaughter in Archaeo-Historic Societies* (Cambridge, 2019), pp. 213–25 (p. 213).

culture. The working skills of medieval craftsmen and the remarkable resourcefulness of book users left their marks in parchment and on manuscripts, in scrape-marks, knife-cuts, scribbles, and careful inscriptions. What unites the practices and processes explored in these chapters are commitments to resilience, durability, and making well, in addition to sparing use, recycling, and resourcefulness. This manifested as making parchment durable, repairing it, avoiding waste, recycling pieces of parchment, protecting books, writing into the marginal spaces of books, and circulating books second-hand. These phenomena were achieved through human agency and involved considerable skill. This study celebrates this fact, and highlights the agency of parchmeners, scribes, binders, menders, annotators, owners and donors. Furthermore, though this book has only fleetingly referred to modern-day craftsmanship, I contend that the study of parchment production *then* might be best undertaken by studying parchment craftsmanship *now* – and this is an exciting avenue for future research.[7]

Returning to my central argument, this book breaks down the notion of 're-use' into two key, closely linked ideas: durability and recyclability. The potential for a wide variety of re-uses depends on the durability of book materials. Durability starts with medieval craftsmen making book materials well, in ways that enhance skin's stable, resilient qualities. Chapter 1 emphasised that the unique materiality of animal skin enabled its transformation into remarkably durable parchment. This long-lasting nature was cultivated through good craftsmanship, but also through care. Efforts to ensure longevity included repair (also discussed in Chapter 1) which was occasionally an opportunity for decorative flourish. Writing on the covers of books served purposes of decoration or identification (Chapter 2) and this might influence a book's chances of survival. The physical durability of medieval manuscripts (whether parchment, paper, or a mix) was promoted in several ways: by protecting the integrity of the book structure (as seen in Chapter 2), by binding or wrapping the book block (again, Chapter 2), and by attempting to provide secure conditions for future storage (Chapter 4). Inscriptions in books show the lengths taken to ensure that manuscripts endured, whether that meant passing a book on to a trustworthy owner, practical means such as chaining, or taking things yet further by proclaiming an anathema upon thieves.

The second core aspect of re-use this book engages with is recycling. This of course relies on the longevity of book materials (especially parchment), so the two key ideas are interdependent. Many people made the most of the long-lasting nature of parchment and took advantage of its latent potential for recycling in a variety of contexts. Chapter 1 presented off-cuts, trimmings and other by-products of parchment production that were efficiently recycled for making glue and size. In Chapter 2, recycling in books was interpreted inclusively, encompassing everything from narrow slices of parchment in the form

---

[7] I am grateful to J. D. Sargan for our personal correspondence in articulating this idea. Others have embarked on craft-conscious scholarship, as noted elsewhere in this book, such as the calligrapher Patricia Lovett, the conservator Jiří Vnouček, and the academic Jonathan Wilcox, and modern-day hand-made parchment is produced by the team at William Cowley.

of reinforcing strips, larger pieces such as off-cuts and whole (or nearly whole) leaves salvaged as wrappers or palimpsests. Chapter 3 examined an array of markings in books' margins, which re-used those spaces for abstract doodles, name-tagging and other playful or ephemeral purposes, but also for future reference and for cultivating memory. Lastly, Chapter 4 explored patterns of book circulation, such as second-hand sales by London stationers, common-profit books for ongoing re-use, the University *cautio* and *electio* systems, and gifts of books between members of communities such as Exeter Cathedral. As this summary of the two-fold interpretation of re-use suggests, the chapters gathered here offer numerous specific findings with implications for other fields of study.

Chapter 1 has much to offer zooarchaeologists, and those interested in craftsmanship, trade networks, and codicological recipes. It also contributes a highly detailed account of parchment production. The first chapter showed that parchment, made from the skins and hides of animals, was a by-product of animal husbandry (for meat or wool products). The supply of animal skins was integrated into medieval agricultural supply chains. The chapter analysed parchment-making processes through the material traces in parchment, and through contemporary medieval recipes which recorded fifteenth-century concerns about how to make parchment well, to avoid waste, and to last for a long time. Finally, it revealed that when skins and hides were damaged, people responded to that damage by finding ways around it, or by repairing it.

The second chapter presented examples of parchment recycled in books. Overall, the chapter contributes in many ways to the wider field of fragmentology. Parchment was repurposed as reinforcing strips, quire guards, flyleaves, pastedowns, limp covers, and palimpsests. It was valued for its material properties, and this offered opportunities to recycle parchment in order to sustain other books. This chapter again has plenty to offer anyone studying craftsmanship or specific techniques of book production. This chapter particularly extends the existing codicological scholarship on off-cuts, limp covers, and palimpsests.

Chapter 3 addressed the re-use of margins and flyleaves for opportunistic markings. Manuscripts from the Bodleian Library's Douce and Laudian collections provided examples of a range of marks, including doodles, tentative efforts towards writing such as signatures, alphabets, and short phrases, as well as recipes, charms, and verses. These marks suggest that people used books for ephemeral purposes, but also as a repository to cultivate memorisation, and for future reference. These findings contribute to the art historical study of non-verbal markings, and suggest affinities with contemporary interpretation of doodling from the perspective of cognitive psychology. The motivations for verbal markings will be of interest to palaeographers, and for those who study short forms of prose and poetry such as recipes and lyrics. Categorising these diverse markings in these ways immediately and dramatically expands the study of marginalia.

In Chapter 4, notes written into manuscripts provided evidence of second-hand circulation. This chapter offers detailed discussion of second-hand book sales, book prices and loan chests, topics acknowledged to be challenging because of the scattered nature of the evidence. It also describes a variety of book re-uses not usually brought together in this fashion by other book historians, including case studies focussing on common-profit books, pledges and gifts. This chapter particularly attends to the motivations and relationships represented by such notes inscribed in books. Books could act like chantries, and realising the book's potential for prayers depended on ensuring the shelf life of the physical book.[8]

The book as a whole offers new ways of thinking about late medieval book production. Book history, like many forms of historical inquiry, is often concerned with uncovering the economic imperatives that guide the course of history. An economically focussed historiography produces one kind of narrative about the past, though it risks overlooking other stories about manuscript culture. This study retrieves and investigates in detail the active choices made by fifteenth-century book producers and users to make durable and re-usable books. What is more, these decisions were not always driven solely by cost, by effort required, or resource scarcity. As this book has shown, the use-values attributed to books and their materials could change over time. Of course, decisions to make durable books or to avoid waste often intersected with economic necessity. This study acknowledges this, but moves away from the assumption that economic considerations always constitute the bottom line. Fifteenth-century people were also concerned to make and to re-use books in ways enabled by the materials, technology, tools, aesthetics, and expectations of their time, and they used books to express identity, perform relationships, and display their religious convictions. They also had fun doodling and writing playful lyrics into the margins of their books. All of these activities left traces on books that are best explained by an inclusive narrative of re-use.

---

[8] An idea explored by Jamieson Weetman, James Willoughby and others, see Chapter 4 for details.

Bibliography

Manuscript sources

Cambridge, Cambridge University Library
MS Dd.v.76
MS Dd.viii.2
MS Ee.i.13
MS Ff.vi.31

Cambridge, Gonville and Caius College Library
MS 17/133
MS 23/12
MS 107/176
MS 247/473
MS 492/261

Cambridge, St John's College Library
MS E.2
MS F.22
MS S.35
MS S.54

Cambridge, Trinity College Library
MS O.7.37 (MS 1365)
MS O.8.36
MS R.3.22
MS R.14.45

Durham, Durham Cathedral Library
MS C.III.18

Eton, Eton College Library
MS 39
MS 42
MS 101
MS 117

Exeter, Exeter Cathedral Library
MS 3505B
MS 3512
MS 3513
MS 3516
MS 3520

London, British Library
MS Cotton Julius D.viii
MS Harley 218
MS Harley 641
MS Harley 993
MS Harley 2336
MS Sloane 4
MS Sloane 73
MS Sloane 1313
MS Sloane 2584
MS Sloane 3481
Royal MS 5 C III
Royal MS 8 D X

London, Gray's Inn
MS 8

London, Lambeth Palace Library
MS 472

Oxford, Bodleian Library
MS Ashmole 33
MS Ashmole 52
MS Ashmole 366
MS Ashmole 750
MS Ashmole 1280
MS Ashmole 1494
MS Auct. D.1.11
MS Auct. D.3.6
MS Auct. D.4.5
MS Auct. D.5.11
MS Auct. D.5.13
MS Auct. D.5.14
MS Auct. F.5.30
MS Barlow 24
MS Bodley 68
MS Bodley 87
MS Bodley 110
MS Bodley 123
MS Bodley 251
MS Bodley 252
MS Bodley 268
MS Bodley 279
MS Bodley 300
MS Bodley 315
MS Bodley 333
MS Bodley 355
MS Bodley 436

MS Bodley 442
MS Bodley 461
MS Bodley 463
MS Bodley 516
MS Bodley 563
MS Bodley 565
MS Bodley 643
MS Bodley 676
MS Bodley 648
MS Bodley 686
MS Bodley 689
MS Bodley 696
MS Bodley 720
MS Bodley 721
MS Bodley 731
MS Bodley 741
MS Bodley 744
MS Bodley 749
MS Bodley 750
MS Bodley 751
MS Bodley 757
MS Bodley 787
MS Bodley 794
MS Bodley 809
MS Bodley 810
MS Bodley 812
MS Bodley 830
MS Bodley 842
MS Bodley 858
MS Bodley 859
MS Bodley 866
MS Canon. misc.128
MS Digby 2
MS Digby 14
MS Digby 15
MS Digby 20
MS Digby 24
MS Digby 230
MS Douce 1
MS Douce 25
MS Douce 33
MS Douce 52
MS Douce 54
MS Douce 60
MS Douce 78
MS Douce 84
MS Douce 103
MS Douce 109

MS Douce 126
MS Douce 141
MS Douce 156
MS Douce 228
MS Douce 257
MS Douce 302
MS Douce 322
MS Douce 323
MS Douce 335
MS Douce 372
MS Douce 369
MS e Mus. 1
MS e Mus. 16
MS e Mus. 23
MS e Mus. 35
MS e Mus. 39
MS e Mus. 42
MS e Mus. 53
MS e Mus. 54
MS e Mus. 76
MS e Mus. 110
MS e Mus. 111
MS e Mus. 116
MS e Mus. 124
MS e Mus. 146
MS e Mus. 187
MS e Mus. 212
MS e Mus. 229
MS e Mus. 232
MS e Mus. 198*
MS Laud misc.36
MS Laud misc.414
MS Laud misc.444
MS Laud misc.609
MS Laud misc.735
MS Laud misc.739
MS Lyell 32
MS Lyell 33
MS Lyell 36
MS Rawl. C.35
MS Rawl. C.86
MS Rawl. C.299
MS Rawl. D.403
MS Rawl. D.1220
MS Rawl. poet.163
MS Selden supra.56

Oxford, Hertford College
MS 4 (formerly MS 2)

Oxford, University College
MS 91
MS 97

San Marino, CA, Henry E. Huntington Library
MS HM 114
MS HM 129
MS HM 132
MS HM 144
MS HM 744
MS HM 19918
MS HM 27187

Worcester, Worcester Cathedral Library
MS F.12
MS F.37
MS F.72
MS F.114
MS F.121
MS F.161
MS Q.15
MS Q.93

Manuscript and early printed works cited

Cambridge, Cambridge University Library
MS Ee.4.20

Cambridge, Corpus Christi College, Parker Library
MS 164

Cambridge, Peterhouse College
MS 114
MS 154

Exeter, Exeter Cathedral Library
MS 3501 (the Exeter Book)

Hertfordshire, Hatfield House
Cecil Papers, Box S/1

Italy, Bologna, Biblioteca Universitaria
MS 1456

Lancashire, Stonyhurst College
MS *Summa de Officiis Ecclesiasticis* (now Stonyhurst Boardman MS XXVII)

Lincoln, Lincoln Cathedral Library
MS 91 (the Thornton manuscript)

London, British Library
MS Add. 48978
MS Arundel 155
MS Cotton Tiberius A.ix
MS Sloane 88

Oxford, Bodleian Library
Douce BB 200
MS Auct. D.inf.2.4
MS Auct. R.sup.1
MS Eng. poet.a.1 (the Vernon manuscript)

Oxford, Lincoln College
MS lat.113

Reykjavík, Árni Magnússon Institute
AM 666 b 4to

San Marino, CA, Henry E. Huntington Library
MS EL 26 C 9 (the Ellesmere Chaucer)

Sweden, National Library of Sweden
MS Isl. Perg. 4 No. 15

Sweden, Uppsala, University Library
MS C.494

Wormsley, Wormsley Library
MS 12 (the Byland Bede)

Primary sources

A Choice of Anglo-Saxon Verse, ed. R. Hamer (London, 1977).
The Crafte of Lymmyng and the Maner of Steynyng: Middle English Recipes for Painters, Stainers, Scribes and Illuminators, ed. M. Clarke, EETS OS 347 (Oxford, 2016).
The Defective Version of Mandeville's Travels, ed. M. C. Seymour, EETS OS 319 (Oxford, 2002).
English Wycliffite Sermons, ed. A. Hudson, 5 vols. (Oxford, 1983).
A Facsimile Edition of the Vernon Manuscript: Oxford, Bodleian Library MS Eng. Poet. A. 1, ed. W. Scase, Bodleian Digital Texts 3 (Oxford, 2012).
The Holy Bible, Containing the Old and New Testaments, with the Apocryphal Books, in the Earliest English Versions Made from the Latin Vulgate by John Wycliffe and His Followers, ed. J. Forshall and F. Madden, 4 vols. (Oxford, 1850).

John Mirk's Festial, ed. S. Powell, EETS OS 335, 2 vols. (Oxford, 2009–11).
John the Blind Audelay: Poems and Carols, (Oxford, Bodleian Library, MS Douce 302), ed. S. G. Fein (Kalamazoo, 2009).
The Master of Game: The Oldest English Book on Hunting, ed. W. A. Baillie-Grohman and F. N. Baillie-Grohman (New York, 1909, repr. Philadelphia, 2005).
The Minor Poems of John Lydgate, ed. H. N. MacCracken, EETS OS 192 (London, 1934).
Richard Morris's Prick of Conscience: A Corrected and Amplified Reading Text, ed. R. Hanna and S. Wood, EETS OS 342 (Oxford, 2013).
The Romance of Guy of Warwick: Edited from the Auchinleck Manuscript in the Advocates' Library, Edinburgh, and from MS 107 in Caius College, Cambridge, ed. J. Zupitza 3 vols., EETS ES 49 (London, 1887).
Secular Lyrics of the XIVth and XVth Centuries, ed. R. H. Robbins (Oxford, 1952 and 1961).
Treatise on the Astrolabe, ed. S. Eisner (Norman, 2002).
Vulgaria, ed. M. R. James (Oxford, 1926).
Yorkshire Writers: Richard Rolle of Hampole and His Followers, ed. C. Horstmann, 2 vols. (London, 1896).

Secondary sources

Aberth, J., *An Environmental History of the Middle Ages: The Crucible of Nature* (London, 2013).
Adams, J., 'Thomas Hunt's Monograms', *The Library* 22:2 (2021), 376–82.
Albarella, U., '"The Mystery of Husbandry": Medieval Animals and the Problem of Integrating Historical and Archaeological Evidence', *Antiquity* 73:282 (1999), 867–75.
——, 'Size, Power, Wool and Veal: Zooarchaeological Evidence for Late Medieval Innovations', in *Environment and Subsistence in Medieval Europe: Papers of the Medieval Europe Brugge 1997 Conference*, ed. G. de Boe and F. Verhaeghe (Zellik, 2007), pp. 19–30.
——, 'Tawyers, Tanners, Horn Trade and The Mystery of The Missing Goat', in *The Environmental Archaeology of Industry*, ed. P. Murphy and P. E. J. Wiltshire, Symposia of the Association for Environmental Archaeology 20 (Oxford, 2003), pp. 71–83.
Amtower, L., *Engaging Words: The Culture of Reading in the Later Middle Ages* (New York, 2000).
Andrade, J., 'What Does Doodling Do?', *Applied Cognitive Psychology* 24 (2010), 100–06.
Andrews, F., ed., *Ritual and Space in the Middle Ages: Proceedings of the 2009 Harlaxton Symposium* (Donington, 2011).
Animal, Vegetable, Mineral: Ethics and Objects, ed. J. J. Cohen (Washington, 2012).
The Archimedes Palimpsest: Catalogue and Commentary, ed. R. Netz, W. Noel, N. Tchernetska, N. Wilson, 2 vols. (Cambridge, 2011).
'Archimedes Project', 'Archimedes Palimpsest', online <http://www.archimedespalimpsest.org/>.
Arnheim, R., *The Power of the Centre: a Study of Composition in the Visual Arts* (Berkeley, London, 1988).
Art into Life: Collected Papers from the Kresge Art Museum Medieval Symposia, ed. C. G. Fisher and K. L. Scott (East Lansing, 1995).
Aston, T. H., and R. Faith, 'The Endowments of the University and Colleges to circa 1348', in *The History of the University of Oxford: The Early Oxford Schools*, ed J. I. Catto (Oxford, 1984), pp. 265–309.
Avrin, L., *Scribes, Script and Books: The Book Arts from Antiquity to the Renaissance* (London, 1991; repr. Chicago, 2010).
B., H. M., 'Documents and Records II: The Wanderings of a Manuscript', *The Bodleian Quarterly Record* 2:17 (1918), 118–20.

Badham, S., *Medieval Church and Churchyard Monuments* (Oxford, 2011).
Bahr, A., 'Miscellaneity and Variance in the Medieval Book', in *The Medieval Manuscript Book: Cultural Approaches* (Cambridge, 2015), pp. 181–98.
Bain, H., 'Binding Marvell: Form and Content in Book Arts', *Andrew Marvell Newsletter* 5:1 (2013), 9–16.
Baker, N., *Double Fold: Libraries and the Assault on Paper* (New York, 2001).
Bale, A., 'Belligerent Literacy, Bookplates and Graffiti: Dorothy Helbarton's Book', in *Book Destruction in the West, from the Medieval to the Contemporary*, ed. A. Smyth and G. Partington (Basingstoke, 2014), pp. 89–111.
Barron, C. M., 'What Did Medieval London Merchants Read?', in *Medieval Merchants and Money: Essays in Honour of James L. Bolton*, ed. A. Martin and D. Matthew (London, 2016), pp. 43–70
Baswell, C., 'Talking Back to the Text: Marginal Voices in Medieval Secular Literature', in *The Uses of Manuscripts in Literary Studies: Essays in Memory of Judson Boyce Allen*, ed. C. C. Morse, P. R. Doob, and M. C. Woods (Michigan, 1992), pp. 121–60.
Beadle, R., 'English Autograph Writings of the Later Middle Ages', in *Gli autografi medievali: problemi paleografici e filologici: atti del Convegno di studio della Fondazione Ezio Franceschini, Erice 25 settembre-2 ottobre 1990*, ed. P. Chiesa and L. Pinelli (Spoleto, 1994), pp. 249–68.
——, 'Robert Elyot – Another Manuscript', *The Library* 5th s. 32:4 (1977), 371–72.
Beal, P., *A Dictionary of English Manuscript Terminology 1450–2000* (Oxford, 2008).
Bearman, F. A., 'The Origins and Significance of Two Late Medieval Textile Chemise Bookbindings in the Walters Art Gallery', *Journal of the Walters Art Gallery: Essays in Honor of Lilian M. C. Randall* 54 (1996), 163–87.
'Beasts 2 Craft project', online <https://sites.google.com/palaeome.org/ercb2c/home?authuser=0>.
Bell, H. E., 'The Price of Books in Medieval England', *The Library* 4th s. 17 (1937), 312–32.
Bennett, J., 'Powers of the Hoard: Further Notes on Material Agency', in *Animal, Vegetable, Mineral: Ethics and Objects*, ed. J. J. Cohen (Washington, 2012), pp. 237–72.
——, *Vibrant Matter: A Political Ecology of Things* (Durham, 2010).
Bennett, T., and P. Joyce, ed., *Material Powers: Cultural Studies, History and The Material Turn* (London, 2010).
Binski, P., *Medieval Death: Ritual and Representation* (London, 1996).
A Biographical Register of the University of Cambridge to 1500, ed. A. B. Emden (Cambridge, 1963).
A Biographical Register of the University of Oxford to A. D. 1500, ed. A. B. Emden, 3 vols. (Oxford, 1957).
Blayney, P. W. M., *The Stationers' Company Before the Charter, 1403–1557* (London, 2003).
Bloxam, J., 'The Beast, the Book and the Belt: An Introduction to the Study of Girdle or Belt Books from the Medieval Period', in *Breaking and Shaping Beastly Bodies: Animals as Material Culture in the Middle Ages*, ed. A. Pluskowski (Oxford, 2007), pp. 80–97.
Bodleian Libraries, Oxford, *Medieval Libraries of Great Britain*, online <http://mlgb3.bodleian.ox.ac.uk>.
Boffey, J., 'Manuscript and Print: Books, Readers and Writers', in *A Companion to Medieval Poetry*, ed. C. Saunders (Oxford, 2010), pp. 538–54.
—— and C. M. Meale, 'Selecting the Text: Rawlinson C. 86 and some other books for London readers', in *Regionalism in Late Medieval Manuscripts and Texts: Essays Celebrating the Publication of a Linguistic Atlas of Late Medieval English*, ed. F. Riddy (Cambridge, 1991).
——, *Manuscript and Print in London c.1475–1530* (London, 2012).
Boivin, N., *Material Cultures, Material Minds: The Impact of Things on Human Thought, Society, and Evolution* (Cambridge, 2008).
'The Book and the Silk Roads' project (2019–21), Old Books New Science lab, at the University of Toronto, online <https://oldbooksnewscience.com/aboutobns/lab-projects/>.

Books, Collectors and Libraries: Studies in the Medieval Heritage, ed. A. G. Watson (London, 1985).
Book Destruction in the West, from the Medieval to the Contemporary, ed. A. Smyth and G. Partington (Basingstoke, 2014).
'Book of Kells' exhibition, Trinity College Dublin.
Book Production and Publishing in Britain 1375–1475, ed. J. Griffiths and D. Pearsall (Cambridge, 1989).
The Book Trade and Its Customers 1450–1900: Historical Essays for Robin Myers, ed. G. Mandelbrote, A. Hunt and A. Shell (New Castle, 1997).
Borland, J., 'Unruly Reading: The Consuming Role of Touch in the Experience of a Medieval Manuscript', in *Scraped, Stroked, and Bound: Materially Engaged Readings of Medieval Manuscripts*, ed. J. Wilcox (Turnhout, 2013), pp. 97–114.
Bosworth-Toller Anglo-Saxon Dictionary, online <http://www.bosworthtoller.com>.
Boyle, M., 'William Wey's Itinerary to the Holy Land: Bodleian Library, MS. Bodl. 565 (c.1470)', *Bodleian Library Record* 28:1 (2015), 22–36.
——, *Writing the Jerusalem Pilgrimage in the Late Middle Ages* (Cambridge, 2021).
Bozzolo, C., and E. Ornato, *Pour une histoire du livre manuscrit au Moyen Âge: Trois essais de codicologie quantitative* (Paris, 1983).
Breaking and Shaping Beastly Bodies: Animals as Material Culture in the Middle Ages, ed. A. Pluskowski (Oxford, 2007).
'Broken Books' project, online <http://brokenbooks.org/brokenBooks/home.html?demo=1>
Brown, B., 'Objects, Others, and Us (The Refabrication of Things)', *Critical Inquiry* 36:2 (2010), 183–217.
——, 'Thing Theory', *Critical Inquiry* 28:1 (2001), 1–22.
Brown, M. P., *Understanding Illuminated Manuscripts: A Guide to Technical Terms*, revised by E. C. Teviotdale and N. K. Turner (Los Angeles, 2018).
Brunius, J., *From Manuscripts to Wrappers: Medieval Book Fragments in Swedish National Archives*, Skrifter utgivna av Riksarkivet 35 (Växjö, 2013).
Buringh, E., *Medieval Manuscript Production in the Latin West: Explorations with a Global Database* (Leiden, 2011)
Burton, J., 'Documenting the Lives of Medieval Nuns', in *Recording Medieval Lives: Proceedings of the 2005 Harlaxton Symposium*, ed. J. Boffey and V. Davis (Donington, 2009), pp. 14–24.
Bynum, C. W., *The Resurrection of the Body in Western Christianity, 200–1336* (New York, 1995).
Calhoun, J., 'The World Made Flax: Cheap Bibles, Textual Corruptions, and the Poetics of Paper' *PMLA* 126 (2011), 327–44.
——, *The Nature of the Page* (Philadelphia, 2020).
The Cambridge History of Libraries in Britain and Ireland, I: to 1640, ed. E. Leedham-Green and T. Webber (Cambridge, 2013).
The Cambridge History of the Book in Britain, II: 1100–1400, ed. N. Morgan and R. M. Thomson (Cambridge, 2014).
The Cambridge History of the Book in Britain, III: 1400–1557, ed. L. Hellinga and J. B. Trapp (Cambridge, 2014).
Camille, M., 'Preface', in *Mirror in Parchment: The Luttrell Psalter and The Making of Medieval England* (London, 2013).
——, *Image on the Edge: The Margins of Medieval Art* (London, 1992).
Carruthers, M. J., *The Book of Memory: A Study of Memory in Medieval Culture* (Cambridge, 2008).
Carus-Wilson, E. M., 'The Overseas Trade of Bristol', in *Studies in the English Trade in the 15th Century*, ed. E. Power and M. M. Postan (London, 1933, repr. 2006), pp. 183–246.
A Catalogue of Chaucer Manuscripts, ed. M. C. Seymour, 2 vols. (Aldershot, 1995).
Catalogue of Manuscripts Containing Anglo-Saxon, ed. N. R. Ker (Oxford, 1957).

Catalogue of Manuscripts Containing Middle English Romances, ed. G. Guddat-Figge (München, 1976).
A Catalogue of Manuscripts Preserved in the Library of the University of Cambridge, ed. C. Hardwick and H. R. Luard, 5 vols. (Cambridge, 1856–67).
Catalogue of the Collection of Medieval Manuscripts Bequeathed to the Bodleian Library, Oxford by James P. R. Lyell, ed. A. C. de la Mare (Oxford, 1971).
Catalogue of the Manuscripts of Balliol College, Oxford, ed. R. A. B. Mynors (Oxford, 1963).
Catalogue of the Medieval and Renaissance Manuscripts c.1300–c.1500 from the Collection of T. R. Buchanan in the Bodleian Library, Oxford, ed. P. Kidd (Oxford, 2000).
Catalogus Codicum MSS. Qui in Collegiis Aulisque Oxoniensibus Hodie Adservantur, ed. H. O. Coxe, 2 vols. (Oxford, 1852).
Cavallo, A. S., *Medieval Tapestries in the Metropolitan Museum of Art* (New York, 1993).
Cavanaugh, S. H., 'A Study of Books Privately Owned in England 1300–1450' (unpublished doctoral thesis, University of Pennsylvania, 1980).
Champion, M., *Medieval Graffiti: The Lost Voices of England's Churches* (London, 2015).
Chartier, R., *Inscription and Erasure: Written Culture from the Eleventh to the Eighteenth Century*, trans. A. Goldhammer (Philadelphia, 2007).
Chaytor, H. J., *From Script to Print: An Introduction to Medieval Vernacular Literature* (London, 1974).
'A Chest for Treasures (and Books)', online <https://exhibitions.lib.cam.ac.uk/linesofthought/artifacts/a-chest-for-treasures-and-books/>.
Christianson, C. P., 'Evidence for the Study of London's Late Medieval Manuscript-Book Trade', in *Book Production and Publishing in Britain 1375–1475*, ed. J. Griffiths and D. Pearsall (Cambridge, 1989), pp. 87–108.
——, *A Directory of London Stationers and Book Artisans, 1300–1500* (New York, 1990), online <http://hdl.handle.net/2027/heb.08874.0001.001>.
'Cistercians Project', online <http://cistercians.shef.ac.uk/>.
Clanchy, M., *From Memory to Written Record: 1066–1307* 3rd edn (Oxford, 2013).
Clarke, M., *The Art of All Colours: Mediaeval Recipe Books for Painters and Illuminators* (London, 2001).
Clarkson, C., *Limp Vellum Binding and Its Potential as a Conservation Type Structure for the Rebinding of Early Printed Books: A Break with Nineteenth and Twentieth Century Rebinding Attitudes and Practices* (Oxford, 1982 repr. 2005).
——, 'Rediscovering Parchment: The Nature of the Beast', *The Paper Conservator: Vellum and Parchment, The Journal of the Institute of Paper Conservation* 16 (1992), 5–26.
Clemens, R., and T. Graham, *Introduction to Manuscript Studies* (Ithaca, 2007).
Clement, R. W., 'A Survey of Antique, Medieval, and Renaissance Book Production', in *Art into Life: Collected Papers from the Kresge Art Museum Medieval Symposia*, ed. C. Garrett Fisher and K. L. Scott (East Lansing, 1995), pp. 9–47.
Cloonan, M. V., *Early Bindings in Paper: A Brief History of European Hand-made Paper-Covered Books with a Multilingual Glossary* (London, 1991).
Cobban, A., *English University Life in the Middle Ages* (London, 2002).
Coleman, J., *Public Reading and the Reading Public in Late Medieval England and France* (Cambridge, 1996).
Collectanea, ed. C. R. L. Fletcher, Oxford Historical Society 1st s. 5 (Oxford, 1885).
A Companion to Medieval Poetry, ed. C. Saunders (Oxford, 2010).
A Companion to the Early Printed Book in Britain 1476–1558, ed. V. Gillespie and S. Powell (Cambridge, 2014).

Cowgill, J., M. de Neergaard, and N. Griffiths, *Knives and Scabbards* (Woodbridge, 2000).
Cowley, William, ethics statement, online <http://www.williamcowley.co.uk/ethical/>.
Cox, J. C., *Notes on the Churches of Derbyshire: The Hundred of Morleston and Litchurch and General Supplement*, 4 vols. (Chesterfield, 1879).
Craig-McFeely, J., 'Digital Image Archive of Medieval Music: The Evolution of a Digital Resource', *Digital Medievalist* 3 (2007/8) online <http://digitalmedievalist.org/journal/3/mcfeely/>.
Crane, S., 'Introduction: Animal Discourses and Animal Studies', *New Medieval Literatures* 12 (2010), 117–19.
Criticism and Dissent in the Late Middle Ages, ed. R. Copeland (Cambridge, 1996).
Da Rold, O., 'Materials', in *The Production of Books in England 1350–1550*, ed. A. Gillespie and D. Wakelin (Cambridge, 2011), pp. 12–33.
——, *Paper in Medieval England: From Pulp to Fictions* (Cambridge, 2020).
Dagenais, J., 'Decolonizing the Medieval Page', in *The Future of the Page*, ed. P. Stoicheff and A. Taylor (London, 2004), pp. 37–70.
Dahmus, J., *William Courtenay Archbishop of Canterbury 1381–1396* (London, 1966).
Davey, F., *The Itineraries of William Wey* (Oxford, 2010).
Davies, R. T., *Medieval English Lyrics* (London, 1963).
Davis, L. F., 'Fragments and Fragmentology in the Twenty-First Century' Stanford Text Technologies webinar, 23 April 2020, online < https://www.youtube.com/watch?v=JQ-XGFZolF8>.
Davis, N. Z., *The Gift in Sixteenth-Century France* (Oxford, 2000).
de Boe, G, and F. Verhaeghe, ed., *Environment and Subsistence in Medieval Europe: Papers of the Medieval Europe Brugge 1997 Conference*, 9 (Zellik, 2007).
de Hamel, C., *Cutting Up Manuscripts for Pleasure and Profit* (Charlottesville, 1996).
——, *Medieval Craftsmen: Scribes and Illuminators* (London, 1992).
de Neergaard, M., 'The Use of Knives, Shears, Scissors and Scabbards, in *Knives and Scabbards* (Woodbridge, 2000), pp. 51–61.
Declercq, G., 'Introduction: Codices Rescripti in the Early Medieval West', *Early Medieval Palimpsests, Bibliologia* 26 (Turnhout, 2007), 7–22.
Derolez, A., *The Palaeography of Gothic Manuscript Books from the Twelfth to the Early Sixteenth Century* (Cambridge, 2003).
A Descriptive Catalogue of the Manuscripts in the Library of Corpus Christi College, Cambridge, ed. M. R. James, 2 vols. (Cambridge, 1912).
A Descriptive Catalogue of the Manuscripts in the Library of Eton College, ed. M. R. James (Cambridge, 1895).
A Descriptive Catalogue of the Manuscripts in the Library of Gonville and Caius College, ed. M. R. James, 2 vols. (Cambridge, 1907–08).
A Descriptive Catalogue of the Manuscripts in the Library of Lambeth Palace, ed. M. R. James and C. Jenkins (Cambridge, 1930–32).
A Descriptive Catalogue of the Manuscripts in the Library of Sidney Sussex College, Cambridge, ed. M. R. James (Cambridge, 1895).
A Descriptive Catalogue of the Manuscripts in the Library of St. John's College Cambridge, ed. M. R. James (Cambridge, 1913).
A Descriptive Catalogue of the Medieval Manuscripts in Worcester Cathedral Library, ed. . M. Thomson and M. Gullick (Cambridge, 2001).
A Descriptive Catalogue of the Medieval Manuscripts of All Souls College Oxford, ed. A. G. Watson (Oxford, 1997).

A Descriptive Guide to the Manuscripts of the 'Prick of Conscience', ed. R. E. Lewis and A. McIntosh, Medium Aevum Monographs, n.s., 12 (Oxford, 1982).

Design and Distribution of Late Medieval Manuscripts in England, ed. M. Connolly and L. R. Mooney (York, 2008).

Dictionary of Medieval Latin from British Sources, ed. R. E. Latham and others, online <http://www.dmlbs.ox.ac.uk/publications/online>.

Diet and Craft in Towns: The Evidence of Animal Remains from the Roman to the Post-Medieval Periods, ed. D. Serjeantson and T. Waldron, British Archaeological Reports, British Series 199 (Oxford, 1989).

The Digital Index of Medieval English Verse, based on the Index of Middle English Verse (1943) and its Supplement, ed. L. Mooney, D. W. Mosser, E. Solopova, D. Thorpe, D. Hill Radcliffe (1965), online <http://www.dimev.net>.

Douglass, R., 'Ecocriticism and Middle English Literature', *Studies in Medievalism* 10 (1998), 136–63.

Doyle, A. I., 'Codicology, Palaeography, and Provenance', in *A Facsimile Edition of the Vernon Manuscript: Oxford, Bodleian Library MS Eng. Poet. A. 1*, ed. W. Scase, Bodleian Digital Texts 3 (Oxford, 2012), pp. 1–19.

——, 'The English Provincial Book Trade Before Printing', in *Six Centuries of the Provincial Book Trade in Britain*, ed. P. Isaac (Michigan, 1990), pp. 13–29.

Doyle, A., 'Romans, Han Dynasty Were Greenhouse Gas Emitters: Study', Reuters 3 October 2012, online <http://uk.reuters.com/article/2012/10/03/us-climate-romans-idUSBRE89212020121003>.

Duffy, C., 'The Discovery of a Watermark on the St Cuthbert's Gospel using Colour Space Analysis', *Electronic British Library Journal* 2 (2014), 1–14, online <http://www.bl.uk/eblj/2014articles/article2.html >.

Dyer, C., 'Sheepcotes: Evidence for Medieval Sheepfarming', *Medieval Archaeology* 39 (1995), 136–64.

——, *Everyday Life in Medieval England* (London, 2000).

——, *Lords and Peasants in a Changing Society: The Estates of the Bishopric of Worcester, 680–1540* (Cambridge, 1980)

——, *Making a Living in the Middle Ages: The People of Britain 850–1520* (London, 2009).

——, *Standards of Living in the Later Middle Ages: Social Change in England, c. 1200–1520* (Cambridge, 1998).

Eckenrode, T. R., 'English Cistercians and Their Sheep During the Middle Ages', *Cîteaux: Commentarii Cistercienses* 24 (1973), 250–66.

Edwards, A. S. G., 'Medieval Manuscripts, the Collector, and the Trade', in *The Cambridge Companion to the Medieval English Manuscript*, ed. O. Da Rold and E. Treharne (Cambridge, 2020), pp. 284–94.

—— and D. Pearsall, 'The Manuscripts of the Major English Poetic Texts', in *Book Production and Publishing in Britain 1375–1475*, ed. J. Griffiths and D. Pearsall (Cambridge, 1989), pp. 257–78.

The Ellesmere Chaucer: Essays in Interpretation, ed. M. Stevens and D. Woodward (San Marino, 1997).

Engaging with Nature: Essays on the Natural World in Medieval and Early Modern Europe, ed. B. A. Hanawalt and L. J. Kiser (Notre Dame, 2008).

The English Library Before 1700, ed. F. Wormald and C. E. Wright (London, 1958).

The Environmental Archaeology of Industry, ed. P. Murphy and P. E. J. Wiltshire Symposia of the Association for Environmental Archaeology 20 (Oxford, 2003).

Ervynck, A., B. Hillewaert, A. Maes, and M. Van Strydonck, 'Tanning and Horn-Working at Late- and Post-Medieval Bruges', in *The Environmental Archaeology of Industry*, ed. P. Murphy and P. E. J. Wiltshire, Symposia of the Association for Environmental Archaeology 20 (Oxford, 2003), pp. 60–70.

Experiences of Charity, 1250–1650, ed. A. M. Scott (Farnham, 2015).
Farrell, J., *The Leathersellers' Company: A Short History* (London, 2008).
Ferdinand, C. Y. 'Library Administration (c. 1475–1640)', in *The Cambridge History of Libraries in Britain and Ireland, I: to 1640*, ed. E. Leedham-Green and T. Webber (Cambridge, 2013), pp. 565–591.
——, 'Magdalen College and the Book Trade, 1450–1550', in *The Book Trade and Its Customers 1450–1900: Historical Essays for Robin Myers*, ed. G. Mandelbrote, A. Hunt, and A. Shell (New Castle, 1997), pp. 175–87.
Fiddyment, S., B. Holsinger et al., 'Animal Origin of 13th-Century Uterine Vellum Revealed Using Noninvasive Peptide Fingerprinting', *Proceedings of the National Academy of Sciences* 112:49 (2015), 15066–71.
——, M. D. Teasdale, J. Vnouček, É. Lévêque, A. Binois and M. J. Collins, 'So You Want To Do Biocodicology? A Field Guide to the Biological Analysis of Parchment', *Heritage Science* 7 (2019), 1–35.
Finlay, M., *Western Writing Implements in the Age of the Quill Pen* (Penrith, 1990).
Fischer, F., C. Fritze, G. Vogeler, ed., *Codicology and Palaeography in the Digital Age II* (Norstedt, 2011).
Flannery, M. C., 'Privy Reading', in *Spaces for Reading in Later Medieval England*, ed. M. C. Flannery and C. Griffin (Basingstoke, 2016), pp. 149–64.
Fleming, J., *Graffiti and the Writing Arts of Early Modern England* (London, 2001).
Fleming, P. W., 'Charity, Faith and the Gentry of Kent 1422–1529', in *Property and Politics: Essays in Later Medieval English History*, ed. T. Pollard (Gloucester, 1984), pp. 36–58.
Food in Medieval England: Diet and Nutrition, ed. C. M. Woolgar, D. Serjeantson, and T. Waldron (Oxford, 2006).
Foot, M., 'Bookbinding 1400–1557', in *The Cambridge History of the Book in Britain, III: 1400–1557*, ed. L. Hellinga and J. B. Trapp (Cambridge, 2014), pp. 109–27.
——, 'English Decorated Bookbindings', in *Book Production and Publishing in Britain 1375–1475*, ed. J. Griffiths and D. Pearsall (Cambridge, 1989), pp. 65–86.
Foys, M., 'The Remanence of Medieval Media', in *The Routledge Handbook of Digital Medieval Literature*, ed. J. Boyle and H. Burgess (Oxford, 2017).
'Fragmentarium' project, online <https://fragmentarium.ms>
Frankis, P. J., 'Two Minor French Lyric Forms in English', *Neuphilologische Mitteilungen* 60 (1959), 66–71.
Freeman, C., 'Feathering the Text', in *Rethinking Chaucerian Beasts*, ed. C. Van Dyke (Basingstoke, 2012), pp. 33–47.
Frow, J., 'Matter and Materialism: A Brief Pre-History of the Present', in *Material Powers: Cultural Studies, History and The Material Turn*, ed. T. Bennett and P. Joyce (London, 2010), pp. 25–37.
Fuchs, R., 'Old Restorations and Repairs in Manuscripts', *Care and Conservation* 6 (2002), 224–41.
The Future of the Page, ed. P. Stoicheff and A. Taylor (London, 2004).
Gabriel, A. L., ed., *The Economic and Material Framework of the Medieval University* (Indiana, 1977).
Gameson, R., 'The Medieval Library (to c.1450)', in *The Cambridge History of Libraries in Britain and Ireland, I: to 1640*, ed. E. Leedham-Green and T. Webber (Cambridge, 2013), pp. 13–50.
——, *The Earliest Books of Canterbury Cathedral: Manuscripts and Fragments to c. 1200* (London, 2008).
Gayk, S., and R. Malo, 'The Sacred Object', *JMEMS* 44:3 (2014), 458–67.
Gee, S., 'The Printers, Stationers and Bookbinders of York before 1557', *Transactions of the Cambridge Bibliographical Society* 12:1 (2000), 27–54.

Getty, P., and H. G. Fletcher, *The Wormsley Library: A Personal Selection by Sir Paul Getty* (London, 1999).
Gilchrist, R., *Medieval Life: Archaeology and the Life Course* (Woodbridge, 2012).
Gillespie, A., 'Bookbinding and Early Printing in England', in *A Companion to the Early Printed Book in Britain 1476–1558*, ed. V. Gillespie and S. Powell (Cambridge, 2014), pp. 75–94.
——, 'Bookbinding', in *The Production of Books in England 1350–1550*, ed. A. Gillespie and D. Wakelin (Cambridge, 2011), pp. 150–72.
—— and D. Wakelin, 'Introduction', in *The Production of Books in England 1350–1550*, ed. A. Gillespie and D. Wakelin (Cambridge, 2011), pp. 1–11.
——, keynote lecture, 4th Biennial BABEL Working Group Meeting: 'Off the Books', Toronto, Canada (9 October 2015).
Gli autografi medievali: problemi paleografici e filologici: atti del Convegno di studio della Fondazione Ezio Franceschini, Erice 25 settembre–2 ottobre 1990, ed. P. Chiesa and L. Pinelli (Spoleto, 1994).
Goddard, S. H., 'Probationes Pennae: Some Sixteenth-Century Doodles on the Theme of Folly Attributed to the Antwerp Humanist Pieter Gillis and His Colleagues', *Renaissance Quarterly* 41 (1988), pp. 242–67.
Gould, K., 'Terms for Book Production in a Fifteenth-Century Latin-English Nominale (Harvard Law School Library MS. 43)', *The Papers of the Bibliographical Society of America* 75:1 (1985), 75–99.
Gray, D., 'Introduction', in *The Oxford Book of Late Medieval Verse and Prose* (Oxford, 1989), pp. 3–44.
Gray, G. J., *The Earliest Cambridge Stationers & Bookbinders, and the First Cambridge Printer* (Oxford, 1904).
Gregson, N., and L. Crewe, *Second-hand Cultures* (Oxford, New York, 2003).
Griffin, C., 'Instruction and Information from Manuscript to Print: Some English Literature 1400–1650', *Literature Compass* 10 (2013), 667–76.
——, 'Reconsidering the Recipe: Materiality, Narrative and Text in Later Medieval Instructional Manuscripts and Collections', in *Manuscripts and Printed Books in Europe 1350–1550: Packaging, Presentation and Consumption*, ed. E. Cayley and S. Powell (Liverpool, 2013), pp. 135–49.
——, *Instructional Writing in English, 1350–1650: Materiality and Meaning* (Oxford, 2019).
Griffiths, J., *Diverting Authorities: Experimental Glossing Practices in Manuscript and Print* (Oxford, 2014).
Grindley, C. J., 'Reading Piers Plowman C-Text Annotations: Notes toward the Classification of Printed and Written Marginalia in Texts from the British Isles 1300–1641', in *The Medieval Professional Reader at Work: Evidence from Manuscripts of Chaucer, Langland, Kempe, and Gower*, ed. K. Kerby-Fulton and M. Hilmo (Victoria, 2001), pp. 73–141.
Grömer, K., G. Russ-Popa and K. Saliari, 'Products of Animal Skin from Antiquity to the Medieval Period', *Annalen des Naturhistorischen Museums in Wien, Serie A für Mineralogie und Petrographie, Geologie und Paläontologie, Anthropologie und Prähistorie* 119 (2017), 69–93.
Guide to Medieval and Renaissance Manuscripts in the Huntington Library, ed. C. W. Dutschke, 2 vols. (San Marino, 1989).
Gullick, M., 'From Parchmenter to Scribe: Some Observations on the Manufacture and Preparation of Medieval Parchment Based Upon a Review of the Literary Evidence', in *Pergament, Geschichte, Struktur, Restaurierung und Herstellung*, ed. P. Rück (Sigmaringen, 1991), pp. 145–57.
——, 'The Bindings', in *A Descriptive Catalogue of the Medieval Manuscripts in Worcester Cathedral Library*, ed. R. M. Thomson, and M. Gullick (Cambridge, 2001), pp. xvii–xlviii.
—— and N. Hadgraft, 'Bookbindings', in *The Cambridge History of the Book in Britain, II: 1100–1400*, ed. N. Morgan and R. M. Thomson (Cambridge, 2014), pp. 95–109.

Gumbert, J. P., 'Codicological Units: Towards a Terminology for the Stratigraphy of the Non-Homogeneous Codex', *Segno e testo: International Journal of Manuscripts and Their Transmission* 2 (2004), 17–42.
——, 'On Folding Skins, According to Gilissen', *Gazette du livre medieval* 43 (2003), 47–51.
——, 'Skins, Sheets, and Quires', in *New Directions in Later Medieval Manuscript Studies: Essays from the 1998 Harvard Conference*, ed. D. Pearsall (York, 2000), pp. 81–90.
——, 'The Sizes of Manuscripts: Some Statistics and Notes', in *Hellinga Festschrift / Feestbundel / Mélanges: Forty-Three Studies in Bibliography Presented to Prof. Dr. Wytze Hellinga on the Occasion of his Retirement from the Chair of Neophilology in the University of Amsterdam at the End of the Year 1978*, ed. W. Hellinga and A. R. A. Croiset van Uchelen (Amsterdam, 1981), pp. 277–88.
Hadgraft, N., 'English Fifteenth Century Book Structures' (unpublished doctoral thesis, University College London, 1997).
Hanna, R., *Introducing English Medieval Book History: Manuscripts, their Producers and their Readers* (Liverpool, 2013).
——, *London Literature, 1300–1380* (Cambridge, 2005).
Hardman, P., 'Bodleian Library, MS Ashmole 33: Thoughts on Reading a Work in Progress', in *Middle English Texts in Transition: A Festschrift Dedicated to Toshiyuki Takamiya on his 70th Birthday*, ed. S. Horobin and L. R. Mooney (York, 2014), pp. 88–103.
——, 'Domestic Learning and Teaching: Investigating Evidence for the Role of "Household Miscellanies" in Late-Medieval England', in *Women and Writing c.1340–c.1650: The Domestication of Print Culture*, ed. A. Lawrence-Mathers and P. Hardman (York, 2010), pp. 15–33.
Hatcher, J., 'Mortality in the Fifteenth Century: Some New Evidence', *Economic History Review* 39 (1986), 19–38.
Hector, L. C., *The Handwriting of English Documents* (Dorking, 1980).
Heller, S., 'The Cognitive Benefits of Doodling', *The Atlantic*, 9 July 2015, online <http://www.theatlantic.com/entertainment/archive/2015/07/doodling-for-cognitive-benefits/398027/>.
Hellinga Festschrift / Feestbundel / Mélanges: Forty-Three Studies in Bibliography Presented to Prof. Dr. Wytze Hellinga on the Occasion of his Retirement from the Chair of Neophilology in the University of Amsterdam at the End of the Year 1978, ed. W. Hellinga and A. R. A. Croiset van Uchelen (Amsterdam, 1981).
Henderson, F., *The Whole Hog: Nose to Tail Eating* (London, 2004).
Hilmo, M., 'The Power of Images in the Auchinleck, Vernon, Pearl, and Two Piers Plowman Manuscripts', in *Opening Up Middle English Manuscripts: Literary and Visual Approaches*, ed. K. Kerby-Fulton, M. Hilmo and L. Olson (Ithaca, London, 2012), pp. 153–205.
Hinks, J., 'The Beginnings of the Book Trade in Leceister', in *The Moving Market: Continuity and Change in the Book Trade*, ed. P. Isaac and B. McKay (New Castle, 2001), pp. 27–38.
A History of the County of Hampshire, ed. H. A. Doubleday and W. Page, 5 vols. (London, 1903).
A History of the County of Oxford: The University of Oxford, ed. H. E. Salter and M. D. Lobel (London, 1954).
The History of the University of Oxford: Late Medieval Oxford, ed. J. I. Catto and T. A. R. Evans (Oxford, 1992).
The History of the University of Oxford: The Early Oxford Schools, ed. J. I. Catto (Oxford, 1984).
Hobson, G. D., *English Binding Before 1500*, The Sandars Lectures 1927 (Cambridge, 1929).
Hoffman, T., *Guilds and Related Organisations in Great Britain and Ireland: A Bibliography*, online <http://www.bbk.ac.uk/lib/elib/databases/tom-hoffman/tom-hoffman-bibliography-on-the-guilds>.

Holsinger, B., 'Of Pigs and Parchment: Medieval Studies and the Coming of the Animal', *PMLA* 124 (2009), 616–23.

——, 'Parchment Ethics: A Statement of More Than Modest Concern', *New Medieval Literatures* 12 (2010), 131–36.

——, 'Ecocodicology; Or, Is The Book A Byproduct?', in *The Parchment Inheritance: Animals, Archives, and the Making of Culture from Herodotus to the Digital Age* (forthcoming).

Horobin, S., 'The Scribe of Bodleian Library MS Bodley 619 and the Circulation of Chaucer's Treatise on the Astrolabe', *Studies in the Age of Chaucer* 31 (2009),109–24.

House of Commons, 'Vellum: Printing Record Copies of Public Acts', 11 May 2016, online <http://researchbriefings.parliament.uk/ResearchBriefing/Summary/CBP-7451>.

Humanism in Fifteenth-Century Europe, ed. D. Rundle, Medium Aevum Monographs, n.s. 30 (Oxford, 2012).

Illuminated Manuscripts in the Bodleian Library Oxford, ed. O. Pächt and J. J. G. Alexander, 3 vols. (Oxford, 1966–73).

The Index of Middle English Prose, Handlist IV: A Handlist of Douce Manuscripts containing Middle English Prose in the Bodleian Library, ed. L. Braswell (Cambridge, 1987).

The Index of Middle English Prose, Handlist VIII: Manuscripts Containing Middle English Prose in Oxford College Libraries, ed. S. J. Ogilvie-Thomson (Cambridge, 1991).

The Index of Middle English Prose, Handlist X: Manuscripts in Scandinavian Collections, ed. I. Taavitsainen (Cambridge, 1994).

The Index of Middle English Prose, Handlist XI: Manuscripts in the Library of Trinity College, Cambridge, ed. L. R. Mooney (Cambridge, 1995).

The Index of Middle English Prose, Handlist XIII: Manuscripts in Lambeth Palace Library, Including Those Formerly in Sion College, ed. O. S. Pickering and V. M. O'Mara (Cambridge, 1999).

The Index of Middle English Prose, Handlist XVI: Manuscripts in the Laudian Collection, Bodleian Library, Oxford, ed. S. J. Ogilvie-Thomson (Cambridge, 2000).

The Index of Middle English Prose, Handlist XVII: Manuscripts in the Library of Gonville and Caius College, Cambridge, ed. K. A. R. Schmidt (Cambridge, 2001).

The Index of Middle English Prose, Handlist XIX: Manuscripts in the University Library, Cambridge (Dd-Oo), ed. M. Connolly (Cambridge, 2009).

Index of Printed Middle English Prose, ed. R. E. Lewis, N. F. Blake and A. S. G. Edwards (New York, 1985).

Interpreting and Collecting Fragments of Medieval Books, ed. L. L. Brownrigg and M. M. Smith (Los Altos Hills, 2000).

Ivy, G. S., 'The Bibliography of the Manuscript Book', in *The English Library Before 1700*, ed. F. Wormald and C. E. Wright (London, 1958), pp. 32–65.

Jackson, H. J., *Marginalia: Readers Writing in Books* (Toronto, 2001).

Jervis, B., *Pottery and Social Life in Medieval England: Towards a Relational Approach* (Oxford, 2014).

John Gower: Trilingual Poet: Language, Translation and Tradition, ed. E. Dutton, with J. Hines, and R. F. Yeager (Cambridge, 2010).

Johnson, E. J., 'Scarring, Tears, Veins and Hair: The Imperfections of Medieval Parchment', The Ohio State University Libraries, online <https://library.osu.edu/blogs/rarebooks/2008/12/01/107/>.

Johnson, E., 'The Poetics of Waste: Medieval English Ecocriticism', *PMLA* 127.3 (2012), 460–76.

Johnston, M., and M. Van Dussen, 'Introduction: Manuscripts and Cultural History', in *The Medieval Manuscript Book: Cultural Approaches*, ed. M. Johnston and M. Van Dussen (Cambridge, 2015), pp. 1–16.

Joyce, P., and T. Bennett, 'Introduction', in *Material Powers: Cultural Studies, History and The Material Turn*, ed. T. Bennett and P. Joyce (London, 2010), pp. 1–21.
Justice, S., 'Inquisition, Speech, and Writing: A Case from Late Medieval Norwich', in *Criticism and Dissent in the Late Middle Ages*, ed. R. Copeland (Cambridge, 1996), pp. 289–322.
Kalof, L., *Looking at Animals in Human History* (London, 2007).
Kay, S., 'Legible Skins: Animals and the Ethics of Medieval Reading', *postmedieval: a journal of medieval cultural studies* 2 (2011), 13–32.
Keefer, S. L., and R. H. Bremmer Jr., 'Introduction', in *Signs on the Edge: Space, Text and Margin in Medieval Manuscripts*, ed. S. L. Keefer and R. H. Bremmer Jr., Mediaevalia Groningana n.s. 10 (Leuven, 2007), pp. 3–6.
Keene, D., and A. R. Rumble, 'Trades and Marketing', in *Survey of Medieval Winchester*, 3 vols. (Oxford, 1985), pp. 249–365.
Kelly, R., 'Another Slice', *The Spectator*, 30 January 2016, online <https://www.spectator.co.uk/article/another-slice>.
Ker, N. R. *Pastedowns in Oxford Bindings* (Oxford, 2000).
——, 'Oxford College Libraries before 1500', in *Books, Collectors and Libraries: Studies in the Medieval Heritage*, ed. A. G. Watson (London, 1985), pp. 301–20.
——, 'Robert Elyot's Books and Annotations', *The Library* 5th s. 30 (1975), 233–37.
——, 'The Books of Philosophy Distributed at Merton College in 1372 and 1375', in *Books, Collectors and Libraries: Studies in the Medieval Heritage*, ed. A. G. Watson (London, 1985), pp. 331–78.
——, *Fragments of Medieval Manuscripts Used as Pastedowns in Oxford Bindings*, Oxford Bibliographical Society 3rd s. 4 (Oxford, 2004 for 2000).
——, *Records of All Souls College Library, 1437–1600* (Oxford, 1971).
Kinch, A. *Imago Mortis: Mediating Images of Medieval Death in Late Medieval Culture* (Leiden, 2013).
Kleineke, H., 'Civic Ritual Space and Conflict in Fifteenth-Century Exeter', in *Ritual and Space in the Middle Ages: Proceedings of the 2009 Harlaxton Symposium*, ed. F. Andrews (Donington, 2011), pp. 165–78.
Knowles, D., and R. N. Hadcock, *Medieval Religious Houses: England and Wales* (London, 1953).
——, *Religious Orders in England*, 3 vols. (Cambridge, 1962).
Kowaleski, M., 'Town and Country in Late Medieval England: The Hide and Leather Trade', in *Work in Towns 850–1850*, ed. P. J. Corfield and D. Keene (Leicester, 1990), pp. 57–73.
——, *Local Markets and Regional Trade in Medieval Exeter* (Cambridge, 2003).
Kwakkel, E., 'A Love Story Hidden in a Hat', Tumblr, online <http://erikkwakkel.tumblr.com/post/55554381477/a-love-story-hidden-in-a-hat-you-are-looking-at-a>.
——, 'Broidery on a Medieval Page', Tumblr, online <http://erikkwakkel.tumblr.com/post/52258862048/broidery-on-a-medieval-page-holes-in-the-pages-of>.
——, 'Commercial Organization and Economic Innovation', in *The Production of Books in England 1350–1550*, ed. A. Gillespie and D. Wakelin (Cambridge, 2011), pp. 173–91.
——, 'Cultural Residue in Medieval Manuscripts', in *The Medieval Manuscript Book: Cultural Approaches*, ed. M. Johnston and M. Van Dussen (Cambridge, 2015), pp. 60–76.
——, 'Destroying Medieval Books – and Why That's Useful', Tumblr, online <https://medievalbooks.nl/2014/10/31/destroying-medieval-books-and-why-thats-useful/>.
——, 'Discarded Parchment as Writing Support in English Manuscript Culture', *Manuscripts Before 1400, English Manuscript Studies 1100–1700* 17 (2013), 238–61.
——, 'Halloween (4): Stabbed, Cut and Stitched Back Together', Tumblr, online <http://erikkwakkel.tumblr.com/post/65552828979/halloween-4-stabbed-cut-and-stitched-back>.

——, 'Holsterbooks and Off-cut Manuscripts', Bodleian Library Manuscript Masterclass, University of Oxford (24 February 2014).

——, 'Late Medieval Text Collections: A Single Author Typology Based on Single-Author MSS', in *Author, Reader, Book: Medieval Authorship in Theory and Practice*, ed. E. Kwakkel and S. Partridge (Toronto, 2012), pp. 56–79.

——, 'Medieval Kids' Doodles on Birch Bark', Tumblr, online <http://erikkwakkel.tumblr.com/post/67681966023/medieval-kids-doodles-on-birch-bark-heres>.

——, 'Party Time', Tumblr, online <http://erikkwakkel.tumblr.com/post/107251005026/party-time-the-first-and-last-text-line-on-the>.

—— and S. Partridge, ed., *Author, Reader, Book: Medieval Authorship in Theory and Practice* (Toronto, 2012).

Lahey, S., 'Offcut Zone Parchment in Manuscripts from Later Medieval England: A Corpus-Based Study' (unpublished doctoral thesis, University of Victoria, 2021).

Lähnemann, H., 'Recycling Parchment: Manuscript Fragments in Medieval Dresses', ICON Paper Conservation group, 1 May 2020, online <https://historyofthebook.mml.ox.ac.uk/2020/05/01/recycling-parchment/>.

——, 'Text und Textil. Die beschriebenen Pergamente in den Figurenornaten', in *Heilige Röcke: Kleider für Skulpturen in Kloster Wienhausen*, ed. C. Klack-Eitzen et al. (Regensburg, 2013), pp. 71–78.

The Language of Bindings Thesaurus, 'Ligatus' project, online <http://www.ligatus.org.uk/lob/>.

Langwe, M., *Limp Bindings from the Vatican Library* (Sollerön, 2013).

Leedham-Green, E., 'University Libraries and Book-sellers', in *The Cambridge History of the Book in Britain, III: 1400–1557*, ed. L. Hellinga and J. B. Trapp (Cambridge, 2014), pp. 316–53.

Les tablettes à écrire de l'Antiquité à l'Epoque Moderne, ed. É. Lalou, *Bibliologia* 12 (Turnhout, 1992).

Lewisohn, C., *Abstract Graffiti* (London, 2011).

Lindkvist, H., 'Richard Rolle's "Meditatio de Passione Domini"', *Skrifter Utgifna af K. Humanistiska Vetenskaps-Samfundet i Uppsala* 19:3 (1917), 34–59.

Livesey, S. J., 'Proportions in Late-Medieval Universities: An Examination of Two Treatises', *Revue d'histoire des textes* 16 (1986, 1988), 283–310.

Logan, F. D., *Runaway Religious in Medieval England, c. 1240–1540* (Cambridge, 2002).

The Long Fifteenth Century: Essays for Douglas Gray, ed. H. Cooper and S. Mapstone (Oxford, 1997).

'Lost Manuscripts' project, online <https://www.lostmss.org.uk/project>.

Lovatt, R., 'College and University Book Collections and Libraries', in *The Cambridge History of Libraries in Britain and Ireland, I: to 1640*, ed. E. Leedham-Green and T. Webber (Cambridge, 2013), pp. 152–77.

——, 'Two Collegiate Loan Chests in Late Medieval Cambridge', in *Medieval Cambridge: Essays on the Pre-Reformation University*, ed. P. N. R. Zutshi (Cambridge, 1993), pp. 129–65.

Lovett, P., slunk vellum, online <https://www.patricialovett.com/tag/slunk-vellum/>

Madan, F., 'Day-Book of John Dorne, Bookseller in Oxford, A.D. 1520', in *Collectanea*, ed. C. R. L. Fletcher, Oxford Historical Society 1st s. 5 (Oxford, 1885), pp. 73–177.

Makers and Users of Medieval Books: Essays in Honour of A. S. G. Edwards, ed. C. M. Meale and D. Pearsall (Cambridge, 2014).

Mann, J., 'Price and Value in Sir Gawain and the Green Knight', *Essays in Criticism* 36 (1986), 294–318.

Manuscripts and Printed Books in Europe 1350–1550: Packaging, Presentation and Consumption, ed. E. Cayley and S. Powell (Liverpool, 2015).

Marland, P., and J. Parham, 'Remaindering: the Material Ecology of Junk and Composting', *Green Letters: Studies in Ecocriticism* 18:1 (2014), 1–8.

Martini, A., 'Ritual Consecration in the Context of Writing the Holy Scrolls: Jews in Medieval Europe between Demarcation and Acculturation', *European Journal of Jewish Studies* 2 (2017), 174–202.

Mason, R., 'Tradition of Recording UK Laws on Vellum May Be Saved', the *Guardian*, 15 February 2016, online <http://www.theguardian.com/politics/2016/feb/15/lords-overruled-recording-laws-vellum-goat-calf-skin>.

Maxted, I., *Exeter Cathedral Library: a Concordance of Medieval Catalogues and Surviving Manuscripts* (Exeter, 1987).

McKenzie, D. F., *Bibliography and the Sociology of Texts*, The Panizzi Lectures (Cambridge, 1999).

McKitterick, R., 'Palimpsests: Concluding Remarks', *Early Medieval Palimpsests, Bibliologia* 26 (Turnhout, 2007), 145–51.

The Medieval Books of Merton College, ed. F. M. Powicke (Oxford, 1931).

Medieval Cambridge: Essays on the Pre-Reformation University, ed. P. N. R. Zutshi (Cambridge, 1993).

A Medieval Farming Glossary of Latin and English Words, ed. J. L. Fisher, revised by A. Powell and R. Powell (Essex, 1997).

Medieval Libraries of Great Britain: A List of Surviving Books, ed. N. R. Ker, Royal Historical Society Guides and Handbooks 3, 2nd edn (London, 1941; 1964).

The Medieval Manuscript Book: Cultural Approaches, ed. M. Johnston and M. Van Dussen (Cambridge, 2015).

Medieval Manuscripts in British Libraries, ed. N. R. Ker and A. J. Piper, 5 vols. (Oxford, 1969–2002).

The Medieval Professional Reader at Work: Evidence from Manuscripts of Chaucer, Langland, Kempe, and Gower, ed. K. Kerby-Fulton and M. Hilmo (Victoria, 2001).

The Medieval Translator: The Theory and Practice of Translation in the Middle Ages, ed. R. Ellis (Cambridge, 1989).

Meyer, J., 'Parchment Production: A Brief Account', in *Scraped, Stroked, and Bound: Materially Engaged Readings of Medieval Manuscripts*, ed. J. Wilcox (Turnhout, 2013), pp. 93–96.

Middle English Dictionary, gen. ed. R. E. Lewis, online <http://quod.lib.umich.edu/m/med/>.

Middle English Texts in Transmission: A Festschrift Dedicated to Toshiyuki Takamiya on his 70th Birthday, ed. S. Horobin and L. R. Mooney (York, 2014).

Mills, R., *Suspended Animation: Pain, Pleasure and Punishment in Medieval Culture* (London, 2006).

Mooney, L. R., and E. Stubbs, *Scribes and the City: London Guildhall Clerks and the Dissemination of Middle English Literature, 1375–1425* (York, 2013 repr. 2014).

——, S. Horobin, and E. Stubbs, *Late Medieval English Scribes*, online <http://www.medievalscribes.com>.

Morrison, S. S., *Excrement in the Late Middle Ages: Sacred Filth and Chaucer's Fecopoetics* (Basingstoke, 2008).

——, *The Literature of Waste: Material Ecopoetics and Ethical Matter* (Basingstoke, 2015).

Morton, T., *Ecology Without Nature: Rethinking Environmental Aesthetics* (Cambridge, London, 2007).

The Moving Market: Continuity and Change in the Book Trade, ed. P. Isaac and B. McKay (New Castle, 2001).

Muzerelle, D., *Vocabulaire codicologique*, online <http://codicologia.irht.cnrs.fr>.

Mynors, R. A. B., *Durham Cathedral Manuscripts to the End of the Twelfth Century* (Oxford, 1939).

Nardizzi, V., 'Medieval Ecocriticism', *postmedieval: a journal of medieval cultural studies* 4.1 (2013), 112–23.

The National Archives, 'Currency Calculator', online <http://www.nationalarchives.gov.uk/currency/default0.asp#mid>.

New Directions in Later Medieval Manuscript Studies: Essays from the 1998 Harvard Conference, ed. D. Pearsall (York, 2000).
Norfolk Medieval Graffiti Survey, online <http://www.medieval-graffiti.co.uk>.
Nottingham Special Collections, 'Money', online, <https://www.nottingham.ac.uk/manuscriptsandspecialcollections/researchguidance/weightsandmeasures/money.aspx>.
O'Connell, M., 'The Marginal Obsession with Marginalia', *The New Yorker*, 26 January 2012 <http://www.newyorker.com/books/page-turner/the-marginal-obsession-with-marginalia>.
O'Connor, T., 'Thinking About Beastly Bodies', in *Breaking and Shaping Beastly Bodies: Animals as Material Culture in the Middle Ages*, ed. A. Pluskowski (Oxford, 2007), pp. 1–10.
Opening Up Middle English Manuscripts: Literary and Visual Approaches, ed. K. Kerby-Fulton and L. Olson (Ithaca, 2012).
Orme, N., *Education and Society in Medieval and Renaissance England* (London, 1989).
——, *Medieval Schools: From Roman Britain to Renaissance England* (New Haven, London, 2006).
——, *Minor Clergy of Exeter Cathedral Biographies: 1250–1548* (Exeter, 2013).
Owen, K., 'Traces of Presence and Pleading: Approaches to the Study of Graffiti at Tewkesbury Abbey', in *Wild Signs: Graffiti in Archaeology and History*, ed. J. Oliver and T. Neal (Oxford, 2010), pp. 35–46.
Oxford English Dictionary, online <http://www.oed.com>.
Parkes, M. B., *Their Hands Before Our Eyes: A Closer Look at Scribes*, The Lyell Lectures, Oxford, 1999 (Aldershot, 2008).
——, 'The Planning and Construction of the Ellesmere Manuscript', in *The Ellesmere Chaucer: Essays in Interpretation*, ed. M. Stevens and D. Woodward (San Marino, 1997), pp. 41–47.
——, 'The Provision of Books', in *The History of the University of Oxford: Late Medieval Oxford*, ed. J. I. Catto and T. A. R. Evans (Oxford, 1992), pp. 407–83.
——, 'Thomas Hunt and the Oxford Book-Business in the Late Fifteenth Century', *The Library* 7th s. 17:1 (2016), 28–39.
Paston Letters and Papers of the Fifteenth Century, ed. N. Davis, 2 vols (Oxford, 1971), online <http://name.umdl.umich.edu/Paston>.
Pearsall, D., and E. Salter, *Landscapes and Seasons of the Medieval World* (London, 1973).
Pegues, F., 'Philanthrophy and the Universities of France and England', in *The Economic and Material Framework of the Medieval University*, ed. A. L. Gabriel (Indiana, 1977), pp. 69–80.
Pen in Hand: Medieval Scribal Portraits, Colophons and Tools, ed. M. Gullick (Walkern, 2006).
Pergamena New York, 'Manuscript Uterine Calf Parchment', online <http://www.pergamena.net/parchment-products/manuscript-uterine-calf-parchment>.
Pergament, Geschichte, Struktur, Restaurierung und Herstellung, ed. P. Rück (Sigmaringen, 1991).
Perkins, N., and A. Wiggins, *Romance of the Middle Ages* (Oxford, 2012).
Perry, R., 'The Material Text: Reading, Identity, and the Late Medieval Book', London Medieval Society Colloquium: 'Who Read What in the Middle Ages?', Queen Mary University London (17 November 2012).
—— and S. Kelly, 'Whittington's Gift: Reconstructing the Lost Common Library of London's Guildhall' project (Leverhulme Trust 2020–2023).
Philip, I., *The Bodleian Library in the Seventeenth and Eighteenth Centuries*, The Lyell Lectures, Oxford, 1980–81 (Oxford, 1983).
Pickwood, N., 'The Use of Fragments of Medieval Manuscripts in the Construction and Covering of Bindings on Printed Books', in *Interpreting and Collecting Fragments of Medieval Books*, ed. L. L. Brownrigg and M. M. Smith (Los Altos Hills, 2000), pp. 1–20.

Pollard, G., 'Medieval Loan Chests at Cambridge', *Bulletin of the Institute of Historical Research* 17 (1939–40), 113–29.
——, 'On the Repair of Medieval Bindings', *The Paper Conservator* 1 (1976), 35–36.
——, *Notes for a Directory of Cat Street: Oxford Before A.D. 1500*, Bodleian Library Archive, Catalogue of the Papers of Graham Pollard, compiled by E. Potter (1937/1988).
The Post-Historical Middle Ages, ed. E. Scala and S. Frederico (Basingstoke, 2009).
Pouzet, J-P., 'Book Production Outside Commercial Contexts', in *The Production of Books in England 1350–1550*, ed. A. Gillespie and D. Wakelin (Cambridge, 2011), pp. 212–38.
——, 'Southwark Gower: Augustinian Agencies in Gower's Manuscripts and Texts – Some Prolegomena', in *John Gower: Trilingual Poet: Language, Translation and Tradition*, ed. E. Dutton, with J. Hines, and R. F. Yeager (Cambridge, 2010), pp. 11–25.
Price, L., *How to Do Things with Books in Victorian Britain* (Princeton, 2013).
Probable Truth: Editing Medieval Texts from Britain in the Twenty-First Century, ed. V. Gillespie and A. Hudson (Turnhout, 2013).
The Production of Books in England 1350–1550, ed. A. Gillespie and D. Wakelin (Cambridge, 2011).
Promissory Notes on the Treasury of Merits: Indulgences in Late Medieval Europe, ed. R. N. Swanson (Boston, 2006).
Property and Politics: Essays in Later Medieval English History, ed. T. Pollard (Gloucester, 1984).
Pulsiano, P., 'Jaunts, Jottings and Jetsam in Anglo-Saxon Manuscripts', *Florilegium* 19 (2002), 189–216.
Quarto Catalogue, II: Laudian Manuscripts, ed. H. O. Coxe and R. W. Hunt (Oxford, 1858–1885; repr. 1973).
Quarto Catalogue, III: Catalogi Codicum Manuscriptorum Bibliothecae Bodleianae Pars Tertia Codices Graecos et Latinos Canonicianos Complectens, ed. H. O. Coxe (Oxford, 1854).
Quarto Catalogue, IX.i: Digby Manuscripts, ed. W. D. Macray, R. W. Hunt, A. G. Watson, A. Thomas, reproduction of the 1883 catalogue (Oxford, 1999).
Quarto Catalogue, V: Catalogi Codicum Manuscriptorum Bibliothecae Bodleianae Partis Quintae Fasciculus Primus (-Quintus) Ricardi Rawlinson Codicum Classes [A-D] Complectens, ed. W. D. Macray (Oxford, 1862–1900).
Quarto Catalogue, X: A Descriptive, Analytical and Critical Catalogue of the Manuscripts Bequeathed Unto the University of Oxford by Elias Ashole: Also of Some Additional MSS. Contributed by Kingsley, Lhuyd, Borlase and Others, ed. W. H. Black, 2 vols. (Oxford, 1845–66).
Ramirez, J., *Illuminations: The Private Lives of Medieval Kings*, Oxford Film and Television collaboration with the British Library for the BBC, 2013.
Ranft, P., *Medieval Theology of Work: Peter Damian and the Medieval Religious Renewal Movement* (New York, 2016).
Raven, J., *The Business of Books: Booksellers and the English Book Trade, 1450–1850* (London, 2007).
Raymond, J., *Pamphlets and Pamphleteering in Early Modern Britain* (Cambridge, 2006).
Reading Skin in Medieval Literature and Culture, ed. K. L. Walter (Basingstoke, 2013).
Recording Medieval Lives: Proceedings of the 2005 Harlaxton Symposium, ed. J. Boffey and V. Davis (Donington, 2009).
Reed, R., *Ancient Skins, Parchments and Leathers* (London, 1972).
——, *The Nature and Making of Parchment* (Leeds, 1975).
Regionalism in Late Medieval Manuscripts and Texts: Essays Celebrating the Publication of a Linguistic Atlas of Late Medieval English, ed. F. Riddy (Cambridge, 1991).
The Register of Congregation, 1448–1463, ed. W. A. Pantin and W. T. Mitchell, Oxford Historical Society, n.s. 22 (Oxford, 1973).

Reiter, E. H., 'Recycling the Written Word: Manuscript Fragments and Late Medieval Readers', in *Interpreting and Collecting Fragments of Medieval Books*, ed. L. L. Brownrigg and M. M. Smith (Los Altos Hills, 2000), pp. 189–204.

Rethinking Chaucerian Beasts, ed. C. Van Dyke (Basingstoke, 2012).

Reynolds, A., 'Introduction', in *Privy Tokens: Waste Paper in Early Modern England* (unpublished), pp. 1–25.

Richardson, M., *Middle-Class Writing in Late Medieval London* (London, 2011).

Ringler Jr., W. A., *Bibliography and Index of English Verse in Manuscript 1501–1558*, prepared and completed by M. Rudick and S. J. Ringler (London, 1992).

Robertson, K., 'Medieval Things: Materiality, Historicity, and the Premodern Object', *Literature Compass* 5 (2008), 1060–80.

Robinson, P. R., 'The "Booklet": A Self-Contained Unit in Composite Manuscripts', *Codicologica: Essais typologiques* 3 (1980), 46–69.

Rosewell, R., *Medieval Wall Paintings* (Oxford, 2014).

Rouse, R. H., and M. A. Rouse, 'The Vocabulary of Wax Tablets', in *Vocabulaire du livre et de l'écriture au Moyen Age: Actes de la table ronde Paris 24–26 septembre 1987*, ed. O. Weijers (Turnhout, 1989), pp. 220–30.

Rubin, M., *Charity and Community in Medieval Cambridge* (Cambridge, 1987).

Rudd, G., *Greenery: Ecocritical Readings of Late Medieval English Literature* (Manchester, 2007).

Rudy, K. M., 'Dirty Books: Quantifying Patterns of Use in Medieval Manuscripts Using a Densitometer', *Journal of Historians of Netherlandish Art* 2.1–2 (2010), 1–26.

——, *Postcards on Parchment: The Social Lives of Medieval Books* (New Haven, London, 2015).

Rundle, D., and S. Mandelbrote, 'Corrigenda', in N. R. Ker, *Fragments of Medieval Manuscripts Used as Pastedowns in Oxford Bindings* 3rd s. 4 (Oxford, 2004 for 2000), pp. †1–29.

——, 'Parliament and the Vellum Debate, Part I', online, 6 March 2016, <https://bonaelitterae.wordpress.com/2016/03/06/parliament-and-the-vellum-debate-part-i/>.

——, POxBo, part of the 'Lost Manuscripts' project, <https://www.lostmss.org.uk/pastedowns-oxford-bindings-online-poxbo>.

Rust, M. D., *Imaginary Worlds in Medieval Books: Exploring the Manuscript Matrix* (Basingstoke, 2007).

Ruzzier, C., 'The Miniaturisation of Bible Manuscripts in the Thirteenth Century: A Comparative Study', in *Form and Function in the Late Medieval Bible*, ed. E. Poleg and L. Light (Leiden, 2013), pp. 105–25.

Ryder, M. L., 'The Biology and History of Parchment', in *Pergament, Geschichte, Struktur, Restaurierung und Herstellung*, ed. P. Rück (Sigmaringen, 1991), pp. 25–33.

Ryley, H., 'Constructive Parchment Destruction in Medieval Manuscripts', *Book 2.0* 7 (2017), 9–19.

——, 'Redrafted and Double-Wrapped: Binding a Medieval English Romance', *The New Bookbinder* 39 (2019), 17–23.

Salisbury, J., *The Beast Within: Animals in the Middle Ages* (London, 2011).

Sapart, C. J., G. Monteil, M. Prokopiou, et al., 'Natural and Anthropogenic Variations in Methane Sources During the Past Two Millenia', *Nature* 490 (2012), 85–88.

Sargan, J. D., 'The Scarlet Letter: Experimentation, Design and Copying Practice in the Coloured Capitals of MS Digby 86', in *Interpreting MS Digby 86: A Trilingual Book from Thirteenth-Century Worcestershire*, ed. S. Fein (York, 2019), pp. 219–54.

Sargent, M. G., 'What do the numbers mean? A Textual Critic's Observations on some Patterns of Middle English Manuscript Transmission', in *Design and Distribution of Late Medieval Manuscripts in England*, ed. M. Connolly and L. R. Mooney (York, 2008), pp. 205–44.

Saul, N., *English Church Monuments in the Middle Ages: History and Representation* (Oxford, 2009).
Sawyer, D., 'Practical Ideas of the Book: Books Present and Absent in Medieval Catalogues' unpublished conference paper (Harlaxton, 2019).
——, *Reading English Verse in Manuscript c.1350–1500* (Oxford, 2020).
Scala, E., and S. Frederico, 'Introduction', in *The Post-Historical Middle Ages*, ed. E. Scala and S. Frederico (Basingstoke, 2009), pp. 1–12.
Scase, W., 'Reginald Pecock, John Carpenter and John Colop's "Common Profit" Books: Aspects of Book Ownership and Circulation in Fifteenth-Century London', *Medium Ævum* 61:2 (1992), 261–70.
Scattergood, V. J., 'Two Medieval Book Lists', *The Library* 5th s. 23:3 (1968), 236–39.
Scholla, A., 'Libri sine asseribus: zur Einbandtechnik, Form und Inhalt mitteleuropäischer Koperte des 8. bis 14. Jahrhunderts' (unpublished doctoral thesis, University of Leiden, 2002).
Schramm, W. L., 'The Cost of Books in Chaucer's Time', *Modern Language Notes* 47 (1933), 139–45.
Sciacca, C., 'Stitches, Sutures, and Seams: "Embroidered" Parchment Repairs in Medieval Manuscripts', *Medieval Clothing and Textiles* 6 (2010), 57–92.
Scott-Warren, J., 'Reading Graffiti in the Early Modern Book', *Huntington Library Quarterly* 73 (2010), 363–81.
Scott, A. M., 'Experiences of Charity: Complex Motivations in the Charitable Endeavour, c. 1100–c.1650', in *Experiences of Charity, 1250–1650*, ed. A. M. Scott (Farnham, 2015), pp. 1–14.
Scott, K. L., 'Past Ownership: Evidence of Book Ownership by Merchants in the Later Middle Ages', in *Makers and Users of Medieval Books: Essays in Honour of A. S. G. Edwards*, ed. C. M. Meale and D. Pearsall (Cambridge, 2014), pp. 150–77.
Scott, K., 'Representations of Scribal Activity in English Manuscripts, c. 1400–1490: A Mirror of the Craft?', in *Pen in Hand: Medieval Scribal Portraits, Colophons and Tools*, ed. M. Gullick (Walkern, 2006), pp. 115–50.
Scraped, Stroked, and Bound: Materially Engaged Readings of Medieval Manuscripts, ed. J. Wilcox (Turnhout, 2013).
Seetah, K., *Humans, Animals, and the Craft of Slaughter in Archaeo-Historic Societies* (Cambridge, 2019).
——, 'The Middle Ages on the Block: Animals, Guilds and Meat in the Medieval Period', in *Breaking and Shaping Beastly Bodies: Animals as Material Culture in the Middle Ages*, ed. A. Pluskowski (Oxford, 2007), pp. 18–31.
Selections From the Correspondence and Memoranda of Cely Family Merchants of the Staple AD 1475–1488, ed. H. E. Malden (London, 1900), online <http://www.r3.org/on-line-library-text-essays/the-cely-papers/>.
Sennett, R., *The Craftsman* (London, 2008).
Serjeantson, D., 'Animal Remains and the Tanning Trade', in *Diet and Craft in Towns: The Evidence of Animal Remains from the Roman to the Post-Medieval Periods*, ed. D. Serjeantson and T. Waldron, British Archaeological Reports, British Series 199 (Oxford, 1989), pp. 129–46.
Seymour, M. C., 'The English Manuscripts of Mandeville's Travels', *Edinburgh Bibliographical Society Transactions* 4:5 (1966), 169–210.
Shailor, B., *The Medieval Book: Illustrated from the Beinecke Rare Book & Manuscript Library* (Toronto, 1991).
Shepherd, S. H. A., 'The Ashmole Sir Ferumbras: Translation in Holograph', in *The Medieval Translator: The Theory and Practice of Translation in the Middle Ages*, ed. R. Ellis (Cambridge, 1989), pp. 103–21.

——, 'Four Middle English Charlemagne Romances: A Revaluation of the Non-Cyclic Verse Texts and the Holograph Sir Ferumbras' (unpublished doctoral thesis, University of Oxford, 1988).
Sheppard, J., *Census of Western Medieval Bookbinding Structures to 1500 in British Libraries* (Cambridge, 1997).
Sherman, W. H., 'The Reader's Eye: Between Annotation and Illustration', Keble Medieval and Renaissance Research Cluster, Keble College, Oxford (8 February 2013).
——, *Used Books: Marking Readers in Renaissance England* (Philadelphia, 2008).
Signs on the Edge: Space, Text and Margin in Medieval Manuscripts, ed. S. L. Keefer and R. H. Bremmer Jr., Mediaevalia Groningana n.s. 10 (Leuven, 2007).
Simpson, J., 'Bonjour Paresse: Literary Waste and Recycling in Book 4 of Gower's "Confessio Amantis"', *Proceedings of the British Academy* 151 (2007), 257–84.
Six Centuries of the Provincial Book Trade in Britain, ed. P. Isaac (Winchester, 1990).
Skemer, D. C., *Binding Words: Textual Amulets in the Middle Ages* (Philadelphia, 2006).
Smith, M. M., 'Preface', in *Interpreting and Collecting Fragments of Medieval Books*, ed. L. L. Brownrigg and M. M. Smith (Los Altos Hills, 2000), pp. xi–xv.
——, *The Title Page, its Early Development, 1460–1510* (London, 2000).
Smyth, A., 'Burning to Read: Ben Jonson's Library Fire of 1623', in *Book Destruction in the West, from the Medieval to the Contemporary*, ed. A. Smyth and G. Partington (Basingstoke, 2014), pp. 34–54.
——, 'Cutting and Authorship in Early Modern England', *Authorship* 2:2 (2013), online <http://dx.doi.org/10.21825/aj.v2i2.790>.
—— and G. Partington, 'Introduction', in *Book Destruction in the West, from the Medieval to the Contemporary*, ed. A. Smyth and G. Partington (Basingstoke, 2014), pp. 1–14.
Solopova, E., *Manuscripts of the Wycliffite Bible in the Bodleian and Oxford College Libraries* (Liverpool, 2016).
Somerset, F., '"No Man May Serue to Two Lordis": The Lollard Glossed Gospels as Spiritual Advice in John Colop's Common-Profit Book, CUL Ff.6.31', *JEBS* 22 (2019), 73–92.
Spaces for Reading in Later Medieval England, ed. M. C. Flannery and C. Griffin (Basingstoke, 2016).
Steel, K., *How to Be a Human: Animals and Violence in the Middle Ages* (Columbus, 2011).
Stevens, C., and R. Verhé, 'Primary Production of Raw Materials', in *Renewable Bioresources: Scope and Modification for Non-Food Applications* (Oxford, 2004).
Stevenson, J., *The Church Historians of England*, 5 vols. (London: Seeleys, 1853).
Stinson, T., 'Counting Sheep: Potential Applications of DNA Analysis to the Study of Medieval Parchment Production', in *Codicology and Palaeography in the Digital Age II*, ed. F. Fischer, C. Fritze, G. Vogeler (Norstedt, 2011), pp. 191–207.
Stock, B., *The Implications of Literacy: Written Language and Models of Interpretation in the Eleventh and Twelfth Centuries* (New Jersey, 1983).
Stoddard, R. E., 'Looking at Marks in Books', *The Gazette of the Grolier Club* n.s. 51 (2000), 27–47.
Stonor Letters and Papers 1290–1483, ed. C. L. Kingsford (London, 1919), online <http://name.umdl.umich.edu/ACA1723.0001.001>.
Storm van Leeuwen, J., 'Review of Agnes Scholla's Thesis: Libri sine asseribus', *Quaerendo* 35:1 (2005), 150–52.
Strand, A., 'The Examination and Conservation of a Medieval Manuscript with Embroidered Repairs', *Care and Conservation* 8 (2005), 113–22.
——, Uppsala Library, 'A Medieval Book Mended with Silk Thread', online <https://web.archive.org/web/20131017052042/http://www.ub.uu.se/en/Just-now/Projects/Completed-projects/A-medieval-book-mended-with-silk-thread/>.

Studies in the English Trade in the 15th Century, ed. E. Power and M. M. Postan (London, 1933, repr. 2006).
Suffolk Medieval Graffiti Survey, online <http://www.medieval-graffiti-suffolk.co.uk>.
A Summary Catalogue of Western Manuscripts in the Bodleian Library at Oxford Which Have Not Hitherto Been Catalogued in the Quarto Series: Collections Received Before 1660 and Miscellaneous MSS. Acquired During the First Half of the 17th Century, ed. F. Madan et al., 7 volumes (Oxford, 1953).
A Summary Catalogue of Western Manuscripts in the Bodleian Library at Oxford Which Have Not Hitherto Been Catalogued in the Quarto Series: Collections and Miscellaneous MSS. Acquired During the Second Half of the 17th Century, ed. H. H. E. Craster and N. Denholm-Young (Oxford, 1937).
Swanson, R. N., 'Praying for Pardon: Devotional Indulgences in Late Medieval England', in *Promissory Notes on the Treasury of Merits: Indulgences in Late Medieval Europe*, ed. R. N. Swanson (Leiden, 2006), pp. 215–40.
Szirmai, J. A., *The Archaeology of Medieval Bookbinding* (Aldershot, 1992).
Taavitsainen, I., 'Middle English Recipes: Genre Characteristics, Text Type Features and Underlying Traditions of Writing', *Journal of Historical Pragmatics* 2:1 (2001), 85–113.
Teasdale, M. D., N. L. van Doorn, et al., 'Paging Through History: Parchment as a Reservoir of Ancient DNA for Next Generation Sequencing', *Philosophical Transactions of the Royal Society B: Biological Sciences* 370:1660 (2015), 20130379, online <http://dx.doi.org/10.1098/rstb.2013.0379>.
Thomas Hoccleve: A Facsimile of the Autograph Manuscripts, ed. J. A. Burrow and A. I. Doyle EETS SS 19 (Oxford, 2002).
Thompson, D. V., 'Medieval Parchment Making', *The Library* 4th s. 16 (1935), 113–17.
——, 'Trial Index to Some Unpublished Sources for the History of Medieval Craftsmanship', *Speculum* 10 (1935), 410–31.
——, *The Materials and Techniques of Medieval Painting* (New York, 1956).
Thomson, D., *A Descriptive Catalogue of Middle English Grammatical Texts* (London, 1979).
Thomson, R. M., 'Parchment and Paper, Ruling and Ink', in *The Cambridge History of the Book in Britain, II: 1100–1400*, ed. N. Morgan and R. M. Thomson (Cambridge, 2014), pp. 75–84.
Thorpe, D. E., 'Young Hands, Old Books: Drawings by Children in a Fourteenth-Century Manuscript, LJS MS. 361', *Cogent Arts and Humanities* 3: 1 (2016), 1–18.
Timmerman, A., 'Of Dirty Books and Bread', online <http://recipes.hypotheses.org/2859>.
Tohma, S., 'Making & Testing Iron Gall Ink', online <https://www.westdean.org.uk/study/school-of-conservation/blog/books-and-library-materials/making-testing-iron-gall-ink>.
Tschichold, J., *The Form of the Book* (London, 1991).
Turner, N. K., 'The Materiality of Medieval Parchment: A Response to "The Animal Turn"', *Revista Hispánica Moderna* 71 (2018), 39–67.
The Uses of Manuscripts in Literary Studies: Essays in Memory of Judson Boyce Allen, ed. C. C. Morse, P. R. Doob, and M. C. Woods (Michigan, 1992).
Ustick, W. L., '"Parchment" and "Vellum"', *The Library* 4th s. 16 (1936), 439–40.
Veale, E., *The English Fur Trade in the Later Middle Ages*, London Record Society 38 (London, 2003).
Veblen, T., *Theory of the Leisure Class* (New York, 1967).
Victoria History of the County of Wiltshire, ed. R. B. Pugh and E. Crittall, 18 vols. (London, 1956).
Vnouček, J., 'The Manufacture of Parchment for Writing Purposes and the Observation of the Signs of Manufacture Surviving in Old Manuscripts', *Care and Conservation* 8 (2005), 74–92.
Vocabulaire du livre et de l'écriture au Moyen Age: Actes de la table ronde Paris 24–26 septembre 1987, ed. O. Weijers (Turnhout, 1989).
Wakelin, D., and C. Burlinson, 'Evidence for the Construction of Quires in a Fifteenth-Century English Manuscript', *The Library* 7th s. 9:4 (2008), 383–96.

——, *Designing English: Early Literature on the Page* (Oxford, 2018).
——, 'Editing and Correcting', in *Probable Truth: Editing Medieval Texts from Britain in the Twenty-First Century*, ed. V. Gillespie and A. Hudson (Turnhout, 2013), pp. 241–59.
——, 'England: Humanism Beyond Weiss', in *Humanism in Fifteenth-Century Europe*, ed. D. Rundle (Oxford, 2012), pp. 265–305.
——, 'Recording Ownership, Recording the Self: Gunthorpe's Example', unpublished paper, 47th International Congress on Medieval Studies, Kalamazoo (May 2012).
——, *Scribal Correction and Literary Craft: English Manuscripts 1375–1510* (Cambridge, 2014).
——, '"Thys ys my boke": Imagining the Owner in the Book', in *Spaces for Reading in Later Medieval England*, ed. M. C. Flannery and C. Griffin (Basingstoke, 2016), pp. 13–33.
Walter, K. L., 'Introduction', in *Reading Skin in Medieval Literature and Culture*, ed. K. L. Walter (Basingstoke, 2013), pp. 1–10.
Warrington, B, 'Conservation Report on the Pembroke Fragments', online <https://www.english.cam.ac.uk/manuscriptslab/conservation-report-on-the-pembroke-fragments/>.
Watson, B., 'Oodles of Doodles? Doodling Behaviour and its Implications for Understanding Palaeoarts', *Rock Art Research* 25 (2008), 35–60.
Weetman, J., 'Testamentary Piety and Charity in London, 1279–1370' (unpublished doctoral thesis, University of Oxford, 2013).
The Western Manuscripts in the Library of Trinity College, Cambridge: A Descriptive Catalogue, ed. M. R. James, 4 vols. (Cambridge, 1900–04).
Whalley, J. I., *Writing Implements and Accessories from the Roman Stylus to the Typewriter* (London, 1975).
White Jr., L., 'The Historical Roots of Our Ecologic Crisis', *Science* 155:3767 (1967), 1203–07.
White, T., research project: 'Working Theories of the Late Medieval Book'.
Wilcox, J., 'Introduction: The Philology of Smell', in *Scraped, Stroked, and Bound: Materially Engaged Readings of Medieval Manuscripts*, ed. J. Wilcox (Turnhout, 2013), pp. 1–14.
Wild Signs: Graffiti in Archaeology and History, ed. J. Oliver and T. Neal (Oxford, 2010).
Willoughby, J., 'Universities, Colleges and Chantries', in *A Companion to the Early Printed Book in Britain, 1476–1558*, ed. V. Gillespie and S. Powell (Cambridge, 2014), pp. 207–24.
Women and Writing c.1340–c.1650: The Domestication of Print Culture, ed. A. Lawrence-Mathers and P. Hardman (York, 2010).
Woodcock, M., 'England in the Long Fifteenth Century', in *A Companion to Medieval Poetry*, ed. C. Saunders (Oxford, 2010), pp. 501–19.
Woods, C., 'Conservation Treatments for Parchment Documents', *Journal of the Society of Archivists* 16:2 (1995), 221–38.
Woolgar, C. M., 'Meat and Dairy Products in Late Medieval England', in *Food in Medieval England: Diet and Nutrition*, ed. C. M. Woolgar, D. Serjeantson, and T. Waldron (Oxford, 2006), pp. 88–101.
Work in Towns 850–1850, ed. P. J. Corfield and D. Keene (Leicester, 1990).

Index

The Abbey of the Holy Ghost 117
Alphabets 118, 125–28
  specimen alphabet 126
Amateurism 36–37, 37 n.112, 73, 73 n.54, 95
Anathema 175
Animal
  by-products (*see also* hide; skins) 19–25, 28–33, 41, 47–48, 50
  ethics (*see also* baiting; slaughter) 27–30
  husbandry (*see also* cattle; selective breeding; sheep) 19, 24, 28–33, 41
Astrological texts 72, 86, 88
Audelay or Awdelay, John 'the Blind' 105–07, 117, 121

Baiting (*see also* slaughter) 28, 31
Bale, John 4, 61, 66
Balsall or Balsalle, Thomas (fellow of Merton College, Oxford) 178
Barnard Castle, Thomas of (founded the chest at Peterhouse College, Cambridge) 171
Beaulieu Abbey (Cistercian foundation in Hampshire) 31–32, 48
Bible 12, 23, 99, 115, 128, 158, 160, 166, 169, 176, 180 (*see also* Wycliffite Bible, Vulgate Bible)
  Corinthians 12, 12 n.61
  illuminated 167
  Isaiah 99
  Psalms 120 n.56, 128, 128 n.91, 134
Biocodicology 15
Bisham Montague (Augustinian Priory in Berkshire) 75
Black Death 31, 33
Bodleian Library, Oxford collections
  Ashmole 69
  Auctarium 154
  Bodley 154
  Digby 69, 72 n.49
  Douce 69, 109, 118, 124
  Laudian 109, 118, 124

Bonhommes or Bonshommes
  of Ashridge, Buckingham 167
  of Edington, Wiltshire 167–68, 181
Bookbinding(s) (*see also* binder's waste; limp covers; re-use of parchment by bookbinders; wrappers) 5, 15–17, 21, 26, 31, 56, 62–63, 74–76, 77, 79–82, 82–95, 137, 143, 152, 159, 162
  boards 21, 62–63, 80–82, 84–85, 92, 95, 113, 137, 162
  leather 62, 81–86, 90, 92, 162
  cost 62, 62 n.4, 83, 88–90, 95, 143
Booklets 20, 51 n.182, 74–79, 84 n.109, 86, 116
Book of Hours 80
Book trade (*see also* stationers and second-hand booksellers) 23, 66, 144–46, 149–54, 156
  definition 144–45
Breton *lais*, *Les Deux Amants* and *Graelent* (in Old Norse translations) 64
Bristol 33
Bruges 53
Brut (prose) 117, 117 n.49, 130,
Butchery 27, 29, 30, 31–32, 40, 185
Buxhale or Boxhole, John (scribe) 161
Bygonell or Byconyll, William (gave books to All Souls College, also executor to Archbishop Henry Chichele) 178
Byland Abbey (Cistercian foundation in Yorkshire) 26, 158, 158 n.69
Bylton, Peter 145, 152–53
By-products 11, 15, 19–25, 29–33, 29 n.66, n.69, 41, 47–48, 50, 73, 74, 90
Byrkhed or Birkhede, John 178

Cambridge 6 n.30, 80, 163–64, 177
  Clare Hall 175–76
  Peterhouse College 171
Canterbury 4, 80, 176, 178
Carols 94
Catalogues
  medieval 83–84, 143
  modern 4, 17, 154–56

Cattle   21, 29–33, 41, 53, 59
  calves   21, 23, 27
Cautio system (*see also* loan chests;
  pledges)   156, 163–72, 176, 187
Chace, Thomas (Chaplain to Humphrey, Duke
  of Gloucester)   168–69
Chaining books   114
  at Exeter Cathedral Library   173–75
  at Merton College Library   179–80
Charity   12, 71, 142–43, 151, 170–77, 181–82
Charms   139
  for curing wounds (in French)   135 n.117
  for staunching blood, (the 'Flum Jordan'
    charm)   132–33
Chaucer, Geoffrey   2, 74, 76 n.71
  The Canterbury Tales   13, 120–23
  Ellesmere Chaucer   26
  'To Rosemounde'   75 n.65
  Treatise on the Astrolabe   90, 98
  Troilus and Criseyde   3, 75
Chestur, John (scribe)   178
Chichele, Henry (Archbishop of Canterbury,
  founder of All Souls College)   178, 179
Christianson, C. Paul   17, 144–54
Cistercian
  Beaulieu Abbey (Cistercian foundation in
    Hampshire)   31–32, 48
  Byland Abbey (Cistercian foundation in
    Yorkshire)   26, 158, 158 n.69
  houses in Yorkshire (Rievaulx, Fountains
    Abbey)   32
Colop
  John   146–49, 149 n.27
  Richard (parchmener, stationer)   30, 145–49,
    152–53
Commentaries   131, 157, 166, 175, 179
  on the Epistles of Paul   162
  Postillae on the Bible (by Nicholas of
    Lyra)   54
Commodities (*see also* the Staple)   20, 29–30,
  50, 63, 141
Common-profit books   71–72, 71 n.46, 141,
  146–49, 152, 181–82, 183
  BodL, MS Douce 25   69–72, 146, 183
  CUL, MS Ff.vi.31   71 n.47
  London, Lambeth Palace Library, MS
    472   146–49
Communities   32–33, 142, 144, 153, 175–81

Confessor's manual   88, 91
Courtenay
  Richard (nephew of William
    Courtenay)   169–71, 176, 177
  William (Archbishop of Canterbury, uncle
    of Richard Courtenay)   169–71, 176, 176
    n.158, 159, 177
Craftsmanship   1, 7, 9–10, 24, 30, 33–34, 34–50,
  58, 67, 102, 144, 185–86
Cutting   44, 47–48, 48 n.170, 50–51, 68, 74–79,
  88–89, 97, 116, 121 n.63, 185–86

Damage (*see also* holes; parchment grades;
  repair)   3, 20, 35, 44, 50–59
Death (*see also* baiting; slaughter)   22, 27–28,
  46, 151–52, 157, 165, 171, 172–81, 185
  blow   53–54
  stain (*mort-de-sang*, visible in BodL, MS
    Bodley 251)   54
Discard   3–4, 13–14, 73, 79, 185
DNA analysis   15, 21
Doodles (*see also* sketches)   105–06, 108, 111,
  113, 120–24, 128, 129, 135
  definition   120–21
  of heads or faces   122–23
Dorman, John   166
Dorse (also dorsal stripe)   26–27
Duncan, Thomas (endowed the Dunken
  or Duncan chest at the University of
  Oxford)   169, 170
Durham Cathedral Chapter   32

Ecocriticism   8, 9, 13–15, 185
Edward I   30
Edward III   32
Electio system   142, 179–80
Elyot, Robert (Vice-Provost of Eton)   81 n.90,
  157–58
Ephemerality   5, 7, 17, 51, 64–65, 66 n.32, 68–69,
  91, 96, 110, 120–24, 139
Erasure   7, 98–99, 110, 117, 135, 135 n.119, 155, 164,
  168 n.124, 169, 178 n.167
Esteby, John (scribe, vicar of Banbury)   161
Eton College, Windsor   152, 157–58
Evesham   83, 83 n.102
Exeter   88, 88 n.127, 151, 155
  Book, *see* Riddle 24
  Cathedral   175, 180–81

Fylham, William (Chancellor of Exeter Cathedral) 56, 180
Keys, Roger (Precentor of Exeter Cathedral) 175
Lacy, Edmund (Bishop of Exeter Cathedral) 173–75, 177, 180
Stevens, John (Canon of Exeter Cathedral) 175
Webber, Henry (Dean of Exeter Cathedral) 180–81
Eyburhale or Eborall, T. 154

Fasciculus morum 91, 93
Feathers (*see* quills)
Festial (by John Mirk) 116
FitzJames, Richard (Bishop of Chichester, also Warden of Merton College, Oxford) 178–79
Flaying (skins to make parchment) 34, 40–42, 54–55
Flyleaves (*see also* pastedowns) 20, 51, 61, 65–67, 76, 79–82, 86, 99, 105–07, 112–15, 117–20, 122 n.69, 123, 126, 128, 129, 131 n.109, 132–39, 151, 152, 153, 156, 157 n.65, 165 n.106, 162 n.88, 165, 169, 174, 175, 176, 178
Fragments 3–4, 15, 63–68, 74–76, 84–85, 155, 176, 187
Fylham, William (Chancellor of Exeter Cathedral) 56, 180

Gardyner, Richard (fellow of Oriel College) 165
Gift-giving 142, 154, 158, 159, 160, 172–81
Gilding 23, 47, 51, 161, 175
Gillyng, John (monk of Byland Abbey, Yorkshire) 158
Gloucester, Humphrey Duke of 168
Glue (*see also* recipes for making horn glue and for stockfish glue; size) 20, 29, 47–48, 56–58, 69, 73, 103
Goats 21–22, 27, 29
Golden Section or Rule 112
Gower, John (*Confessio Amantis*) 14, 97 n.163, 121, 125, 130, 130 n.102, 137–39
Gradual 81–82, 82 n.95
Graffiti (*see also* signatures) 6–7, 6 n.30, 107, 129–30
Grosseteste, Robert 175

Guilds 30–31
  Leathersellers' Company 30
  Skinners Company 30, 48
  Stationers' Company (*see also* stationers) 145, 153
  Mistery of Textwriters and Limners 30, 145, 152–53, 153 n.50
  Whitetawyers 31
Gunthorpe, John (Dean of Wells) 150–51

Handwriting (*see also* writing; pen trials) 4–6
  anglicana 125, 126
  mixed anglicana-secretary 69, 77, 126, 132, 136, 166
  secretary 77, 118, 125, 126, 129, 131, 134, 137–39, 149, 158, 177, 178, 179
  textura 80, 82, 99–101, 138–39, 165, 175, 177
Helbarton, Dorothy 130
Henry V 170
Henry VI 30, 178
Hide (*see also* parchment; skin; vellum) 16, 19–59, 22 n.24, 73
Hoccleve, Thomas 77 n.73, 118, 129
Holbroke, John (endowed the chest at Peterhouse College, Cambridge) 171
Holgate, Thomas 166
Hopton, Richard (Head Master of Eton College) 152

Jews, expulsion of 164

Kame (or Thame), William, *The Northern Homily Cycle* 56
Killum, John (grocer; *see also* his executor John Colop) 146–49
Knife (*see also* shears; tools) 37, 40, 44–48, 54–55, 74, 97, 121, 186
  fleshing 37
  penknife 74, 97

Langlay, Thomas (vicar of Northbourne, Kent) 158
Langton, John (Bishop of Chichester, Chancellor of England) 167, 170
Leather 21, 25–26, 29–31, 36–37, 107,
  covers 62, 81–86, 90, 162
Leland, John 4, 61, 66
Letters 76 n.71, 79, 109

The Libelle of Englysche Polycye 30 n.73
Limp covers (*see also* wrappers) 63, 82–95
  medieval terms for 82–84
Literacy 3, 107–8, 129, 130, 144
Loan chests (*see also cautio* system) 142, 160, 163–72, 177, 181, 182, 187
  at the University of Cambridge
    Billingford (now at Corpus Christi College) 163
    Peterhouse College 171
  at the University of Oxford
    Celton (or Selton) 163, 166, 170
    Dunken (or Duncan) 163–65, 169, 170
    Langton 163, 167–68, 169, 170
    Robury (or Roubury) 163, 165, 169
    St Frideswide 170
    Vienna (or Vienne) 163
    Waugham (or Vaughan and Hussey) 163, 170
    Winton 163, 168
London 30, 67, 145–46, 149–54, 156, 157
  Bridge 153
  Paternoster Row 152
  St Paul's 145, 153
  Westminster Abbey 6
Lydgate, John 25, 28, 58, 74, 77, 118, 129
  'The Debate of the Horse, Goose, and Sheep' 25, 28
  Troy Book 58 n.219

Mandeville's Travels 118, 126, 128
Manuscripts
  definition 4–5
  Byland Bede 26
  Ellesmere Chaucer 26
  Exeter Book (*see* Riddle 24)
  medieval terms for 5–6
  Thornton manuscript 46
  Vernon manuscript 26–27
Manyman or Menyman, William 157
Margins 51, 56, 71 n.45, 80 n.87, 99–101, 105–40, 141, 158, 162
  marginalia definition 105–8
Martinmas (11 November) 41
The Master of Game (Edward, Duke of York) 31, 53
Material turn 9–11
Martyrology of Usuardus 157

Medical texts (*see also* charms) 35–36, 77, 80, 122, 125, 132, 134, 161
'The Meditation on the Five wounds of Christ' (1410) 46
Memory 109, 124, 131–34, 139, 173–77
Mirk, John (*Festial*) 116
Missal of Hereford use 97
Moleyns, Katerine (Prioress of Kyngton, Wiltshire) 146 n.22

Newton, William (a Bonhomme of Edington, Wiltshire) 167–68
The Northern Homily Cycle (by William Kame or Thame) 56
Norwich Cathedral Priory 32
Nose-to-tail 19, 19 n.2, 23, 33, 47

Oak galls 24–25, 65, 131–32
Off-cuts 45, 48, 51, 68–73, 88, 109, 146, 161
Ownership 3, 131–32, 140–44, 156, 175–76, 181
  marks of 129–31, 150, 156
Oxford 6 n.30, 67, 80, 145, 161, 163–71, 179
  All Souls College 157–58, 179
  Balliol College 168
  Bodleian Library 69, 109
  Catte Street 145
  Exeter College 151
  Merton College 178–79

Palimpsests 61–62, 65–68, 77–79, 95–103
  recipe for making 98
Paling, Robert 154
Palmer, William (Precentor of Crediton church) 151
Paper 13, 20–21, 61–63, 74–79, 76 n.71, 82 n.92, 83, 85, 88, 91, 94, 110, 116, 118, 120, 122, 126, 137 n.124, 144, 155
Parchment (*see also* fragments; off-cuts; parchmeners; size)
  hair 25–26, 35, 42, 44, 54–55
  hide 16, 19–59, 22 n.24, 73
  Fellmongers 30 n.75, 31–32, 32 n.87
  grades (*see also* scabby) 20, 24, 26, 31, 39–40, 51, 52, 69–72, 71 n.47, 86, 88, 94, 114, 161
  recipes for making 35–59
  scabby 40, 51–52, 53 n.187
  skin 19–59, 20 n.11, 22 n.23, 69–71, 73, 83–86, 90 n.130, 107

Parchmeners (or parchment-makers)   10, 19, 19 n.3, 28, 30–34, 37, 39–44, 47–50, 55, 68
   London parchmeners 1370–1467 known by name   30–31
   Colop, Richard (parchmener, stationer)   30, 145–49, 152–53
   Gay, Richard and wife (Winchester)   42
Pastedowns (see also flyleaves)   4, 20, 62–63, 79–82, 86, 113, 118, 126, 128, 129, 131–32, 156, 157, 158, 159, 165, 166
Pen trials   120–21, 124–28, 132
Pergamon (Bergama in western Anatolia, Turkey)   21
Piers Plowman   14, 117
Pledges (see also *cautio* system; loan chests)   163–72
Polychronicon (by Ranulf Higden)   150
Pontoise, John of (Bishop of Winchester, endowed the Winton chest at the University of Oxford)   168
Prayers   6–7, 55, 105, 114, 122, 125, 128, 134, 135, 162 n.88, 170–73, 177–88
The Prick of Conscience   63 n.16, 72, 97, 98, 101, 102, 118–20, 122–23
'Privity of the Passion' (Thornton manuscript)   46
Pumice (see also stanchgrain)   25, 49, 97–98

Quills   24–25
Quire guards   63, 76–79, 82, 102, 107

Recipes   16, 19, 24–25, 35–59, 98, 108, 122, 125, 131–34, 139, 184
   for curing wounds (in French; see also charms)   135 n.117
   for gilding an initial   23
   for making horn glue   47
   for making ink   24, 24 n.36, n.37, 36, 37, 131–32
   for making leather   36
   for making parchment   35–59
   for making palimpsests   98
   for making stanchgrain   36, 48–49, 52, 98 n.168
   for making stockfish glue   47 n.166
   for recycling parchment into cheverel   55
   for spiced and sugared wine   132
   for staunching blood (the 'Flum Jordan' charm; see also charms)   132–33

Recycling (see re-use)
Reinforcing strips   3, 74–76
Repair (see also damage; sewing; stitching)   12, 20, 47, 55 n.202, 56–59
   decorated   58–59
Re-use of parchment
   as bishop's mitre stiffening (see also Breton lais)   63–64
   destructive   62, 66, 69, 79, 80, 83, 86, 96–97, 107, 111, 185
   in books
      as flyleaves   79–82, 157 n.65
      as limp covers or wrappers   82–95
      as pastedowns   79–82
      as quire guards   76–79
      as reinforcing strips   74–76
   to wipe jakes, scour candle sticks, rub boots   62
   to wrap groceries and soap   62, 66
Riddle 24 (Old English, in the Exeter Book)   22–23
Robury, Gilbert (judge, endowed the Robury chest at the University of Oxford)   165, 170
Rolle, Richard   46, 175
Romances   85, 88, 93
   Guy of Warwick   22
   Richard Cœur de Lion   115
   Sir Firumbras   93
   Titus and Vespasian   122, 125
Rotherham   91
Rule of Gregory   25

Scientific texts   36, 77, 85–86, 90–91, 98
Second-hand   2, 12, 141–54, 154–81
   definition of   142
Selective breeding   35, 35 n.103
Selton, William (Canon of Wells, endowed the Celton or Selton chest at the University of Oxford)   166, 170
Sentences (by Peter Lombard)   57, 162
Sermons   73 n.54, 75, 77–79, 80, 81 n.90, 116, 157 n.65, 161, 162, 165, 168
Sever, Henry (Warden of Merton College, Oxford)   178–80
Sewing (see also stitching)   11, 56–59, 64, 74–76, 76–79, 81, 82–95, 90 n.129
   guards or stays (see reinforcing strips)

Shambles, the (or Fleshambles, in York)   27, 40
Shears (*see also* knife; tools)   48, 48 n.170, 74
Sheep   20 n.11, 21–22, 24–34, 40 n.124, 41, 52 n.185, 53
    lambs   23, 27, 31, 52 n.185
Sherborne (Dorset)   88
Signatures (*see also* ownership)   81, 108, 118, 125, 129–31, 135 n.118, 137
Sixteenth century   2–4, 61, 62, 64–67, 74 n.60, 80, 155
Size (*see also* glue)   20, 23, 36, 47–48, 69, 73
    of animals   29, 35, 40–41
    of books   26–27, 69, 71, 109, 136 n.121, 160, 162
    of margins   108–17, 125 n.85
    of off-cuts   45, 48, 69
    of parchment   40, 45, 48, 50, 56, 58, 74, 79 n.79, 86, 89–95,
Sketches   120, 123–24
Skin (*see also* parchment; vellum)   19–59, 20 n.11, 22 n.23, 69–71, 73, 83–86, 90 n.130, 107
Slaughter   27–32, 41, 53
Speculum ecclesie   69–72
St Albans Abbey   32
Stanchgrain   36, 48–49, 52, 98
Staple, the   30
Stationers
    and second-hand booksellers   145–54
        Bylton, Peter (also known to be a bookbinder)   145, 152–53
        Chirche or Cherch, Robert   145, 153
        Cok, Edmund   145–46
        Colop, Richard (also a parchmener)   30, 145–49, 152–53
        Elys, John   145–46
        Lokton, Thomas   145–46
        Lyonhill, David   145–46, 150–51
        Marleburgh or Marlburgh, Thomas   145–46, 153
        de Nessefylde, William   145–46, 149–50, 50 n.28
        Pye, John   145–46, 150, 152, 153–54
        Sampson, John   145–46, 150
        Veysey, Thomas   145–46, 151
    at the University of Oxford   164–65
        Coke, Christopher   165 n.108
        Doll or Dolle, John   164–65

Godsond, John   164–67
Hunt, Thomas   165
More, John   164–5
The Stationers' Company   145, 153
Stitching   56–59, 86, 89–95, 90 n.130
Sustainability   1, 5, 8–15, 23–25, 27–33, 35, 43–44, 48, 50–59, 62, 67, 79, 85, 95, 111–12, 132, 149, 170, 181
    definitions   11, 11 n.56, n.57
Swan, Richard   158
Syon Abbey   157

Taillour, John (textwriter, executor to Peter Bylton)   153
Tillney, John   177
Thing theory   9
Titchfield (Premonstratensian house)   83, 83 n.102
Tools
    harowe or herse   34, 40, 44–48, 57, 68
    knife   37, 40, 44–48, 54–55, 74, 97, 121, 186
    lunellarium (or *lunellum*)   46–47
    penknife   74, 97
    shears   48, 48 n.170, 74
Trithemius, Johannes, *De laude scriptorum*   76 n.71

Uterine vellum   23–24

Vaughan, Sir Thomas (endowed the Waugham or Vaughan and Hussey chest)   170 n.129
Vellum (*see also* parchment; skin; uterine vellum)   20 n.11, 22, 36–38, 94
Verses   72, 108, 123 n.76, 128, 131, 134–39
    'Besse Bunting' (a Middle English version of the French *Bele Aeliz* lyric)   137–39
    'Kyng Harry'   134
    'Love ys had whyll monney doth lest'   136
    'Love ys hade whyll sylver dothe laste'   137
    'The Tribulations of Marriage'   134–36
Vulgaria (by William Horman)   23, 25
Vulgate Bible   99, 158, 169

Washing (skins to make parchment)   41–42, 55
Waste   3, 13–18, 19 n.2, 20, 28–30, 39, 47–50, 56, 65–67, 107, 185
    binder's waste   64–67

Wax
   seal   130
   tablets   6–7, 110, 120, 139
Wey, William (a Bonhomme of Edington,
   Wiltshire)   181
Wrappers (*see also* limp covers)   63, 82–95, 162
   n.88
William Cowley parchment makers   30, 47,
   186 n.7
Winchester   32, 42
Writing (*see also* alphabets; pen trials;
   signatures; verses; *Vulgaria*)
   exercises   124–30
   on things   6–7, 105, 109, 139–40
Wyntershulle, William (note in CUL, MS
   Ee.4.20)   23 n.28
Wycliffe, John
   De Mandatis   180

Rosarium theologie   77, 102
Sunday epistle sermons (extracts)   77–79
Translation of the four Gospels   118
Wycliffite Bible   12, 115–16
Wykeham, William of   179

Yngham or Ingham, John de (fellow of Clare
   Hall)   176
York   145
   Byland Abbey (Cistercian foundation in
      Yorkshire)   26, 158, 158 n.69
   Cistercian houses in Yorkshire (Rievaulx,
      Fountains Abbey)   32
   Edward Duke of   31, 53
   Gillyng, John (monk of Byland Abbey,
      Yorkshire)   158
   the Shambles (or Fleshambles)   27, 40

YORK MEDIEVAL PRESS PUBLICATIONS

York Manuscript and Early Print Studies

This new series builds on and expands York Medieval Press' Manuscript Culture in the British Isles. It aims to further the study of handwritten and early print sources for literature and intellectual history in the pre-modern period, and champions an interconnected mode of analysis for the textual, material and cultural, whether the focus is local, regional, national or transnational. It welcomes contributions providing critical approaches to manuscript studies, history of the book, cultural history, philology and editing, whether monographs, edited collections, or catalogues.

Series Editors
Orietta Da Rold (Cambridge)
Holly James-Maddocks (York)

Advisory Committee
Alexandra da Costa (Cambridge), Marilena Maniaci (Cassino), Linne Mooney (York), Nicola Morato (Liège), Máire Ní Mhaonaigh (Cambridge), David Rundle (Kent), Elaine Treharne (Stanford)

1 *Manuscript Culture and Medieval Devotional Traditions: Essays in Honour of Michael G. Sargent*, edited by Jennifer N. Brown and Nicole R. Rice
2 *Saints' Legends in Medieval Sarum Breviaries: Catalogue and Studies*, Sherry L. Reames
3 *Scribal Cultures in Late Medieval England: Essays in Honour of Linne R. Mooney*, edited by Margaret Connolly, Holly James-Maddocks and Derek Pearsall

Details of other York Medieval Press volumes are available from Boydell & Brewer Ltd

www.ingramcontent.com/pod-product-compliance
Lightning Source LLC
Chambersburg PA
CBHW080837230426
43665CB00021B/2864